Quicksilver Messenger Service The Shamen Prince Black Flag Radiohead
Adams Robbie Williams Scaggs
The B-52's Lenny Kravitz Pulp
Spencer Davis Group Nick Drake Garth Brooks
Steely Dan Blondie Blodwyn Pig Fatboy Slim Nico
Genesis Minutemen Alice Cooper Sting
Wayne County Mike Oldfield Johnny and Edgar Winter The Catherine Wheel
Haley and his Comets Sepultura Magma Hole R.E.M.
The Family Stone George Michael
Joplin Billy Bragg Eric Clapton
Catatonia The Charlatans Throwing Muses
l.d. lang Bee Gees Run-D.M.C Family Laura Nyro
Dukes Wire Soul Asylum Buffalo Springfield
Arthur Brown Southern Culture On The Skids
Club Leftfield Van Morrison Rush
Jamiroquai Joe Satriani
Boys Grand Funk Railroad Marc Bolan
Nick Cave The Teardrop Explodes
Traffic Spirit
Suzi Quatro Joe Cocker George Clinton
The Smiths Soft Machine Los Lobos Blue Öyster Cult
Chicago The Police Buddy Holly
Generator Robert Palmer John Lee Hooker
Velvet Underground Jackson Browne The Band
Emerson, Lake & Palmer Jane's Addiction Violent Femmes Metallica
Charles Roy Orbison Rory Gallagher
The Residents
The Everly Brothers Curtis Mayfield
Led Zeppelin Counting Crows
Cream The Only Ones
The Mission Stone Temple Pilots
Madonna Booker T. and the MG's Black Sabbath
Nash & Young Alternative TV Steve Miller

THE BOOK OF
rock

Philip Dodd

PAVILION

THE BOOK OF ROCK is a gallery of

saints, sinners, martyrs and magicians.

Each of them has left their mark on the half-century of musical history we know as rock'n'roll. They may have cast a lengthy shadow from the heights of legend over all that followed. Or they may have added, for one brief shining or sullied moment, a flavour, a colour or a sound that was in tune with the mood of the times. Whatever their contribution, in this book democracy is everything. The aristocrats of rock rub shoulders with its journeymen and artisans, they jostle with crazed guitar heroes, introverted songwriters and cult artists barely known outside a circle of fiercely loyal and protective fans. Here are the flamboyant and the reclusive, the sensitive and the outrageous. The hip, the hyped and the hyper. The OTT, the AOR and the DOA. Together they represent the performers of a maverick circus.

To those who rock'n'rolled, we salute you.

First published in Great Britain in 2001 by Pavilion Books Ltd. London House, Great Eastern Wharf, Parkgate Road, London SW11 4NQ. www.pavilionbooks.co.uk

Text © 2001 Philip Dodd. Design and layout © Pavilion Books Ltd. The moral right of the author has been asserted. Designed by Wherefore Art?

A CIP catalogue record for this book is available from the British Library.

ISBN 1 86205 2921

Set in RotisSerif

Colour origination in Hong Kong by Bright Arts

Printed and bound in Italy by Giunti Industrie Grafiche, Prato

2 4 6 8 10 9 7 5 3 1

This book can be ordered direct from the publisher. Please contact the Marketing Department. But try your bookshop first.

'What is rock?' – this was the question that had to be resolved before this

Book Of Rock could be compiled. We took the view, shared by most rock reference editors, that rock'n'roll has survived by evolution for nigh on fifty years by adapting, raiding and influencing other musics. So around the acts who would always be racked under R for Rock are also the musicians from other genres who have either had a major influence on rock artists or enjoyed a significant crossover audience: hence James Brown, Bob Marley, Public Enemy and Kiss fan Garth Brooks. The next decision was to include 500 entries – enough, we felt, to create a book that could be genuinely catholic and not unduly predictable. Some 100 entries were self-evident, the real Hall of Famers. Not to include the Beatles, Dylan, the Grateful Dead, Hendrix, Nirvana, the Sex Pistols or the Stones would be criminally negligent in a Book Of Rock. A further 150 acts were almost automatic selections – which left some 250 where debate was free to rage, and rage it did. The final choice is necessarily subjective, but our aim was to convey the full spectrum of rock music, from critics' favourites to commercial megastars. It was also essential not to ignore those bands who had had an impact at a particular moment, but who might later have fallen out of favour or by the wayside: Fanny, the first all-female rock band of any note, or Gong and Tangerine Dream, never mainstream but the flag-carriers for a raft of blissed-out acts in the 1990s. The entries are organised in A-Z order by the name of the act or musician – using the form of name the band generally used on their own releases. One of the joys of organising the book alphabetically has been the serendipitous juxtaposition of neighbours: Moby and Moby Grape, or Kate Bush and the Butthole Surfers, for example. Note that Howlin' Wolf and Muddy Waters appear under H and M respectively; P J Harvey, the band as opposed to Polly Harvey herself, appear under P. Each entry lists biographical dates*, recording career and music. Where possible, the dates of birth – and when relevant death – are given for each individual artist or for the key or enduring members of a band, although in the world of the music business, the information available on birth dates is often contradictory or deliberately confusing. Under Recording career, for artists who went solo after a period as a band member we have given their solo recording career dates (viz. Paul Weller following his time with the Jam and the Style Council). And finally, under Sounds, we have selected up to three albums for each entry to provide an interesting and representative sample of their work, including the first release dates of each album. We have generally not included any compilations or Best Of's since that is an obvious, though no less valid, way to be introduced to any act's repertoire. And clearly, for prolific greats like David Bowie or Frank Zappa we can only scratch the surface. Above all this book is not intended to be a definitive encyclopedia, but to celebrate the variety, the fun and the weirdness of rock. Applying too rigid an approach to rock history goes against its very grain. After all, it is only rock'n'roll and nothing to get hung about!

* Please note that dates are presented by day/month/year.

ABBA

Once upon a time there was no strife in Abba-land. The populace of the kingdom was content, having the time of their lives; divorce, fragmentation and regrets were not yet on the horizon. Following that exuberant, jump-suited Eurovision explosion in April 1974 when 'Waterloo' blew away the competition, Abba had discovered its essential being: seriously good melodies from two seriously good songwriters in Benny and Björn, quaintly quirky syntax and Agnetha's legendary

Swedish rear (much to the annoyance of Norwegian-born Anni-Frid). You could call it all a smörgåsbord of popular music, except you can't dance to a smörgåsbord. Always much more than aural candy, Abba were far from forgotten when they went into exile, courtesy of a decade of wedding discos, before their triumphant restoration in the 1990s, with a little help from friends like U2 - who played 'Dancing Queen' on the Zoo TV tour - Björn Again, Erasure, Alan Partridge and *Muriel's Wedding*.

"I suppose we were the ideal team: the two girls were the faces and the two boys the artists. There was no way people were ever going to pay to see Benny and me performing." Björn Ulvaeus

Key members: Benny Andersson 16/12/46, Agnetha Fältskog 5/4/50, Anni-Frid Lyngstad 15/11/45, Björn Ulvaeus 25/4/45 • Recording career: 1972 - 1982

Sounds: Arrival 1976, The Album 1977, Super Trouper 1980

ABC

Their music was praised yet faintly damned as 'perfect pop', the covert suggestion being that there really wasn't much of great substance once you dug down below the surface of ABC's white soul sound. Singer and main man Martin Fry's studied blend of Bowie and Ferry (and the occasional dodgy haircut) only heightened suspicions that this was little more than clever, but synthetic, pastiche. It was Fry who had corralled the remnants of a Sheffield-based post-punk outfit called Vice Versa, steering them towards his own tastes for Earth Wind & Fire and Chic. Later he was so impressed by the production values on a Dollar single that the group hooked up with ex-Buggle Trevor Horn to create their finest moment, 1982's *The Lexicon Of Love*, a wide-screen sonic movie of an album. Sadly they peaked there and then, and with the departure of David Palmer and Steve Singleton, 'The Look Of Love' was thereafter firmly retrograde.

"I wanted a name that would put us first in the phonebook, or second if you count Abba." Martin Fry

5

Key members: Martin Fry 9/3/58, David Palmer 29/5/61, Steve Singleton 17/4/59, Mark White 1/4/61 • Recording career: 1982 - present

Sounds: The Lexicon Of Love 1982, How To Be A... Zillionaire! 1985, Skyscraping 1997

AC/DC

"The critics may not like us - as Angus said, **we put out the same album every year with a different cover!** But the kids still like it." Malcolm Young

The schoolboy tie and short trousers started out as a gimmick and ended up a trademark: Angus Young was still sporting them at the ripe old age of 40-something. It was an odd counterpoint to the blast of AC/DC's metal, which had all the rollicking roister of a heavy night out in Glasgow, from where the Young brothers had been transplanted to Australia. Fronted by Bon Scott, a high-energy screamer and fellow Scot, who possessed plenty of attitude (and some minor convictions),

they neatly coincided with punk's late-70s rasp, and built on their live skills to deliver the breakthrough album *Highway To Hell*. Alas, it proved to be the last exit for Scott, who died after a monster drinking binge in 1980; replacement Brian Johnson pluckily held the *forte* as they wheeled out their show, with little evolution, through the next two decades. 'Rock And Roll Ain't Noise Pollution', they sang, but an AC/DC gig - their true home - was essentially tinnitus-inducing.

Key members: Brian Johnson 5/10/47, Bon Scott 9/7/46 (died 19/2/80), Cliff Williams 14/12/49, Angus Young 31/3/59, Malcolm Young 6/1/53 • Recording career: 1974 - present

Sounds: High Voltage 1976, Highway To Hell 1979, Ballbreaker 1995

Adam and the Ants

Like all the great moments of teen idol-dom, the piratical swashbuckle of Adam and the Ants swished by in a blur. During a couple of years in the early 1980s the chief Ant seemed to be omni-present, his art school heritage standing him in good stead as the then-new (and possibly wild) frontier of the promo video business was transfixed by a combination of narrative fantasies, undeniably good looks, and a penchant for pantomime-style costumes, underlaid with those bounding Burundi drums and overlaid with Ant's weird yodel of a voice. Barely a trace remained of his punk phase, when the Ants had been managed by the legendary Jordan and landed a brief appearance in Derek Jarman's movie *Jubilee*. But the boy who worshipped Diana Dors found his moment and then, with wisdom beyond his years, disbanded the Ants at their peak. The Antpeople mourned, but Adam had understood the timing perfectly.

"The essence of pop is brilliant songs. The rest is sex, subversion, style and humour."

Adam Ant

Key member: Adam Ant (Stuart Goddard) 3/11/54 • Recording career: 1978 - 1982 • Sounds: Dirk Wears White Sox 1979, Kings Of The Wild Frontier 1980

He smiles, he's modest, clean-living, successful and politically right-on: a regular performer for the benefit circuit. Worse, he's a fine songwriter. So where's the catch? Well, maybe, just maybe, after the unprecedented chart success of '(Everything I Do) I Do It For You', and those really quite annoying parentheses, he tumbled into the AOR honey trap too readily. And what followed definitely eroded his reputation as a decent rocker - Adams himself was an Eddie Cochran fan. Indeed, on first emerging as a solo artist - after a period spent writing songs for the likes of Bachman-Turner Overdrive and Kiss - he had been dubbed a Springsteen copyist. A slot at the US segment of Live Aid and the well-judged 'Summer Of '69' helped him build credibility, but, after 'Everything' had played itself to death in the Summer of '91, that cred slipped dramatically, and *NME* reported that by late that year even Bryan hated the song... A late-1990s re-invention found him duetting with Mel C and working with Chicane.

"Most people wouldn't know who I was if I fell on them."

Bryan Adams

8

Born: 5/11/59 • Recording career: 1979 - present • Sounds: Cuts Like A Knife 1983, Reckless 1984, Waking Up The Neighbours 1991

Aerosmith

> "We've cleaned up now... Well, our minds are just as dirty as ever!"
>
> Joe Perry

With seemingly inexhaustible energy, Steve (father of Liv) Tyler and his fellow Aerosmiths spent three decades leaping gaily above the criticism that they were simply an ersatz Stones. Sure, Tyler was an acrobatic performer who came complete with a set of patent Mick Jagger lips, with a guitar-toting partner in Joe Perry (although it was Tyler whose face later grew to resemble the rugged terrain of Keef's). Both bands loved the blues, but the boys in the attic admired the Beatles as much as Led Zep and Cream: their harmonies were pure Fab Four. The USA's biggest heavy rock band, with Kiss, of the 1970s, they worked and played hard, but showed through Tyler's often thoughtful, occasionally ironic, lyrics a more reflective side to their personalities. After the requisite split caused by irreconcilable differences in the late 70s, it was rap that brought them back into the spotlight in 1986, as Aerosmith teamed up with Run-D.M.C. to record a steaming version of their 1977 single 'Walk This Way'. And thus re-invigorated, they merrily continued to strut their stuff.

Key members: Tom Hamilton 31/12/51, Joey Kramer 21/6/50, Joe Perry 10/9/50, Steven Tyler 26/3/48, Brad Whitford 23/2/52 • **Recording career:** 1973 - present

Sounds: Toys In The Attic 1975, Rocks 1976, Pump 1989

The Allman Brothers Band

Somewhere around 1970, down below the Mason-Dixon line, the monster of Southern rock stirred itself out of hibernation, seduced by the bottleneck guitar work of Duane Allman, the session musician's musician. Even if he and brother Gregg had never worked together, Duane's duetting and duelling with Clapton on 'Layla' would have assured his slice of posterity. With the Brothers Band's bubbling rhythm section supporting his bluesy magic, Dickey Betts not far behind, and Gregg's organ and vocals laced with bourbon, their two nights at Fillmore East recorded in March 1971 showcased the band at its live best. But that same October Duane was killed in a motorbike smash at just 24. His stunned colleagues carried on; then a year later bassist Berry Oakley also died on *his* bike. Dickey Betts picked up the pieces that remained (Gregg was either out of it and/or marrying Cher), but the Stars And Bars were forever lowered at half mast.

"You better be pickin', man, if you come to play in my band. Come to play, not to show off your clothes."

Duane Allman

Key members: Duane Allman 20/11/46 (died 29/10/71), Gregg Allman 8/12/47, Dicky Betts 12/12/43, Jai Johanson 8/7/44, Berry Oakley 4/4/48 (died 11/11/72), Butch Trucks 11/5/47

Recording career: 1969 - 1981 & 1990 - present • Sounds: At Fillmore East 1971, Eat A Peach 1972, Brothers and Sisters 1973

Sometimes lost between the cracks of punk history, Alternative TV provided a soapbox for Mark Perry, aka Mark P, who was the founder and editor-in-chief of one of the all-time great fanzines - *Sniffin' Glue*. Just as he was able to expound his vision of what punk should be about through the pages of his fanzine, Alternative TV gave Perry the chance to stand and deliver a verbal blast of intellectual content that most punk bands might have boggled at. Surrounded by an aggressive aural maelstrom including tape edits and sound effects, an evening with Mark and the boys always promised to be stimulating, rarely comfortable. Their recordings were limited (an early release, 'Love Lies Limp', was given away as a flexi-disc with the fanzine) but benefited from production by John Cale - the Velvets, along with the Stooges and Frank Zappa, were a Perry favourite. His cohorts came and went, but a reformed ATV hit back in 1981 and yet again in the mid-90s.

"I didn't get into punk to destroy it or because I was dissatisfied with it.

I suppose I found out that I was dissatisfied with it." Mark Perry

Alternative TV

Key member: Mark Perry 1957 • **Recording career:** 1977 - present • **Sounds:** The Image Has Cracked 1978, Strange Kicks 1981, My Life As A Child Star 1994

The intricate harmonies and acoustic guitarwork of America (a trio of USAF brats who had met up at school in the UK) led to a label as 'the poor man's Crosby, Stills, Nash & Young'. The jibe was unnecessary: it was more a case of them being in tune with the soft rock groove of the early 1970s, as their single 'A Horse With No Name' galloped towards the top of the charts on both sides of the Atlantic. Returning to the land of their name, they continued in much the same vein, garnering enough kudos to attract sidemen of the calibre of Joe Walsh and Tom Scott and coming under the silken tutelage of George Martin for four albums. Dan Peek's departure in 1977 - to pursue his Christian beliefs - essentially put the kibosh on the original set-up, although the remaining duo continued doggedly touring and occasionally recording.

America

"We like to play close to the audience -
we would probably sound at our best in your living room." Gerry Buckley

12

Key members: Gerry Buckley 12/9/52, Dewey Bunnell 19/1/51, Dan Peek 1/11/50 • Recording career: 1972 - 1977 (as trio), 1979 - 1985 & 1994 - present (as duo)

Sounds: America 1972, Holiday 1974, America/Live 1978

"Predictable is a bore.

That's why I'm not successful." Mark Eitzel

American Music Club

It's one of those imponderables that music aficionados love to ponder: how come San Francisco's American Music Club could be acclaimed by the critical fraternity of the early 90s - leading light, the mercurial Mark Eitzel, was voted *Rolling Stone*'s Songwriter of the Year in 1991 - but be pretty much ignored by the buying public? Maybe they were just too much of an acquired taste. Eitzel's vision of a lonely but resilient low life, down but never quite out for the count, was a stark mix of Nick Drake and Ian Curtis, laid over a country-cum-punk sound - Eitzel had lived in England during the heyday of the Pistols. American Music Club's fanbase in the UK always stood by them and was the only territory where their 1989 album (significantly titled *United Kingdom*) was released, after a deal with BMG ran into problems. In the end Eitzel shut the Club down, but his solo career snagged the same reefs.

Key members: Mark Eitzel 30/1/59, Bruce Kaphan 7/1/55, Tim Mooney 6/10/58, Dan Pearson 31/5/59, Vudi (Mark Pankler) 22/9/52 • Recording career: 1986 - 1995

Sounds: California 1988, Everclear 1991, Mercury 1993

Amon Düül II

"When the development stops,
the group finishes."
John Weinzierl

14

The more musically gifted sibling of twin factions that emerged from a Munich commune in the late 1960s, the umlaut-heavy Amon Düül II was the house band of the German underground movement. They applied the philosophy of unstructured communal living to a number of fluid line-ups and their freedom of experimentation could alternate anywhere between blistering riffs or extensive improvisations, backed up by lightshows à la early Pink Floyd (although they dismissed the comparison themselves).

Performances were erratic but rarely without interest - never a Düül moment. Their mix of guitar, sax, bongos and organ was suitably avant-garde as they represented the outer edge of a phalanx of contemporary German bands: Can, Faust, Tangerine Dream. Around 1980 even this most flexible of bands caved in, although it refused to lie down completely and reared up again intermittently (including a variant Welsh strain fronted by the band's one-time bassist Dave Anderson) like some latter-day Hydra.

Key members: Chris Karrer, Renate Knaup, Peter Leopold, John Weinzierl • **Recording career:** 1969 - present • **Sounds:** Yeti 1970, Dance Of The Lemmings 1971, Wolf City 1972

Tori Amos

"The only place
where I've never felt guilty or shameful
is playing."

Resolutely her own woman, Tori (born Myra Ellen) Amos turned unflinching self-scrutiny into an art form. She was in dire need of a musical catharsis after her first outing with the raunchily marketed, nauseatingly named *Y Kant Tori Read* was rejected by all and sundry. She licked her wounds and, relying on the spirit and natural musical ability that had got her a place at Baltimore's esteemed Peabody Institute aged five, returned to a powerful, percussive piano sound.

Brought over to a sympathetic UK by Atlantic Records, her stripped-away songs - the most soul-bearing of which was 'Me And A Gun', Tori's raw account of her own experience of rape - launched a slew of fessing-up female writers. Straddling her piano, legs akimbo and orange locks flowing, she was a Net nerd's dream, but beyond the visuals there was much more going on. As anyone who experienced her later albums discovered, this was a talent with few horizons.

Born: 22/8/63 • Recording career: 1988 - present • Sounds: Little Earthquakes 1992, Under The Pink 1994, From The Choirgirl Hotel 1998

Laurie Anderson

Where art meets rock there is a fine line between experimentation and pretension, but Laurie Anderson, for the most part, walked it with poise rather than pose. As part of the SoHo avant-garde scene she developed a blend of music media and 'found' noises (her debut in the Rochester, Vermont had the local inhabitants accompanying her on car horns), but it was 'O Superman', with its hypnotic, Vocoder-repeated "uh uh uh", that broke her into a mainstream which otherwise would have remained blissfully unaware. Warner Bros picked her up, but a series of albums warning against a soul-less techno-world hovered on the fringes, despite collaborators of the stature of Peter Gabriel, Lou Reed and Nile Rodgers. As Anderson herself pointed out, this was hardly surprising - what everyone in the music biz thought was 'new' had been standard fare in the avant-garde for over half a century.

"I'm an artist because it's one of the few things you can do in this country in which there are no rules."

Born: 5/6/47 • Recording career: 1981 - present • Sounds: Big Science 1982, United States 1985, Strange Angels 1989

"I can recall copying the sound of the coalman who use to come round...
Just a step away from singing the blues." Eric Burdon

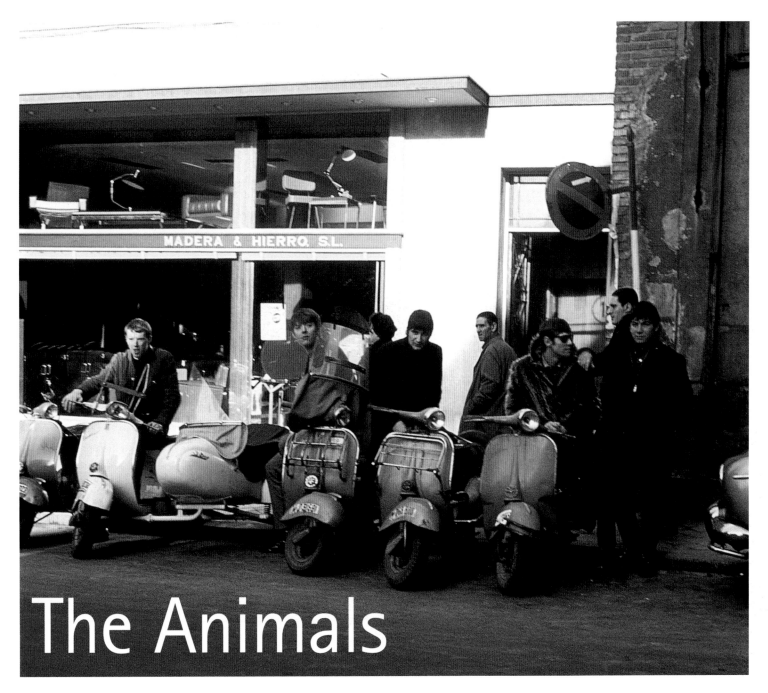

The Animals

They were a posse of Geordie lads steeped in a love of black R&B. Eric Burdon added his gritty voice to Alan Price's fluid organ-based arrangements, and Mickie Most, who'd spotted them at Newcastle's Club-A-Go-Go, paired them with some brilliantly picked covers. Their rendition of Josh White's version of 'House Of The Rising Sun' hit the jackpot - instrumental in making Dylan go electric, it is their lasting testament. Then animal instinct took over, and they turned on

themselves, despite producing singles as timeless as Barry Mann/ Cynthia Weil's 'We Gotta Get Out Of This Place'. Price left after an ego clash with Burdon and Chas Chandler took a career shift to manage the Jimi Hendrix Experience. Before Burdon recruited Californian funk-blues outfit War as his backing band, he tried out a Summer of Love sound and a revised line-up that included Zoot Money and Policeman Andy Summers, but as so often, the raw original was by far the best.

Key members: Eric Burdon 11/5/41, Chas Chandler 18/12/38, Alan Price 19/4/42, Dave Rowberry 27/12/43, John Steel 4/2/41, Hilton Valentine 21/5/43 • **Recording career:** 1964 - 1966, reformed 1976 & 1983

Sounds: The Animals 1964, Animalisms 1966, Wind Of Change 1967

Anthrax

"Some people love the cover of Fistful Of Metal,
'cos it's just the sickest thing,
but some people take one look at it and puke!" Scott Ian

Fuelled on adrenaline and firing out thrash metal at the speed of white noise, the Anthrax epidemic was in full flood in the late 1980s, with their unrelenting drive and surfer street style. They were the brainchild of Scott Ian - sole survivor of the original line-up - whose passion for punk (the band later covered 'God Save The Queen') and horror/comic books (Stephen King and Judge Dredd both inspired songs) finally seduced thrash metal panjandrum Johnny Z to put out their debut

album - *Fistful Of Metal* - on his Megaforce label. Its cover illustration, a fist smashing its way through a face, was on the borderline of good taste, but laid the groundwork for a cluster of albums on which they found a ready audience for their - albeit juvenile - humour. Their spoof rap song 'I'm The Man' in fact presaged a collaboration with Chuck D. of Public Enemy on 'Bring The Noise', which helped them ride out the drop in metal popularity and head off across the 1990s.

Key member: Scott 'Not' Ian 31/12/63 • **Recording career:** 1983 - present • **Sounds:** Among The Living 1987, Attack Of The Killer B's 1991, Sound Of White Noise 1993

Naturally shy, but open to persuasion... The reticence that led certain unsympathetic journalists to use the nickname Joan Armourplating might well have prevented her talent from reaching a wider audience, but she was blessed not only with that mellifluous, honest voice, but also a string of talented producers (Glyn Johns, Steve Lillywhite) and sessionmen (Clarence Clemons, Georgie Fame and Sly and Robbie) who helped spread the word. Self-taught on piano and acoustic guitar, her two early albums -

including a duo recording with Pam Nestor, which was marketed under Armatrading's name - failed to spark, until Johns' touch on the 1976 album *Joan Armatrading* delivered her career start-up and stand-out track 'Love And Affection'. Tougher on 'Me Myself I', rockier on 'Walking Under Ladders', Joan's lyrics always hit home with plenty of melancholy, but little self-pity. Usually disappearing back to songwriting after each album release, her career has now plateaued - or remained delightfully constant.

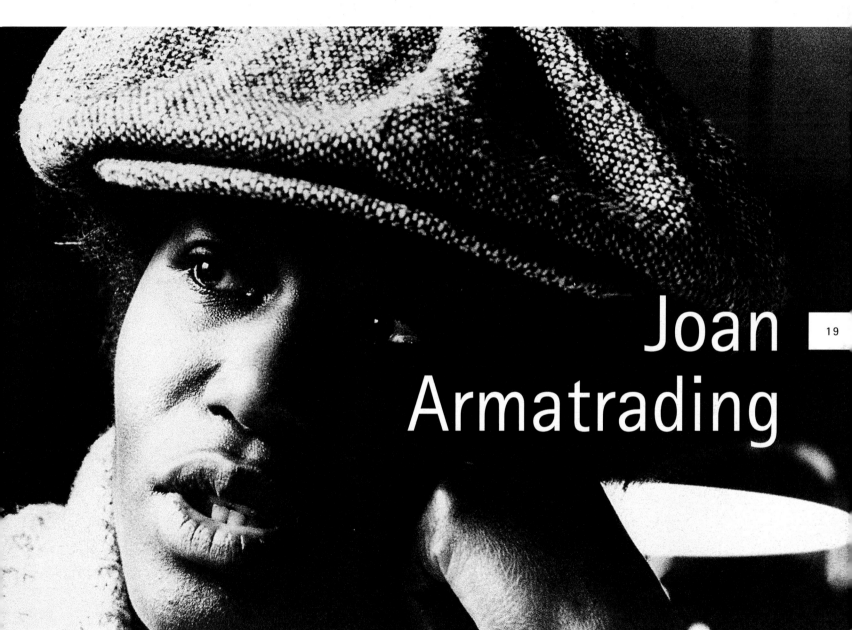

Joan Armatrading

"I'd be very uncomfortable **if all my songs were about me.**
I always say you must be a very big-headed person
to write everything that you write about yourself."

Born: 9/12/50 • Recording career: 1972 - present • Sounds: Joan Armatrading 1976, Show Some Emotion 1977, Me Myself I 1980

Aztec Camera

Amid the synth-driven sounds of the early 1980s, Aztec Camera shed a shaft of light. Light, but not necessarily slight, since Roddy Frame - to all intents and purposes Aztec Camera, with assorted musicians - had a finely tuned sense of melody, harmony

"I used to wear anoraks and play semi-acoustic guitar. Now I'm less precious, more careless." Roddy Frame

and lyrics. Nothing to frighten the horses, but plenty to mull over. In his teens in East Kilbride he'd followed the crowd with a short-lived punk band, but his true colours emerged on softer-edged ballads and by the time he was 19 his band was supporting Elvis Costello on a US tour. Their semi-acoustic romances were flavoured with a hint of Latin and a grace note of jazz - uncomplicated stuff which sometimes fought against over-production: on the album *Love* there were five producers in addition to Frame. But such was his overall dominance that in 1990 the support act at Aztec Camera gigs, solo and unplugged, was... Mr Roddy Frame.

Key member: Roddy Frame 29/1/64 • Recording career: 1982 - present • Sounds: High Land, Hard Rain 1983, Stray 1990, Dreamland 1993

The B-52's

It seems entirely appropriate that the B-52's, whose debut gig had been at a party in Athens, Georgia, were the (inspired) choice to sing the 1994 *Flintstones* movie theme as the BC-52's - because they had been living in a cartoon-like, time-warp celebration since the 1970s. You knew that if you joined these crazy, beehived, go-go-booted dudes for a trip to Planet Claire or Mesopotamia, you were going to have a goooood time. Their kitsch-retro image was oh so exquisitely post-modern, but it didn't really matter if the group's lyrics were left-field, as their groove was right on (shortly before his death,

"We just did our own thing: a combination of rock'n'roll, Fellini, game-show host, corn and mysticism."

Fred Schneider

John Lennon named them one of his favourite acts). They had slightly outstayed their own party by the mid-80s and, after guitarist Ricky Wilson's death in 1985, hibernated for four years before bouncing back with 'Love Shack' - these B-52s never quite bombed.

21

Key members: Kate Pierson 27/4/48, Fred Schneider 1/7/51, Keith Strickland 26/10/53, Cindy Wilson 28/2/57, Ricky Wilson 19/3/53 (died 12/10/85) • Recording career: 1979 - present

Sounds: The B-52's 1979, Wild Planet 1980, Cosmic Thing 1989

Bad Brains

"We're a gospel group, preaching a word of unity." Darryl Jennifer

Dr Know's blistering guitar attack could comfortably take on all-comers in the thrash punk speed stakes, but unlike many of the other performers in that particular arena his skills had been honed in the technically demanding field of jazz-fusion. Beneath the velocity was serious virtuosity. Yet Bad Brains had no hesitation in delivering the prescribed levels of attack and volume when they allied themselves with British punks (a gig supporting the Damned in the UK only fell through because of work permit problems) and joined the hardcore scene in Washington DC alongside the likes of Minor Threat and Black Flag. What marked them out was the inclusion, particularly on their first, cassette-only release, of loping reggae on tracks like 'I Luv I Jah' and 'Leaving Babylon'. The musicality of the band underpinned the flexibility of vocalist HR, volatile in voice and person: he was once arrested for assaulting his co-members.

Key members: Earl Hudson 17/12/57, HR (Paul Hudson) 11/2/56, Darryl Jenifer 22/10/60, Dr Know 15/9/58 • Recording career: 1981 - present

Sounds: Rock For Light 1983, I Against I 1986, God Of Love 1995

Badfinger

"It gets a drag when a gig advertises you as Paul McCartney's group." Pete Ham

One of the genuinely tragic tales of the music business took a dramatic twist when Badfinger's Tom Evans hanged himself eight and a half years after his fellow band member (and co-writer of 'Without You') Pete Ham had similarly taken his own life. All had seemed possible for Badfinger when a demo tape found its way to Paul McCartney, who was signing acts for the nascent Apple Corps. Macca wrote their first single 'Come And Get It' and they benefited from the Beatles' patronage, including appearances on 'Imagine' and at the Concert for Bangla Desh. However, despite the Liverpudlian roots of Tom Evans and guitarist Joey Molland, and some Fab Fourish vocals, Badfinger proved beyond doubt their own writing capabilities on tracks like 'No Matter What' and 'Without You', the latter subsequently turned by Harry Nilsson into a US/UK Number One. But at that point management problems and financial shenanigans conspired to start unravelling the plot.

Key members: Tom Evans 5/6/47 (died 19/11/83), Mike Gibbins 12/3/49, Pete Ham 27/4/47 (died 24/4/75), Joey Molland 21/6/48 • Recording career: 1969 - 1983

Sounds: No Dice 1970, Straight Up 1972, Wish You Were Here 1974

'We Shall Overcome' was Joan Baez's gift to the activists of the 1960s - and equally a millstone for the rest of her career. The song's chanted chorus echoed around demonstrations, marches and sit-ins throughout the decade, and far beyond. Baez used the combination of her pure voice and striking looks to promote a range of issues that included civil and human rights abuses and opposition to the draft, even setting up her own Institute for the Study of Non-Violence in Carmel, California. Her commitment to these causes doubtless held back the progress of her career - one side of the album *Where Are You Now, My Son?* was devoted to recordings of a US bombing raid on Hanoi. Baez remained the darling of the left, but alienated those who wanted to remember her as half of folk-rock's golden couple: she'd had a romance with Bob Dylan in the mid-60s, a relationship she reflected on in her most commercial album *Diamonds & Rust*.

Joan Baez

"Have you ever sung something for 26 years? You'd have a right to be fed up."

24

Born: 9/1/41 • Recording career: 1960 - present • Sounds: Joan Baez In Concert, Vol. 1 1962, Diamonds & Rust 1975, Play Me Backwards 1992

Hank Ballard

"If I'd had fame and money,
I probably would have ended up
**strung out
on some kind
of drug.**"

The shock value which early rock'n'roll revelled in was foreshadowed by R'n'B artists like Hank Ballard, whose early singles with their non-too-subtle, earthy lyrics managed to offend radio station programmers. Ballard (his cousin Florence was later one of the Supremes) laid out his stall from the outset in 'Work With Me Annie' - "Let's get it when the gettin's is good... Gimme all my meat" - which topped the R&B charts in 1954, leading to a string of Annie-based songs, and releases like 'Sexy Ways' and 'Open Up Your Back Door'. Ballard's influence was acknowledged by James Brown, whose revue Ballard joined in the late 1960s, and the Allman Brothers, but he missed out on personal mega-success when the B-side of a Hank Ballard and the Midnighters single was re-recorded by Chubby Checker - 'The Twist' swept the charts, and Ballard's version, though it sold a million, was sidelined.

The Band

"Back a couple of years ago, **we'd play and people would call it nostalgia.** Lately they've been calling it music again." Rick Danko

Apparently as unassuming as their non-name suggested, the Band emerged on an unsuspecting world in the aftermath of the Summer of Love, when word went around that Bob Dylan's backing band were releasing an album. The four Canadians and one Arkansan (Levon Helm) had in fact paid their dues - and built up their tight empathy - backing rockabilly singer Ronnie Hawkins before coming to Dylan's attention, when he invited Helm and Robertson to be part of the backing band at his famous 'electric' gig. Working with Dylan on *The Basement Tapes* the band developed their own songwriting skills to match their instrumental and vocal talents. *Music From Big Pink* - named after the pink house they shared near Woodstock - was a revelation of a rustic, pre-rock'n'roll world, drawing on a rich heritage of North American folklore and music, a furrow they ploughed through to their (overblown and premature) farewell concert on Thanksgiving Day 1976.

Key members: Rick Danko 9/12/43 (died 10/12/99), Levon Helm 26/5/42, Garth Hudson 2/8/37, Richard Manuel 3/4/43 (died 6/3/86), Robbie Robertson 5/7/44

Recording career: 1968 - 1978 & 1994 - 1996 • Sounds: The Band 1969, Music From Big Pink 1968, Northern Lights - Southern Cross 1975

Bangles

The ad that recently graduated Susanna Hoffs placed in a local paper set the tone, seeking fellow musicians into "the Beatles, Byrds and Buffalo Springfield". The Peterson sisters responded and, with bassist Annette Zilinskas, the quartet of California girls were off and dreaming of becoming the Fab Four. Their efforts on the 'paisley underground' circuit of LA caught the eye and ear of Prince, who presented them with 'Manic Monday' (written under the pseudonym Christopher). The single broke them as a fresh-sounding and feisty act with great harmonies, now featuring Michael Steele on bass; despite her name, the band remained all-girl. The quirky 'Walk Like An Egyptian' kept their freshness going, but by the time of 1989's MOR ballad 'Eternal Flame' - a reference to Elvis's grave - media focus on Susanna Hoffs was starting to threaten their egalitarian ideals. Shortly afterwards bang went the Bangles, until a re-union rekindled the flame in the year 2000.

"It's often difficult for people to accept us **because we're not easy to pigeonhole."** Michael Steele

27

Key members: Susanna Hoffs 17/1/57, Debbi Peterson 22/8/61, Vicki Peterson 11/1/58, Michael Steele 2/6/54 • Recording career: 1982 - 1989

Sounds: All Over The Place 1985, Different Light 1986, Everything 1988

Barclay James Harvest

"I'm amazed where we are without a cross-the-board single.
It must say something
for the quality of the music." John Lees

Frequently consigned to the footnotes of rock history, Barclay James Harvest - constantly slagged off by the press as Moody Blues copyists - outlasted the majority of their critics and continued recording for over a quarter of a century with a virtually unchanged personnel: the first member to leave departed after 13 years. The Oldham-based quartet were label-mates with Pink Floyd on EMI's Harvest (it's never clear whether the label was named after the band or not). Both were blues fans offering a melodic take on the underground music scene, though BJH's blend of folk, classical and art rock, with flashy keyboards, live orchestral arrangements and the then novel Mellotron just never cut it commercially, although they had a massive college following. Their 1977 album *Gone To Earth* contained the brave riposte track 'Poor Man's Moody Blues', but by then they must have observed the Floyd's global success with some degree of envy. Nonetheless their hardcore fans remained loyal and ardent.

Key members: Les Holroyd 12/3/48, John Lees 13/1/47, Mel Pritchard 8/1/48, Stuart Wolstenholme 15/4/47 • Recording career: 1968 - present

Sounds: Barclay James Harvest 1970, Everyone Is Everybody Else 1974, Berlin: A Concert For The People 1982

Syd Barrett

"Syd one day decided the answer to Pink Floyd's problems was to introduce two saxophonists and a girl singer. **We said 'Yeah, yeah. Good idea, Syd'.**" Roger Waters

The Floyd's lost pretty boy - born Roger, but dubbed Syd after a jazz drummer in his native Cambridge - Barrett provided the final flourish to the (then) Tea Set. From his knowledge of the blues, Syd came up with The Pink Floyd Sound (after bluesmen Pink Anderson and Floyd Council), and became the group's main songwriter and frontman, adding his improvisationally spacey guitar. Those familiar with *Dark Side Of The Moon* are often surprised to discover the whimsical fantasy of Syd's lyrics (the "gnome called Grimble Gromble"). Sadly that spacey guitar got spacier and more hallucinogenic and by late 1967 Syd had reached a state of virtual catatonia. He parted company with the Floyd, and his 1970 brace of solo albums were his final offering, much treasured by Barrett cultists: he has lived a reclusive lifestyle since, but emerged unannounced at Abbey Road during the 1975 recording of 'Shine On You Crazy Diamond', the Floyd's tribute to him...

29

Born: 6/1/46 • Recording career (solo): 1969 - 1970 • Sounds: The Madcap Laughs 1970, Barrett 1970

Bauhaus

When vocalist Peter Murphy was selected to appear in a Maxell Tapes ad, being windblown by the sound on the tape, few people would necessarily have recognised him as the hyperactive lead singer - with a vocal style worthy of the undead - of the dark force that was Bauhaus. The energy and aggression of guitarist Daniel Ash alongside Murphy was perfect fodder for the early days of the post-punk pre-goth underground. Some of Bauhaus's art-school theatricality could be traced in a direct line to Iggy Pop and Bowie, whose 'Ziggy Stardust' the band covered (tongue in cheek to a certain extent) in 1982. It was their biggest hit, although the song they left behind as a monument was their debut, 'Bela Lugosi's Dead', with its lugubriously descending bass riff and the mix of horror movie and erotic morbidity that first caught the attention of the Small Wonder label, which also launched the Cure.

> "We use white light -
> **coloured lights are
> for Christmas trees."**
>
> Peter Murphy

Key members: Daniel Ash 31/7/57, Kevin Haskins 19/7/60, David Jay 24/4/57, Peter Murphy 11/7/57 • Recording career: 1979 - 1983

Sounds: Mask 1981, Press The Eject And Give Me The Tape 1982, Burning From The Inside 1983

Beyond all that California sunshine, the sand and the broad smiles lay some dark, swirling waters - not least the complex relationship that existed between the Wilson brothers and their father Murry. "Our father beat the shit out of us, but beautiful music would always melt his heart," said Dennis. The surfing paradise evoked by the Beach Boys' early singles was equally ambiguous. Dennis was the surfer ("he'd disappear every Saturday and Sunday he could," remembered Murry),

while Brian - who acted out his father's songwriting aspirations - just could not relate to the whole beach party image. He retreated, first into his bedroom, then into his own paranoias, and tried to reject the past. *Pet Sounds* became a critically lauded masterpiece, but what does the world still remember? Brian's surfing tunes... In the words of friend Terry Melcher, "He convinced surfers those songs were written by someone who was out there hanging ten". Little wonder he cracked up.

The Beach Boys

"The ideas on Pet Sounds were Brian's, but we all sang harmonies, which anyone with ears will realise." Bruce Johnston

Key members: Al Jardine 3/9/42 , Bruce Johnston 27/6/44, Mike Love 15/3/41, Brian Wilson 20/6/42, Carl Wilson 21/12/46 (died 6/2/98), Dennis Wilson 4/12/44 (died 28/8/83)

Recording career: 1961 - present • Sounds: All Summer Long 1964, Pet Sounds 1966, Surf's Up 1971

"They were loud, obnoxious and ugly, and a lot of fun.
The whole point was to be terrible –
and admit it." Original drummer Kate Schellenbach

If you were feeling uncharitable, and their snotty smugness *really* irritated you, the Beastie Boys could be easily dismissed as middle-class white boys who took rap away from its roots, and homogenised it for white audiences. The truth was that they were bright enough to see the huge potential of doing just that: their debut album *Licensed To Ill* was CBS's fastest-selling album. Blessed with the rap magic of Rick 'Def Jam' Rubin, the title of their infectious first hit, '(You Gotta) Fight For Your Right (To Party)', said it all: from Daddy's up-scale Manhattan apartment that was pretty much the only thing to fight for. By their second album, *Paul's Boutique* - after a hiatus of three years - their innate intelligence had persuaded them to attempt a cross-influence indulgence, before they got funky and matured into an entrepreneurial empire boasting their own Grand Royal label and magazine.

Beastie Boys

Key members: Michael 'Mike D' Diamond 20/11/65, Adam 'King Ad-Rock' Horowitz 31/10/66, Adam 'MCA' Yauch 15/8/67 • **Recording career:** 1983 - present

Sounds: Licensed To Ill 1986, Paul's Boutique 1989, Hello Nasty 1998

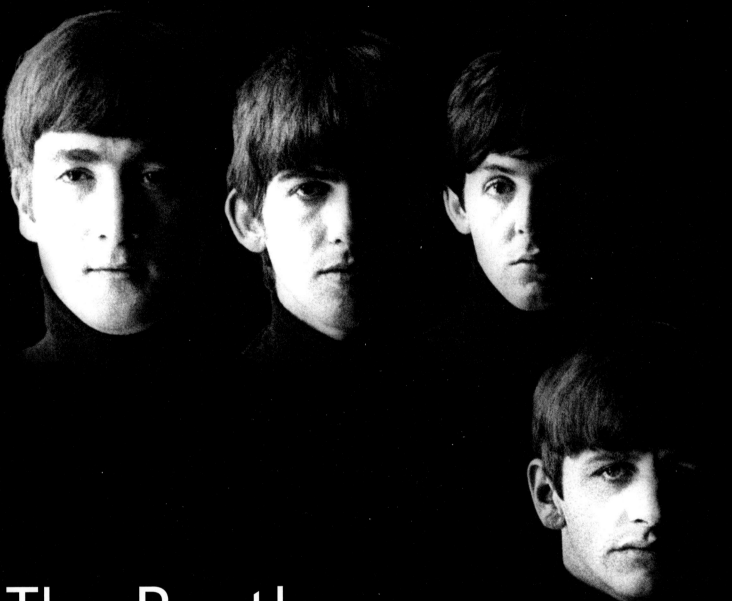

The Beatles

When Robert Freeman shot the Beatles for the cover of their November 1963 album *With The Beatles*, he caught them on the brink of a dazzling transition from pop group to phenomenon. The songs were Lennon and McCartney's, but the styling was down to Brian Epstein - although Paul later observed "People used to say we were manipulated. We were never manipulated." That same month this combination of melody and image seduced the Royal Command Variety Performance. *The Daily Mirror* was moved to coin the phrase 'Beatlemania', and from here on they were public property ("it was just bedlam, madness," said George) and on a roll, with a million copies of 'I Want To Hold Your Hand' pre-sold and the USA ripe for invasion. The only thing missing from the moody cover shot was the Merseyside humour which bubbled underneath all the packaging and that had been essential in making those moptops quite so loveable.

"Brian put us in suits, and we made it very, very big.

But we sold out.

The Beatles' music died then." John Lennon

Key members: George Harrison 24/2/43, John Lennon 9/10/40 (died 8/12/80), Paul McCartney 18/6/42, Ringo Starr 7/7/40 • **Recording career:** 1962 - 1970

Sounds: With The Beatles 1963, Revolver 1966, Sgt. Peppers Lonely Hearts Club Band 1967

Beck walks down the streets of New York, beatbox in hand, like the Freewheelin' Bob Dylan crossed with the Midnight Cowboy. The 18-year-old Beck moved out to the Big Apple in 1989, quitting Los Angeles, where he had grown up with his mother (an acolyte of Andy Warhol's Factory) and discovered the joys of the Delta blues, a music he first responded to in the mid-1980s when synth pop was prevalent.

In Manhattan's Lower East Side he found the punk scene was also discovering country blues. Looped through Beck's own grab bag of eclectic tastes, and backed by a hip hop beat, he created what he called 'talking blues', and his MTV-friendly single 'Loser' was immediately linked with the Slacker generation, a tag he tried to shrug off. At turns gloomy, funky and hilarious, Beck's pet hate was any kind of label.

Beck

34

"There was this whole kinda punk-rock-folk scene
and noise-music chaos-poetry-underground-basement-
40-ounce-malt-liquor-being-crazy scene going on."

Born: Beck Hansen 8/7/71 • Recording career: 1993 - present • Sounds: Mellow Gold 1994, Odelay 1996, Midnite Vultures 1999

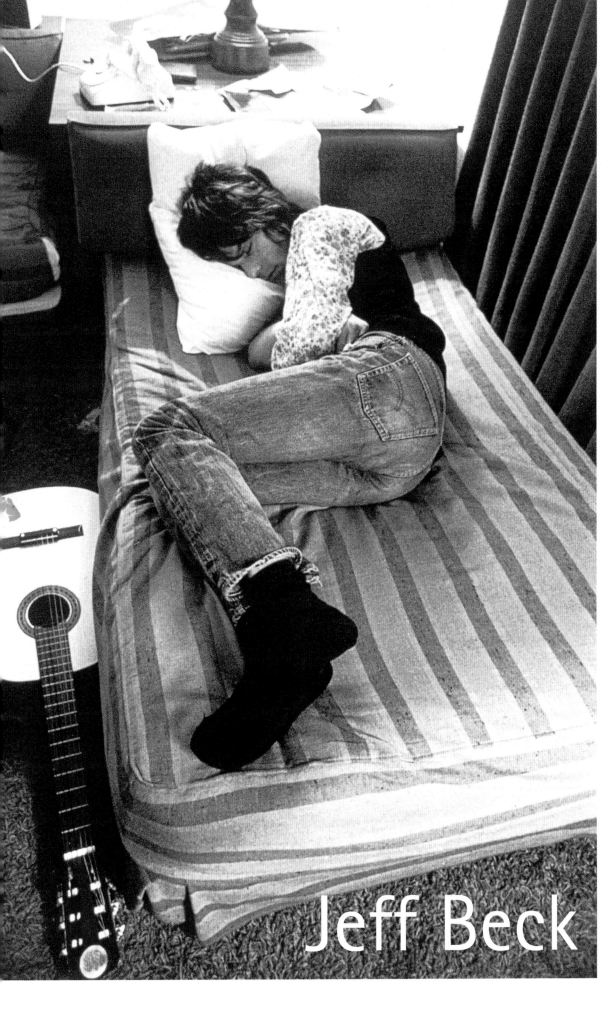

Jeff Beck

"We used to do a lot of booze, **and I'd drop plectrums all the time.** The embarrassment of looking for them on stage during a song wasn't worth it."

It's always slightly disconcerting to look down the list of Jeff Beck recordings and find his hit single 'Hi Ho Silver Lining', nestling amid the history of this massively influential guitarist's guitarist. The 'Hi Ho' escapade was part of a brief involvement with Mickie Most following Beck's departure from the Yardbirds, where he had inherited the mantle of Clapton and Page. His first Jeff Beck Group had a wonderful line-up, including Rod Stewart, Ron Wood and Nicky Hopkins, and their hard blues, following Beck's fuzz-box, feedback and distortion-flavoured lead, was dynamite (including the relationship between Stewart and Beck). The band fell apart, leaving the door open for Led Zep: the story of Beck's career was a tale of never quite seizing the moment (he cancelled a chance to perform at Woodstock, for example). Various subsequent groups and supergroups - and forays into fusion with Jan Hammer - were often inspiring, but he remains one of rock's under-achievers.

35

Born: 24/6/44 • Recording career: 1965 - present • Sounds: Beck-ola 1969, Blow By Blow 1975, Jeff Beck's Guitar Shop 1989

Bee Gees

By the time the Bee Gees had arrived back in the UK from Australia and come under Robert Stigwood's guidance, the Beatles were turning serious, leaving a gap in their wake for teenage fans who found the ex-moptops too old, too distant. Possessing a neat line in harmonies, topped by Robin's ever-distinctive falsetto, and some melodious ballads, the brothers Gibb launched swiftly into a string of hits: 'New York Mining Disaster 1941', 'Massachusetts', 'Words'. Yet by 1969 it looked like their moment might have passed, as Robin tried a solo career, and the highlight for the others was Maurice's wedding to Lulu. But back together, and after a couple of fallow years, the Stigwood connection came spectacularly good as he introduced the Bee Gees to

Dusty In Memphis co-producer Arif Mardin and some funky Miami rhythm sections, and then asked them for a few numbers for a movie he was developing. Saturday Night Fever was about to break out.

"If we hadn't been related, we would probably never have gotten back together." Robin Gibb

Key members: Barry Gibb 1/9/46, Maurice Gibb 22/12/49, Robin Gibb 22/12/49 • Recording career: 1963 - present • Sounds: Odessa 1969, Main Course 1975, Saturday Night Fever (soundtrack) 1977

"Some people are into Jesus because of the story.
Some people are into Elvis.
I'm into Muhammad Ali." Ben Folds

The instrumental icon of rock'n'roll has always been the electric guitar (just as the sax is in jazz). The piano was always a lesser partner - maybe through memories of cosy Victorian parlours, or more likely the logistical difficulties of transporting, tuning and amplifying an acoustic piano. So it was a breath of fresh air when Chapel Hill, North Carolina native Ben Folds decided to centre a band around his slightly battered grand. In fact

it took a starring role. Supported by bass and drums - the Ben Folds Five was actually a trio - and with a clutch of songs usually leavened by lyrical playfulness, Folds' barrelhouse rhythmic playing (he'd previously performed both as a percussionist and bassist) rocked at its heart. There was more than a touch of Joe Jackson and Billy Joel in his voice, though he strongly proclaimed a desire not to be seen as a singer-songwriter.

Ben Folds Five

37

Key members: Ben Folds 12/9/66, Darren Jessee 8/4/71, Robert Sledge 9/3/68 • Recording career: 1996 - 2000

Sounds: Ben Folds Five 1995, Whatever And Ever Amen 1997, The Unauthorized Biography Of Reinhold Messner 1999

Chuck Berry

"If you tried to give rock'n'roll another name, **you might call it 'Chuck Berry'."** John Lennon

Long live rock'n'roll. Chuck Berry wrote its manifesto: 'Roll Over Beethoven' summing up in three words the new disregard for the establishment. His guitar-driven blues were buzzed up with a country twang and Berry's witty take on automobiles and school: John Lennon thought his lyrics were the key element ("they were fantastic - even though we didn't know what he was saying half the time"). When Berry emerged from a decidedly dodgy jail sentence in 1964, he found that the Beatles and the Stones had both covered his material - Keith Richards went further, proudly claiming "I lifted every lick he ever played" - while the Beach Boys had been rejigging his riffs for their surfing needs. Berry cruised on, churning out even more classics, finding his greatest chart success with 'My Ding-A-Ling' in 1972 and - occasionally - colliding with the law and the tax man, although his attitude was "I just take what's my due".

Born: 18/10/26 • Recording career: 1955 - 1987 • Sounds: One Dozen Berrys 1958, St. Louis To Liverpool 1964, Back Home 1970

"Big Star was never a household word.

Every time I'd run into somebody who'd heard of the band,

the expression 'small world' would invariably come up." Jody Stephens

Big Star

Big Star are proof that talent will not necessarily out. The group produced three albums, all of which figure consistently in critics' polls and which were later re-discovered by acts like R.E.M. and the Replacements - and yet the band lives on in a kind of mythical penumbra. Alex Chilton, former vocalist for the Memphis-based Box Tops, brought his fresh-voiced, blue-eyed soul to a distillation of all that Big Star had heard on the airwaves, including the ringing guitars of the Byrds and the power pop of the Who. But their debut, *#1 Record*, disappeared due to minimal distribution; co-founder Chris Bell left, acrimoniously, before their second release, which equally vanished (Bell's talent was later snuffed out in a car crash). By the third album Big Star was really just Chilton - despite the presence of Steve Cropper on guitar, the LP remained unreleased for four years. All the ingredients for a cult future were present, and so it proved.

Key members: Chris Bell 12/1/51 (died 27/12/78), Alex Chilton 28/12/50, Andy Hummel 26/1/51, Jody Stephens 4/10/52 • Recording career: 1972 - 1975

Sounds: #1 Record 1972, Radio City 1974, Third/Sister Lovers 1978

Zing boom! Everybody's favourite Icelandic pixie sometimes gave the impression she was all space child, but the giggling elfin face masked a shrewd brain. Björk Gudmundsdóttir had a long pedigree of music-making: as a child prodigy she released an album at barely eleven. After working with a number of punk/goth bands, she and the Sugarcubes coalesced, signed to One Little Indian, and garnered most attention because of her extraordinary voice. It was capable of accelerating from whisper to yell like a Formula One car, as she later demonstrated on the solo single 'It's Oh So Quiet' - dismissed by some Björkists, but harking back to a previous jazz-influenced solo album, *Gling-Glo*. Post-Cubes, the Nellee Hooper-produced *Debut* of 1993 was sparkling, mixing unexpected atmospherics, techniques and textures (including Talvin Singh's exquisite strings), as well as a song recorded in a club loo. There were plenty of surprises to come.

Björk

"I could be more in control, but I don't want to be. I'm always thirsty for surprise."

Born: Björk Gudmundsdóttir 21/11/65 • Recording career: 1977 - present • Sounds: Debut 1993, Post 1995, Homogenic 1997

"There's no new music ever, period."

I interpret Keith Richards in the same way Keith Richards interpreted Muddy Waters and Chuck Berry." Rich Robinson

The Black Crowes

Shake Your Money Maker, the Crowes' debut album, spurred critics to iterate the patently obvious: here was a band steeped in early 1970s British rock. Vocalist Chris Robinson possessed the visuals of Mick Jagger and the vocal holler of Paul Rodgers and Rod Stewart - all skinny legs and velvet flares, obscured by a permanent haze of incense. His younger brother Rich, meanwhile, was the guitarist-cum-curator, employing an open tuning in tribute to Muddy Waters. Their distillation of the Stones,

Humble Pie and Free was way out of time in the early 90s, but they were righteously proud to be authentic. *The Southern Harmony And Musical Companion* broadened out the sound with gospel girl singers on 'Sting Me' counterpointing the hard riffing of 'Remedy', and the two brothers (whose fall-outs were frequently Gallagherian) later funked up their "bell-bottomed blues" on 1994's *Amorica*. However, as the rest of the world discovered retro, their formula ultimately became somewhat restrictive.

Key members: Johnny Colt 1/5/66, Marc Ford 13/4/66, Steve Gorman 17/8/65, Ed Hawrysch 27/5/57, Chris Robinson 20/12/66, Rich Robinson 24/5/69

Recording career: 1990 - present • Sounds: Shake Your Money Maker 1990, The Southern Harmony And Musical Companion 1992, By Your Side 1999

Black Flag

There was never much compromise with Black Flag, whether in the hardcore commitment of their music or the politically driven literacy of Henry Rollins, who added the essential brandish to the band. A succession of vocalists had careened over the top of Greg Ginn's crazy-horse guitar and Dukowski's grinding bass - with the arrival of Rollins, there was suddenly an extra level of depth, along with some real-world humour. The first album with Rollins, *Damaged*, proved just *too* damaged for MCA: the band's own label, SST, took it on and with Ginn (a UCLA economics graduate) at the helm, built itself into a major player in hardcore/indy with artists including Hüsker Dü, Dinosaur Jr. and Sonic Youth. In fact it was Ginn who would fold Black Flag after a couple of years of prolific output to concentrate on SST, while Rollins headed off to a solo career of music, poetry and publishing.

"People refer to our attitude as 'legendary', but we never thought of it as being any great statement - it was just the way Black Flag did things."

Greg Ginn

Key members: Chuck Dukowski 1/2/54, Greg Ginn 8/1/54, Henry Rollins 13/2/61 • Recording career: 1978 - 1986 • Sounds: Damaged 1981, In My Head 1985, Who's Got The 10½? 1986

Black Sabbath

"It's a satanic world. The Devil's more in control now and

happier than ever before." Geezer Butler

One of a seemingly inexhaustible seam of bands who emerged from the Midlands in the late 60s, each blessed with a self-deprecating sense of humour (viz. Slade), Black Sabbath virtually defined heavy metal. Their roots were in jazzy rock, before they heavied things up and, armed with a Denis Wheatley-ish name, burst on the scene with albums like *Paranoid*, pulsating with power and flirting with the occult. Much of the imagery was cosmetic - bat-biting apart - but terrified protectors of the world's young folk. Detested by critics, Sabbath releases were lapped up by their fan base, until Tony Iommi's musical yearnings and Ozzy's alcoholic explorations tore the original band apart. With future line-ups including the likes of Cozy Powell and Ian Gillan, and at worst lurking perilously close to Spinal Tap territory, fans dreamt of an authentic reformation because, as Ozzy Osbourne freely admitted, the only true Sabbath line up was the one with himself, Iommi, Geezer and Ward.

Key members: Terry 'Geezer' Butler 17/7/49, Tony Iommi 19/2/48, Ozzy Osbourne 3/12/48, Bill Ward 5/5/48 • Recording career: 1970 - 1998

Sounds: Black Sabbath 1970, Paranoid 1970, Master Of Reality 1971

Beale Street, Memphis was where Bobby 'Blue' Bland mastered his craft in the early 1950s, alongside B.B. King. Bland's own career didn't find its feet until he was in his late twenties, when, fresh from military service, he was matched by the Duke record label with a brass-rich band led by arranger/trumpeter Joe Scott, who - with other band members - would write much of Bland's material. His ability to handle both shouting blues and quiet ballads (he was a great admirer of Perry Como) brought him a sequence of R'n'B hits - including 'I Pity The Fool' and 'Turn On Your Love Light' - that rarely reached the mainstream charts, making him a well-kept, much cherished secret. Rod Stewart, like Van Morrison a long-time fan of Bland's, covered 'It's Not The Spotlight', and a tie-up with Four Tops producer Steve Barri created a measure of crossover success in the mid-1970s. Meanwhile Bobby kept on touring and touring, often back with B.B..

"Sometimes people classify you as a blues singer and nothing else - I do a variety of things, but what I have to rely on is the blues."

Bobby Bland

44

Born: 27/1/30 • Recording career: 1951 - present • Sounds: Two Steps From The Blues 1961, Dreamer 1974, Here We Go Again 1982

Blind Faith

Maybe Blind Faith had the perfect rock'n'roll career more sussed than anyone - including themselves - knew. From conception to dissolution in less than seven months during 1969, one transatlantic Number One album containing a couple of corking tracks, plus a money-spinning stadium tour of the States. Then call it a day: not bad. The quartet - Clapton and Baker from the disbanded Cream, Traffic's Steve Winwood, and bassist Grech plucked mid-tour from Family - were unsure if the public would accept this manufactured supergroup: the band's name suggested as much. Their album (with a controversial cover featuring a naked pre-teen model) was a swift creation, Side Two containing one 15-minute filler aptly titled 'Do What You Like', but Clapton's 'Presence Of The Lord' endures. Unhappy with the musical results, their final gig was on 20th August 1969. Perhaps Clapton gained most: the support on their tour was Bonnie and Delaney, which opened another chapter.

"We didn't rehearse enough, didn't get to know each other enough. We didn't go through enough trials and tribulations before the big time came." Eric Clapton

Key members: Ginger Baker 19/8/39, Eric Clapton 30/3/45, Rick Grech 1/11/46 (died 17/3/90), Steve Winwood 12/5/48 • Recording career: 1969 • Sounds: Blind Faith 1969

Possessors of one of the rock cognoscenti's favourite nonsense names, Blodwyn Pig were - for a short while - at the vanguard of progressive blues courtesy of guitarist Mick Abrahams, who had left Jethro Tull's original line-up to allow his bluesy guitar the room to express itself more freely. Another angle of attack was provided by sax player Jack Lancaster, who indulged in simultaneous multi-sax playing in the fine tradition of Rahsaan Roland Kirk and provided a jazz overtone to the slide skills of Abrahams. After their debut album - with suitably piggy artwork - and its successor had hit the UK Top Ten, and despite a strong live presence often showcasing Abrahams' version of Cream's 'Cat's Squirrel', the guitarist headed for pastures new, and saxman Lancaster took over, even changing the name to Lancaster's Bombers (a pun for all you planespotters). Abrahams then picked up the Blodwyn moniker and intermittently returned, recording again in the 1990s.

"A lunatic gave us the name!
This fella called Graham who had just come home after spending four years as a Buddhist monk." _{Mick Abrahams}

Blodwyn Pig

46

Key members: Mick Abrahams 7/4/43, Ron Berg, Jack Lancaster, Andy Pyle • **Recording career:** 1969 - 1970 & 1991 - 1996 • **Sounds:** Ahead Rings Out 1969, Getting To This 1970

Debbie Harry's name and look dominated Blondie, even though the musicianship throughout the band was excellent. Harry's boyfriend and co-writer Chris Stein put it this way: "It all comes together through her, but I don't think it's really built *on* her". Already in her thirties when the band took off, Debbie was the Brigitte Bardot of the 1970s ("she was a sort of continental punk, I guess"), and with a little help from Chinnichap's Mike Chapman, the combination of

"Women are going to be the new Elvises.

That's the only place for rock'n'roll to go."

Debbie Harry

1960s girl group/punk energy and Harry's odd, flat delivery was rolled out with 'Denis', their cover of NYC quintet Randy and the Rainbows' 'Denise'. Soon no self-respecting red-blooded male was without a Debbie poster on his wall, and through 1979 and 1980 they packed in the hits, including Giorgio Moroder's re-routing of the group into disco ('Heart Of Glass'). Though solo projects delayed the break-up, by 1982 it was time to move on. As Harry remarked, "You do get tired of bleaching your hair out".

Blondie

47

Key members: Clem Burke 24/11/55, Jimmy Destri 13/4/54, Nigel Harrison 24/4/51, Debbie Harry 1/7/45, Frank Infante, Chris Stein 5/1/50 • **Recording career:** 1976 - 1982 (reformed 1999 - present)

Sounds: Blondie 1976, Plastic Letters 1977, Parallel Lines 1978

"Our blues is a crazy blues.
A lot of us are nuts and music is our outlet."

Al Kooper

BS&T's attempt to introduce other forms of music into 1960s rock was the brainchild of Al Kooper, who had previously proved his worth with the Blues Project (including fellow Bloodster Steve Katz) and a credit as organist on Dylan's 'Like A Rolling Stone'. Enhancing a core quartet with a brass section that included future luminary Randy Brecker, the outfit brought together elements of pop, jazz and Motown as it paraded covers by the toniest of songwriters - Harry Nilsson, Tim Buckley,

Randy Newman, Goffin and King. The project showed much promise but both Kooper and Brecker decided to quit and the second album was fronted by vocalist David Clayton-Thomas. Although the album was a massive hit, containing three gold US singles including 'Spinning Wheel' ("What goes up, must come down"), its classical aspirations - there was an Erik Satie re-work - caused some observers to suggest that the original jazz-rock outfit might have lost its way. They were right.

Blood, Sweat & Tears

Key members: Randy Brecker 27/11/45, Bobby Colomby 20/12/44, Jim Fielder 4/10/47, Dick Halligan 29/8/43, Steve Katz 9/5/45, Al Kooper 5/2/44, Fred Lipsius 19/9/43, Jerry Weiss 1/5/46
Recording career: 1968 - 1980 • **Sounds:** Child Is Father To The Man 1968, Blood, Sweat & Tears 1969, Blood, Sweat & Tears 3 1970

"We're absolutely determined to **make every note mean something emotionally** and not to add or subtract from that."

Paul Buchanan

Three albums in over twelve years: very good for credibility, but you need a patient, understanding record label. There is an extremely considered aspect to the work of three Glasgow University post-graduates whose home-studio doodlings were on the verge of release when their first label (RSO) collapsed. It could have been the end of the story, but local audio company Linn Products began using the Blue Nile's demos to demonstrate the quality of their product range - and set up Linn Records to boot. Their synthy softness provided little obvious single material, but the debut album was hailed as ideal nocturnal listening. The world waited, and waited, and five years later *Hats* appeared, another lush collage of sound. Now in their thirties, the band were encouraged to tour by fan Rickie Lee Jones, and Annie Lennox's cover of 'Downtown Lights' provided extra exposure. It was another seven years before the third album. Watch this space.

The Blue Nile

Key members: Robert Bell, Paul Buchanan, Paul Joseph Moore • Recording career: 1981- present • Sounds: A Walk Across The Rooftops 1984, Hats 1989, Peace At Last 1996

"Are you familiar with the film Spinal Tap? It's bit like that. In fact we're living Spinal Tap!" Eric Bloom

The svengali-like figure of *Crawdaddy* writer Sandy Pearlman hovered over the Cult. He moulded them, not in his own image, but into that of a post-Altamont sub-Satanic biker outfit, as well as supplying lyrics that were always curiously cryptic. The Cult members, previously incarnated in line-ups such as the psychedelic Soft White Underbelly (a name they later used for club dates), bolted fast heavy metal onto Donald Roeser's blues-based guitar solos and lashings of stage flash.

Occasionally the imagery - their logo was the symbol of Cronos - threatened to weigh them down, but there was usually something half-way intelligent to save each album, including lyrics by Patti Smith, Allen Lanier's one-time girlfriend. Following the career-boosting 1976 album *Agents Of Fortune*, the upbeat hit '(Don't Fear) The Reaper' was replete with West Coast harmonies. The band were teetering on the edge less of darkness than AOR - for Cultists a far more terrifying prospect.

Blue Öyster Cult

50

Key members: Eric Bloom 11/12/44, Albert Bouchard 24/5/47, Joe Bouchard 9/11/48, Allen Lanier 25/6/46, Donald 'Buck Dharma' Roeser 12/11/47 • Recording career: 1972 - present

Sounds: Tyranny And Mutation 1973, Agents Of Fortune 1976, Extraterrestrial Live 1982

Blur

Mockney it might have been, but what Blur's *Parklife* lacked in genuine East End credentials it made up for with sheer chutzpah, as the art-school boys mugged their way, with mouthy confidence, through a vision of an England made up of betting shops, pubs and Radio 4's Shipping Forecast, topped off by Phil (*Quadrophenia*) Daniels' streetwise rap. The album - evoking the spirit of Ray Davies, Steve Marriott, Andy Partridge and Madness - rescued the band from near disaster, after the quartet had found their original guise as quasi-Happy Mondays with a barrel-load of attitude losing out when grunge overwhelmed baggy. The Britpop wave salvaged their irrepressible humour. After the whole overblown, in retrospect highly embarrassing, battle royal with Oasis (in fact Suede were the much more deadly enemy), Blur moved on and decided to grow up: their 1999 album *13* - rating Mach One on the emotional scale - marked a new maturity.

"We are not shaping up to be the next Rolling Stones. No way are we doing another twenty years." Damon Albarn

Key members: Damon Albarn 23/3/68, Graham Coxon 12/3/69, Alex James 21/11/68, Dave Rowntree 8/5/64 • Recording career: 1990 - present

Sounds: Modern Life Is Rubbish 1993, Parklife 1994, 13 1999

Marc Bolan

"I never thought it would be real. Marc Bolan is an illusion."

The wheels fell off Marc Bolan's career far too soon - the world of pop he revitalised had moved on. When the Beatles abdicated in 1970, rock had got serious and grown beards: the counter-culture didn't seem to have unadulterated fun any more. The poet-fantasist Bolan, always changing faces - he'd been a rock'n'roller, Mod, then flower child - woke up, soldered his teenage love for Elvis and Cochran onto a rhythm section that was all beef and no bongos, shortened his band's name, and unleashed 'Ride A White Swan'. For a couple of years T-Rextasy was rampant, in the vanguard of glam rock. It wasn't punk that marked the downturn - the Damned were big fans - just the arrival of younger, slimmer teen idols. Bolan's car crash created snide jokes ('Tie A Yellow Mini Round The Old Oak Tree') and a shrine for fans who kept a little bit of Marc in their hearts.

Born: Mark Feld 30/9/47 (died 16/9/77) • Recording career: 1965 - 1977 • Sounds: A Beard Of Stars 1970, Electric Warrior 1971, The Slider 1972

Bon Jovi

Whatever else, Bon Jovi laid to rest the assumption that metal bands were universally blessed with lank hair and unholy hygiene problems. Jon Bon Jovi, né Bongiovi, was the photogenic fulcrum, pretty enough to enjoy an intermittent film career. Backing him, the guitar of Richie Sambora: they'd met when Jon was working at Manhattan's Power Station studios, using downtime to record demos. Early Bon Jovi had far too much hair and suffered no little abuse for their appearance. It all changed after they were paired with songwriter Desmond Child - who co-wrote two US Number One singles ('Livin' On A Prayer', 'You Give Love A Bad Name') - and started using focus groups of kids to test-market track selection. Stardom ensued. After a hiatus for solo projects and family matters the band returned to form, never straining any boundaries but undemandingly comfortable - their 'best of' album *Crossroads* was the UK's biggest selling album of 1994.

"I'd much rather not be playing than in a band that's big on image." Jon Bon Jovi

53

Key members: Jon Bon Jovi 2/3/62, David Bryan 7/2/62, Richard Sambora 11/7/59, Alex John Such 14/11/56, Tico Torres 7/10/53 • **Recording career:** 1984 - present

Sounds: Slippery When Wet 1986, New Jersey 1988, Keep The Faith 1992

The Bonzo Dog Doo-Dah Band

"Looking very relaxed, Adolf Hitler on vibes... In the corner, Eric Clapton on ukulele... Digging General de Gaulle on accordion - really wild, General."

From 'The Intro & The Outro'

Crazy name, crazy guys. The Bonzos were a mix of music hall, Kenny Ball's Jazzmen and *The Goon Show*, the kind of humour that made people, especially duffle-coated Englishmen, chortle throughout the 1950s and 60s. Their fluid art school personnel - simply whoever turned up on the night when they started out - included the 1920s enthusiasms of Roger Spear, the mimicry of Neil Innes (later of the Rutles), the majestic humour of Viv Stanshall, and the spoon-playing of... Sam Spoons. An appearance in the Beatles' *Magical Mystery Tour* helped promote their debut 1967 album *Gorilla*, as did performances on kids' TV show *Do Not Adjust Your Set* - a springboard for various Pythons - while Paul McCartney produced, as Apollo C. Vermouth, their big hit, Innes's 'I'm The Urban Spaceman'. The joke dwindled by the early 70s and they scattered: Innes to Python sideman, Stanshall to voice-over *Tubular Bells*, Rodney Slater to local government officer...

Key members: Vernon Dudley Bohay-Nowell 29/7/32, Neil Innes 9/12/44, Rodney Slater 8/11/44, Larry Smith 18/1/44, Roger Ruskin Spear 29/6/43, Sam Spoons 8/2/42, Vivian Stanshall 21/3/43 (died 5/3/95)

Recording career: 1966 - 1971 • Sounds: Gorilla 1967, The Doughnut In Granny's Greenhouse 1968, Tadpoles 1969

"I love music and I love people.

Together we have understanding, expression and communication." Booker T. Jones

The backbone of the Memphis label Stax sound, where their spare, tight-knit sound featured behind the likes of Otis Redding and Wilson Pickett, the MG's (for Memphis Group) brought together sax player and organist Booker T. alongside Ozark Mountain boy Cropper - the band was calmly integrated -and eventually their jam session-produced solo number 'Green Onions' sprouted forth. Bass legend Duck Dunn was not on that recording (it was original bassist Lewis Steinberg), but the later version of the quartet became the best known, their hits including 'Soul Limbo', BBC-TV's long-time cricket *Test Match Special* theme (American readers please change channels). Steve Cropper not only played a mean guitar, he also had co-writing credits on 'Knock On Wood', 'Soul Man' and 'In The Midnight Hour'; he and Duck starred in the Blues Brothers band. A fond visual memory: the group's *Abbey Road* instrumental tribute, *McLemore Avenue*, complete with road-crossing cover photo!

55

Booker T. and the MG's

Key members: Steve Cropper 21/10/41, Donald 'Duck' Dunn 24/11/41, Al Jackson Jr 27/11/35 (died 1/10/75), Booker T. Jones 12/11/44 • Recording career: 1962 - 1977 & 1994

Sounds: Green Onions 1962, Soul Dressing 1964, McLemore Avenue 1970

"I want to write a song that people will some day hear
and be reminded of something they did years ago.
Maybe 'I Don't Like Mondays' will be the one." Bob Geldof

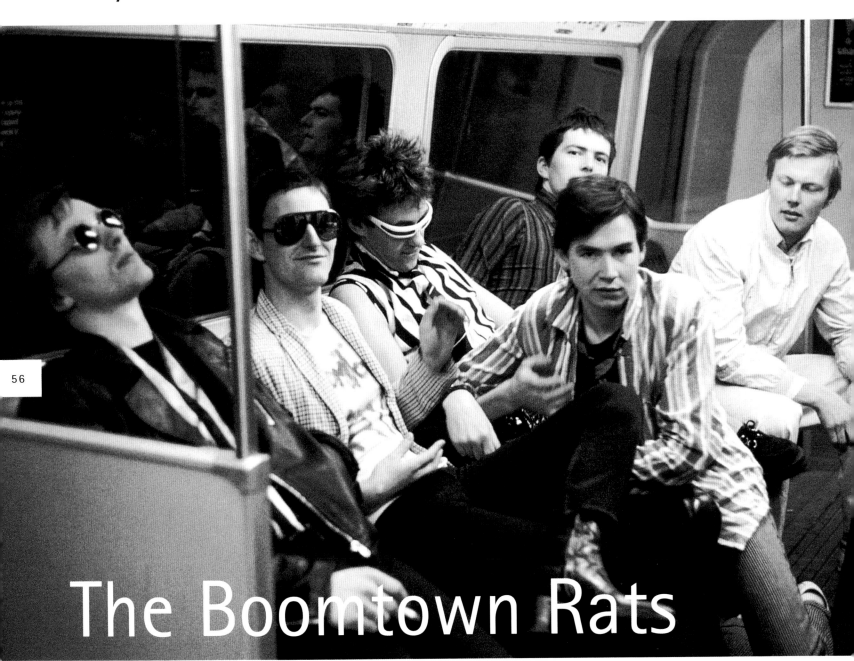

56

The Boomtown Rats

A move to London in 1976 put Dublin's Boomtown Rats - named after a line from a Woody Guthrie bio-pic - onto the mainline of punk's birth, an opportunity they embraced with vigour. Fronted by ex-music journalist and motormouth Bob Geldof, they were never mainstream punk - far too talented for that. A couple of singles in they delivered 'Rat Trap', an acerbic thing of beauty, and on a tour of the USA (a territory that largely ignored them) picked up the idea for

'I Don't Like Mondays' from the kind of schoolkid shooting spree that back then was still something of a rarity. It was the best thing they ever did - thereafter the Boomtown started to go bust: the early 1980s were enlivened primarily by Geldof's appearance as Pink in the movie version of Pink Floyd's *The Wall* and a bizarre fan riot in Greece. Following 1984 and the whole Band Aid/Live Aid extravaganza, the Rats dispersed, leaving Geldof to knighthood and sanctification.

Key members: Pete Briquette 2/7/54, Gerry Cott 16/6/54, Simon Crowe 1/4/48, Johnnie Fingers (John Moylett) 10/9/56, Bob Geldof 5/10/54, Garry Roberts 16/6/54 • Recording career: 1977 - 1985

Sounds: The Boomtown Rats 1977, A Tonic For The Troops 1978, The Fine Art Of Surfacing 1979

It is extraordinary still to recall the debut album of Boston, essentially the home-made tapes of Polaroid boffin Tom Scholz plus various Beantown musicians, racing to eight million copies on release, and almost double that in the USA alone by 1994. Scholz's tapes were barely amended and simply enhanced by contributions from the rest of the band to produce some solid rock featuring power riffs, twin guitar solos and intricate harmonies: the single 'More Than A Feeling' became an

AOR anthem (influencing Kurt Cobain's 'Smells Like Teen Spirit' amongst others). Scholz's reclusive recording obsessions frustrated the Epic label, and during an eight-year hiatus following Boston's second album the rest of the band melted away, leaving Scholz and vocalist Delp for the 1994 release *Walk On*, before another lengthy gap. Scholz meantime had successfully invented and marketed the Rockman mini amp for guitarists - and music was increasingly an unnecessary sideline.

Boston

57

"I had enough visions of grandeur at Polaroid.
I've already gone further than I expected. It's all downhill from here." Tom Scholz

Key members: Brad Delp 12/6/51, Barry Goudreau 29/11/51, Sib Hashian 17/8/49, Tom Scholz 10/3/47, Frank Sheehan 26/3/49 • Recording career: 1976 - 1987 & 1994

Sounds: Boston 1976, Don't Look Back 1978, Third Stage 1986

David Bowie

"My interest in music dissipated during the 80s **as I realised that I was more important."**

Early stripped-to-basics David Bowie was a little too late in the day for the folk-rock boom and 'The Laughing Gnome' failed to offer him a stairway to stardom. Bowie, who'd spent time working with Lindsay Kemp's mime/dance outfit, simply raided the costume trunk and, like some old-style music-hall act, rummaged around to invent a repertory company of characters ("I feel like an actor when I'm onstage, rather than a rock artist"). On *Hunky Dory* he proudly announced his manifesto of ch-ch-ch-changes; from then on the now familiar cast emerged: Ziggy, Aladdin, soul boy, Thin White Duke, rock'n'roller and art(iste). Equally brilliant at absorbing musical cultures, from the New York underground to the gloss of Philly, Bowie would glance over his shoulder at the imitators and camp-followers, before flouncing off to leave them floundering in his wake. "If it works, it's out of date," was his declared philosophy. The gnome nearly always had the last laugh.

Born: David Jones 8/1/47 • Recording career: 1964 - present • Sounds: Hunky Dory 1971, The Rise And Fall Of Ziggy Stardust And The Spiders From Mars 1972, Low 1977

What you see is what you get with Billy Bragg. Whether in the former Eastern bloc or Latin America, he took along his Burns guitar and a backpack of straight-talking songs and convictions, just as he had done throughout the 1980s, when, with Thatcherism at full pelt, he might well have been sidelined like a musical Michael Foot. But with defiant humour, he kept digging away, supporting the Miner's Strike, mobilising Red Wedge, honing his songwriting - given a boost by Kirsty MacColl's

hit cover of 'New England' - and always lightening, as in that song, a review of contemporary Britain and world injustice with the prospect of personal happiness. Even with the added constraints of speech-making, journalism and TV presenting, Bragg continued straight as a die, and though he broadened his palette to include human and sexual politics ('Sexuality' in 1991) and a fine collaboration with Jeff Tweedy's Wilco, it was a brave observer who would accuse him of ever selling out.

Billy Bragg

"When a folk club artist goes out with his guitar,
he might think he's James Taylor or Bob Dylan.
I still think I'm the Clash."

Born: 20/12/57 • Recording career: 1983 - present • Sounds: Brewing Up 1984, Don't Try This At Home 1991, William Bloke 1996

Garth Brooks

Gene Simmons watch out.... Traces of Garth Brooks' early exposure to the Kiss experience of the 1970s re-emerged in the controlled theatricality of his shows, which took country to new heights. The son of noted 1950s country artist Colleen Carroll, Brooks was persistent enough in his dream of success to survive a first fruitless, demoralising trip out to Nashville. On his second attempt, he forced a break, and, like a pumped-up rodeo calf released from the stalls, rocketed full-pelt into the arena. His classic voice and heartfelt delivery steered his second album *No Fences* to sales of fifteen million copies and then some; *Ropin' The Wind*, the follow-up, was a double rock and country Number One. Records for sales units, audiences and awards tumbled. Singing up for gay rights and confessing past adultery on talk shows, here was a country boy for the VH-1 generation.

"My biggest influence through junior high was Kiss.
That was my thing."

Born: 7/2/62 • Recording career: 1989 - present • Sounds: No Fences 1990, Ropin' The Wind 1991, Sevens 1997

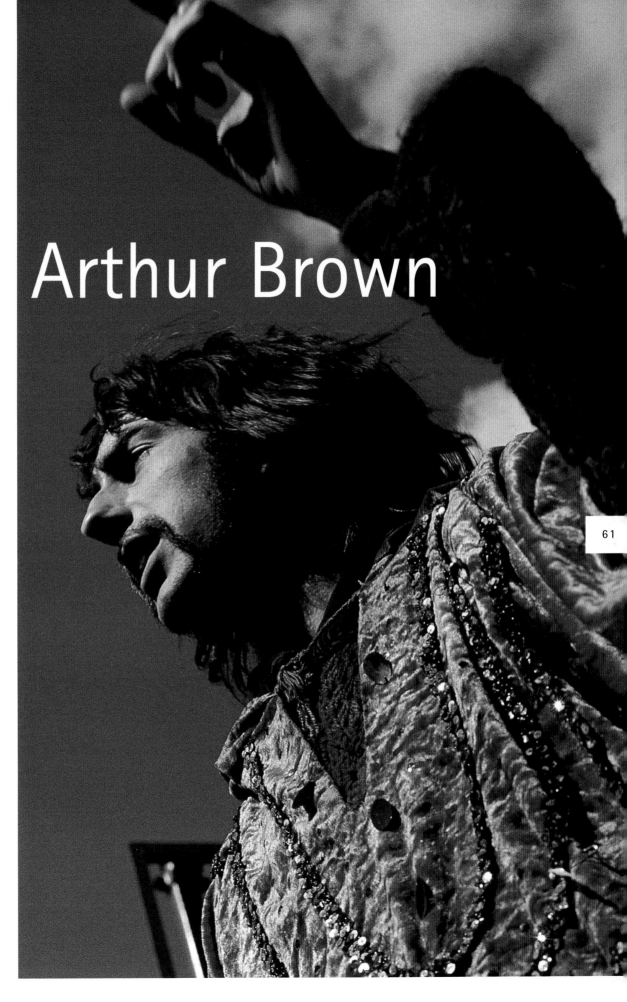

"We represented a different approach altogether

to what the pop music thing was all about."

Arthur Brown usually appeared on stage with his hair in flames, in keeping with his most celebrated single, 'Fire'. It was an illusion, of course - the effect created by a craftily constructed helmet - and his self-styled Crazy World Of Arthur Brown was as sane as the rest of the late 60s underground. Arthur's roots were in R&B - his elastic voice capable of as many variations as his namesake James. Using a cocktail of make-up, psychedelia and blues - and a band that at one point included future ELP drummer Carl Palmer - the Arthur Brown experience centred around the leader's lengthy discourse-cum-operetta on sin and damnation. His debut album was co-produced by Pete Townshend (who recorded a 'Fire' tribute in 1989) but the follow-up remained unreleased for two decades. Brown meantime headed for Texas to a life of carpentry, and an occasional band called the Even Crazier World Of...

Arthur Brown

61

Born: 24/6/42 • Recording career: 1968 - present • Sounds: The Crazy World Of Arthur Brown 1968

James Brown

The whipcracking energy of Mr Dynamite was as tight as those pants and the discipline imposed on his backing bands: "I don't allow anybody to get high, or get drunk, and they got to wear a uniform". His revue, captured in all its glory on the groundbreaking 1963 record *Live At The Apollo*, established the live album as a viable genre, and highlighted all the Brown attributes. He teased his audiences, working them up, simmering them down, before the famous finale in which he feigned collapse but always, always, came back for more. Fierce ambition - "I wanted to be somebody, to *be* somebody" - meshed with both social conscience and patriotism ('America Is My Home'), but above all with that Groove - scratch guitar, funky bass riffs, brass stabs. Pure rhythm, above which JB could gospelise the audience, laying the groundwork for both 1970s funk (listen to the Bootsy Collins groove on 'Papa's Got A Brand New Bag') and 80s hip-hop.

"God made me... But I created the myth."

Born: 3/5/33 • Recording career: 1956 - present • Sounds: Live At The Apollo 1963, Say It Loud, I'm Black And I'm Proud 1969, The Payback 1973

Jackson Browne

As politically and socially committed as Billy Bragg or Joan Baez, Jackson Browne brought to West Coast music a sense of reflection more refined than, say, the Eagles' generally hedonistic approach, though it was the Eagles who provided a high-profile platform for his songs: Browne co-wrote 'Take It Easy' with Glenn Frey and also contributed to 'James Dean' and 'Doolin-Dalton'. An earlier, though ephemeral, patron had been Nico, who included three of his songs on *Chelsea Girls*.

His solo albums were enhanced by some top session musicians, including Jim Keltner on drums, mandolin supremo David Lindley and the Byrds' Clarence White, but they never threatened to overshadow the gentle power of his songs. Able to transcend personal grief through writing, 1976's album *The Pretender* - a US Number Five - was recorded after the suicide of his first wife. A later, much-publicised, break-up with actress Daryl Hannah inspired the 1993 release *I'm Alive*.

"Being able to play live is like mother's milk to me."

Born: 9/10/48 • Recording career: 1972 - present • Sounds: Late For The Sky 1974, The Pretender 1976, I'm Alive 1993

Roy Buchanan

"He was the first great rock guitarist I ever heard... **Wonderful, just wonderful.**"

Robbie Robertson

Described in the title of a PBS documentary as 'The Best Unknown Guitarist In The World', Roy Buchanan is that lodestone of rock music, the musician's musician - a low-profile, technically brilliant guitarist, to be played late at night and savoured with awe. Jeff Beck, Eric Clapton and the Band's Robbie Robertson were all celebrants of the preacher's son whose Fender Telecaster graced, by his own reckoning, hundreds of recordings. An R'n'B apprenticeship in LA led to stints with Dale Hawkins, the rockabilly singer, and the unrelated rock'n'roller Ronnie Hawkins, alongside some solo releases, including a version of 'Green Onions' with Steve Copper. The much-awaited breakthrough never came; he claimed to have been considered by the Stones as a replacement for Brian Jones, but he might not have wanted it. Shy, reticent, he carried his own doubts and demons: after several suicide attempts, he hanged himself in a Virginia police cell after an arrest for drunkenness.

Born: 23/9/39 (died 14/8/88) • Recording career: 1959 - 1988 • Sounds: Roy Buchanan 1972, Live Stock 1975, When A Guitar Plays The Blues 1986

He tried hard to downplay comparisons with his father, but there was no mistaking the vocal connection. Just as Tim Buckley had swooped and soared across his albums, so the son he'd left behind had a range that spanned octaves of emotion. Some considered Jeff to be potentially the better songwriter, yet his own early death in a swimming accident on the Mississippi river bequeathed a slender legacy including a couple of live recordings, and one much-lauded album. *Grace* (praised on release, not just in rosy-tinted respectful retrospect) included, as well as his own work, characterful covers of Leonard Cohen's 'Hallelujah' and the Elkie Brooks number 'Lilac Wine': live, he performed MC5's 'Kick Out The Jams' over a sparse band with whom he could rock as well as retreat, and out of Greenwich Village word was spreading fast about another talented Buckley. Thanks to some additional, posthumously released, material there is a bequest (but still too little) to let us recall him, and ponder what might have been.

"I want the idea and the sound of the idea to intoxicate - not the voltage."

Jeff Buckley

Born: 17/11/66 (died 29/5/97) • Recording career: 1992 - 1997 • Sounds: Grace 1994, Sketches For My Sweetheart The Drunk 1998, Mystery White Boy 2000

"The trick of writing is **to make it sound like it's all happening for the first time.**"

Tim Buckley

His thirst for exploration was both his characteristic temperament and his downfall. Discovered by Zappa's manager Herb Cohen, and initially bracketed with the West Coast folk-rock movement - he was signed to the label of the moment, Elektra - Tim Buckley built a loyal audience for his early releases, seduced by the poetry, range and expressiveness of his tenor voice on songs like 'Morning Glory' (later covered by Blood, Sweat & Tears, whose John Fielder was a long-time associate). But by 1971 on *Starsailor* he had embraced the sounds of John Coltrane and Ornette Coleman, employing his voice as an additional, nearly atonal, instrument: the stylistic change dismayed his core fans, and Buckley hit lean times. He returned with another surprise, the earthy, rootsy, horny *Greetings From LA*, and was working on an ambitious album project in 1975 when his explorations ended in a Santa Monica morgue following a morphine/heroin overdose.

Born: 14/2/47 (died 29/6/75) • Recording career: 1966 - 1974 • Sounds: Goodbye And Hello 1967, Starsailor 1970, Greetings From LA 1972

The mark left by Buffalo Springfield was significant, despite a short and turbulent time together. After a while the tensions between three major-league songwriters were bound to tell - Stills and Furay were effectively the band's leaders, with Neil Young comparatively taking a back seat: the quintet had come together in 1966 when the Canadians Martin, Palmer and Young joined forces with Stills and Furay. As folk-rock trumpeted its last fanfare, announcing the dawn of the country rock movement, their melodic songs and harmonies were there at its onset. 1967's 'For What It's Worth' ("Stop, children, what's that sound?"), written by Stills, captured a contemporary mood of public concern at establishment excess, specifically police over-reaction to an anti-Vietnam demo in LA. Later inter-personnel feuds, between Stills and Young in particular, scattered the Springfield's final line-up, but the resulting diaspora of musicians was impressive, including Crosby, Stills, Nash & Young, Loggins and Messina, and Poco.

Buffalo Springfield

"I was trying to be Boss Cat and keep the thing in order, and someone like Neil or Bruce was instantly going to rebel. So there was chaos." Steven Stills

Key members: Richie Furay 9/5/44, Dewey Martin 30/9/42, Bruce Palmer 9/46, Steven Stills 3/1/45, Neil Young 12/11/45 • Recording career: 1966 - 1968

Sounds: Buffalo Springfield 1967, Buffalo Springfield Again 1967, Last Time Around 1968

Kate Bush

"I don't really see myself as a performer.

That's hard for me when I have to come out and expose myself and be the saleswoman of the hour."

When EMI presented Kate Bush to an unsuspecting world in 1978, the impact was immediate. 'Wuthering Heights', her Emily Bronte-inspired mini-drama, with its piercing, little-girlish vocals and serious dance movements, was an unlikely UK Number One. It represented the culmination of careful cultivation by EMI, introduced to her by Pink Floyd's Dave Gilmour: they decided to be patient and nurture the then 15-year-old whose already finished songs included an early version of 'The Man With The Child In His Eyes'. She studied dance and mime, notably with Lindsay Kemp, and played the pub circuit. Four years later it paid off, with a debut album that was both rounded and perceptive. Taking her music out on the road, though, proved so exhausting she never toured again and rarely appeared live - video became her creative outlet instead. Hardly prolific, Kate Bush's role in the 1990s was as an elder sister to Björk and Tori Amos.

Born: 30/7/58 • Recording career: 1978 - present • Sounds: The Kick Inside 1978, Hounds Of Love 1985, The Sensual World 1989

"I don't go looking for weird shit,
but it seems like it comes for me." Gibby Haynes

This band were fond of bizarre nomenclature - an earlier formation revelled in the moniker of Ashtray Baby Heads, and their albums included *Rembrandt Pussyhorse* and *Locust Abortion Technician* - but Butthole Surfers was not their choice, just a song that a DJ mistakenly thought was the band's name. Never mind, it suited them, as they took hardcore punk into weirder, more psychedelic realms than had existed before (and may never grace our world again). With music able to embrace Oriental drones, industrial noise and manic laughter, and a stage show that could at any one time feature simulated sex, urination and jello-covered nude dancers, the Surfers were no shrinking violets. They also subverted their own influences with parodies of Black Sabbath and the wonderfully named *Hairway to Steven*, complete with Zep-style symbols - John Paul Jones later produced the band. Their calculated outrage was either found pretentious... or hilarious.

Butthole Surfers

Key members: Gibby Haynes 1957, King Coffey, Paul Leary, Theresa Nervosa (Theresa Naylor), Jeff Pinkus • **Recording career:** 1984 - present

Sounds: Butthole Surfers 1983, Locust Abortion Technician 1987, Hairway To Steven 1988

Buzzcocks

Punk - musically - was really all about singles: short, sharp bursts of adrenaline, and anger. The Buzzcocks understood that, and could go head to head with any other punk outfit for speed of attack, but they also grafted on top of that a pop awareness that gave their singles a little extra finesse - few of their contemporaries could have delivered the 1978 classic 'Ever Fallen In Love?' Standing in a direct line from the Ramones to the Britpoppers of the 1990s, the Buzzcocks were the creation of Howard Devoto and Pete Shelley, inspired to get up and play by the Sex Pistols as they in turn would prove inspirational. After participating in seminal punk moments like the 100 Club Festival of

"The New Wave is not just about music.

It is a challenge to consider everything you do, think and feel."

Pete Shelley

September 1976, Devoto fled the coop to launch the edgy post-punk outfit Magazine; Shelley carried on with his concerns of adolescent love and life. Following 1979's *A Different Kind Of Tension* the Buzzcocks ran out of momentum, but were poised to encourage a new generation.

Key members: Howard Devoto 1955, Steve Diggle, Steve Garvey, John Maher, Pete Shelley 17/4/55 • Recording career: 1977 - 1981 & 1991 - present

Sounds: Another Music In Another Kitchen 1978, Love Bites 1978, Singles - Going Steady 1981

"We always hated the idea of being put into any kind of pigeon-hole. That's why we kept changing our style." Roger McGuinn

The picture-perfect pose of the Byrds' first manifestation was hot off the success of their cover of Dylan's 'Mr Tambourine Man', complete with trademark 12-string guitar and triple harmonies: Roger McGuinn and Gene Clark had been performing as a duo until David Crosby added the third voice. After their chart success, they set out to explore

The Byrds

psychedelia on 'Eight Miles High'. The song was criticised for its 'drug' references ("we weren't totally unaware of the innuendo," admitted McGuinn), but was more about a group obsession with flying. Gene Clark departed shortly afterwards - partly because "he got uptight in airplanes" - and as other differences erupted, including fisticuffs on stage, Crosby left too, followed by all bar McGuinn, who observed "Like most groups, we just got too big for our breeches": he outlasted every new Byrd, including a brief visitation by Gram Parsons. No other formation, though, truly bested the one that had patented folk-rock.

Key members: Gene Clark 17/11/44 (died 24/5/91), Michael Clarke 3/6/44 (died 19/12/93), David Crosby 14/8/41, Chris Hillman 4/12/42, Roger McGuinn 13/7/42 • Recording career: 1965 - 1973

Sounds: Mr Tambourine Man 1965, The Notorious Byrd Brothers 1968, Sweetheart Of The Rodeo 1968

And then there were two. Cabaret Voltaire started out as a trio of Sheffield teenagers, inspired by the mechanics of Can and the ambience of Eno, who patched together tapes of noises to amuse themselves at teenage parties. As the punk ethic emerged they adopted the same attitudes of anti-stardom, but concentrated instead on their individual take on *musique concrète*, and the Dadaist spirit of the original Cabaret Voltaire (a shortlived club set up in Zurich during the late 1910s). By the time they signed for Factory Records, they had settled on the collages of samples, loops and tape effects which would form the basis for acts like Depeche Mode and the Human League. After original member Christopher Watson departed, they almost went stale. But then the house movement discovered and embraced them and they celebrated their new-found fashion on *Groovy, Laid Back And Nasty*, emerging in the 1990s revitalised and ambient, fully justified (and ancient).

Cabaret Voltaire

"The first Roxy album was what got us going - the Eno influence: that element of non-music alongside music."

Mal Mallinder

Key members: Richard H. Kirk, Stephen 'Mal' Mallinder • **Recording career:** 1978 - 1994

Sounds: Red Mecca 1981, The Covenant, The Sword And The Arm Of The Lord 1985, Groovy, Laid Back And Nasty 1990

"Plenty of people out there were trying to do hard rock.

I thought I'd slide into a slot nobody had covered."

The embodiment of laid-back, J.J. (for Jean-Jacques) adopted the initials to differentiate himself from the Velvets' John Cale. At the time he was a good ole boy out on the road, packing a weary croak of a singing voice, and a pure, blues-inspired guitar sound. Heading from Oklahoma to LA in 1964 with long-time pal Leon Russell, his band - Johnnie Cale and the Valentines - and session work gave him a living, until a job with Delaney and Bonnie Bramlett brought him to Eric Clapton's attention. The latter's patronage (including the majestic covers of 'After Midnight' and 'Cocaine') did much to spread the word about Cale's style of vocals and guitar, which Mark Knopfler would later take on and weave into his own personal cloth of gold. But Cale, ever the modest troubadour seemed untroubled and his solo albums carried on spinning much the same fabric - in the title of his debut release, just doing it *Naturally*.

J.J. Cale

Born: 5/12/38 • Recording career: 1967 - present • Sounds: Really 1972, Troubadour 1976, Travel-Log 1990

Can

"All you can try to do is set up little cells, which may grow or not, but
music is not to make revolutions." Irmin Schmidt

Like Amon Düül II, Can began their life as a collective in the late 1960s, the principal difference between the two being Can's strong links to the mainstream of European avant-garde music: both Holger Czukay and Irmin Schmidt were alumni of Karl-Heinz Stockhausen. Michael Karoli, one of Schmidt's own pupils - he was teaching modern classical music - helped ease his teacher towards the sounds of the Velvet Underground. The result: Can's proto-techno bass lines and machine-like drum sounds,

percussive keyboards and industrial guitar, producing music that was remarkably funky. Original vocalist Malcolm Mooney supplied an odd mixture of crazed moans and monologues (too crazed, in fact - he suffered a breakdown and left to be replaced by the Japanese Damo Suzuki). After signing with Virgin in the 1970s Can moved more mainstream, including some former Traffic sidemen and a guest appearance by Dave Gilmour, co-writer of their only hit 'I Want More'.

Key members: Holger Czukay 24/3/68, Michael Karoli 29/4/48, Jaki Liebezeit 26/5/38, Irmin Schmidt 29/5/37 • Recording career: 1968 - 1979 (reformed 1989)

Sounds: Tago Mago 1971, Future Days 1973, Landed 1975

"His attitude was that we were the only thing and everything else sucked. A Coltrane solo or a Mingus tune might be acceptable, **but other than that we were God's gift to planet Earth."** Zoot Horn Rollo of the Magic Band

By the time he retired in 1982 to a trailer in the Mojave Desert to concentrate on painting and sculpture, Don Van Vliet, progenitor of the Captain, had created a highly personal landscape of words and music. After high school days spent alongside Frank Zappa, he formed his first Magic Band playing off-centre R'n'B: their first single was 'Diddy Wah Diddy', and there was always a resonance of Howlin' Wolf in Beefheart's vocals. A move towards free-form music caused him problems with record labels, despite the presence of a young Ry Cooder on 1967's *Safe As Milk*, so Zappa took his old friend under his wing and onto his own label. The next release, *Trout Mask Replica* - an album written in eight and a half hours (and frankly sometimes sounding it) - was a cult success, its deliberately off-key approach so challenging even hardened critic Lester Bangs declared it had shattered his skull like a bomb.

Captain Beefheart

75

Born: Don Van Vliet 5/1/41 • Recording career: 1966 - 1982 • Sounds: Safe As Milk 1967, Trout Mask Replica 1969, Doc At The Radar Station 1980

The Cardigans

"Girls are fine as long as they're put out in front as a mascot. When it turns out she might do it even better than the boys, people are very surprised." Nina Persson

The happy smiling people of the Cardigans came from the land of the midnight sun and Abba (Jönköping, specifically). Peter Svensson and Magnus Sveningsson had previously played in a number of local metal bands and retained a particular fondness for Thin Lizzy and Black Sabbath - covers of 'Mr Crowley' and 'Sabbath Bloody Sabbath' later featured in the Cardigans' repertoire. Yet it was the lighter, lounge-style delivery of their upbeat pop songs, as fresh as a wind-dried woolly, and often fleshed out with a production sound that was 1930s Palm Court tea room in atmosphere, which caught the public's imagination. Their debut release, *Emmerdale*, was album of the year in Sweden, but had been heard very little outside their home country - it needed the inclusion of 'Lovefool' on the soundtrack of Baz Luhrmann's funky movie version of *Romeo & Juliet* to propel their third album, *First Band On The Moon*, into the stratosphere.

Key members: Lasse Johansson, Bengt Lagerberg, Nina Persson, Magnus Sveningsson, Peter Svensson • Recording career: 1994 - present • Sounds: Emmerdale 1994, Life 1995, Gran Turismo 1998

Mary Chapin Carpenter

She always was a straight shooter, with an unflamboyant personal style, some honest songs and a business-like, no-nonsense stage presence. Not one of the Nashville mafia, Mary Chapin Carpenter grew up in Washington DC and attended Brown University; her stagecraft and songwriting was perfected during hard work on the Washington club circuit between semesters. Right from her debut album, *Hometown Girl*, she delivered uptempo country with a splash of the blues, a nod in the direction of her mother's favourite Woody Guthrie albums, and an awareness of the 1970s pop that she had grown up with. This seamless blend made her a natural pioneer of the new female country movement (motto: no big hair, no rhinestones). She also possessed a nice line in humour - shown off on 'I Feel Lucky' and 'Shut Up And Kiss Me' - which sat easily alongside the moving 'Come On, Come On' and her heartfelt rendition of Lucinda Williams' 'Passionate Kisses'.

"There's so few of us women in country music, and it's harder for us to break through, so we've tended to be a bit more distinctive."

77

Born: 21/2/58 • Recording career: 1987 - present • Sounds: Come On, Come On 1992, Stones In The Road 1994, A Place In The World 1996

"I think if it wasn't for writing I probably would've wound up dead or totally lost."

By the age of twenty, New Yorker Jim Carroll had already published various volumes of poetry as well as his teenage journals called *The Basketball Diaries*, which was adapted for a 1995 film featuring Leonardo DiCaprio. He'd also crashed out at Patti Smith's and hung out with Andy Warhol. Moving to California to kick a heroin habit, Carroll joined forces with a band called Amsterdam who needed a lyric writer. After returning to New York he landed a recording contract via Rolling Stones Records - Keith Richards jammed with the re-named Jim Carroll Band - and released *Catholic Boy* in 1980, with dying-embers-of-punk instrumental and vocal mannerisms. Carroll's breakthrough song was 'People Who Died', which he described as a life-affirming elegy to friends who'd variously perished from ODs, Vietnam, murder, suicide and disease. Released shortly before John Lennon's killing, it hit a nerve. Subsequent musical outings were less momentous, and in the end Carroll returned to the timelessness of the spoken word.

Jim Carroll

Born: 1/8/1950 • Recording career: 1980 - present • Sounds: Catholic Boy 1980, Dry Dreams 1982, Pools Of Mercury 1998

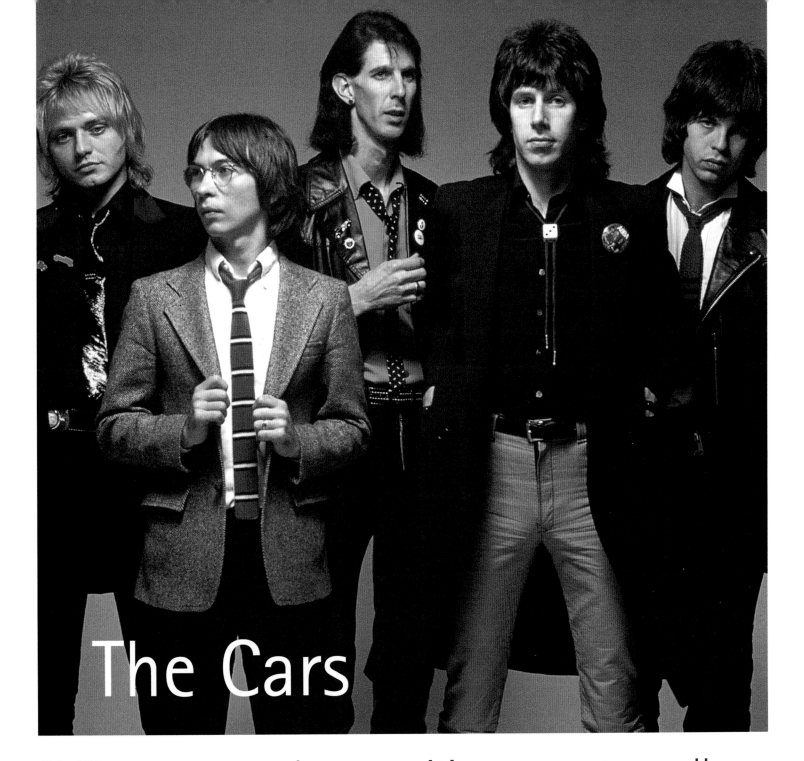

The Cars

"I like our name because it's so easy to spell.
It's real authentic. It's pop art, in a sense." Ric Ocasek

They wanted to be as crisp and snappy as the new wave of cool detachment they represented. Ric Ocasek and his co-driver Ben Orr had been knocking around in various bands through the 1970s, but performances at Boston's Rat Club firmed up their act, perfected on home demos - all synth drums and choppy guitar - one of which became a major local radio request. It was 'Just What I Needed', their first single, featured on a debut album that contained three crisp hits, including 'My Best Friend's Girl', and which secured multi-million sales. The formula changed little through the early 1980s, as individual band members spent more time on outside production duties (Ocasek notably with Bad Brains and Suicide) and solo work. The flagging band was perked up by 1984's 'Drive', selected by the Live Aid organisers as an incongruous but strangely moving aural backdrop to the images of suffering, but it was effectively their last gasp.

Key members: Elliot Easton 18/12/53, Greg Hawkes, Ric Ocasek 23/3/49, Ben Orr 9/8/55 (died 3/10/00), David Robinson 2/4/53 • Recording career: 1978 - 1987

Sounds: The Cars 1978, Candy-O 1979, Heartbeat City 1984

"I do it the way I feel it.
Take it or leave it – that's the way I do it."

An appearance at Glastonbury in 1994 marked the adoption of the Man In Black by a new generation. The alt.rockers had found a new icon courtesy of Def American's Rick Rubin, who signed Cash and leased him some fresh life. By then he'd been a recording artist for nearly four decades, ever since Sam Phillips at Sun Studios had dubbed him Johnny - which Cash initially hated. From 'Cry Cry Cry' onwards his powerful baritone, over guitar and slap bass, drove a series of hits, but in the 1960s a self-destructive downturn involved an unhealthy combination of drink, divorce, a near fatal car crash and brushes with the law (although for someone whose classic albums included *Live At San Quentin*, his own time in jail was minimal). Rescued by marriage to June Carter, co-writer of 'The Ring Of Fire', and his discovery of evangelical zeal, he recovered - and the Highwayman rode on.

Johnny Cash

Born: 26/2/32 • Recording career: 1955 - present • Sounds: Orange Blossom Special 1964, Johnny Cash At Folsom Prison 1968, American Recordings 1994

Cerys Matthews' voice dripped South Wales - as distinctive as laver bread, as powerful as the famed Pontypool front row, and with a gravelly tone not heard since Bonnie 'Lost In France' Tyler. Initially releasing singles on Crai, a local indie label, Catatonia proudly picked up the banner of Welsh rock'n'roll, a banner for years forlornly paraded by Man and later the Manic Street Preachers; and suddenly you couldn't move for bands from the principality. Although media attention, Blondie-style, inevitably tended to gravitate towards Cerys, the strength of their 1998 album *International Velvet* was in the ensemble around her, and the passion of songs like 'Mulder And Scully' and 'Road Rage'. After a steady start, the album built an unstoppable momentum to a UK Number One slot, and the icing on the cake was Cerys's 1999 duet on 'Baby It's Cold Outside' with Mr Green Green Grass himself, Tom Jones.

Catatonia

"Bugger standing on stage having the adulation of thousands -
give me a sink."
Cerys Matthews

Key members: Paul Jones 5/4/60, Cerys Matthews 11/4/69, Owen Powell 9/7/67, Aled Richards 5/7/69, Mark Roberts 3/11/69 • Recording career: 1993 - present

Sounds: Way Beyond Blue 1996, International Velvet 1998, Equally Cursed And Blessed 1999

"Coming from Norwich is an advantage.

I'm sure if we'd been living in London we'd have disappeared up our own bottoms by now." Neil Sims

The Catherine Wheel

The aircraft-carrier flatness of Norfolk has never been a particularly successful launchpad for budding rock bands. Nevertheless Wilde Club, a Norwich-based indie label, catapulted the Catherine Wheel to attention in 1991. Formed by guitarists Brian Futter and Rob Dickinson (cousin of Iron Maiden's Bruce), the band's reliance on the wonder of wah-wah, effects boxes and a certain onstage inertia found them being categorised as 'shoegazers', along with bands like Lush, Ride and Moose. Certainly

that had been the mood of their first mainstream releases *Ferment* and *Chrome*, but they made a change of gear in 1995. Their songs had always offered shape and melody, but on *Happy Days* - an album that, like much of their output, benefited from the design talents of Storm Thorgerson (of *Dark Side Of The Moon* fame) - they dispensed with most of their previous effects. From now on the music was tougher and heavier, although their lyrics remained as addictively and moodily obsessive as ever.

Key members: Rob Dickinson 23/7/65, Brian Futter 7/12/65, Neil Sims 4/10/65 • **Recording career:** 1991 - present • **Sounds:** Ferment 1992, Happy Days 1995, Wishville 2000

"I'd hate to go down in history as the man who spawned a thousand goth bands."

Nick Cave chose his collaborators carefully. Some he worked with in person - the fellow Aussies who transported their Birthday Party to the UK for the dawn of the 1980s, and later an eclectic coterie including Lydia Lunch, PJ Harvey, the chirrupy Kylie Minogue and film director Wim Wenders. Others were the ghosts of vinyl past: the Birthday Party's debut release was Nancy Sinatra's 'These Boots Are Made For Walking'; the Bad Seeds' released Elvis's 'In The Ghetto'; and the Seeds' 1986 covers album *Kicking Against The Pricks* included 'Hey Joe' and a dark reworking of Jimmy Webb's classic 'By The Time I Get To Phoenix'. But Cave's own work was equally original. His Tom Waits meets Leonard Cohen voice could be brooding, gruff or intense on tales of doomed souls and murderous deeds, but could also handle elegantly crafted ballads like 'The Ship Song'. A poet, novelist and playwright, he was set to evolve for years.

Nick Cave

83

Born: 22/9/57 • Recording career: 1980 - present • Sounds: From Her To Eternity 1984, Kicking Against The Pricks 1986, Let Love In 1994

Tracy Chapman

Cometh the hour... Alone with her guitar, dwarfed by Wembley's twin towers at Nelson Mandela's 70th birthday concert in September 1988, Tracy Chapman played the gig of her life. Stevie Wonder had been unable to appear on stage at the appointed time, and so her slot was unexpectedly extended. The audience revelled in her vulnerability, and suddenly her recently released debut album was Number One in both the UK and US, and the single 'Fast Car' riding high. From a quiet folk background, Tracy was an instant star, although she already had good foundations in her label, Elektra (who had picked her up in the wake of Suzanne Vega's success), a producer who'd worked with Joan Baez, and a manager whose client list included Neil Young and Joni Mitchell. Comparisons to Joan Armatrading were unavoidable - and not entirely unjustified - but more likely showed up the paucity of support for black female singer/songwriters that had existed since the 1970s.

"I didn't know you had to have a percentage of humour on every album you put out."

Born: 30/3/64 • Recording career: 1988 - present • Sounds: Tracy Chapman 1988, Crossroads 1989, New Beginning 1995

The melodians of 'rave on', the Charlatans provided the essential theme tune for Madchester's summer of 1990: 'The Only One I Know', a funky dose of 60s pop with swirling Hammond organ from Rob Collins. As floppy and baggy as the best of them, they were looking set fair for an unassailable progress, until a number of setbacks intervened. They encountered name-clash problems in the States (forcing them to tour as Charlatans UK), bassist Martin Blunt underwent a breakdown and Rob Collins spent four months in jail, after being implicated in an armed robbery. Worse, Madchester's merry carnival was soon over, and the band dangerously dated - yet they struck back with *The Charlatans*, a UK Number One album. Within a year, there was a further crushing blow when Collins was killed in a car accident, but the remaining Charlatans drew on their communal resilience for 1997's *Tellin' Stories* - the final track simply 'Rob's Theme'.

The Charlatans

"To most people we're a superficial rock band, but there's always something going on in the background."

Tim Burgess

Key members: John Baker 1969, Martin Blunt 21/4/64, Jon Brookes 1969, Tim Burgess 30/5/67, Rob Collins 23/2/63 (died 22/7/96) • **Recording career:** 1990 - present

Sounds: Some Friendly 1990, The Charlatans 1995, Tellin' Stories 1997

Ray Charles

For the first years of his career, Ray Charles Robinson - he dropped the surname out of deference to the champion boxer Sugar Ray - subscribed to the Nat King Cole school of smooth jazz, but a revelatory contact in the mid-1950s with rough and ready, gospel-fervent, blues guitarist Guitar Slim changed his whole approach. Suddenly, on songs like 'I've Got A Woman', a new Ray Charles was apparent: fusing the gospel sound and blues, his pounding piano backed by horns rather than choir. The father of soul brought the passion of the church to everything he did. Smiling, laughing and liberated, his whole body was in motion; this was the Ray Charles who stole the show on 'We Are The World'. A talented songwriter - 'What I'd Say' was widely covered - he successfully explored both jazz (*Genius + Soul = Jazz*) and country ('I Can't Stop Loving You'). Blind from the age of seven, Charles remained a true visionary.

"I always tell record companies:
'Let me do the music and you do the marketing'."

Born: 23/9/30 • Recording career: 1949 - present • Sounds: The Genius Of Ray Charles 1959, Genius + Soul = Jazz 1961, Modern Sounds In Country And Western Music 1962

> **"Our music is made from natural impulses. There's no cynical exploitation."**
>
> Ed Simons

All they wanted to do was spin some records and do a bit of DJ'ing at their own club night, Naked Under Leather. Tom Rowlands (the long-haired Brother) and Ed Simons, both Manchester University students, eventually invested a few hundred quid in making a track that they could play, calling themselves the Dust Brothers as homage to a Stateside production team. Their own hip hop/rave wave of beats, breaks and frequent sirens - that first track was called 'Song To The Siren' - became an in-demand re-mix sound. Come a first album, the US outfit objected to their name and so they went chemical, stirring in Noel Gallagher, Beth Orton of Portishead and Tim Burgess of the Charlatans when they needed to add a little vocal spice to the mix. Live shows were visually low-fi, with the pair nursing their samplers, but on an album like *Surrender* they could rock out as hard as anyone.

The Chemical Brothers

Key members: Tom Rowlands 11/1/71, Ed Simons 9/6/70 • **Recording career:** 1993 - present • **Sounds:** Exit Planet Dust 1995, Dig Your Own Hole 1997, Surrender 1999

Neneh Cherry

Entertainment was in her blood and her upbringing. The daughter of a Swedish artist and a percussionist from West Africa, she was raised by her stepfather, the late and very great jazz trumpeter Don Cherry, in New York. Consequently Neneh had bags of cosmopolitan chutzpah when she moved to London to flatshare with Ari Up from the Slits. After adding vocals and percussion to Rip Rig + Panic, the 1980s dub/funk/jazz outfit, she re-emerged fully fledged in 1989 with the *Raw Like Sushi* album, as a rap-snappy urban sophisticate and (inner city) mama who was pregnant, confident and outspoken - "wot is she like?" Her exotic looks, the sassiness of 'Buffalo Stance' and the dreaminess of 'Man Child' were that season's flavour, but illness delayed a follow-up, and 'Seven Seconds', her world music duo with Youssou N'Dour was - fans hoped - not an indicator of her allotted timespan of fame.

"You don't have to be a great musician to make great records. You just have to have a lot of good ideas."

Born: 10/3/64 • Recording career (solo): 1989 - present • Sounds: Raw Like Sushi 1989, Homebrew 1992, Man 1996

Though they formed in Chicago, the band moved fairly swiftly out to LA to work with producer/manager James William Guercio, and it was Hollywood rather than the Windy City that set the tone for their jazz-rock fusion. Their first outings had been relatively earthy, under the name Chicago Transit Authority, but after their name had been shortened and their logo created, it was showbiz (and a string of hits) all the way, including 1976's smoochadelic 'If You Leave Me Now'.

Much derided for naming their albums like *Rocky* movies - by 1998 they'd managed to reached *Chicago 25* - their line-up for such a large band was astonishingly stable, broken after eleven albums only by the death of guitarist Terry Kath. Fellow jazz-rockers like Blood Sweat And Tears and Electric Flag had long since foundered, and cynical onlookers considered Chicago by far the smartest outfit for wising up to the limitations of the genre and opting for commercial success.

Chicago

"We got sick and tired of our songs getting chopped up, and tried to condense things. We may have left a little bit of our artistic integrity behind." Danny Seraphine

Key members: Peter Cetera 13/9/44, Terry Kath 31/1/46 (died 23/1/78) Robert Lamm 13/10/44, Lee Loughnane 21/10/46, James Pankow 20/8/47, Walter Parazaider 14/3/45, Danny Seraphine 28/8/48 • Recording career: 1969 - present • Sounds: Chicago Transit Authority 1969, Chicago V 1972, Chicago VIII 1975

Eric Clapton

"No matter what direction rock goes in, it has to stay with the blues. **That's the spine and body of it."**

Eric Clapton has always been caught up in the blues, "because of its rawness". The 1994 release of *From The Cradle*, an album of 16 blues classics, marked a full circle in his journey through the by-roads of the genre. As a teenager in Britain, Clapton studied, note by note, the licks of guitarists Big Bill Broonzy, Blind Lemon Jefferson and Son House (and harmonica player Little Walter) to become a fully committed disciple, purist enough to quit the Yardbirds because he thought - correctly - they were becoming too commercial. His reputation could have survived on the powerhouse legacy of Cream alone, but it was the tapestry of his own life that added extra understanding. Whether his own addictions or the personal tragedy of his son Conor's death ("my soul went dead to music"), the mature Clapton could draw on a deep resource of ragged emotion. There was no need to copy any more.

Born: 30/3/45 • Recording career: 1964 - present • Sounds: 461 Ocean Boulevard 1974, MTV Unplugged 1992, From The Cradle 1994

Out on the streets, in their sub-urban guerrilla mode, the Clash put a snap, crackle and snarl into punk rock, but were always skating on thinnish ice, given their studied image, political agenda and simplistic slogans. The Clash were a great punk band, no question, but there was often a lingering thought that they had to come a cropper. Yet their reputation survived and grew: *Rolling Stone* magazine voted *London Calling* the best album of the 1980s, as the best of their traits shone through. The passion and intensity overcame any musical defects, and a genuine idealism saw off snide remarks about Joe Strummer's supposedly privileged background and Mick Jones' fake London accent. And their style was spot on. Strummer had much admired Malcolm McLaren's attention to sartorial detail, and their outfits, whether leather or boiler suits, perfectly matched their own tag as 'the last gang in town'.

"I think people ought to know that we're anti-fascist, we're anti violence, we're anti-racist and we're pro-creative. We're against ignorance." Joe Strummer

The Clash

Key members: Nicky 'Topper' Headon 30/5/55, Mick Jones 26/6/55, Paul Simonon 15/12/55, Joe Strummer 21/8/52 • **Recording career:** 1977 - 1985

Sounds: The Clash 1977, London Calling 1979, Combat Rock 1982

George Clinton

"Before I heard them, I was planning to be a mechanical draftsman.
But P-Funk's music opened my mind up to the idea that
there are no barriers except the ones you believe."

Dr Dre

George frees his mind, and if his credo holds true, his ass will surely follow. The self-styled Dr Funkenstein created the P-Funk empire, encompassing the mother of all Parliaments and the Funkadelic army. His own early doo-wop outfit, the Parliaments, had pottered through the 1950s and 60s, but it was exposure to Iggy Pop and MC5, to Hendrix, Sly Stone and Zappa, and copious amounts of acid that created the new Clinton administration - lengthy workouts, a stage show that incorporated the best/worst of Alice Cooper and the Butthole Surfers, and a vision encapsulated by 'One Nation Under A Groove'. George straddled its two manifestations - the more commercial Parliament, the experimental Funkadelic - educating alumni like Bootsy Collins and Maceo Parker, until the edges blurred. Clinton seemed to lose the plot in the 1980s, before rebuilding himself with a helping hand from Prince and no little respect from the generation of Dr Dre.

Born: 22/7/40 • Recording career: 1958 - present • Sounds: Mothership Connection 1976, One Nation Under A Groove 1978, Computer Games 1982

93

The Coasters

White audiences of the late 1950s - safe in the cosseted surroundings of consumer boomtown suburbia - were still distinctly wary of the animal energy of R'n'B. The Coasters, with a touch of humour, went a long way to making its crossover much more palatable, aided and abetted by the whip-smart Bronx songwriter/producers Jerry Leiber and Mike Stoller (Elvis's 'Hound Dog' team) who began working with the R'n'B vocal group then called the Robins. Reconfigured as the

Coasters, they set out their stall with a string of story-song hits: first 'Searchin'', featuring a detective theme, before the big Number One of 'Yakety Yak', a brilliantly topical cameo of the ever-widening generation gap, laced with the honking sax of King Curtis, the fifth Coaster, and Bobby Nunn's ultra-bass "Don't talk back". Mike Stoller dubbed these Coasters' mini-sketches 'playlets' - but following 'Charlie Brown' and 'Poison Ivy', the jokes wore thin and the audience thinner.

Key members: Carl Gardner 29/4/28, Billy Guy 20/6/36, Leon Hughes 20/6/36, Bobby Nunn 1925 (died 5/11/86) • **Recording career:** 1956 - 1967 • **Sounds:** The Coasters 1958, One By One 1960

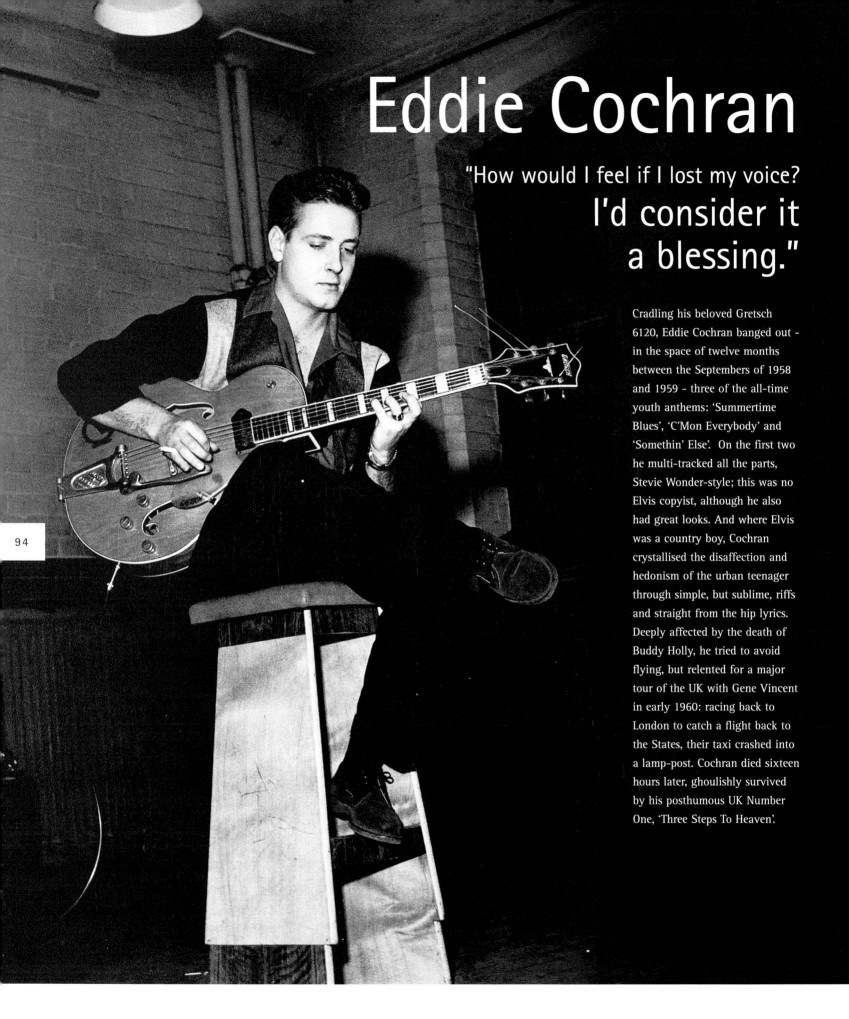

Eddie Cochran

"How would I feel if I lost my voice? I'd consider it a blessing."

Cradling his beloved Gretsch 6120, Eddie Cochran banged out - in the space of twelve months between the Septembers of 1958 and 1959 - three of the all-time youth anthems: 'Summertime Blues', 'C'Mon Everybody' and 'Somethin' Else'. On the first two he multi-tracked all the parts, Stevie Wonder-style; this was no Elvis copyist, although he also had great looks. And where Elvis was a country boy, Cochran crystallised the disaffection and hedonism of the urban teenager through simple, but sublime, riffs and straight from the hip lyrics. Deeply affected by the death of Buddy Holly, he tried to avoid flying, but relented for a major tour of the UK with Gene Vincent in early 1960: racing back to London to catch a flight back to the States, their taxi crashed into a lamp-post. Cochran died sixteen hours later, ghoulishly survived by his posthumous UK Number One, 'Three Steps To Heaven'.

Born: 3/10/38 (died 17/4/60) • Recording career: 1955 - 1960 • Sounds: Singin' To My Baby 1957, The Eddie Cochran Memorial Album 1960

Joe Cocker's flailing arms, parodied by John Belushi on *Saturday Night Live*, always gave the impression of a man who was out of control, an impression sometimes heightened by Cocker's lifestyle: it belied a deep, respectful passion for R'n'B, and Ray Charles in particular. After paying hard-earned dues around northern clubs, his rise to fame was swift: a UK Number One single with his cover of 'With A Little Help From My Friends' (the friends included Jimmy Page and Steve Winwood), and notable appearances at Woodstock and the Isle of Wight. The rambling, shambling Mad Dogs & Englishmen tour of the US, organised by Leon Russell in 1970, was a saga of exhaustion (sixty gigs in three months) and self-destruction, and the strain nearly did for him. But Cocker was made of Sheffield steel, re-emerging to duet with Jennifer Warnes on 'Up Where We Belong' and jump-start his career.

Joe Cocker

"I've always done me theatricality bit
of throwing me arms about."

95

Born: 20/5/44 • Recording career: 1964 - present • Sounds: With A Little Help From My Friends 1969, Mad Dogs & Englishmen 1970, Have A Little Faith 1994

Cocteau Twins

"Please don't write that we eat. **We don't like the fans to think that we eat.**"

Robin Guthrie

The Cocteau Twins - often, with a bassist, a threesome - seemed to have successfully cornered the market for the use of the adjective 'ethereal' before Enya intervened. Liz Fraser's vocals were variously described as incomprehensible or incoherent, particularly by critics flummoxed by her decision to use her voice as though it was another instrument (or to sing in an ancient Scots tongue) over the effect-heavy experiments or lush, floating textures created by Guthrie. When they headed south to London from Stirlingshire, they recorded their debut album *Garlands* in just over a week and just under £1000: it was an immediate indie hit and the beginning of a cult. Their life as a couple was kept scrupulously private and the mystique heightened by the lack of band photos on their album sleeves. Then in 1990, a surprise: a new release, *Heaven Or Las Vegas* with damn-near audible words... Would things ever be the same again?

Key members: Elizabeth Fraser 29/8/58, Robin Guthrie 4/1/62 • Recording career: 1982 - 1996 • Sounds: Treasure 1984, Blue Bell Knoll 1988, Heaven Or Las Vegas 1990

Leonard Cohen

A latecomer to recording at 34,
Leonard Cohen could have been
the object of an undergraduette's
infatuation: a wrinkled, wordy and
worldly wise father figure with a
dirty mind, the Serge Gainsbourg
of the English-speaking world.
Already a published poet and
writer, he had been performing in
his native Canada to jazz piano
accompaniment since the late
1950s, but was sprung into the
music business though a meeting
in New York with singer Judy
Collins, who recorded his
'Suzanne'. Cohen's own lugubrious
performances of songs discussing
loneliness, love and hate, delivered
with minimal accompaniment
(although he might convene an
occasional band for events like the
Isle of Wight festival) lasted him
well through a series of albums
into the mid-1970s. When punk
arrived he was dismissed as a
boring old fart, but a tribute
album released in 1991 found
Nick Cave, the Pixies and R.E.M.
all lining up to pay their respects.

"It took
poverty, not
courage,
to get me
performing.
As a novelist I had
good reviews but
no career."

Born: 21/9/34 • Recording career: 1968 - present • Sounds: Songs Of Leonard Cohen 1968, New Skin For Old Ceremony 1974, I'm Your Man 1988

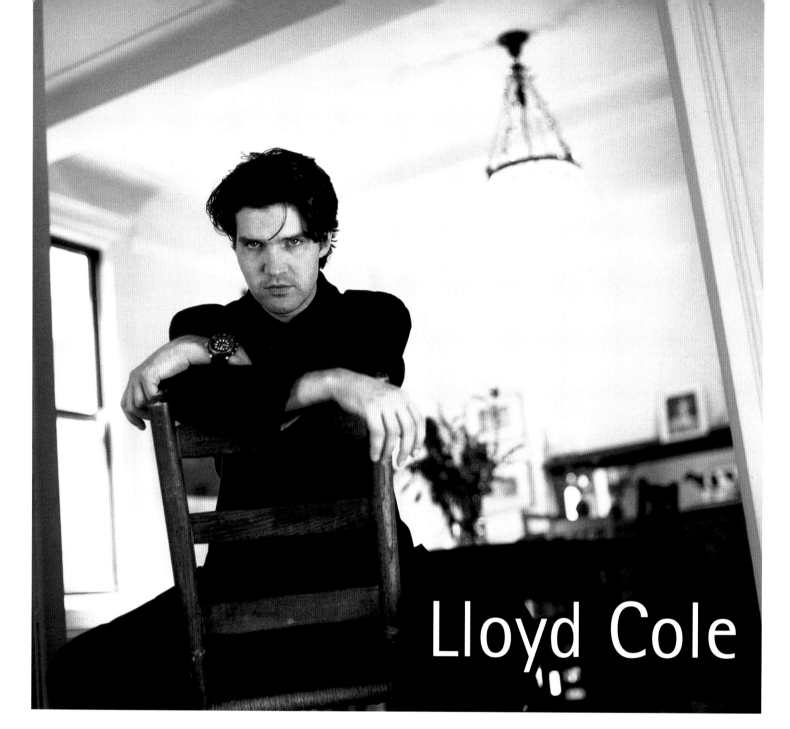

Lloyd Cole

"Look, I'm making records because

I was an 11-year-old kid who loved T. Rex

and a 16-year-old who read New Musical Express."

After his Commotions split up in 1989, the lone Lloyd Cole was never quite as successful, suggesting that his literate lyrics and model-look delivery worked best when he was underpinned by the band's Byrds-like guitar on singles like 'Perfect Skin'. Emerging onto the UK college circuit in the mid-80s, the Commotions' package was self-consciously intellectual - songs replete with references to French existentialists, dress code frequently black polo-neck, and demeanour suitably pallid.

When they dropped their worst excesses, the band picked up some serious sales with 1985's *Easy Pieces* (though they never achieved much in the States), and while *Mainstream* reached UK Number Two, the Commotions had commoved their best. In his solo guise, Cole pursued a Lou Reed infatuation - critics had frequently noted his similar vocal inflections - to the extent of employing Reed drummer Fred Maher to produce his debut; his future releases were patchily received.

Born: 31/1/61 • **Recording career:** 1984 - present • **Sounds:** Rattlesnakes 1984, Easy Pieces 1985, Don't Get Weird On Me, Babe 1991

"There's a cat I'm trying to get across to people. His name is Albert Collins, he's a smooth guitarist who plays around Texas and he's good, real good. **One of the best in the world."** Jimi Hendrix

Albert Collins

Success was a long time coming for Albert Collins, who steadfastly worked the clubs of Texas throughout the 1950s, alongside a phalanx of bluesmen including Johnny 'Guitar' Watson and Clarence 'Gatemouth' Brown. Collins had his own nicknames, most famously 'Master of the Telecaster', the instrument he favoured for his minor-inflected Texas shuffle blues, using intense clusters of treble notes, so precise that his sound was dubbed 'cool' (although his live performances were storming).

From the debut instrumental single, 'The Freeze', to 1992's albums *Molten Ice* and *Frozen Alive!*, chill-out titling was an (over)worked trademark of a career mileposted by moments when patrons gamely tried to introduce Collins to a broader audience. California blues band Canned Heat promoted him, Alligator Records in Chicago gave him a fresh start, and following a Live Aid appearance in 1985, Collins was seemingly on the cusp of the mainstream before cancer intervened.

Born: 1/10/32 (died 24/11/93) • Recording career: 1958 - 1993 • Sounds: Truckin' With Albert Collins 1969, Frozen Alive! 1981, Showdown 1985

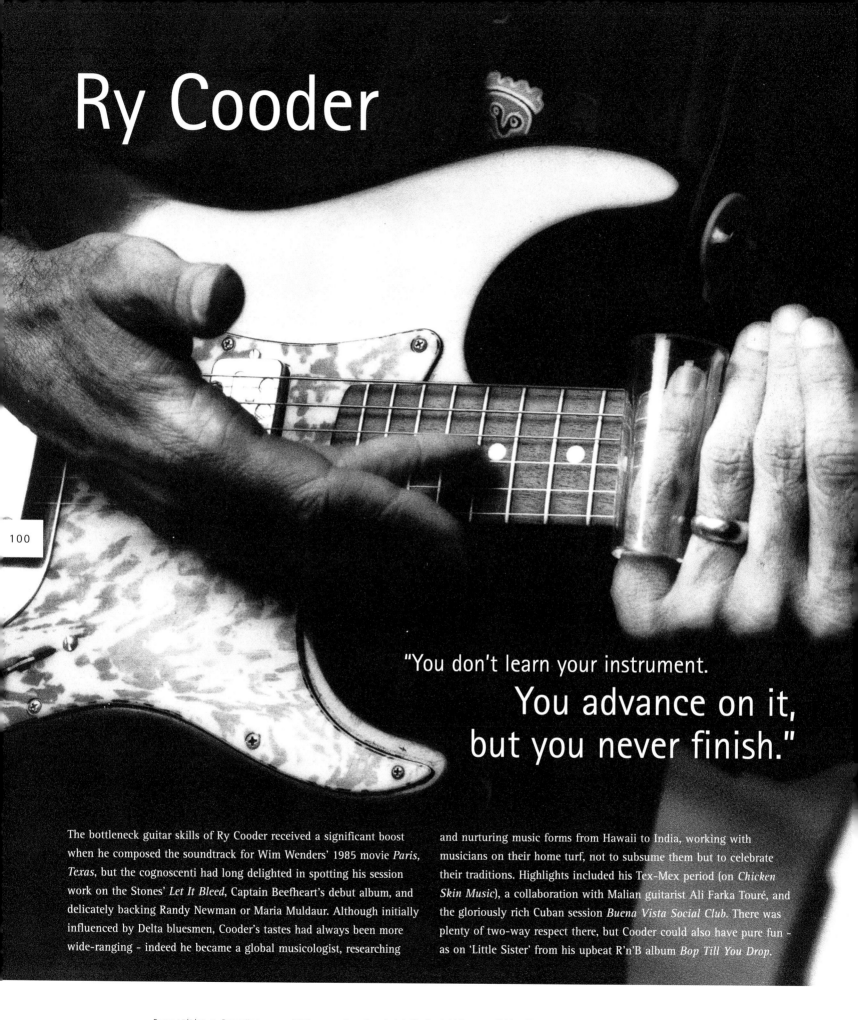

Ry Cooder

"You don't learn your instrument.
You advance on it, but you never finish."

The bottleneck guitar skills of Ry Cooder received a significant boost when he composed the soundtrack for Wim Wenders' 1985 movie *Paris, Texas*, but the cognoscenti had long delighted in spotting his session work on the Stones' *Let It Bleed*, Captain Beefheart's debut album, and delicately backing Randy Newman or Maria Muldaur. Although initially influenced by Delta bluesmen, Cooder's tastes had always been more wide-ranging - indeed he became a global musicologist, researching and nurturing music forms from Hawaii to India, working with musicians on their home turf, not to subsume them but to celebrate their traditions. Highlights included his Tex-Mex period (on *Chicken Skin Music*), a collaboration with Malian guitarist Ali Farka Touré, and the gloriously rich Cuban session *Buena Vista Social Club*. There was plenty of two-way respect there, but Cooder could also have pure fun - as on 'Little Sister' from his upbeat R'n'B album *Bop Till You Drop*.

Born: 15/3/47 • Recording career: 1970 – present • Sounds: Into The Purple Valley 1971, Chicken Skin Music 1976, The Buena Vista Social Club 1997

"Modulation, shading, dynamics, progression, emotion.
Every essential quality – he had it all." Jerry Wexler

Sam Cooke

The very manner of his death was a shock: a squalid shooting in an LA motel involving alleged rape, all diametrically at odds with the Cooke persona - pure, groomed, in control. These adjectives applied equally to his voice and life: he ran his own management and publishing, and his record label SAR sourced bright talent including the Womacks, Billy Preston and Lou Rawls. A Baptist minister's son, Cooke first swayed gospel audiences with his earnest, gliding phrases, but when a move to secular material beckoned he was quick to realise the potential it offered, although he initially adopted a pseudonym, Dale Cook, to avoid offending purists. 'You Send Me', from 1957, was one of *the* seminal soul records, also bringing crossover acceptance - and although some of his later songs were rather too saccharine, he returned to earthier ways on 'Bring It On Home To Me', and suggested a nascent political consciousness on the posthumously released 'A Change Is Gonna Come'.

Born: 22/1/31 (died 11/12/64) • Recording career: 1956 - 1964 • Sounds: The Wonderful World Of Sam Cooke 1960, Night Beat 1963, Sam Cooke At The Copa 1964

"I've always said Alice has a love affair with his audience. But where most entertainers pet their audience, Alice rapes 'em." Vincent Furnier

Alice Cooper

Mr Vincent Furnier and friend request the pleasure of your company. The boa was an integral part of the theatricality of Alice Cooper - originally the band's name, then adopted by Furnier as a sobriquet - which rescued the collection of Phoenix, AZ school chums from their reputation as 'the worst band in LA'. Even Frank Zappa, the patron saint of lost causes and freaks, could do little with Alice, so they re-located to Detroit, home of MC5 and the Stooges, and forged a fruitful link with producer Bob Ezrin. They fine-tuned their fusion of hard rock and stage props - baby dolls, electric chairs... and boas - towards teenage anthems like 'I'm Eighteen' and 'School's Out', and huge-selling albums with enough kudos to feature Nilsson, Donovan and Bolan. Cooper later turned to Hollywood, golf, and alcohol, before re-applying the make-up to become an MTV icon, and gratefully acquiescing to the worship of *Wayne's World* ("We are not worthy").

Born: Vincent Furnier 4/2/48 • Recording career: 1969 - present • Sounds: Love It To Death 1971, Billion Dollar Babies 1973, Welcome To My Nightmare 1978

A blur of lyrics and pent-up anger, Elvis (Declan McManus's choice of name nearly backfired when the King died in the year of his first release) spewed out ideas and spiky comments at a furious rate, but always with an articulate sense of wordplay and songcraft. Discarding his previous band, Flip City, when Stiff Records asked him to go solo, was the first of many re-inventions, and

"I'm never ever going to stick around long enough to churn out a load of mediocre crap like all those guys from the 60s."

Costello's lack of compromise has left a few corpses along the way. His first manifestation, all huge specs, awkward body posture and dazzling songs - 'Alison', 'My Red Shoes' - was a stunning debut, but only that year's model. He was soon testing new musical ground: the jazzier explorations of the under-rated *Trust*; Nashville on the Billy Sherrill-produced *Almost Blue*. Whether sparking off Presley's backing band, Tom Waits, Roger McGuinn, the Brodsky Quartet or Burt Bacharach, Costello's well was unlikely to run dry too soon.

Elvis Costello

Born: Declan McManus 25/8/54 • Recording career: 1977 - present • Sounds: My Aim Is True 1977, This Year's Model 1978, Imperial Bedroom 1982

Counting Crows

"To the outside world,
I'm the cute one, I'm the quiet one, I'm the funny one,
and I'm the sad one." Adam Duritz

When Van Morrison failed to show for his own induction ceremony at the Rock'n'Roll Hall of Fame in January 1993, a comparatively unknown band performed in the great man's stead. The Counting Crows' rendition of Morrison's 'Caravan' excited industry mavens, and their debut *August And Everything After*, produced by former Dylan sideman T-Bone Burnett, was much anticipated. Its first track, 'Round Here', opened with vocalist Adam Duritz and guitarist David Bryson echoing their early days as an acoustic duo in San Francisco,

before the rest of the Crows kicked in with a take on R.E.M. (ringing guitars), the Band (rootsy mandolin and a splash of accordion) and Van himself (both in the vocal delivery, and some tasty Hammond organ supplied by Charlie Gillingham). Meanwhile Duritz's wordy - sometimes too indulgent - lyrics offset the clean sound with tales of grunge-friendly despair. Although music critics later fell out of love with the band, their loyal fanbase, which dated from the early 1990s, stood firm and waited for the band to deliver a truly great album.

Key members: David Bryson 5/11/61, Adam Duritz 1/8/64, Charlie Gillingham 12/1/60, Matt Malley 4/7/63, Ben Mize 2/2/71, Dan Vickrey 26/8/66

Recording career: 1993 - present • Sounds: August And Everything After 1993, Recovering The Satellites 1996, This Desert Life 1999

Country Joe and the Fish

"There was this revolution in songwriting

that took place in the 1960s

and I just happened to pick the Vietnam War to write about." Country Joe McDonald

Out of a tradition of Woody Guthrie, jug bands and protest songs - lead singer Joe McDonald had been named after Stalin - the Fish filtered the Bay Area's folk scene through a handful of hallucinogens and stood proudly at the crossroads of Haight-Ashbury. They brought together the ideals of contemporary radicalism (their first release was the anti-Vietnam number 'I-Feel-Like-I'm-Fixin'-To-Die Rag') and a hippie lifestyle, which made them natural bookings for the Fillmore and the

Avalon Ballroom in San Francisco, and the festival highlights of Monterey and Woodstock. Country Joe played the latter as effectively a solo gig, with just bass and drums, but it was the guitar of Barry 'The Fish' Melton - the only consistent member with McDonald in a band which boasted five different line-ups in as many years - who was primarily responsible for the psychedelically laid-back Fish sound, captured at its best on *Electric Music For The Mind And Body*.

Key members: Country Joe McDonald 1/1/42, Barry Melton 1947 • Recording career: 1967 – 1971 (reformed 1976)

Sounds: Electric Music For The Mind And Body 1967, I Feel-Like-I'm-Fixing-To-Die 1967, Together 1968

Wayne County

"If I'd stayed Wayne, I could've got a lot further, **but growing tits freaked people out.** It said I'm serious, I'm not putting on an act."

Just a regular downhome Georgia boy, Wayne County was rock'n'roll's original in-your-face transvestite. Arriving in the Big Apple, he gravitated towards Warhol's Factory crowd and New York's alternative theatre, alongside Patti Smith and Holly Woodlawn, of 'Walk On The Wild Side' fame. With the Ramones leading the way, Wayne found the NY music scene a perfect stage for his pure trash, platinum blonde-bewigged persona. However, while other bands like Blondie were picking up deals, Wayne proved too risky, armed (usually with a dildo) and, for the times, dangerous: songs included '(If You Don't Want To Fuck Me) Fuck Off'. So he shipped over to the UK, formed the Electric Chairs, was embraced by the punk movement as a flamboyant older sister, and a German label finally released some examples of the County canon. After hormone treatment in the 80s, Wayne transmogrified to Jayne, emerging in the 1990s to record *Deviation*.

Born: Does a gentleman ask a lady her age? • Recording career: 1978 - present • Sounds: The Electric Chairs 1978, Rock'n'Roll Resurrection 1981, Deviation 1994

"The whole rock'n'roll lifestyle...

Well, basically, we never had one." Margo Timmins

The bleak country-blues that set the tone of the Cowboy Junkies' early releases was matched by their cost-effective recording techniques. Their first album, recorded at a friend's house, was refreshingly low-tech; the second, 1988's *The Trinity Session*, was named after the Toronto church in which the tracks had been laid down during a 14-hour session - total cost in the region of $200; total sales one million copies. The *sotto voce* drawl of Margo Timmins seemed to be equally prudent (she later had

voice training to help increase her volume), but it suited their take with a twang on the Velvet Underground. The Velvets influence had come via her brother Michael's earlier music-making with his childhood friend Alan Anton - and Lou Reed applauded their version of 'Sweet Jane'. As Michael Timmins' songwriting developed, the sparseness of the initial Junkies sound seemed to be potentially limiting, and from *Pale Sun, Crescent Moon* onwards they began to add a flurry of raw passion.

Cowboy Junkies

Key members: Alan Anton 22/6/59, Margo Timmins 27/6/61, Michael Timmins 21/4/59, Peter Timmins 29/10/65 • Recording career: 1986 - present

The Trinity Session 1988, Pale Sun, Crescent Moon 1993, Miles From Our Home 1998

"Are we born in the wrong time?
If we can save rock'n'roll,
we're born at just the right time." Poison Ivy Rorschach

108

The Cramps

If rock'n'roll ever needed a saviour, the Cramps could provide its Noah's Ark. Fronted by the frenetic Lux Interior and the ice-cool Poison Ivy, they first brought their ragout of rockabilly, psychedelia and garage, aka psychobilly, to the masses - well the cultish hordes at least - in the mid-1970s. In their own inimitable way, they were as musicologically important as Ry Cooder, driven by a quest to unearth the obscure 1950s and 60s material they revered. The Cramps survived

regular label changes and fluctuating personnel (sometime band members included Fur Candy Del Mar and Slim Chance), always maintaining a cracked sense of humour that first saw the light of night at CGBG's. Underlaid by a fulsome guitar sound that meant a bassist was generally superfluous to requirements, tracks like 'Bikini Girls With Machine Guns' and 'I Wanna Get In Your Pants' confirmed that the essence of rock'n'roll, was, for the time being, in safe hands.

Key members: Lux Interior (Erick Purkhiser) 1948, Poison Ivy Rorschach (Kirsty Wallace) 1954 • Recording career: 1978 – present
Sounds: Songs The Lord Taught Us 1980, A Date With Elvis 1986, Flamejob 1994

"I decided that I no longer cared about what the media thought of me or my band. As far as I'm concerned **they can kiss my Irish ass."** Dolores O'Riordan

The Cranberries

There was a touching provincial awkwardness about the Cranberries. The Hogan brothers and Fergal Lawler were, to be honest, going nowhere fast in their native Limerick - especially with the joke name Cranberry Saw Us - when they acquired a new singer and lyricist. Immediately Dolores O'Riordan added looks, attitude (though at first she had been agonisingly shy in front of audiences) and a mystical blend of lilting vocals and breaking-voice yelp that moved even seasoned critics like Greil Marcus to observe that she summoned "landscapes and poses of the Pre-Raphaelites". The UK and Ireland remained resistant to their charms until they found success in the States - a graveyard for most non-US bands at that time bar Radiohead. Suddenly everyone fell victim to their Gaelic charms and their ability to be by turns plaintive and declamatory, particularly on the seething 'Zombie', a response to the Warrington bombing. The Cranberries caught the wave and tapped the source.

Key members: Mike Hogan 29/4/73, Noel Hogan 25/12/71, Fergal Lawler 4/3/71, Dolores O'Riordan 6/9/71 • **Recording career:** 1991 - present

Sounds: Everybody Else Is Doing It, So Why Can't We? 1993, No Need To Argue 1994, To The Faithful Departed 1996

Robert Cray took blues to fresh levels of popularity as a frontline member of the 1980s/90s blues revival. The title of his 1986 release, *Strong Persuader*, suggested how the allure of his fluid Stratocaster style had attracted a new audience to the sometimes introspective and insular world of the blues; Clapton was an early admirer, and covered 'Bad Influence' on his album *August*. Cray learnt his guitar chops from listening to Albert Collins (and toured with the master in the mid-1970s), but equally from Steve Cropper and Jimi Hendrix, whose pyrotechnics were sometimes evident in his playing. A warm soul voice led him towards a couple of more mainstream - and, for some, over-slick - albums, but he was never in danger of straying too far from the real blues, and it was in no small measure thanks to Cray that John Lee Hooker and Buddy Guy enjoyed a high profile in their later years.

Robert Cray

"I couldn't see myself playing rock'n'roll, **singing about trees and stuff."**

Born: 1/8/53 • Recording career: 1980 - present • Sounds: Bad Influence 1983, Strong Persuader 1986, Shame And A Sin 1993

Although the trio pre-dated Clapton and Baker's Blind Faith, this was less a contrived supergroup, more a coming together of like-minded blues-rockers. Baker and Clapton persuaded Jack Bruce to leave a lucrative Manfred Mann gig before Cream broke cover in 1966, immediately establishing their trademark power blues and extended jam/improvisations. Initially drawing heavily on the Delta blues repertoire they had added more original material by their second album, the Dayglo-bright *Disraeli Gears*.

With songs by Jack Bruce, the group's main singer, and poet Pete Brown, it included the classics 'White Room' and 'Strange Brew', and the timeless riff of 'Sunshine Of Your Love'. Their lengthy, potentially self-indulgent, workouts - Baker's pounding drum solos, Clapton just being God - were always in danger of turning sour, and the band agreed, bidding farewell with two gigs at the Royal Albert Hall in November 1968. But they cleared the ground for Led Zep and left behind some absolutely corking tracks.

Cream

"Until we came to America we were just an ordinary English provincial group. Then the bubble burst. We thought we were God's gift." Eric Clapton

Key members: Ginger Baker 19/8/39, Jack Bruce 14/5/43, Eric Clapton 30/3/45 • Recording career: 1966 - 1969 • Sounds: Fresh Cream 1966, Disraeli Gears 1967, Wheels Of Fire 1968

The Creation

"There was a riot of imagination.

Kenny was interpreting our music in a crude fashion with paints on a screen."

Jack Jones

Considering their relatively brief career, the Creation left behind a mark not just as power-poppers on a par with the Who and the Kinks, but also as the inspiration for Alan McGee's Creation record label - future nurturing ground of the Jesus & Mary Chain, Primal Scream and Oasis. Twenty years earlier it was Tony Stratton-Smith and Shel Talmy who steered the fortunes of this 'freakbeat' foursome. Creation's pair of 1966 singles - 'Making Time' and 'Painter Man', later a hit for Boney M. -

dispatched high-quality, though low-charting, blasts of mod-pop. Largely ignored, other than in Germany, Creation's R'n'B-influenced psychedelia, onstage painting sessions, and guitarist Kenny Pickett's use of a violin bow on his guitar (pre-Jimmy Page) had potential. But the group splintered, and despite sporadic revivals (one including Ron Wood) they disappeared, virtually without trace, until the mid-1990s, reforming to release an album on, where else, Creation Records.

Key members: Bob Garner, Jack Jones 8/11/44, Eddie Phillips 15/8/45, Kenny Pickett 3/9/47 (died 10/1/97) • Recording career: 1966 - 1968 (reformed 1993 - 1996)

Sounds: We Are Paintermen 1967

Creedence Clearwater Revival

"John Fogerty was an Old Testament, shaggy-haired prophet." Bruce Springsteen

They hailed from the Bay Area, but their heart - particularly leading light John Fogerty's - resided in the Bayou. Previously called the Blue Velvets, and then, embarrassingly, the Golliwogs (a record company attempt to compete with the British invasion), CCR took control of their development, coming good on the magnificent 'Proud Mary', the first of a rolling river of crisply disciplined hit singles released at a time when the concept album was king. Their 1950s rock'n'roll sound -

'Travelin' Band' from *Cosmo's Factory* was perilously close to 'Good Golly Miss Molly' - was imbued with the spirit of the Mississippi Delta, evoked by John Fogerty's expressive voice. Hip enough to appear at Woodstock, they managed to keep the critics on side, but eventually began to be dismissed as 'just' a singles act. Internal tensions raised their own bad moon, and after Tom Fogerty abandoned his brother, the group tottered on as a trio before submerging in the swamps.

Key members: Doug 'Cosmo' Clifford 24/4/45, Stu Cook 25/4/45, John Fogerty 28/5/45, Tom Fogerty 9/11/41 • Recording career: 1968 - 1972

Sounds: Green River 1969, Willy And The Poor Boys 1969, Cosmo's Factory 1970

Crosby, Stills, Nash & Young

The harmonies of CSN&Y could not have been closer, but their individual personalities proved less compatible. In their early rosy days, Stephen Stills, fresh from Buffalo Springfield, and ex-Byrd David Crosby waylaid Graham Nash while he was touring the States with the Hollies. To boost the trio's instrumental strength, Stills' former colleague Neil Young was drafted in for Woodstock - where they played an acoustic set as CS&N and an electric set with Young. The debut album *Déjà Vu* served up two million advance orders, songs from all four, and contributions from John Sebastian and Jerry Garcia, while

Young's 'Ohio', written in response to the Kent State University shootings, presented them as the sweet voice of the anti-war movement. Inner tensions (ego and drugs the usual suspects) broke up the group at their peak, and after various reshuffles the next CSN&Y album did not appear until 1988 - the surprisingly cohesive *American Dream*.

> "I already had a good solo career going, and before I would join I wanted to make sure that the 'and Young' bit was right in there."
>
> Neil Young

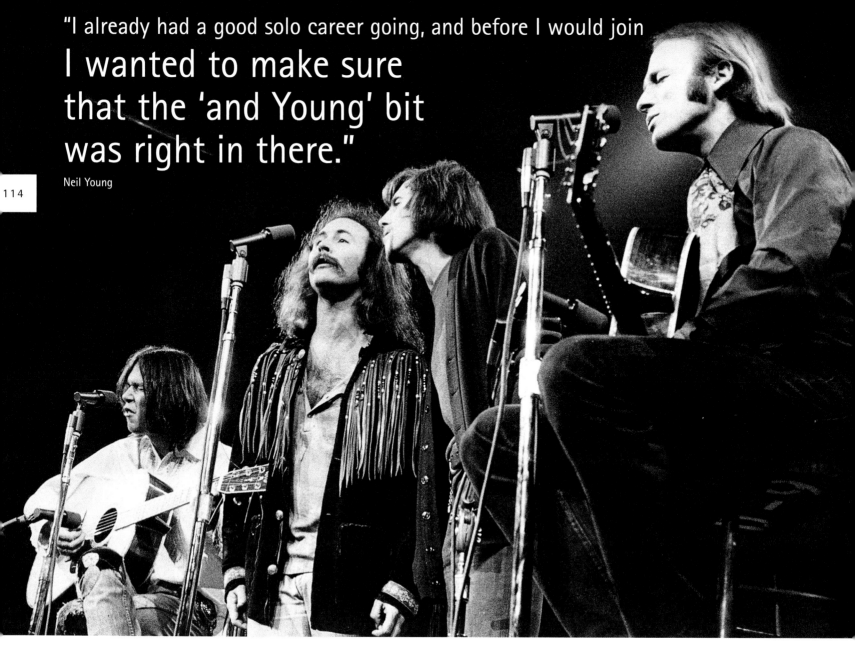

Key members: David Crosby 14/8/41, Graham Nash 2/2/42, Stephen Stills 3/1/45, Neil Young 12/11/45 • Recording career: 1970 - 1971 (reformed 1988 - 1989)

Sounds: Déjà Vu 1970, 4-Way Street 1971, American Dream 1988

Sheryl Crow

"I had this horrible stigma of being a backing singer. **It took five years for anyone to take me seriously.**"

Follow your vision: Sheryl Crow never abandoned hers. Inheriting a musical dream from her parents (her father Wendell played some tastefully muted trumpet on 'We Do What We Can'), and following a music degree and a period teaching, Crow took her chances in LA. She worked as a singer on Michael Jackson's *Bad* tour, earnt writing credits with Wynona Judd and provided b.v.s for Don Henley and Rod Stewart. Though her work with Jackson led to offers to record in a similar vein, she was confident enough to stick to her own sound, even convincing A&M to ditch a complete album because it was too slickly produced. Instead, her debut album *Tuesday Night Music Club* emerged from weekly improv sessions at producer Bill Bottrell's Pasadena studio: a feel-good, relaxed set that was a sleeper before exploding with the release of 'All I Wanna Do' - Crow's perfect music for cruising, best of all on Santa Monica Boulevard.

115

Born: 11/2/62 • Recording career: 1993 - present • Sounds: Tuesday Night Music Club 1993, Sheryl Crow 1996, The Globe Sessions 1998

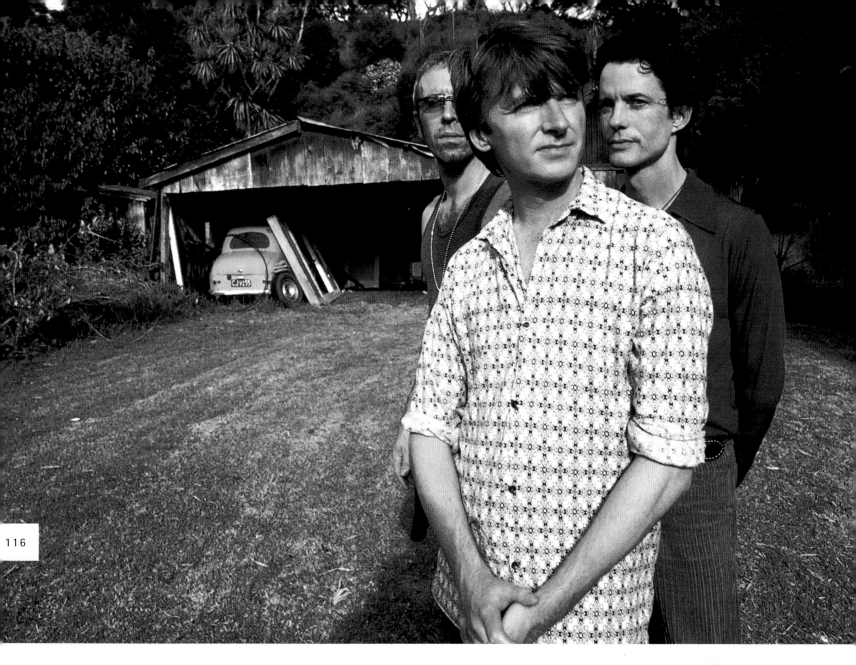

"I've always liked a tinge of melancholy in songs,

and I find that even on a perfect day anxieties are always close." Neil Finn

Crowded House were the unlikely progeny of Aussie 70s art-rockers Split Enz (imagine Roxy Music à la Sparks), which the Kiwi Neil Finn joined while his brother Tim was already a member. When the Enz fell out and Tim headed off to marry actress Greta Scacchi - he later became a Crowded House resident - Neil launched a new group as a vehicle for his determinedly melodic songs, shipping the trio out to LA and adopting various names until the one based on their cramped living quarters stuck. Their profile perked up after 'Don't Dream It's Over' was performed by Paul Young at 1988's Mandela birthday party. Yet it still took until the albums *Woodface* and *Together Alone* for more than a close-knit group of Householads to appreciate Finn's stone-dead songwriting talent, linked by critics variously with Paul McCartney, Squeeze, the Kinks and the Byrds; Roger McGuinn even joined the band on stage in 1989 to perform some Byrds classics.

Crowded House

Key members: Neil Finn 27/5/58, Paul Hesler 8/1/59, Nick Seymour 9/12/58 • Recording career: 1986 - 1996 • Sounds: Crowded House 1986, Woodface 1991, Together Alone 1993

The Cult

"We are a band able to play in both hard rock and alternative areas. Few bands can do that.

I think we were a little ground-breaking." Billy Duffy

Emerging as the Southern Death Cult in Bradford during 1982, the band carried out a policy of gradually paring away their name on an annual basis, recording as Death Cult in 1983, and emerging as simply the Cult by 1984 - apparently dropping the Death because it was too goth and too restricting. Fronted by Ian Astbury, who originally favoured shamanistic American Indian imagery and costume (he'd spent some time in Canada when he was young), the Cult's musical progression was one of movement across the divide between goth-punk and indie, before forging onwards to hard rock, driven there by Billy Duffy's guitar. In 1985 *Love* had been an exercise in psychedelic rock; by 1987 *Electric*, produced by Def Jam's Rick Rubin, was striding into the territory of AC/DC and Led Zep - ahead of a five-year-long split in 1995 they supported Metallica and Guns N' Roses, who'd recruited one-time Cult drummer Matt Sorum in 1990.

117

Key members: Ian Astbury 14/5/62, Billy Duffy 12/5/59 • Recording career: 1984 - 1994 • Sounds: Love 1985, Electric 1987, Sonic Temple 1989

Culture Club

Boy George proudly declared that he was no musician, that in fact he didn't know how to play *any* instrument. He was an out-and-out rent-a-quote icon with a telegenic look and half-decent soul voice, who never frightened the grannies - they just thought he was cute. Emerging from the 1980s club scene in his smock, dreadlocks and little black hat, George was the acceptable drag queen that Wayne County could never have been, the visual highlight of a band whose drummer, and George's sometime lover, Jon Moss had played with the Damned and Adam Ant. After the breakthrough 'Do You Really Want To Hurt Me', the band's perky tunes - 'Karma Chameleon' among the perkiest - proved flavoursome for two or three years before Boy George's drug problems stymied their progress. Yet they retained a affectionate memory in the heart of those who'd seen them, and the Club reformed in 1998, once some minor lacerations had healed.

"I've been doing the drag queen bit for years, and it was only a way of getting laid." Boy George

Key members: Mikey Craig 15/2/60, Boy George (George O'Dowd) 14/6/61, Roy Hay 12/8/61, Jon Moss 11/9/57 • Recording career: 1982 - 1986 & 1998 - present

Sounds: Kissing To Be Clever 1982, Colour By Numbers 1983, From Luxury To Heartache 1986

The Cure

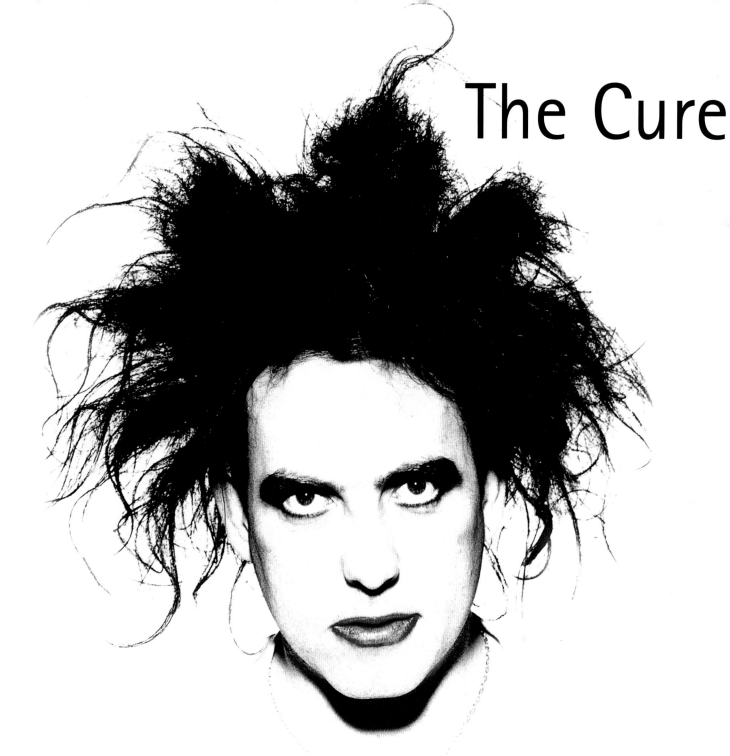

For somebody who preferred to hide behind a layer of white slap, Robert Smith bared his soul in a way that suggested his music-making was as much about therapy as any other kind of motivation. Once he had shed the punkish mood of the Cure's early work - the Albert Camus-inspired 'Killing An Arab' caused some knee-jerk consternation amongst those who hadn't properly listened to its intent - Smith ploughed through band members in a way which

made the title of their 1989 album *Disintegration* only too appropriate; original member and keyboardist Lol Tolhurst lasted the longest, but even that relationship ended up in the law courts. Dubbed 'masters of mope rock', the Cure could certainly provide the necessary ambience to make you feel really good about feeling really down. Yet they always inlaid a few gem-like singles - 'In Between Days', or 'Friday I'm In Love' - to leaven the doom and gloom.

"I find it quite frustrating that I'm so easy-going about this group, and sometimes let it slip. But at least I let it slip upwards."

Robert Smith

Key member: Robert Smith 21/4/59 • **Recording career:** 1978 - present • **Sounds:** Three Imaginary Boys 1979, The Head On The Door 1985, Kiss Me, Kiss Me, Kiss Me 1987

The Damned

"I never expected it to last for a month. **Nobody did...**" Rat Scabies

The first, and for many the finest. The Damned were present in all the right places during the early days of punk - a debut gig at the 100 Club supporting the Pistols, performing at the Mont de Marsan festival. Theirs was the first punk single ('New Rose' b/w a cover of 'Help!') and first album - *Damned Damned Damned* - and they were the first UK punk act to play in the US, at CBGB's in New York. Speed of attack and anger of vocals hid a genuine talent revealed on later albums (Pink Floyd's Nick Mason produced their second), and a sense of the absurd which surfaced on Captain Sensible's whimsical solo hit, Rodgers and Hammerstein's 'Happy Talk'. They collapsed initially in 1978 before they had really got going, but all bar guitarist Brian James re-formed - first as The Doomed until they re-acquired rights to the name - and later, minus Sensible, produced a run of singles success which culminated in a UK Number Three in 1986 with a cover of Barry Ryan's 'Eloise'.

Key members: Brian James 18/2/55, Rat Scabies (Chris Miller) 30/7/57, Captain Sensible (Ray Burns) 23/4/55, Dave Vanian 12/10/56 • Recording career: 1976 - 1987

Sounds: Damned Damned Damned 1977, Machine Gun Etiquette 1979, The Black Album 1980

Hallelujah for Spencer Davis: he it was who brought us the talent of Steve Winwood, not yet 18 years old when 'Keep On Running' hit the UK Number One slot. Guitarist Davis, from a background of skiffle and blues, had joined forces with the Winwood brothers - who had a trad jazz band - and bassist York to pump out some driving R'n'B: their first single was a version of John Lee Hooker's 'Dimples'. Signed by Chris Blackwell, it was another Island discovery, singer/songwriter Jackie Edwards, who provided them with 'Keep On Running' and 'Somebody Help Me', also a Number One. The star of the show, though, was undoubtedly Steve Winwood, whose white soul vocals and organ riffs were the heart of the Davis sound. When he left to join Traffic (brother Muff also quit to become a successful producer/record exec), the Group never recovered, despite some talented replacements, including Nigel Olsson and Dee Murray, later the guts of Elton John's backing band.

The Spencer Davis Group

"When this spotty kid on organ suddenly opened his mouth
I felt a chill down my spine." Noddy Holder

Key members: Spencer Davis 17/7/37, Mervyn 'Muff' Winwood 15/6/43, Steve Winwood 12/5/48, Pete York 15/8/42 • Recording career: 1964 - 1969 & 1973 - 1974

Sounds: The First Album 1965, Autumn '66 1966

Dead Kennedys

Pulling punches was never a Dead Kennedys speciality: their name was guaranteed to give Boston brahmins the screaming habdabs and they relentlessly highlighted liberal hypocrisy: their definitive 'California Über Alles' lampooned Linda Ronstadt's one-time squire Governor Jerry Brown. Jello Biafra (Eric Boucher of Boulder, Colorado) had recruited his troops after witnessing the Sex Pistols' final gig in San Francisco's Winterland Ballroom, but his lacerating lyrics proved too provocative even for US labels looking for homegrown punk acts. So the Kennedys formed their own label, Alternative Tentacles, later home to Hüsker Dü and DOA, and 'Too Drunk To Fuck', despite minimal airplay, even penetrated the UK singles charts. Needless to say, the Powers That Be were constantly on the Kennedys' case, resulting in a prosecution over the artwork of their *Frankenchrist* album (an H.R. Giger poster with self-sodomising penises). The Kennedys won, but were so drained they lost the will to carry on.

"Punk will never die
until something more dangerous replaces it." Jello Biafra

122

Key members: East Bay Ray (Ray Glasser), Jello Biafra (Eric Boucher)17/6/58, Klaus Fluoride, D.H. Peligro • Recording career: 1979 - 1986

Sounds: Fresh Fruit For Rotting Vegetables 1980, Plastic Surgery Disasters 1982, Frankenchrist 1985

Deep Purple

"We took from jazz,
old-fashioned rock'n'roll, the classics.
We were musical
magpies." Jon Lord

To understand the Purple power, crank up the volume on *Made In Japan* (the *Guinness Book Of Records* declared them the world's loudest band - it's official!). Strained backstage relations were subsumed behind the roar of Ian Gillan's voice jousting with Ritchie Blackmore's guitar, each attempting to outstrip each other over a heavy rhythm section and Jon Lord's swirly organ: Gillan is equal to the challenge. The same live album contains 'Smoke On The Water' - testing ground for a million music shop guitarists - as much a Deep Purple trademark as flares, nutshell hats and bulging groins. Once they'd ditched a number of early pop tendencies, and overcome Jon Lord's classical aspirations - though they did release an album with the Royal Philharmonic Orchestra - they concentrated on what they did supremely well, before the best line-up caved in and new boys, including David Coverdale (later of Whitesnake) and Tommy Bolin, tried their hardest to match the glory of Gillan at his finest.

Key members: Ritchie Blackmore 14/4/45, Ian Gillan 19/8/45, Roger Glover 30/11/45, Jon Lord 9/6/41, Ian Paice 29/6/48 • **Recording career:** 1968 - 1976 (reformed 1984 - present)

Sounds: Deep Purple In Rock 1970, Machine Head 1972, Made In Japan 1973

Their self-belief helped them overcome adversity, and Def Leppard's fans stuck with them - the critics were *never* with them - through the departure of original guitarist Pete Willis (a drink problem), the death of guitarist Steve Clark (also alcohol-related) and the car accident that cost drummer Rick Allen his left arm. He persevered, grittily using drum machines and adapted kits, while the band patiently waited for him to recover. Precocious on their debut - Allen was fifteen at the time - their metal was tempered through a punishing touring regime, particularly in the States where Def Leppard were instrumental, along with Iron Maiden, in putting British HM on the map. Their hard-riffing, Mutt Lange-produced, guitar-led energy sold serious millions of albums like *Pyromania* and *Hysteria*: the band repaid their fans by letting them select the title of their 1992 album *Adrenalize*, and were canny enough to keep updating their sound without ever alienating their support.

"We all want to go on stage, pose, wear dinky white boots, tight trousers and have all the girls looking at our bollocks." Steve Clark

Def Leppard

Key members: Rick Allen 1/11/63, Steve Clark 23/4/60 (died 8/1/91), Phil Collen 8/12/57, Joe Elliott 1/8/59, Rick Savage 2/12/60 • Recording career: 1979 - present

Sounds: Pyromania 1983, Hysteria 1987, Slang 1996

Depeche Mode

For all their self-conscious pose, Depeche Mode presented the human face of electro-pop, filtering Kraftwerk's techno sound into a sequence of UK Top 30 hits which provided one of the dominant sounds of the 1980s. Gone was all that guitar, bass and drums nonsense - synths were easier to carry, for one thing - and the whole concept of 'the band' was turned on its head, with only Alan Wilder given a credit as 'musician', the others being 'singer' (Gahan), 'songwriter' (Gore) and

'co-ordinator' (Fletcher): the band's original songwriter Vince Clarke had quit the band in 1981, popping up later in Yazoo and Erasure. Martin Gore took over his duties and covered some demanding lyrical territory - from SM to religious obsession - but the tunes won the day. By the 1990s Dave Gahan's back-of-the-throat voice had racked up an extra notch of power, and they made the step up to stadium stature, although their earnest approach was now sounding a wee bit dated.

"We're in our own little world, really.
We've had all this success
and we're still quite anonymous as people." Dave Gahan

Key members: Andy Fletcher 8/7/60, Dave Gahan 9/5/62, Martin Gore 23/7/61, Alan Wilder 1/6/59 • Recording career: 1981 - present

Sounds: Some Great Reward 1984, Music For The Masses 1987, Songs Of Faith And Devotion 1993

Devo

"In our music we're looking for the big enema, the big catharsis." Gerry Casale

Something bubbled up in Ohio during the late 1970s, as the New York music scene stimulated a response from the youth of the industrial Mid-West, a generation spearheaded by Pere Ubu, Tin Huey, the Dead Boys and Devo. More art school graduates than musicians, Devo's vision was of a world in 'de-evolution', first proclaimed in a video which picked up a film festival award. Their combination of boiler suits, flower pot hats and a sharply pointed deconstruction of the Stones' 'Satisfaction' was granted His Imperial Ziggyness's blessing by Bowie (who introduced the band on their New York debut). But ultimately their tongue-in-cheek games and quirks wore thin and, as Billy Joel once pointed out, their tunes just *didn't* work on the radio. Devo in turn felt that most people had completely failed to grasp their essential humanism, and indeed, as they de-evolved themselves at the end of the 1980s, their influence was being acknowledged by bands like Nirvana and Soundgarden.

Key members: Bob Casale, Jerry Casale, Bob Mothersbaugh, Mark Mothersbaugh, Alan Myers • Recording career: 1976 - 1990 (reformed 1997)
Sounds: Q: Are We Not Men? A: We Are Devo! 1978, Duty Now For The Future 1979, Freedom Of Choice 1980

Dexys Midnight Runners

The original Dexys garb, doffing its cap to the stevedores of New York's docks, was the tougher than tough look for 'Geno', a tribute to Geno Washington and the Northern soul sound Kevin Rowland had grown up with. His single-minded, some said pig-headed, passion was already evident: once 'Geno' charted, the band dumped it from their live show for a while, and Rowland sequestered the masters of their debut album *Searching For The Young Soul Rebels* until contract terms improved.

It was a fierceness that eventually ripped apart the band around him, requiring a series of re-inventions, first to anoraks and pony-tails, and then the raggle-taggle gypsy style of 'Come On Eileen' - complete with fiddles (provided by violin trio The Emerald Express) and mandolins. Most people overlooked the final manifestation - slicked-back Ivy League - on the stream of consciousness *Don't Stand Me Down*, but with Rowland, the unexpected always lay just around the corner.

"People will always laugh at the Dexys.
But I know that what I'm doing is totally honest." Kevin Rowland

127

Key member: Kevin Rowland 17/8/53 • Recording career: 1979 - 1986 • Sounds: Searching For The Young Soul Rebels 1980, Too-Rye-Ay 1982, Don't Stand Me Down 1985

Bo Diddley

"I opened the door for a lot of people, and they just ran through **and left me holding the knob."**

He might not always have reaped the commercial rewards, but Bo Diddley was always a great self-promoter. His rectangular guitar, be-bop goatee and horn-rims were an inspired piece of branding, and his album titles relentlessly reminded consumers whose product they were buying: *Go Bo Diddley*, *Bo Diddley Rides Again*. He created a trademark chunk-a-chunk riff, and his two sidekicks, the glamorous 'Duchess' on guitar alongside the maracas-playing, repartee-swapping Jerome Green, were perfect foils. Mississippi-born, Chicago-raised, and nurtured on a diet of John Lee Hooker and Muddy Waters, Bo was always open to new possibilities. His 1963 album, *Surfin' With Bo Diddley*, was a typical piece of opportunism; some fifteen years later he was opening shows for the Clash, echoing the mark he had left on an earlier generation of Brits, especially the Rolling Stones and the Pretty Things, the latter named after one of his numbers.

Born: Ellas Bates 30/12/28 • Recording career: 1955 - present • Sounds: Bo Diddley In The Spotlight 1960, Bo Diddley Is A Gunslinger 1963, Bo Diddley's Beach Party 1963

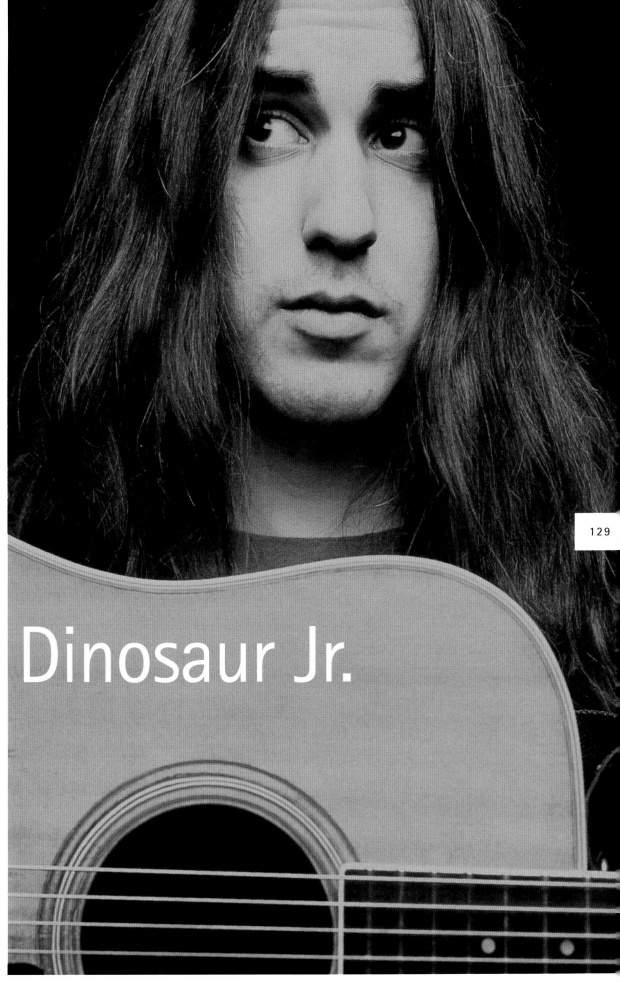

At one time named as a potential candidate for the Nirvana drum stool, J. Mascis was more often tipped as the saviour of the electric guitar, at the heart of his own band Dinosaur Jr. Yet his reticence in front of the press - often perceived as lethargic slackerdom - ensured a lower profile than he deserved. Mascis considered the birth of great rock music to be the sound of the Stooges and the UK punk scene, Sham 69 in particular. There was plenty of that heritage in his guitar sound, cross-fertilised with his fondness for Neil Young, which emerged as angsty lyrics. This meeting point of noise and melody was best displayed on the band's 1988 indie hit single 'Freak Scene', which was a significant precursor of the grunge sound. However, a period of personnel changes followed, an unfortunate interruption at a time when Mascis and his Dinosaur could have been all-conquering.

"At home I still play drums all the time.
I can't really play the guitar."

J. Mascis

Dinosaur Jr.

Key member: J. Mascis 10/12/65 • Recording career: 1985 - 1998 • Sounds: You're Living All Over Me 1987, Bug 1988, Hand It Over 1997

Dion and the Belmonts

For a while there, between 1958 and 1963, between Elvis's call-up and JFK's assassination, Dion DiMucci was the bossman of white rockers, a New York Italian guy with pin-up potential and a wardrobe full of college sweaters. Supported by backing group the Belmonts - a bunch of neighbourhood friends named after an Avenue in the Bronx - he kicked off with Doc Pomus and Mort Shuman's 'A Teenager In Love', tapping into the Brill Building songwriters' ability to articulate teenage concerns. Following a version of Rodgers and Hart's 'Where Or When' Dion shucked off the Belmonts and went solo, producing two more rock/teenage classics, 'Runaround Sue' (debate, despite Dion's explanation, continues to rumble about the song's inspiration) and 'The Wanderer'. He then moved onwards through the blues, dealing with a heroin problem, and via a couple of reunions with the Belmonts, to embrace born-again Christian music. But Dion had no major hit after 1968's inspirational 'Abraham, Martin And John'.

"'Runaround Sue' was written about a chick named Dolores. She was the neighbourhood whore." Dion

Key member: Dion DiMucci 18/7/39 • Recording career: (with the Belmonts) 1958 - 1960, reformed 1967 & 1973, (solo) 1960 - present

Sounds: Lovers Who Wander 1962, Dion 1968, Born To Be With You 1975

> "We got a lot of flak. For a while I was just as happy playing a game of tennis as picking up a guitar."
>
> Mark Knopfler

It came ready minted for the compact disc generation, scratch-free and seamless: *Brothers In Arms*, only marred by the fact that Mark Knopfler's brother David was no longer 'in arms', having quit the band in 1980 to go solo, leaving Mark to let his laidback licks and vocals insinuate their way into the CD players of a yuppie world. And Sting's immortal line "I want my MTV" on 'Money For Nothing' gave a clue to the other secret of the band's success: innovative promo videos which brilliantly camouflaged the band's frankly unprepossessing appearance. By this stage Mark was a guitar icon, invited to guest on Steely Dan's *Gaucho* - the highest of all possible commendations - and laying down mellifluous lines in a style he had demonstrated as early as 'Sultans Of Swing'. While he engaged in outside production work, soundtracks and hobbies like the Notting Hillbillies, the Straits gently ossified behind him, and their reformation in the 1990s broke little new ground.

Dire Straits

Key members: Alan Clark 5/3/52, Guy Fletcher, John Illsley 24/6/49, David Knopfler 27/12/52, Mark Knopfler 12/8/49, Terry Williams 11/1/48 • Recording career: 1978 - 1988 & 1991 - 1993

Sounds: Dire Straits 1978, Making Movies 1980, Brothers In Arms 1985

Lonnie Donegan

The appeal of skiffle frequently remained a mystery to those who were never caught up by its unsophisticated charms. Yet, at its peak, in the late 1950s and early 60s, Lonnie Donegan was the undisputed king of skiffle, after the former trad jazz banjoist broke into the charts with a re-worked Lead Belly number 'Rock Island Line'. His loose pop-folk sound - Britain's first response to Bill Haley - encouraged the next generation of musicians (not least the Beatles-to-be Quarrymen) to get up and have a go. Skiffle was never as sexy as Elvis, but it was rough, ready and accessible: all you needed to perform it was a tea-chest bass, a washboard and an acoustic guitar. After fading somewhat as Beatlemania swept the remains of skiffle away, Donegan left behind the Steptoe-like legacy of 'My Old Man's A Dustman' - but his own career ultimately avoided the scrapheap, as a late 1990s revival proved.

132

"Skiffle was the start of British rock music. It was all about feel rather than content. It had style."

Born: 29/4/31 • Recording career: 1956 - present • Sounds: Tops With Lonnie 1958, Putting On The Style 1978, Muleskinner Blues 1998

"Everyone gives off a certain musical note. I think I'm F sharp."

When he started out, Donovan's esteem for Bob Dylan was such that he featured in the Dylan documentary *Don't Look Back* watching his hero with due reverence, and his imitation was pure flattery: harmonica, denim cap, anti-protest involvement, the works. But in 1966 he swapped cap for kaftan with matching love beads and re-emerged as an iconic flower child on 'Sunshine Superman' (featuring Jimmy Page on guitar) and 'Mellow Yellow' (Paul McCartney on whispering) - some thought the Dylan-style songs were actually better. After a trip to see Maharishi Mahesh Yogi on the banks of the Ganges, he was heavily into meditation. The *Barabajagal* album of 1969, featuring Jeff Beck, promised a new direction, but Donovan disappeared to Ireland (for tax reasons of course) where he tended to lie low - especially in the shadow of his film star children Ione Skye and Donovan Leitch - occasionally emerging to record an F sharp or two.

133

Donovan

Born: Donovan Leitch 10/5/46 • Recording career: 1965 – present • Sounds: Sunshine Superman 1966, A Gift From A Flower To A Garden 1968, Barabajagal 1969

"Everybody seemed like road warrior types, war horses,
an intense hardcore touring band,
very different from Steely Dan's cast of characters." Michael McDonald

The Doobie Brothers

Loosely grouped with other American boogie bands - particularly the Allman Brothers - the Doobies were originally seen, and somewhat dismissed, as little more than a bunch of good-time guys, partly because of their choice of name: West Coast slang for a joint. Although their first album did little to suggest otherwise, they tightened up considerably after creating a two-drummer line-up and adding Tiran Porter's funky bass to *Toulouse Street*, and especially *The Captain And Me* - with 'Long

Train Running' (later a remixed dance hit in 1993) showing off the interplay between their vocal harmonies and a grooving rhythm section. This approach wound down as vocalist Tom Johnston's health proved problematic, and the band entered phase two, joined by two refugees from Steely Dan: Jeff Baxter on guitar, and Michael McDonald, whose white soul voice took them into an AOR direction. Both versions of the Doobies had their merits, but people tended to like one or the other.

Key members: Jeff 'Skunk' Baxter 13/12/48, John Hartman 18/3/50, Michael Hossack 18/9/50, Tom Johnston 15/8/48, Michael McDonald 2/12/52, Tiran Porter, Pat Simmons 23/1/50

Recording career: 1971 - 1984, 1989 - 1991 & 1996 - present • Sounds: The Captain And Me 1973, Stampede 1975, Minute By Minute 1978

"Jim Morrison was possessed by a vision,
by a madness, by a rage to live,
by an all-consuming fire to make art." Ray Manzarek

The Doors

Morrison Hotel rescued the Doors from a period when Jim Morrison's excess weight and weighty excess - "I want to experience everything at least once," he had boasted - was threatening to turn them into a bit of a joke. The rootsier, bluesier *Hotel* got them back on track, and their next release, *L.A. Woman*, a back-to-basics piece of brilliance topped off by 'Riders On The Storm', suggested they had re-kindled the passion of their early days. Back then The Doors had fused Morrison's

sensual theatrics with Robbie Krieger's Chicago blues (and songwriting skills: he wrote 'Light My Fire') and Ray Manzarek's organic organ textures. Jim frequently over-acted as the Lizard King - including an undignified exposure charge in Miami - but his early death, within weeks of *L.A. Woman*'s release, ensured it was the young sex god who remained enshrined, rather than the corporate record exec Morrison thought of becoming: "I kinda like the image. Big office. Secretary..."

Key members: John Densmore 1/12/44, Robbie Krieger 8/1/46, Ray Manzarek 12/2/35, Jim Morrison 8/12/43 (died 3/7/71) • Recording career: 1967 - 1972

Sounds: The Doors 1967, Morrison Hotel 1970, L.A. Woman 1971

"To this day I can't stand Straight Outta Compton. I threw that thing together in six weeks so we could have **something to sell outta the trunk."**

In that confluence of Compton's finest talent called NWA, Dr Dre was the turntable architect, using techniques sharpened at Eve's After Dark club to provide the basis of their gangsta groove. Rapping was never his forte, and it was no surprise that for his massive solo album *The Chronic* he brought in Snoop Doggy Dogg. While NWA had shown the rest of the world a slice of inner-city life it had not heard before (or chosen not to hear), Dr Dre was sampling lashings of George Clinton to create G-Funk: 'Nuthin' But A 'G' Thang' was the West Coast sound of the streets in Summer 1993. Following some unpleasantness (various indictments and a feud with NWA's Eazy-E which only ended on the latter's deathbed), Dr Dre - who had discovered Eminem - was ready to move on from the success of his Death Row Records, returning with a long-awaited second album in 1999.

136

Dr Dre

"What we were doing was a bit of a crusade, thinking about some of the crap that was going on at the time, like Emerson Lake & Palmer.

We were trying to destroy all that." Wilko Johnson

Dr Feelgood

Canvey Island - lurking low in the Thames Estuary - was the stamping ground of all four Feelgoods. Guitarist Wilko Johnson had headed off and away to Newcastle (University) and Nepal, returning to rejoin the others in a no-frills R'n'B band, featuring Lee Brilleaux's unflinching vocals and Wilko's frenetically jerky Telecaster action. Named after a Johnny Kidd and the Pirates track, they became a feature of the emerging pub rock circuit, pulsating and sweaty onstage, studiedly anti-glam offstage, their debut album both monochrome and mono. A third, live, album, *Stupidity*, reached UK Number One, but the anticipated shift up in gears stalled when Johnson left while recording the follow-up. The Feelgood factor was maintained single-handedly by Brilleaux - the rhythm section called it a day in 1982 - and it was at his Dr Feelgood Music Bar on Canvey Island that the final Feelgood album was recorded shortly before his death from cancer aged 41.

137

Key members: Lee Brilleaux 1953 (died 7/4/94), Wilko Johnson 1947, John Martin 1947, John B. Sparks 1953 • Recording career: 1975 - 1993

Sounds: Down By The Jetty 1975, Stupidity 1976, Live In London 1990

Dr John

"I sit at home and write songs.
Don't think about where it came from, it just kinda passes through me."

A native of New Orleans who graduated, *summa cum laude*, from Professor Longhair's boogie-woogie academy, Mac Rebennack was a one-time guitarist who turned to the piano and organ, and headed west to LA to become a prolific session musician. Somewhere along the way he invented an alter ego called Dr John, 'The Night Tripper' - supposedly a response to the Beatles' 'Day Tripper' and inspired by the Big Easy singer Prince Lala - and dressed his skills up with all the regalia of voodoo: robes, head-dresses, necklaces of teeth. Album titles like *Gumbo* proclaimed a bubbling stew of Dixieland jazz, rock'n'roll and funk: hot, horny and steamy, often enhanced by the presence of the Meters and the Neville Brothers, and sometimes by guests like Eric Clapton and Mick Jagger. Dr John's role in setting up AFO (All For One), a co-operative label for black artists, was a testament to the respect he commanded amongst all of the Crescent City's musicians.

Born: Mac Rebennack 21/11/40 • Recording career: 1957 - present • Sounds: Gris-Gris 1968, Dr John's Gumbo 1972, Television 1994

"There were only two or three concerts that felt right.
If I could find a fairly natural connection with something else,
I might move on."

The output that Nick Drake left behind when he died of an overdose aged 26 was as frustratingly slender as the Rizla papers that inspired the title of his debut album *Five Leaves Left*. The three albums he released - he was halfway through recording a fourth at the time of his death - were increasingly introspective, particularly the third, *Pink Moon*, which was both haunting and harrowing. Drake suffered from depression, requiring psychiatric treatment, and eventually became so reclusive - à la Syd Barrett - that the tapes for *Pink Moon* were simply dropped off, as if anonymously, at Island Records' reception desk; performing in front of an audience also proved a problem. The former Marlborough and Fitzwilliam College, Cambridge student was the discovery of Fairport Convention's bassist Ashley Hutchings, and on his first two releases, Drake's intricate guitar was rounded out by various Fairports, especially Richard Thompson. Both albums were rich but gossamer-fragile (critics made comparisons with Van Morrison and Tim Buckley), and their low sales only served to deepen Drake's depression.

Nick Drake

Born: 19/6/48 (died 25/11/74) • Recording career: 1969 - 1974 • Sounds: Five Leaves Left 1969, Bryter Layter 1970, Pink Moon 1972

"When they first played the demo of 'This Wheel's On Fire', I thought **'What a drag'.**"

The theme tune to Jennifer Saunders' masterly comedy series *Absolutely Fabulous* featured her husband Ade Edmondson singing 'This Wheel's On Fire' with Julie Driscoll. It was an affectionate tribute to the Bob Dylan/Rick Danko-written single with which she had had a UK Top Five hit in 1968 as part of Brian Auger's Trinity. A sometime model, Driscoll was working as a secretary for promoter-manager Giorgio Gomelsky when he suggested adding her voice as a third singer to organist Auger's then band Steampacket: the other vocalists, which made for an impressive front-line, were Rod Stewart and Long John Baldry, each taking a turn in front of an R'n'B-jazz backing. After Stewart and Baldry had departed for pastures new, a re-configured Trinity featured Driscoll's soulful voice alone, but after the success of 'This Wheel' she also left, marrying pianist Keith Tippett, and from time to time recording under her married name.

Julie Driscoll

Born: 8/6/47 • Recording career: 1966 - 1994 • Sounds: (with the Brian Auger Trinity) Streetnoise 1968

Duran Duran

"We want to be the band to dance to
when the bomb drops." Simon Le Bon

Vapid or valid - the Duran Duran debate continues. Apart from the certainty that this was the only charting band to feature three unrelated Taylors, there has always been merry dispute about whether the group were a stiff, talentless quintet flattered by great videos, or an act whose songwriting transcended the frills and frippery of New Romanticism. Revisionism later veered towards the latter (heck, Puff Daddy sampled them), despite the 1995 album *Thank You*, with its covers of Dylan,

Elvis Costello and Public Enemy that had several hardcore journalists choking on their disbelief. In the era of 1982's *Rio* the Durans had successfully fingered the pulse of synth-led fashion and - if truth be told - much of the knocking copy was simply jealousy that they had sussed the combination of look and hook that typified 'Girls On Film' (complete with raunchy video by Godley & Creme), and later 'The Reflex'. It was as of its moment as yuppiedom and kohl for the lads.

Key members: Simon Le Bon 27/10/58, Nick Rhodes 8/6/62, Andy Taylor 16/2/61, John Taylor 20/6/60, Roger Taylor 26/4/60 • Recording career: 1981 - present
Sounds: Rio 1982, Notorious 1986, Duran Duran (The Wedding Album) 1993

Ian Dury and the Blockheads

"My mum told me to write a hit single. She was fed up of me being skint and moaning about it." Ian Dury

Ian Dury's songs and Cockney patter were pure music-hall, with tongue firmly in cheek and verbal gymnastics in overdrive, a talent first bruited with the visually remarkable pub-rockers Kilburn and The High Roads (the band featured a seven-foot-tall bassist, a crippled drummer and Dury's own polio-withered body). There he met Chas Jankel, whose keyboards and arrangements added texture and depth to Dury's natural charm and talent. Following his first solo release - *New Boots And Panties!!* - the Blockheads were assembled, and fast became one of the great live bands, with Norman Watt Roy on malevolent bass, Davey Payne on orgasmic sax, and the late Charley Charles on driving drums. The pre-rap rap of 'Hit Me With Your Rhythm Stick', the sardonic stomp of 'Sex'n'Drugs'n'Rock'n'Roll' and the foul-mouthed humour of 'Plaistow Patricia' were never better played than by this line-up. The loss of Dury to cancer in 2000 made us all realise how good he'd been.

Key member: Ian Dury 12/5/42 (died 27/3/00) • Recording career: 1977 - 1999 • Sounds: New Boots And Panties!! 1978, Do It Yourself 1978, Mr Love Pants 1998

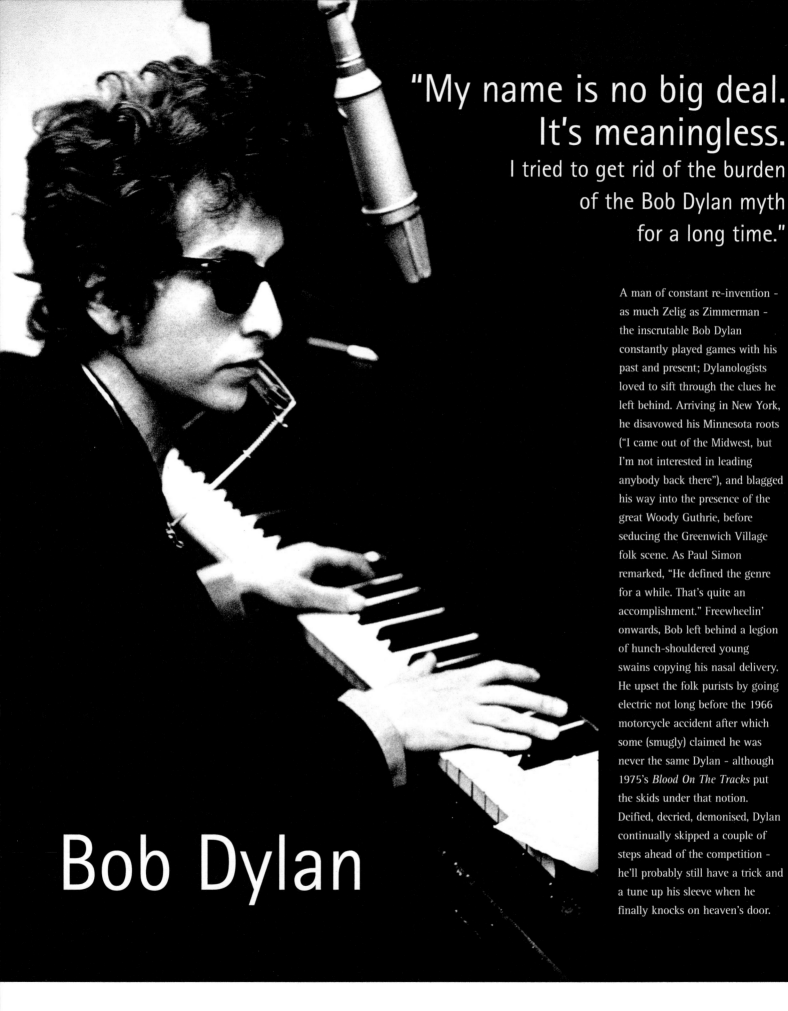

"My name is no big deal. It's meaningless. I tried to get rid of the burden of the Bob Dylan myth for a long time."

A man of constant re-invention - as much Zelig as Zimmerman - the inscrutable Bob Dylan constantly played games with his past and present; Dylanologists loved to sift through the clues he left behind. Arriving in New York, he disavowed his Minnesota roots ("I came out of the Midwest, but I'm not interested in leading anybody back there"), and blagged his way into the presence of the great Woody Guthrie, before seducing the Greenwich Village folk scene. As Paul Simon remarked, "He defined the genre for a while. That's quite an accomplishment." Freewheelin' onwards, Bob left behind a legion of hunch-shouldered young swains copying his nasal delivery. He upset the folk purists by going electric not long before the 1966 motorcycle accident after which some (smugly) claimed he was never the same Dylan - although 1975's *Blood On The Tracks* put the skids under that notion. Deified, decried, demonised, Dylan continually skipped a couple of steps ahead of the competition - he'll probably still have a trick and a tune up his sleeve when he finally knocks on heaven's door.

Bob Dylan

Born: Robert Zimmerman 24/5/41 • Recording career: 1962 - present • Sounds: The Freewheelin' Bob Dylan 1963, Blonde On Blonde 1966, Blood On The Tracks 1975

Eagles

"We're the Oakland A's of rock'n'roll.
On the field we can't be beat. But in the clubhouse, that's another story.
We're completely different people." Glenn Frey

The Eagles' wings were trimmed when Bernie Leadon left the original line-up. A former Flying Burrito Brother, his banjo and mandolin skills provided an authentic country vibe to the rockier sound of Glenn Frey and Don Henley. The latter pair had arrived in LA from Michigan and Texas respectively, joined forces at the Troubadour club, and ended up, with Leadon and Randy Meisner, as Linda Ronstadt's backing band. From the opening cut of their first album - the Frey-Jackson Browne

number 'Take It Easy' - they conjured up a vision of freewheelin' West Coast hedonism that Frey and Henley certainly enjoyed to the full as the capos of the so-called Avocado Mafia. Having been hugely hip, after Leadon's departure they became far too AOR, although 'Hotel California' (for all its pedestrian analogies) could still thrill and chill. Appropriately, later disputes led to Henley's famous comment that they wouldn't reform till hell froze over - which of course it did in 1994...

Key members: Don Felder 21/9/47, Glenn Frey 6/11/48, Don Henley 22/7/47, Bernie Leadon 19/7/47, Randy Meisner 8/3/46, Joe Walsh 20/11/47 • Recording career: 1972 - 1981 (reformed 1994)

Sounds: Desperado 1973, One Of These Nights 1975, Hotel California 1976

Throw away your rhinestones: Steve Earle's in town. His country-outlaw look was no pose. Earle - part of the vanguard of new country alongside Randy Travis and Dwight Yoakam - paid his dues as a musician in Nashville, never quite breaking through until MCA released *Guitar Town* in 1987. An intense, restless soul (with six marriages to date), he collected his outlaw credibility through a number of run-ins with the sheriff's office: Earle was out of action during the mid-1990s after turning himself in to serve a jail sentence for possession. The inclusion of his songs on Emmylou Harris's 1995 comeback album *Wrecking Ball* and the soundtrack of *Dead Man Walking* introduced a wider audience to Earle's hard-boiled country-cum-rock'n'roll songs (Woody Guthrie and Duane Eddy were both important influences), which articulated many of the same blue-collar realities and frustrations that populated the tales of Bruce Springsteen.

145

Steve Earle

"What Springsteen, Mellencamp and me are trying to do is **give the working people a voice.**"

Born: 17/1/55 • Recording career: 1982 - present • Sounds: Guitar Town 1986, Copperhead Road 1988, El Corazón 1997

Earth, Wind & Fire

George Clinton cattily called EW&F "Earth, hot air and no fire" but he did a dis-service to their buoyant blast of pop, rock, funk and soul. The spirit of Sly Stone and James Brown lay behind the slickness of their presentation, a riot of effects, costumes and exuberance, wrapped up in an, at times, excruciating philosophy of Egyptological hokum and universal brotherhood. But anyone who could take the Lennon and McCartney track 'Got To Get You Into My Life' and jazz-funk it up with such panache and *joie de vivre* was a force to be reckoned with. Maurice White, always at the centre of proceedings (the band was named after the elements in his astrological chart), had studied percussion and composition at the Chicago Conservatory. His dynamic arrangements and syncopated riffs propelled tracks like 'September' and 'Boogie Wonderland', blessed with the voice of Philip 'Easy Lover' Bailey. Pure showbiz, but simply marvellous to boogie on down to.

"We're not really interested in getting a hit single. We're more interested in communicating." Maurice White

146

Key members: Philip Bailey 8/5/51, Larry Dunn 19/6/53, Ralph Johnson 4/7/51, Fred White 13/1/55, Maurice White 17/12/41, Verdine White 25/7/51

Recording career: 1971 - 1984 & 1987 - present • Sounds: Head To The Sky 1973, Gratitude 1975, I Am 1979

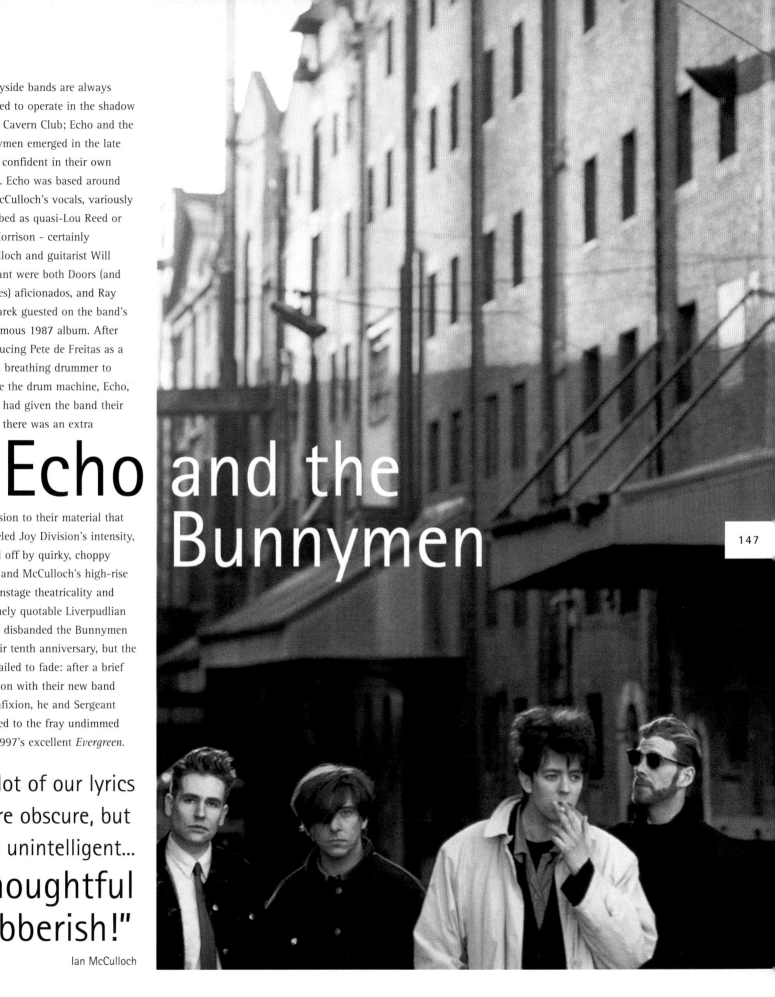

Merseyside bands are always required to operate in the shadow of the Cavern Club; Echo and the Bunnymen emerged in the late 1970s confident in their own image. Echo was based around Ian McCulloch's vocals, variously described as quasi-Lou Reed or Jim Morrison - certainly McCulloch and guitarist Will Sergeant were both Doors (and Stooges) aficionados, and Ray Manzarek guested on the band's eponymous 1987 album. After introducing Pete de Freitas as a living, breathing drummer to replace the drum machine, Echo, which had given the band their name, there was an extra

Echo and the Bunnymen

dimension to their material that paralleled Joy Division's intensity, topped off by quirky, choppy guitar and McCulloch's high-rise hair, onstage theatricality and extremely quotable Liverpudlian lip. He disbanded the Bunnymen on their tenth anniversary, but the echo failed to fade: after a brief diversion with their new band Electrafixion, he and Sergeant returned to the fray undimmed with 1997's excellent *Evergreen*.

"A lot of our lyrics were obscure, but not unintelligent... Thoughtful gibberish!"

Ian McCulloch

Key members: Pete de Freitas 2/8/61 (died 14/6/89), Ian McCulloch 5/5/59, Les Pattinson 18/4/58, Will Sergeant 12/4/58 • Recording career: 1980 - 1992 (reformed 1997 - present)

Sounds: Crocodiles 1980, Ocean Rain 1984, Evergreen 1997

If you've got it, flaunt it. Duane Eddy was unceasing in his use of the word 'twang' - a description of his guitar style, which heavily favoured the bass strings of his beloved Gretsch Chet Atkins - on album titles galore, including *The Twang's The Thang* and *Have 'Twangy' Guitar Will Travel*.... We can forgive him (and his record company) that indulgence, since it was a wondrous sound, bounding forth, laced with plenty of echo provided by a primitive 500-gallon tank employed as a chamber, and accompanied by the occasional confederate yelp from his backing band the Rebels. The Eddy formula was applied to a truckload of Lee Hazlewood-produced singles, of which the most durable proved to be 1960's 'Peter Gunn', the Henry Mancini theme - its driving riff was diligently mastered note by note by a generation of actual and aspirant Hank Marvins. The tell-tale clue that the twang might have outstayed its welcome was probably the fatal crossover title from 1964: *Duane Goes Dylan*.

Duane Eddy

148

"Ever since I have been knee-high to a guitar, I've hated photographers."

Born: 26/4/38 • Recording career: 1958 - 1994 • Sounds: The Twang's The Thang 1960, Twistin' 'n' Twangin' 1962, Duane Eddy 1987

Produce of the San Fernando Valley, the Electric Prunes were working on their surf/garage style when a chance encounter led them to the door of Dave Hassinger, an RCA engineer with credits on the Stones' *Aftermath* album. He steered them to a debut hit single in 1966: 'I Had Too Much To Dream (Last Night)' was a sonic freakout, featuring Ken Williams' fuzz-drunk guitar drowning out Jim Lowe's ominous vocals, which placed them in the frontline of LA's early psychedelic bands.

However the album of the same name included a mere handful of the band's original songs: producer Hassinger was clearly in control, to the extent that by 1968 he had completely re-invented the Prunes, with not one original member in place. Not only that, but the direction he took was pseudo-classical (*Mass In F Minor*). A fossil of this second Prunes age - 'Kyrie Eleison' - can be unearthed on the *Easy Rider* soundtrack.

"The idea was to be an electronically charged recording band. Everybody else was interested in becoming bar bands." Jim Lowe

The Electric Prunes

149

Key members: Jim Lowe, Preston Ritter, James 'Weasel' Spagnola, Mark Tulin, Ken Williams • Recording career: 1966 - 1969

Sounds: The Electric Prunes 1967, Underground 1967, Mass In F Minor 1968

When ELP made their first major appearance, at the Isle of Wight Festival in August 1970, they were no strangers to the main stage. Keith Emerson had been displaying his keyboard acrobatics (as 'the Hendrix of the organ') with the Nice, while Greg Lake had provided basslines for King Crimson. Carl Palmer, formerly of Atomic Rooster and Arthur Brown's band, took up the vacant slot in the trio after discussions with the Hendrix Experience's Mitch Mitchell failed to work out. ELP solidified into a concoction of Emerson's techno flash and classical allusions, Lake's softer ballads and a novelty number or two: 'Benny The Bouncer' on *Brain Salad Surgery* and 'Nut Rocker' from *Pictures From An Exhibition*. But it was the classical fare that dominated, including their re-working of Aaron Copland's 'Fanfare For The Common Man', a surprise hit just before the original line-up split up - a later version of ELP would feature Cozy Powell as the P.

"If you read something good about yourself, you start to think 'Hey, I must be fantastic'. You can end up an egomaniac." Keith Emerson

150

Emerson Lake & Palmer

Key members: Keith Emerson 1/1/44, Greg Lake 10/11/48, Carl Palmer 20/3/47 • Recording career: 1970 - 1978 (reformed 1986 & 1992 -1994)

Sounds: Emerson Lake & Palmer 1970, Pictures At An Exhibition 1971, Brain Salad Surgery 1973

Brian Eno

Eno's time with Roxy Music was an exuberantly extrovert phase for the man who would become a cerebral elder statesman of the music business: his visual impact actually threatened Brian Ferry's dominance. Cue a falling out and Eno's departure. He returned to Suffolk, where as a youngster he had listened to the other-worldly sounds of USAF broadcasts beaming into local airbases, to continue the explorations into tape techniques and modern classical music - Reich, Cage, Riley - that he'd undertaken at art school. Now he could devote his appliance of musical science to a range of activities: his own albums, which moved from idiosyncratic pop to pure ambience (*Music For Airports*); production work for Devo, U2, Talking Heads and Bowie; collaborations with Jah Wobble and James. Constantly challenging, always thinking, Eno was free to go wherever he wanted like an unrestricted musical cosmonaut; indeed, in 1968 he had compiled a manual succinctly entitled 'Music For Non-Musicians.'

151

"I became drawn into music by sonic atmospheres and textures. Suddenly I thought 'This is the best way to paint: **painting with music.'"**

Born: 15/5/48 • Recording career (solo): 1973 - present • Sounds: Here Come The Warm Jets 1974, Another Green World 1975, Ambient #1: Music For Airports 1979

When Melissa Etheridge made the decision to declare her lesbianism publicly at an event celebrating Bill Clinton's inauguration in 1993, her announcement had a radical effect both on her media profile and her album sales. Up till then, the bright flame that Island's Chris Blackwell had cannily spotted when he saw her performing in a Long Beach bar had failed to ignite, certainly commercially, even though her plain, pared-down blues guitar and throaty voice had established a healthy live following and enough credibility to convince Bono to lend the weight of his backing vocals to her second album *Brave And Crazy*. After her coming out the next release, the wryly titled *Yes I Am*, sold over five million copies, and re-asserted the straightforward blues-rock that reflected her admiration for both Janis Joplin (who she inducted into the Rock'n'Roll Hall of Fame) and Bruce Springsteen, with whom she duetted on his 'Thunder Road' for a 1995 *MTV Unplugged* session.

Melissa Etheridge

"I wish everyone came out with 2,000 people applauding them.
Next morning I called my publicists who said 'We know'."

Born: 29/5/61 • Recording career: 1988 - present • Sounds: Melissa Etheridge 1988, Yes I Am 1993, Breakdown 1999

"When you've lived with someone it's hard to talk to them like you would a mate you write songs with, and sometimes it turns into an argument. We're our own worst critics." Dave Stewart

Eurythmics

Already an ex-couple by the time they formed Eurythmics - after an excursion as The Tourists which had produced the hit 'I Only Want To Be With You' - Dave Stewart and Annie Lennox were able to bring a relatively level-headed approach to their music. Their debut album *In The Garden*, including members of Can, was a false start, perhaps a tad too electro-Germanic. But by *Sweet Dreams* they'd established a more accessible formula: slickly produced synth-driven singles, handled with a deftness of touch absent from many similar bands of the day. There was manifestly a human heart beating there, a flavour of their fondness for American R'n'B and soul, which was acknowledged on *Be Yourself Tonight*, with guests Stevie Wonder and Aretha Franklin (the latter duetting with Annie Lennox on the storming 'Sisters Are Doing It For Themselves.') By 1989, Lennox was ready to break away on her own; after a decade of successful solo work, the pair re-formed.

Key members: Annie Lennox 25/12/54, Dave Stewart 9/12/52 • Recording career: 1981 - 1989 & 1999 - present

Sounds: Sweet Dreams (Are Made Of This) 1983, Be Yourself Tonight 1985, Savage 1987

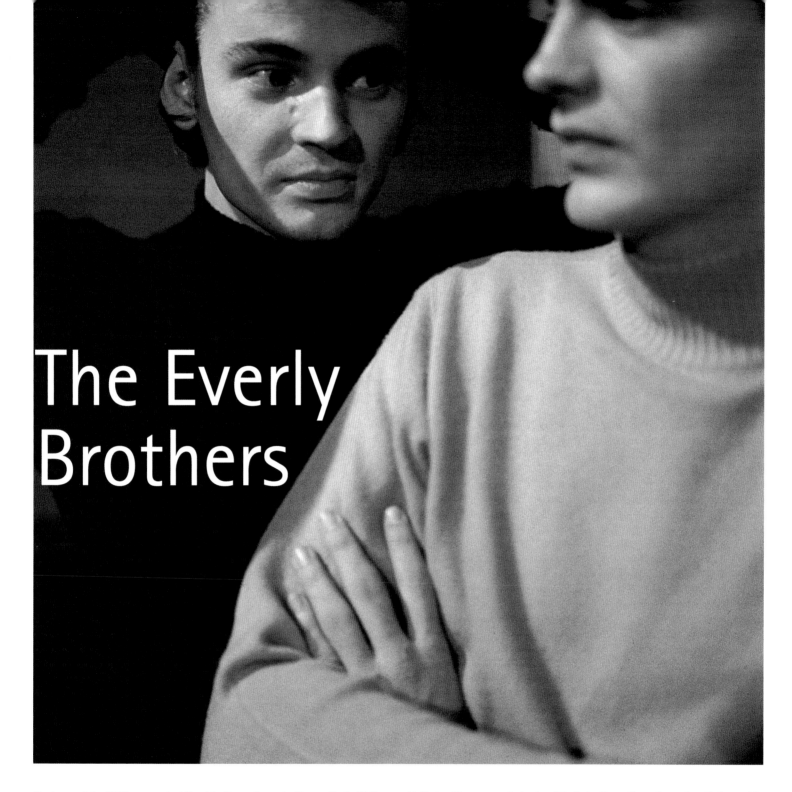

The Everly Brothers

During a July 1973 concert at Knott's Berry Farm in Buena Park, Phil Everly smashed his guitar on stage. Days before, Don had announced "I'm tired of being an Everly Brother", shattering a fraternal partnership which had transferred country-style cadences to rock'n'roll (carefully rehearsed harmonies that both the Beatles and the Byrds would emulate) to create an non-threatening variant. 'Bye Bye Love' and other hits came courtesy of songwriting couple Boudleaux and Felice Bryant - as she described it, "anything they put their voices to seemed to blend like custard". By 1960 the Brothers were hot enough to sign to Warners in a $1 million deal, but in doing so they lost their creative support system.

At first self-composed singles ('Cathy's Clown') performed well, but with young challengers on their heels, a tale of supper clubs and growing animosity played itself out. After their split they remained out of favour until a 1984 reunion album, produced by an admiring Dave Edmunds.

"We're not Grand Ole Opry.
We're not Perry Como.
We're just pop music."

Born: Don Everly 1/2/37, Phil Everly 19/1/39 • **Recording career:** 1956 - 1973 (reformed 1984 - 1988) • **Sounds:** The Everly Brothers 1958, It's Everly Time 1960, Two Yanks In England 1966

Everything But The Girl

Aren't they sweet? Nothing but bedsit tweeness, according to the hard-bitten and jaded. Ben Watt and Tracey Thorn - already and independently signed to the Cherry Red label - met for the first time at college in Hull, forming a personal and professional relationship and naming themselves after the non-PC sign over a local furniture store: 'For your bedroom, etc...' It was a near-perfect pairing, Thorn's rich, seductive voice meshing effortlessly with Ben Watt's harmonies and crystal-clear acoustic guitar.

Their first album, *Eden*, suggested what might come, before *Baby The Stars Shine Bright* delivered luscious horns in a package demonstrating Watt's understanding of the arranging brilliance of Burt Bacharach and John Barry. In the early 1990s he was stricken with the potentially fatal Churg-Strauss Syndrome, but recovered to full strength physically and musically, a period featuring a global hit in 'Missing' and culminating in the drum'n'bass-sensitive and aptly named album *Walking Wounded*.

"Even we got a bit bored with what we were doing." Tracey Thorn

155

Key members: Tracey Thorn 26/9/62, Ben Watt 6/12/62 • Recording career: 1983 - present • Sounds: Eden 1984, Baby The Stars Shine Bright 1986, Walking Wounded 1996

"The Faces are a rock'n'roll band, but Rod's a bit of a folkie at heart." Ian McLagan

Good-time boys on stage and off, the Faces were the party that stayed after closing time at the Small Faces. Lane, McLagan and Jones, the loiterers, chanced upon Rod and Ron - according to legend, in a London pub - as Stewart was on the verge of a solo career: they agreed to let him pursue it alongside his Faces commitments, a tension tautened after his 1971 solo hit 'Maggie May'. Yet at the outset the band pulled together

despite a legendary loose live approach (r'n'booze was the order of the day) and could still deliver a punch: 'Stay With Me' displayed Rod at his croaky finest. However, the departure of Ronnie Lane, myriad hotel bans, Stewart's solo success - his 1975 album *Atlantic Crossing* topped the UK charts - and Wood's alignment with the Stones wound the party up. But at least they'd been fun in an era of frequently po-faced rock seriousness.

156

Faces

Key members: Kenney Jones 16/9/48, Ronnie Lane 1/4/46 (died 4/6/97), Ian McLagan 12/5/45, Rod Stewart 10/1/45, Ron Wood 1/6/47 • Recording career: 1970 - 1974

Sounds: First Step 1970, Long Player 1971, A Nod Is As Good As A Wink... To A Blind Horse 1971

Fairport Convention

"Fairport may not have been the first band to pick up electric instruments
and play folk songs, but they made a success of it,

in their loose, improvised, fun-loving way." Ashley Hutchings

Through all its ups, downs and traumas, Fairport Convention remained constant as a showcase for Britain's finest folk-rock performers, including Richard Thompson and Dave Swarbrick. But the line-up was permanently unsettled, and not only by 'musical differences' - original drummer Martin Lamble died when the band's tour van crashed in 1969; Sandy Denny's alto voice was stilled when she fell down a flight of stairs in 1978. Starting out in the slipstream of Jefferson Airplane,

Fairport (they formally dropped the 'Convention' in the mid-70s) moved increasingly towards an eclectic embracing of traditional native folk music: their acclaimed 1970 live album, *Liege & Lief*, was billed as 'the first British folk/rock LP ever'. But its release only highlighted the contemporary vs roots division within the band, unresolved until the 1980s, when an annual reunion at the village of Cropedy in Oxfordshire turned into a major folk festival, and something approaching stability.

Key members: Sandy Denny 6/1/47 (died 21/4/78), Ashley Hutchings 26/1/45, Martin Lamble 28/8/49 (died 12/5/69), Dave Mattacks 13/3/48, Ian Matthews 16/6/46, Simon Nicol 13/10/50,

Dave Pegg 2/11/47, Dave Swarbrick 5/4/47, Richard Thompson 3/4/49 • Recording career: 1967 - present • Sounds: What We Did On Our Holidays 1969, Liege & Lief 1969, Jewel In The Crown 1995

Faith No More

The full-on, melodic fusion of funk, rap and hardcore that Faith No More straddled (a territory shared with the Red Hot Chilis) was typified by their 1992 album *Angel Dust*, a splendidly sprawling concoction. But they were even more eclectic in their single releases, covering the Commodores' 'Easy' in 1993 and, just before announcing that the band would be no more in 1998, collaborating with the Mael brothers in a re-working of Sparks' 'This Town Ain't Big Enough For The Both Of Us'.

Britain proved a happy hunting ground - especially after the release of *The Real Thing* - while the band struggled to find consistent success in the States, despite steady gigging there since their formation in the early 1980s. By 1988, their original, theatrical singer Chuck Mosely - who had punched out their trademark 'We Care A Lot' - was proving undependable; he was replaced by the equally, if not more, theatrical Mike Patton, a man with super-elastic, supernatural vocal chords.

"We are socially retarded people
in as much as we do a lot of childish things to keep our sanity." Billy Gould

Key members: Mike Bordin 27/11/62, Roddy Bottum 1/7/63, Billy Gould 24/4/63, Jim Martin 21/7/61, Chuck Mosely, Mike Patton 27/1/68 • Recording career: 1985 - 1998

Sounds: Introduce Yourself 1987, The Real Thing 1989, King For A Day... Fool For A Lifetime 1995

"In the new century there will be no more interviews about drugs and Mick."

Her profile in the early years of her fame, nay notoriety, was lived out in the shadow of the Rolling Stones. Before her relationship with Mick Jagger and the whole tabloid shock-horror 'nude in fur coat' episode, Jagger and Keith Richards had been instrumental in the launch of Marianne Faithfull's career, providing 'As Tears Go By' for her debut single. Her convent-girl looks, with an exotic aura provided through a maternal connection with the von Sacher-Masoch family, had caught the eye of the Stones' then manager Andrew Loog Oldham. 'Tears' reached the UK Top Ten, and her presence in the public eye was assured, out and about with Jagger, or as the original *Girl On A Motorbike*. Then she disappeared, stumbling through a down-and-out drug habit that wiped out much of the 1970s before re-emerging with the album *Broken English*, a more careworn and harder-bitten version of the angelic teenager, but still indisputably fighting fit.

Marianne Faithfull

159

Born: 29/12/46 • Recording career: 1964 - present • Sounds: Marianne Faithfull 1965, Broken English 1979, Strange Weather 1987

"The media over-estimates its own importance.

I was on the cover of everything for three years,
but I still only had half a bottle of milk in the fridge." Mark E. Smith

Musicians were obviously reading plenty of Albert Camus during the late 1970s: The Cure's first single, 'Killing An Arab', based on one novel, was released shortly after Mark E. Smith had named his Manchester-based band after *La Chute*. Smith was always at the very epicentre of the Fall, crusading against hypocrisy and ignorance wherever it might foolishly jay-walk across his path (including some co-band members at times). His jaundiced view of the world, delivered in a deadpan *singspiel*, might have proved unendearingly monotonous, but he lightened the load with some trenchant, albeit dark, humour and a healthy dose of rockabilly.

The Fall

Evergreen survivors of the punk movement, the Fall were never really a mainstream band, although in the late 1980s, under the influence of his then wife, guitarist Brix E. Smith, they came pretty close, with Smith sounding positively cheery. When Brix left him for the violinist latterly known as Kennedy, he naturally reverted to his original splenetic fury.

Key member: Mark E. Smith 5/3/57 • Recording career: 1978 - present • Sounds: Live At The Witch Trials 1979, This Nation's Saving Grace 1985, Shift Work 1991

The spawn of a couple of Leicester bands, Family were fronted by the raw and indiscriminate energy of Roger Chapman, who was equally prone to unleash a tambourine at unsuspecting members of the audience, or indulge in fisticuffs with the likes of Bill Graham (the latter event occurred on their Fillmore East debut - they never had much luck in the US). Chapman's distinctive vibrato was backed by a talented prog-rock band - Rick Grech was an original member before heading off to Blind Faith - occasionally nuanced with flute, violins and vibes. Featuring Chapman's co-conspirator Charlie Whitney, and stalwart drummer Rob Townsend, Family took to the road with the kind of gusto that later provided fodder for Jenny Fabian's legendary rock-novel *Groupie*. On their demise, the band left behind memories of a down-to-earth, humorous band whose debut album, *Music In A Doll's House*, many considered to have been far ahead of its time.

Roger would just get carried away. I've seen him split his eye open and he's not known about it until we got off stage. **It wasn't drugs, it was just him."** Rob Townsend

Family

161

Key members: Roger Chapman 8/4/42, Rob Townsend 7/7/47, Charlie Whitney 24/6/44 • Recording career: 1967 - 1973

Sounds: Music In A Doll's House 1968, Family Entertainment 1969, Fearless 1971

Fanny

"I didn't want to play lead guitar. I thought what everybody else thought, **that a chick couldn't play lead."** June Millington

It's time to re-assert the importance of Fanny as a pioneering, all-female rock band, one of the first to get out there and kick some butt. The name, supposedly suggested by George Harrison, was, in the end, a bit of an albatross - leading to dully predictable 'Get Behind Fanny' advertising, and somehow suggesting they were an Archies-style confection. But the Millington sisters and Alice De Buhr were good enough to have backed Barbra Streisand on her *Stoney End* album, while Nicky Barclay formed part of Joe Cocker's Mad Dogs and Englishmen tour. Fanny's proficiency attracted Streisand's producer Richard Perry to oversee their first three albums, and Todd Rundgren their fourth. However, in 1974 June (along with De Buhr) jumped ship and abandoned her sister. Fanny's next version included Patti Quatro, sister of Suzi, who would of course find more commercial success with her particular version of the ballsy rock chick.

Key members: Nicky Barclay 21/4/51, Alice De Buhr 1950, Jean Millington 1950, June Millington 1949 • Recording career: 1970 - 1975 • Sounds: Fanny Hill 1972, Mother's Pride 1975

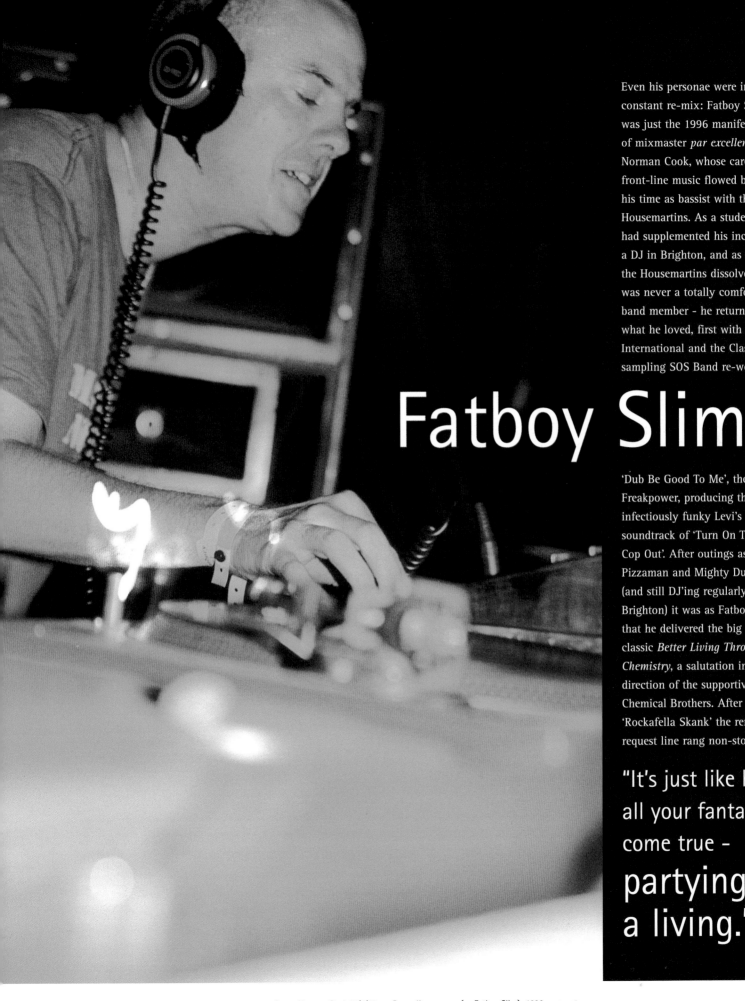

Even his personae were in constant re-mix: Fatboy Slim was just the 1996 manifestation of mixmaster *par excellence* Norman Cook, whose career in front-line music flowed back to his time as bassist with the Housemartins. As a student, Cook had supplemented his income as a DJ in Brighton, and as soon as the Housemartins dissolved - he was never a totally comfortable band member - he returned to what he loved, first with Beats International and the Clash-sampling SOS Band re-work

Fatboy Slim

'Dub Be Good To Me', then as Freakpower, producing the infectiously funky Levi's ad soundtrack of 'Turn On Tune In Cop Out'. After outings as Pizzaman and Mighty Dub Katz (and still DJ'ing regularly in Brighton) it was as Fatboy Slim that he delivered the big beat classic *Better Living Through Chemistry*, a salutation in the direction of the supportive Chemical Brothers. After 'Rockafella Skank' the remix request line rang non-stop.

"It's just like having all your fantasies come true – partying for a living."

Born: Norman Cook 31/7/63 • Recording career (as Fatboy Slim): 1996 - present

Sounds: Better Living Through Chemistry 1996, You've Come A Long Way, Baby 1998, Halfway Between The Gutter And The Stars 2000

Flamin' Groovies

"Forget image and meaning - it's just too rock'n'roll.

We're a loud jukebox." Cyril Jordan

It was always difficult to fit the Flamin' Groovies into a pigeonhole, and so there were periods - notably the mid-1970s - when they found themselves bereft of recording deals. One particular drought came to an end in 1976 with the Sire-released *Shake Some Action*, produced by Dave Edmunds, who was exactly the kind of musician who could appreciate their homage to the garage rock'n'roll of the late 1950s and 60s. Powered by Cyril Jordan's rockin' guitar, the Groovies remained unfashionably loyal to the energy of white R'n'B, British beat and the concise beauty of the three-minute single, even while all around them their hometown of San Francisco was turning itself on to psychedelia. Closer in spirit to bands like MC5 and the Stooges - though possessing none of Iggy's showmanship - the Groovies had some influence on the punk movement and toured the UK with the Ramones in 1976, but by then their power pop obsession seemed more than a little bit dated.

Key members: George Alexander 18/5/46, Cyril Jordan 1948, Roy A. Loney 13/4/46, Tim Lynch 18/7/46, Danny Mihm • Recording career: 1965 - 1986

Sounds: Supersnazz 1976, Teenage Head 1971, Shake Some Action 1976

It can only be one version or the other, and much as we all loved Stevie Nick's sassiness and Lindsey Buckingham's rococo curls, the insistent use of 'Don't Stop' by the Clinton election caravan in 1992 gives the nod to the original line-up. As alumni of John Mayall's Bluesbreakers production line, Mick Fleetwood, John McVie and Peter Green - who'd replaced Eric Clapton when he left to form Cream - formed a sober blues-revering band, with Green's slide-guitar and

writing talents upfront, including the languid 'Albatross' and the future Santana hit 'Black Magic Woman'. However Green crumpled under the pressure, later recovering to continue proselytising for the true blues, and Jeremy Spencer disappeared into a religious cult while on tour in 1971. The remnants of the Macs, joined by Christine McVie (née Perfect) from Chicken Shack, dibbled and dabbled until pairing up with the Nicks/Buckingham duo. Thereafter the soap opera wended its own way.

Fleetwood Mac

"Fleetwood Mac became a living fantasy.
It was basically unreal." Mick Fleetwood

Key members: Lindsey Buckingham 3/10/47, Mick Fleetwood 24/6/47, Peter Green 29/10/46, Danny Kirwan 13/5/50, Christine McVie 12/7/43, John McVie 26/11/45, Stevie Nicks 26/5/48, Jeremy Spencer 4/7/48 • Recording career: 1967 - present • Sounds: Peter Green's Fleetwood Mac 1968, Rumours 1977, Tango In The Night 1987

Focus

The language trap has always been a problem for European bands: France's Téléphone was a classic example of a band stymied outside its homeland because of the English language's stranglehold on rock'n'roll. Focus sidestepped the problem by ditching (dyking?) their native Dutch and concentrating on instrumentals and keyboard/flautist Thijs Van Leer's spooky falsetto yodelling. Alongside him, guitarist Jan Akkerman, built like a Rotterdam docker, played with the finesse of Segovia on tracks like

the mellifluous 'Sylvia' and 'Hocus Pocus'. Both were UK hit singles in 1973, a golden age for the Netherlands with Golden Earring in the charts with 'Radar Love', and Holland playing the finest football of the era. Trace elements of Van Leer's classical training could have pushed Focus into ELP territory, but they maintained their sense of individuality, later enrolling jazz guitarist Philip Catherine to replace Akkerman, and collaborating with P.J. Proby on the improbably named 1978 album *Focus Con Proby*.

"We get into the theatrics strictly through the music." Jan Akkerman

Key members: Jan Akkerman 24/12/46, Thijs Van Leer 31/3/48, Bert Ruiter 26/11/46, Pierre van der Linden 19/2/46 • Recording career: 1971 - 1978 • Sounds: Moving Waves 1971, Focus III 1972

Smoothly working the self-appointed establishment into a right lather, Frankie Goes To Hollywood gave them a glimpse into the gay club subculture - lived for real by Holly Johnson and Paul Rutherford, not a manufactured simulation like the Village People. It frightened the carthorses silly at the BBC, and their pulsating debut single 'Relax' made DJ Mike Read very uptight indeed: a ridiculous ban gave Frankie all the publicity they and producer Trevor Horn could have wished for.

'Relax' was the first of a trio of Number Ones in their *annus mirabilis* of 1984, followed by 'Two Tribes', with Cold War heavyweights slugging it out on the accompanying video, and 'The Power Of Love', a Christmas chart-topper. But by their second album, *Liverpool*, they'd become overblown and self-important (neatly spoofed by Hank Wangford's Edinburgh Festival T-shirt 'Hankie Goes to Holyrood'), and had, fatally, lost sight of the raunchy humour of their glory days.

"Controversy is something extra,
but our records will always stand up on their own." Holly Johnson

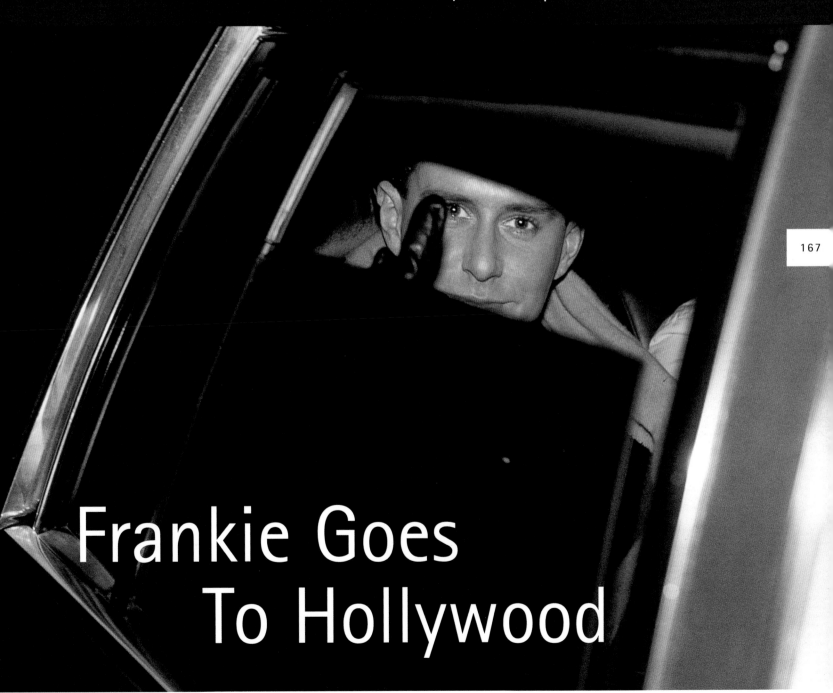

Frankie Goes
To Hollywood

Key members: Peter Gill 8/3/64, Holly Johnson 19/2/60, Brian Nash 20/5/63, Mark O'Toole 6/1/64, Paul Rutherford 8/12/59 • Recording career: 1983 - 1987

Sounds: Welcome To The Pleasuredome 1984

The Queen of Soul reigned on the strength of her voice, a natural asset ("like a national monument in America", according to Keith Richards) which made weak material lustrous, and great songs simply sublime. The daughter of a renowned preacher, Aretha Franklin was recording gospel material for the Checker label at 14, earning comparisons with the mighty Mahalia Jackson. A long stint at CBS/Columbia under the aegis of John Hammond (he said she had "the best voice I've heard since Billie Holiday") is often maligned as the least successful phase of her career, although it produced glorious tracks like 'Today I Sing The Blues'. But *nobody* could deny the magic of her work with Jerry Wexler at Atlantic on 'Respect', 'Natural Woman' and 'Chain Of Fools'. After a somewhat diffuse period in the 1970s spent exploring her roots, collaborations with the Eurythmics and George Michael helped give Franklin renewed profile, and belief in her original, intuitive skills.

"Aretha carries you back to church
in everything that she does."

Al Jackson, Booker T. and the MG's

168

Born: 25/3/42 • Recording career: 1956 - present • Sounds: I Never Loved A Man The Way I Love You 1967, Aretha: Lady Soul 1968, Amazing Grace 1972

Free

"The Free thing was almost too open.

The tension in the spaces was almost unbearable." Paul Rodgers

Pure and unadulterated, Free emerged as keepers of the flickering flame of the British blues in a quartet of beautiful balance. Paul Rodgers's huskily yearning vocals, clothes courtesy of the small ads in *Melody Maker*; Paul Kossoff stretching his timeless guitar licks with his Les Paul's sustain; teenage Andy Fraser's mile-wide bass; rock-steady Simon Kirke 4/4'ing the whole together. Their manifesto was nowhere better proclaimed than on 'All Right Now'. Alexis Korner had suggested that they call themselves Free after his own blues trio Free At Last, and seemingly erupting out of nowhere, they found themselves up amongst the headline acts at the Isle of Wight Festival of 1970. Yet they were never able to build completely on that success, not least through trying to keep Paul Kossoff's drug addiction under control. 1973's 'Wishing Well', Free's final single, was a heartfelt plea from Rodgers to Kossoff - he failed to heed the song's message, and was dead within three years.

Key members: Andy Fraser 7/8/52, Simon Kirke 28/7/49, Paul Kossoff 14/9/50 (died 19/3/76), Paul Rodgers 12/12/49 • Recording career: 1968 - 1973

Sounds: Tons Of Sobs 1968, Fire And Water 1970, Heartbreaker 1973

Fugazi

The ideals of punk - anti-corporate, self-reliant - were sustained for real by Fugazi in all their activity. The band backed up their beliefs with direct action: playing only all-age venues, pushing door prices as low as possible, shunning rip-off merchandise. And in line with their stance that you could not, should not, be a genuine punk act and sign a deal with a mainstream label, they issued albums on their own Dischord Records - selling upwards of 150,000 copies per release purely by word of mouth. Dischord had been set up by singer/guitarist Ian MacKaye in the early 1980s while he was part of Washington DC hardcore outfit Minor Threat (with whom he'd written 'Straight Edge', the freedom-of-choice anthem that launched an ethical crusade). With co-writer Guy Picciotto, MacKaye expanded Fugazi towards funk and ska, but never lost sight of the challenge, responsibility and snap-tight intensity of their punk roots.

> "We play loud, electric guitar music and you'd hope this doesn't mean you have to act like an asshole." Ian MacKaye

Key members: Brendan Canty 9/3/66, Joe Lally 3/12/63, Ian MacKaye 16/4/62, Guy Picciotto 17/9/65 • Recording career: 1988 - present • Sounds: 13 Songs 1990, Repeater 1990, Red Medicine 1995

"We thought we could raise the level of rock lyrics. I think we did a little." Tuli Kupferberg

Down at the Peace Eye Bookstore on New York's East 10th Street, Ed Sanders - publisher of the poetry magazine *Fuck You* - and his neighbour, Beat writer Tuli Kupferberg, listened to the Beatles and the Shangri-Las and decided they'd like a slice of the fun. No spring chickens (Kupferberg was pushing a prehistoric forty at the time) and untrained, other than at what they called the 'Beatnik Academy of the Outlandish Spectacle', they knocked a set of songs together as the Fugs, swinging between the consciously literary on 'Swinburne Stomp' or the joy of carnal pleasure in the three-chord romp of 'Supergirl'. Their Greenwich Village blend of in-jokes, poetry, profanity, and later political satire, was all in the name of art of course, 'Coca-Cola Douche' included. Nonetheless, these Beat Bonzos penetrated the underground semi-consciousness of both the US and UK through the efforts of the avant-garde label ESP and laid important groundwork for a radical alternative to Tin Pan Alley.

171

The Fugs

Key members: Tuli Kupferberg 28/9/28, Ed Sanders 17/8/39, Ken Weaver • Recording career: 1965 - 1969 & 1985 - 1995

Sounds: The Fugs First Album 1965, The Fugs Second Album 1966, Virgin Fugs 1966

Fun Lovin' Criminals

A hit squad of musical magpies, the Fun Lovin' Criminals roamed the side streets of hip-hop and rock, looting hither and thither to swipe their own sonic booty - a perfect end-of-millennium sampler of the previous half-century of musical output. Better still, it also worked live. Meeting at Manhattan's Limelight Club, where Huey was barman, Fast ran the phones, and original drummer Steve 'hung out', the trio bonded on their sense of humour and lashed together a catholic raft

of soul, R'n'B, jazz - whatever they liked - into a set of funky, slinky screenplays. All three were avid movie buffs, and 'Scooby Snacks', a drug-fuelled bank heist fantasy, was a pure (and admitted) Tarantino tribute. By their second full-length, almost sample-free, album *100% Colombian*, the urban groove was more laid-back and jazzier: 'Love Unlimited' delivered an unalloyed tribute to Barry White, and B.B. King, with Lucille of course, guested on 'Mini Bar Blues.'

"When you find people that can laugh in the face of adversity, then you've found your kin." Huey Morgan

Key members: Steve Borovini, Brian 'Fast' Leiser, Mackie, Hugh 'Huey' Morgan 8/8/68 • Recording career: 1995 - present • Sounds: Come Find Yourself 1996, 100% Colombian 1998, Loco 2001

Peter Gabriel

When he abandoned the cocoon of Genesis, Peter Gabriel also jettisoned a wardrobe of fantastical masks and costumes, re-emerging in buttoned-down austerity for his first four solo albums, each given the same title - *Peter Gabriel*. He was aided by a roster of name producers: Bob Ezrin on 'Solsbury Hill', Gabriel's song of release celebrating his new beginning, Steve Lillywhite bringing discipline to 'Games Without Frontiers'. But the richest pickings came with the Daniel Lanois-helmed *So*. It layered accessible rhythms beneath the curiosity for other musics that had led Gabriel to bail out WOMAD (before anyone knew what world music was) and his openness to stimulating collaborations, with Kate Bush on 'Don't Give Up', and later Laurie Anderson, Jimmy Pursey and Tom Robinson. The visual experimentation of his Genesis days also surged back in a series of startling videos, from the hyper-animation of the pulverising 'Sledgehammer', to the monster snails of 'Digging In The Dirt'.

"I wanted to sit at the piano for hours and hours **and just scream,** which was one of the main attractions of rock music for me."

Born: 13/2/50 • Recording career (solo): 1977 - present • Sounds: Peter Gabriel (3) 1980, So 1986, Us 1992

Rory Gallagher

The straightforwardness of Rory Gallagher was no façade: he was as unflashy as the jeans and lumberjack shirt that were his stage costume, and his commitment to the blues guitar was unwavering. After learning the basics of his trade on the Irish showband circuit, he broke away from its razzamatazz to form a tight little trio called Taste, touring with Blind Faith, supporting Cream, appearing at the Isle of Wight Festival. Rory was clearly the star performer, and his dominance caused a split.

He unfussedly set about forming a new trio - Gerry McAvoy on bass was a constant supporter - and returned to yet more touring, swinging out both blues standards and Gallagher originals, his guitar style acknowledging B.B. King and Muddy Waters (the latter in turn invited Gallagher and his Strat to sit in on his *London Sessions*). But a life spent so much on the road brought with it an alcohol-related liver problem, and complications following a transplant cost him his life.

"It's nice to have all these new gadgets,
but in the studio I still like to start more or less live."

Born: 2/3/49 (died 15/6/95) • Recording career: 1968 - 1990 • Sounds: Live In Europe 1972, Irish Tour '74 1974, Calling-Card 1976

"We are most definitely not fucked-up, miserable people.

There are different sides to everybody." Shirley Manson

Garbage

Butch Vig and the remixers Steve Marker and Duke Erikson had played together in the garage band Spooner in the mid-1980s. Come the early 1990s and they had amassed hot production credits, Vig in particular on Nirvana's *Nevermind* and Sonic Youth's *Dirty*, a much in-demand studio in Madison, Wisconsin, but no voice. Enter stage left, Ms Shirley Manson, flickering across their MTV screen as the vocal talent for Angelfish, and they'd found their (Scottish) muse. Vig insisted that

Garbage was a real band, not just a vehicle for the studio, and Manson rose to the challenge, providing a provocative attitude, an unsettling voice and bags of media appeal. They called their sound 'noisy pop' - a friend had early on called their mix of loops and sample experiments 'garbage', hence the name - but it was seductively commercial enough to attract the interest of the Bond movie machine, which signed them up to provide the theme music for *The World Is Not Enough*.

Key members: Duke Erikson, Shirley Manson 3/8/66, Steve Marker, Brian 'Butch' Vig • Recording career: 1995 - present • Sounds: Garbage 1995, Version 2.0 1998

Marvin Gaye

The soothing voice of Marvin Gaye could mend a broken heart, but though "I sang and sang until I drained myself of everything I'd lived through", in the end the soul physician could not heal himself. A turning point in his life was the death in 1970 of Tammi Terrell, his vocal partner on 'Ain't No Mountain High Enough'. Gaye was part of Motown's inner circle (having married Berry Gordy's sister Anna) and being groomed for a solo career, but after Terrell died he laid low before returning to the limelight with his own vision - no longer the Motown conformist - on the socially aware *What's Going On* and the sensual *Let's Get It On*. As he put it, "I got some highways to ride up myself". Though the road ahead was hard - including a difficult divorce - 1982's '(Sexual) Healing' seemed to offer Marvin new hope, but tax problems, drug abuse and suicide attempts thwarted his recovery, ending in the final and fatal confrontation with his father.

"I don't make records for pleasure. I record so that I can help someone overcome a bad time."

Born: 2/4/39 (died 1/4/84) • Recording career: 1957 - 1982 • Sounds: You're All I Need 1968, What's Going On 1971, Let's Get It On 1973

The J. Geils Band

"We tour so often not so much because of the money but because we simply love to play.
I know that sounds weird..." Peter Wolf

Although the Boston-based band bore Jerome Geils's name, the guitarist himself had a relatively low profile compared to his louche colleagues, especially harmonica virtuoso Magic Dick and frontman Peter Wolf. A raconteur, late-night DJ and - for five years - Faye Dunaway's husband, Wolf joined the J. Geils Blues Band as they built up a strong following in New England. Their first two albums reflected the members' blues purism, including covers of John Lee Hooker and Otis Rush numbers, but under the guidance of producer Bill Szymczyk they expanded their range to encompass Motown numbers and the fast-paced R'n'B that the Blues Brothers later favoured. This formula kept them going throughout the 1970s, but shortly after their biggest hit, 1981's 'Centrefold', Wolf left for a solo career - and his loss was noticeable. Dissed by some critics as nothing more than 'a bar band', that was their greatest strength: best sampled loud, live and liquid.

Key members: Stephen Jo Bladd 13/7/42, J. Geils 20/2/46, Seth Justman 27/1/51, Danny Klein 13/5/46, Magic Dick (Richard Salwitz) 13/5/45, Peter Wolf 7/3/45

Recording career: 1970 - 1984 • Sounds: The Morning After 1971, Full House: Live 1972, Monkey Island 1977

Genesis

There was some surprise when drummer Phil Collins stepped out from behind his kit to assume vocal duties for Genesis after Peter Gabriel took his leave. But Collins had been a child actor, had sung in *Oliver!* no less, and was ready for the fray. The Charterhouse schoolboys had recorded their first album while still doing their homework, produced by Jonathan

"I don't mean to sound big-headed, but I don't think we've put a foot wrong in twenty years."

Mike Rutherford

King (also an Old Carthusian). Sales were short of spectacular, but Tony Stratton-Smith of Charisma Records rescued them from oblivion, encouraging their arty-rock inclinations alongside Gabriel's masks and theatrics. When Phil Collins moved upfront, Genesis sidestepped punk and metamorphosed into a mainstream chart act, getting up the noses of sniffy critics by producing what was, in retrospect, a remarkably consistent run of Number One albums, and bolting on equally commercial solo projects: Collins' solo career rarely missing a beat after 'In The Air Tonight' and Mike Rutherford taking a lucrative Saturday job with the Mechanics.

Key members: Tony Banks 27/3/50, Phil Collins 31/1/51, Peter Gabriel 13/2/50, Steve Hackett 12/2/50, Mike Rutherford 2/10/50 • Recording career: 1968 - present

Sounds: Selling England By The Pound 1973, The Lamb Lies Down On Broadway 1974, Abacab 1981

Never the colossus they could have been, Gentle Giant proved difficult to market at a time, in the early 1970s, when fusion of any kind was viewed with suspicion or confusion. The Giant's progenitors were the Shulman brothers, who'd had a minor hit in 1967 with 'Kites' under the name Simon Dupree & The Big Sound (Derek Shulman masquerading as Mr Dupree). Tiring of pop, they created Gentle Giant, but found little commercial response for their combination of jazz, classical music and rock - including the occasional madrigal. It was just all too eclectic, although audiences on the Continent were appreciative and *The Power And The Glory*, a 1974 concept album, brought some US recognition. As punk loomed and threatened their species, Gentle Giant attempted a simpler approach, but it was too late: the group reeked of the past. Their lasting impact came in subsequent careers - Derek Shulman signing Bon Jovi to Polygram, brother Ray producing the Sugarcubes.

"We were pulling the same sized crowds as Genesis, the same people were buying our records. They cracked it because they went commercial about two years earlier." John Weathers

179

Gentle Giant

Key members: Gary Green 20/11/50, Kerry Minnear 2/1/48, Derek Shulman 11/2/47, Phil Shulman 27/8/37, Ray Shulman 8/12/49, John Weathers 2/2/47 • Recording career: 1970 - 1980

Sounds: Gentle Giant 1970, The Power And The Glory 1974, Playing The Fool 1977

When Gomez rummaged through their parents' record collections they discovered new musical virtues; previously they'd been heavy metal headbangers. Ben Ottewell re-played his mother's Nick Drake albums, Ian Ball stumbled across Tom Waits, all of them listened to the blues. Ball organised free-form jams at home in the windswept coastal suburbia of Southport - Lancashire's very own Deauville - and before Gomez had even played live they had self-produced the retro pot-pourri of *Bring It On*. Success was instantaneous - even if some sneered it was just second-generation Jefferson Airplane - and Gomez collected the 1998 Mercury Music Award by fighting off Massive Attack and the Verve. They maintained their enthusiasm onto the second album *Liquid Skin* - experimenting with home-made percussion like the early Floyd

let loose in Abbey Road's storage cupboard - still armed with two devilishly effective weapons: Reggie Pedro's collectable cover artworks, and Ben Ottewell's voice, marinaded in the ghostly light of the blues.

"This is the band that missed punk. Black Flag, the Misfits, I know those names from reading magazines." Ian Ball

Gomez

Key members: Ian Ball, Paul Blackburn, Tom Gray, Ben Ottewell, Olly Peacock • Recording career: 1998 - present

Sounds: Bring It On 1998, Liquid Skin 1999, Abandoned Shopping Trolley Hotline 2000

Gong

The inhabitants of Gong were beamed down to the French countryside in the early 1970s, colonising a rustic little commune not far from Fontainebleau. There they followed the lore and imagination of Gong leader Daevid Allen, an Aussie beatnik who'd travelled to Europe, helped form Soft Machine, and then, after the British authorities refused him re-entry, stayed in France with his partner Gilli Smyth. There Allen convened a gaggle of like-minded musicians who, essentially, cooked up endless improvisations while stoned, indulging in a surfeit of surrealism, pixie hats, whimsical pseudonyms (eg Dingo Virgin and Hi T. Moonweed) and album titles (*Camembert Electrique*). Relocating to the UK and a sympathetic Virgin label, they produced a trippy trio of albums, beefed up musically by Steve Hillage and Tim Blake, before the founder upped and offed, and Gong splintered into a cluster of mini-Gongs, reuniting when the acid house movement landed on their peculiar planet.

181

"With Gong, although there are themes, it's constructed like jazz with a certain amount of improvisation and movement going on." Daevid Allen

Key members: Daevid Allen 13/1/38, Tim Blake 6/2/52, Steve Hillage 2/8/51, Didier Malherbe 22/1/43, Pierre Moerlen, Gilli Smyth • Recording career: 1971 - present

Sounds: Camembert Electrique 1971, The Flying Teapot 1973, Gong Est Mort - Vive Gong 1977

Grand Funk Railroad

They could have been just another American band, melting down an alloy of Cream and Hendrix into power chord heavy metal, but they had an aggressive guru in Terry Knight, a fellow Michigan native who had played with Don Brewer in a previous teenage band. Knight's marketing chutzpah early on landed the band a gig performing to 125,000 fans at the Atlanta Pop Festival of 1969. Suddenly they started shifting albums and singles by the barrel-load: they became one of the

USA's biggest-selling rock bands in 1970, and only the second act, after the Beatles, to sell out Shea Stadium. The critics, however, were vehemently hostile, and the fans loved Grand Funk because of it. Parting company with Terry Knight somewhat acrimoniously in 1972 and signing up with Linda McCartney's brother John Eastman, the band had Number One hits with 'We're An American Band' and a cover of Little Eva's 'The Loco-motion', but hit the end of the line in 1983.

"You guys don't know Grand Funk?
The wild shirtless lyrics of Mark Farner? The bone-rattling bass of Mel Schacher? The competent drumwork of Don Brewer?" Homer Simpson

Key members: Don Brewer 3/9/48, Mark Farner 29/9/48, Mel Schacher 3/4/51 • Recording career: 1969 - 1976 & 1981 - 1983

Sounds: Live Album 1970, We're An American Band 1973, Good Singin', Good Playin' 1976

Grateful Dead

The cult of the Dead existed long before Jerry Garcia passed away, his demise merely elevating the existing hagiography to new levels. Three members had already died, including 'Pigpen' McKernan, whose swirling Hammond organ was integral to the definitive sound, but Garcia was the cornerstone, surviving longer than anyone expected, through heroin addiction and a diabetic coma. In the 1960s he had been the bluegrass purist amid the rock and blues influences of the others, jamming on acid at 710 Ashbury Street, never selling commercially until they went rootsy on *Workingman's Dead* and *American Beauty* and produced deceptively effortless tracks like 'Truckin'' ("we really laboured over the bastard," was Jerry's recollection). Constant touring encouraged generations of

"The Grateful Dead, by and large, are a bunch of perverse gunsels." Bob Weir

Deadheads to camp-follow their shows, with bootlegs encouraged, band and audience stoned in mutual respect. Well, maybe not entirely mutual. What on earth did they find so fascinating, said Garcia, about the Dead playing the same old stuff? "There must be a dearth of fun out there."

183

Key members: Jerry Garcia 1/8/42 (died 9/8/95), Bill Kreutzmann 7/4/46, Phil Lesh 15/3/40, Ron 'Pigpen' McKernan 8/9/45 (died 8/3/73), Bob Weir 6/10/47

Recording career: 1966 - 1981 & 1987 - 1990 • Sounds: Live/Dead 1969, American Beauty 1970, In The Dark 1987

Al Green

The young Al Green, starting out with the family gospel group, got hell from his father for listening to the 'profane' sounds of Jackie Wilson. Like Sam Cooke he had been seduced by the secular charms of R'n'B, but he found no great success until a meeting in the late 1960s with the trumpeter and producer Willie Mitchell, who took Green to Memphis.

There they created an uncluttered, percussive, string-layered, horn-punctuated backdrop for Green's light, sensuous voice. The formula clicked to perfection on 'Let's Stay Together' in 1972, the year he had four million-selling US singles, but was almost getting predictable when, in a torrid episode two years later, a jilted suitor attacked Green (with a bowl of hot grits) and killed herself with his gun. This incident hastened his desire to return to the church, and after joining the ministry, Green found some kind of equilibrium between temporal and religious needs, dividing his time between pastorship and performing.

"If I'd sung pop and failed – oh, I'd be a sinner, sinner, sinner."

FULL GOSPEL
TABERNACLE

DEDICATED TO
THE GLORY OF GOD
DECEMBER 19, 1976

REV. AL GREEN, PASTOR

Born: 13/4/46 • Recording career: 1960 - present • Sounds: Let's Stay Together 1972, Call Me 1973, The Belle Album 1977

Green Day

When purists Fugazi took offence at punk acts who negotiated major label deals, they might have had Green Day specifically in mind: the trio signed to Warners subsidiary Reprise in 1993 after two albums with the independent Lookout. It proved a lucrative decision, since 1994's *Dookie* sold some ten million copies and reached US Number Two, as did the follow-up *Insomniac*. But Green Day were purists too in their own way. Childhood friends Armstrong and Dirnt - from the Berkeley,

California suburb of Rodeo, as dominated by refineries as the Canvey Island of Dr Feelgood - harked back to the Ramones and the British pop-punk of bands like Buzzcocks and Stiff Little Fingers. Apathy, dead-end teenage life, pent-up rage, all packaged up in crackling three-minute blasts; close your eyes and it could have been the 100 Club circa 1977. But maybe Fugazi had a point, since Green Day's 1997 single 'Good Riddance' was adopted as an official theme for golf's PGA Tour.

"We're not your average American band.

We're not shit heads." Mike Dirnt

Key members: Billie Joe Armstrong 17/2/72, Tré Cool 9/12/72, Mike Dirnt 4/5/72 • Recording career: 1989 - present • Sounds: Dookie 1994, Nimrod 1997, Warning: 2000 2000

Groundhogs

The backing band for the likes of John Lee Hooker, Little Walter and Champion Jack Dupree when they visited the UK in the mid-1960s, guitarist Tony McPhee and bassist Pete Cruickshank were then known as John Lee's Groundhogs. Reconstituting in 1968 following a break of a couple of years, the Groundhogs added Ken Pustelnik on drums and moved consciously towards a heavier sound, in step with the progressive rock movement - even ungenerously naming one album *Blues Obituary*. Word spread swiftly about Tony McPhee's searing, soaring guitar work and the band's live strengths, which were combined with a contemporary tolerance for concept albums on *Thank Christ For The Bomb*, *Who Will Save The World?* and *Split*. The latter was a treatise on schizophrenia, lightened by 'Groundhog'

"The Groundhogs are the number one best blues group you have over there,

and they fit in with my type of music perfectly." John Lee Hooker

(McPhee's loyal tribute to Hooker) and their trademark number, the driving 'Cherry Red'. After taking a sabbatical in the mid-1980s, the band, like Groundhog Day, then kept coming round again and again.

Key members: Peter Cruickshank 2/7/45, Tony McPhee 22/3/44, Ken Pustelnik • Recording career: 1968 – 1977 & 1984 - present

Sounds: Blues Obituary 1969, Thank Christ For The Bomb 1970, Split 1971

"I don't care if you think I'm being big-headed.
This is the only rock'n'roll band to come out of LA
that's real and the kids know it." Slash

Saul 'Slash' Hudson used to have a poster on his bedroom wall of Aerosmith's Joe Perry playing a 1959 Sunburst Les Paul Standard; the guitar, once owned by Duane Allman, was later offered to Slash, who delighted in acquiring it. He revered a guitar heritage going back to Townshend, Beck and Clapton which sat at odds with the 'world's most outrageous hard rock band' tag. It was one reason Guns N' Roses stood out from the herd, not just their often bratty obnoxiousness.

When they broke through, with breathtaking speed, they projected a frisson of danger that was perfectly served up on *Appetite For Destruction*, but sating their own appetites drained the band, and eventually the ballads which once had been affecting - 'Sweet Child O'Mine', for example, written for frontman Axl Rose's (ephemeral) bride Erin Everly - became overblown, the excess embarrassing. And Axl became the solitary guardian of the Guns' guttering flame.

Guns N' Roses

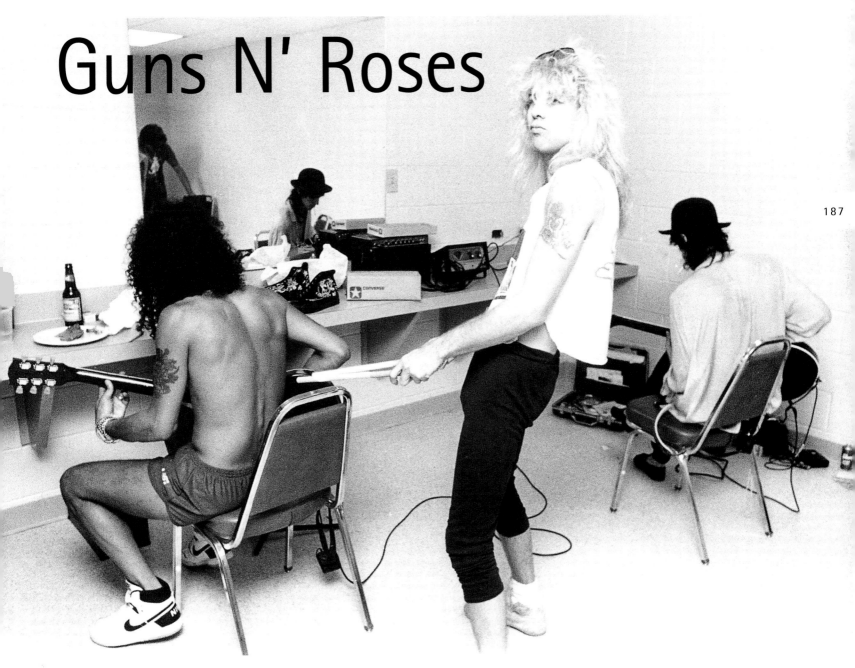

Key members: Steven Adler 22/1/65, Duff McKagan 5/2/64, Axl Rose (William Bailey) 6/2/62, Slash (Saul Hudson) 23/7/65, Izzy Stradlin 8/4/62 • **Recording career:** 1986 - 1994

Sounds: Appetite For Destruction 1987, Use Your Illusion I 1991, Use Your Illusion II 1991

Buddy Guy

Damn right he had the blues. Chicago, the hub of the electric blues, acted as a beacon to Louisiana's Buddy Guy. He was talent-spotted by Willie Dixon, who brought him into the Chess Records fold. There, as part of the house band, he worked with Muddy Waters and Howlin' Wolf, and made recordings as a gutsy singer and guitarist, delivering performances with punch and panache. He wanted to use feedback and distortion with the phased settings of his Fender Strat, but the idea didn't appeal to Chess - not long afterwards one James Marshall Hendrix did exactly that. As for many bluesmen the 1970s and 80s provided thin pickings for Guy, despite a fruitful musical relationship with harmonica player Junior Wells, but the support of Eric Clapton at his Royal Albert Hall blues nights helped foster a much-needed revival in the 1990s, playing alongside admirers like Jeff Beck, Mark Knopfler and Bonnie Raitt.

"Before Muddy died he told me
'Don't let the music die'."

Born: 30/7/36 • Recording career: 1958 - present • Sounds: Buddy Guy And Junior Wells Play The Blues 1972, Damn Right, I've Got The Blues 1991, Feel Like Rain 1993

"Tchaikovsky and Bach is Cadillac music.
We play down-to-earth Ford music."

Bill Haley

Not that long before 'Rock Around The Clock', Bill Haley was still styling himself The Ramblin' Yodeller or performing with his western swing band the Saddlemen. But, realising that R'n'B's high energy could be wedded to country and western, he moved speedily, recording 'Rocket 88' in 1951, and remodelling his band as the Comets. The first single which could genuinely be called rock'n'roll was their 1953 release 'Crazy Man Crazy' - 'Rock Around The Clock', released later, didn't do half as well, but got a second lease of life when the song was included in the movie *The Blackboard Jungle*, going on to sell a million copies (mainly, quaintly, on 78s). Suddenly teenagers were on fire, but when the lights went up they found Haley's kiss-curl chubbiness not quite the rebel they'd expected - he'd never pretended otherwise - and moved on to Elvis. Yet Haley had shown the way, and the yodeller's echo reverberated on.

189

Bill Haley and his Comets

Key member: Bill Haley 6/7/25 (died 9/2/81) • Recording career: 1953 – 1979 • Sounds: Rock'n'Roll Stage Show 1956

Happy Mondays

It's always worth celebrating a band which includes one member listed as performing 'percussion and dancing' - the incessantly mobile Bez - and the Happy Mondays' hedonism and sheer good fun provided the perfect soundscape for the spirit of Madchester. The rumbustiousness of the Mondays' music was channelled through the savvy mastermind of Tony Wilson at Factory. He shrewdly brought in experienced producers to oversee their shenanigans, including John Cale for their debut, and master re-mixers Paul Oakenfold and Steve Osborne. Their *Madchester Rave On* EP led out a pied piper's retinue of Mancunian followers including Stone Roses, James and Inspiral Carpets. They reached an apogee with the 1990 album *Pills'N'Thrills And Bellyaches*, a fresh'n'funky tonic prescribed on singles like 'Kinky Afro' and 'Step On'. But a trip to the Caribbean to record ...*Yes Please!* proved an expensive and excessive episode - "It was lucky no one died," observed one of the survivors - that led to a temporary parting of the ways in the mid-1990s.

"We started making music **as a joke,** something to do. I ended up with the job of having to put the words down." Shaun Ryder

Key members: Mark 'Bez' Berry 18/4/64, Paul Davis 7/3/66, Mark Day 29/12/61, Paul Ryder 24/4/64, Shaun Ryder 23/8/62, Gaz Whelan 12/2/66 • Recording career: 1985 - present

Sounds: Squirrel And G-Man Twenty Four Hour Party People Plastic Face Carnt Smile (White Out) 1987, Bummed 1988, Pills'n'Thrills And Bellyaches 1990

Better known via cover versions of his songs - Bobby Darin, and later the Four Tops, recorded 'If I Were A Carpenter', while Rod Stewart gave an unplugged rendition of 'Reason To Believe' - Tim Hardin failed to achieve similar success for himself. For much of his adult life he was struggling with a heroin addiction, which curtailed his ability to perform live and progressively diluted his muse. After a period serving in the US Marines, Hardin had taken his electric folk to Cambridge, MA and thence to New York, eventually releasing *Tim Hardin I*, with John Sebastian on harmonica and Gary Burton on vibes. Burton's presence was a sign of Hardin's love for jazz, superbly realised on *Bird On A Wire* with a dream support cast including Miroslav Vitous, Ralph Towner and Joe Zawinul. His introspective, cracked-voice songs were always touched with dignity; appropriately, following his death from an overdose at the age of 39, the first retrospective of his fine material was called *Shock Of Grace*.

"I just happened to land in this place where all these songs were. In order to be sung they had to be written."

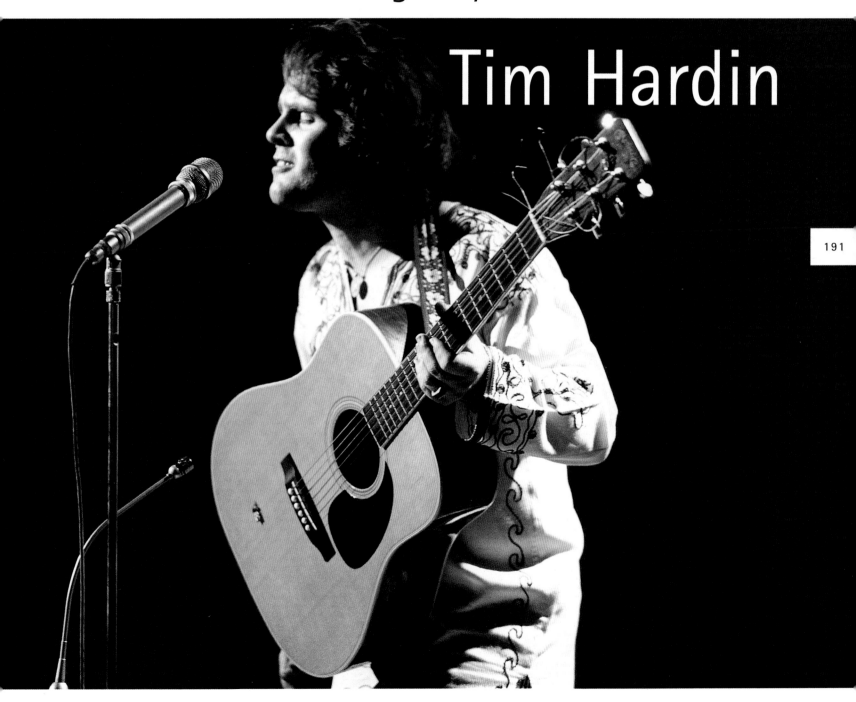

Tim Hardin

191

Born: 23/12/41 (died 29/12/80) • Recording career: 1966 - 1974 • Sounds: Tim Hardin 2 1967, Tim Hardin 3 1968, Bird On A Wire 1971

Ben Harper

While political and moral conviction provided the emotional heart of Ben Harper's music, it was the little-known Weissenborn guitar which supplied its physical mainspring. Built in the 1920s and 30s by Hermann Weissenborn, a Southern California-based instrument maker, this lap-held, hollow-necked acoustic slide guitar was a resonant inspiration for Harper's songs. Backed in the main by no more than bass and drums, the guitar's crystal-clear but rich tones set the scene for his clear-headed stance on contemporary issues. Growing up in a family of musicians, he drew on the honesty of Bob Marley, the technique of Jimi Hendrix and the authenticity of the blues, performing with the likes of Taj Mahal and Brownie McGhee. Harper laid his agenda on the line in his debut album *Welcome To the Cruel World*, juxtaposing in 'Like A King' the inspirational hope of Martin Luther and the brutal nightmare of Rodney - and barely flinched thereafter.

"Justice costs. It's for people who can really afford justice.
So music fills the place of working man's justice."

Born: 28/10/69 • Recording career: 1994 - present • Sounds: Welcome To The Cruel World 1994, Fight For Your Mind 1995, Burn To Shine 1999

"Though I can justify home taping, I'm not in love with it, because I tend to be bootlegged more than most."

'Committed', on his first album, was typical of Roy Harper's uncompromising self-examination: the track recalled his time in mental care, undergoing ECT, after he'd bailed out of a loathed period in the RAF. Travelling and busking, Harper pitched up in London as a streetwise poet-troubadour (*The Sophisticated Beggar* in the title of his debut), and formed a long-lasting friendship with Jimmy Page. Led Zeppelin's third album included 'Hats Off To Harper' and Page was a frequent musical ally, as at a 1973 Rainbow Theatre concert also featuring Keith Moon, Ronnie Lane and Dave Gilmour. Pink Floyd's first manager Peter Jenner now handled Harper's affairs, and the connection led to his best-known appearance, guesting on lead vocals for the Floyd's 'Have A Cigar'. Always highly regarded, Harper remained a uniquely English eccentric, an image he fostered on 1975's 'When An Old Cricketer Leaves The Crease', set to the strains of the Grimethorpe Colliery Band.

Roy Harper

Born: 12/6/41 • Recording career: 1966 - present • Sounds: Stormcock 1971, HQ 1975, Once 1990

194

Somehow Emmylou Harris managed to smile on beyond the shattering loss of her partner Gram Parsons in 1973. One of Parsons' fellow Flying Burrito Brothers had encountered Emmylou in Washington DC, playing clubs and bars after an unsuccessful attempt to break Nashville (and one failed marriage). Inspired by her pure, sweet soprano, Parsons dovetailed Harris into his two albums *GP* and *Grievous Angel.* After his death she forced herself to overcome her distress - and criticism that she was merely a harmonies singer - and by the time of *Elite Hotel,* backed by the tasty Hot Band, was a fully fledged crossover star. She moved closer to traditional country in the 1980s, but, although *Trio,* with Linda Ronstadt and Dolly Parton, was a surefire success, her career seemed to lose its way until 1995, when she stormed back with the 'weird' (her choice of adjective) *Wrecking Ball,* produced by Daniel Lanois, an album which obliterated most everybody's preconceptions.

Emmylou Harris

"The best country music is incredibly simple, **yet very poignant and moving.**"

Born: 2/4/47 • Recording career: 1970 - present • Sounds: Pieces Of The Sky 1975, Cimmaron 1981, Wrecking Ball 1995

"Hawkwind was more like a concept.

There was a lot of love put into it by creative people doing things because they believed in it." Nik Turner

Hawkwind

At the Isle Of Wight Festival in 1970 Hawkwind were delighted to perform. Not that they'd been booked, you understand: they simply turned up and started playing outside the fences. It was all part of the Hawkwind philosophy of free gigs for all; they had formed as an outpost of London's Notting Hill underground movement, their ethos of collectivity entailing ever-changing line-ups, but always true to the spirit of acid improvisation, with a sci-fi twist encouraged through collaborations with writer Michael Moorcock. Though a 'people's band', they still enjoyed the fruits of chart success, one track - 'Silver Machine', from the Greasy Trucker's Party held at the Roundhouse in 1972 - even making the UK Top Three. Tribal members included Stacia (the Bez of the 1970s, just dancing along) and one Ian Kilmister on bass, who was fired after a drug-related incident on one North American tour. Undaunted, Kilmister went off to form Motörhead - for it was Lemmy.

Key members: Dave Brock, Ian 'Lemmy' Kilmister 24/12/45, Nik Turner • Recording career: 1970 - present

Sounds: Space Ritual 1973, Warrior On The Edge Of Time 1975, The Chronicle Of The Black Sword 1985

Heart

"Wilson women have cleavage.
It's in the family. We think it's beautiful."

Nancy Wilson

As a concept, it was a beaut - the Wilson sisters, Ann and Nancy, brunette and blonde, playing heavy rock, kind of Abba with decibels. There was also a touch of the Fleetwood Macs about Heart: Ann was involved with guitarist Roger Fisher, while Nancy was stepping out with his brother, the band's soundman; by the time those relationships ended they had established a mainstream melodic rock style on singles like 'Magic Man' and 'Barracuda'. When the formula threatened to stagnate in the mid-80s, new label Capitol re-focused Heart onto a string of power ballads - 'These Dreams', 'Nothing At All' and 'Alone' (another US Number One for the Steinberg/Kelly songwriting team who'd created 'Like A Virgin' and 'True Colors'). This new lease of life was given an additional fillip when their Bad Animals studios found itself at the centre of Seattle's musical renaissance, and the Wilsons consorted gamely with the new generation of Soundgarden and Pearl Jam.

Key members: Ann Wilson 19/6/51, Nancy Wilson 16/3/54 • Recording career: 1976 - present • Sounds: Dreamboat Annie 1976, Heart 1985, The Road Home 1995

Richard Hell and the Voidoids

Malcolm McLaren loved Richard Hell, loved his look - above all the spiked hair and those ripped, graffitied T-shirts. But Hell was far removed from the deliberate brutishness of the British punks. As a schoolkid, with his chum Tom Miller, he had devoured 19th-century French romantic poetry. Miller assumed the name of a favourite writer (Verlaine) and the pair eventually formed Television. Hell, however, tired of Verlaine's controlling tendencies and re-located to Johnny Thunders' Heartbreakers, but still wanted his own show. So at CBGB's he unleashed the Voidoids alongside the Ramones and Blondie - Hell whirling about the stage dodging the sparring guitars of Bob Quine and

Ivan Julian, singing choppy, punky songs in his strangulated voice. The title track of their first album *Blank Generation* was not, remarked Hell, about oblivion, more to do with re-inventing yourself. And in the early 1980s he did just that, returning to poetry, editing and writing: rock'n'roll had been a temporary, convenient, medium for his messages.

"Britain is inspired by America and American music, but they really don't want to acknowledge it - at least not until 20 years later." Richard Hell

Key members: Marc Bell 15/7/56, Richard Hell (Richard Myers) 2/10/49, Ivan Julian 26/6/55, Robert Quine 30/12/42 • Recording career: 1976 - 1982

Sounds: Blank Generation 1977, Destiny Street 1982

From the outside, Jimi Hendrix is a series of iconic images. The man with attitude and a Carnaby Street mantle draped about his shoulders. The showman virtuoso setting his guitar alight at Monterey. Visual memories crystallising a period of three or four years when Hendrix's meteor burnt brightly. The reality, of course, was somewhat different. Here was a working professional who had paid his dues with the Isley Brothers and Little Richard. An instinctive musician - "the guitar was the snake, and he was the snake charmer," said Bill Graham. A softly spoken man whose tender ballads like 'The Wind Cries Mary' sit alongside the hard riffs of 'Purple Haze' or 'Crosstown Traffic'. A modest performer ("We're just jammin', that's all") and unconfident singer, whose vocal style nevertheless made a huge impact. For all these other sides of the man, long may the icons endure.

198

"If I seem free,
it's because I'm always running."

Jimi Hendrix

Born: 27/11/42 (died 18/9/70) • Recording career: 1966 - 1970 • Sounds: Are You Experienced 1967, Axis: Bold As Love 1967, Electric Ladyland 1968

John Hiatt

The tag 'songwriter's songwriter' is often code for a talented writer who fails to deliver big sales. Certainly John Hiatt remained a relatively well-kept secret, although his songs - highly crafted tales - were covered by Bonnie Raitt ('Thing Called Love'), Suzy Bogguss ('Drive South'), the Searchers and Iggy Pop, which is a pretty eclectic mix. After trying to surf the new wave, Hiatt fetched up on Geffen Records in the early 1980s, but encountered difficult personal times: he later admitted to an alcohol problem. He got back in the groove with the 1987 album *Bring The Family*, accompanied by the musical talents of Ry Cooder, Nick Lowe and ace session drummer Jim Keltner. The four tried to make the combo permanent as Little Village in 1990, but response was muted. Hiatt then brushed up against grunge on *Perfectly Good Guitar* - with Faith No More producer Matt Wallace - before returning to his heartfelt, bitter-sweet scenarios.

"There's lots of stuff I don't remember. **There's lots of years I don't remember."**

Born: 20/8/52 • Recording career: 1974 - present • Sounds: Riding With The King 1983, Bring The Family 1987, Perfectly Good Guitar 1993

Hole

The media attention encircling Courtney Love in her role as 'the widow of Kurt Cobain' almost suggested that she and her band Hole were some gruesome Nirvana cash-in. The truth was that Hole pre-existed their relationship, Love having formed Sugar Baby Doll with Kat Bjelland and Jennifer Finch, later of Babes In Toyland and L7 respectively, before Hole allowed her to become grunge's own Stevie Nicks (Love was a big Fleetwood fan, and covered Nicks' 'Gold Dust Woman'). Her band had *cojones* too, and the singles 'Dicknail' and 'Teenage Whore' set the keynote of their attitude. Frustratingly, their very well regarded album *Live Through This* was released in and overshadowed by the immediate aftermath of Cobain's death in April 1994. Bassist Kirsten Pfaff died two months later from an overdose, and Love went a little off the rails (not surprisingly) before shaping up as an actress, in *The People vs Larry Flynt*, and returning with an even tougher *Celebrity Skin*.

"Hole operates under a democracy."

Courtney Love

Key members: Melissa Auf Der Maur 17/3/72, Eric Erlandson 9/1/63, Courtney Love (Love Harrison) 9/7/65, Kristin Pfaff 1967 (died 16/6/94), Patty Schemel 24/4/67

Recording career: 1990 - present • Sounds: Pretty On The Inside 1991, Live Through This 1994, Celebrity Skin 1998

"We like this kind of music.
Jazz is strictly for
the stay-at-homes."

Buddy Holly

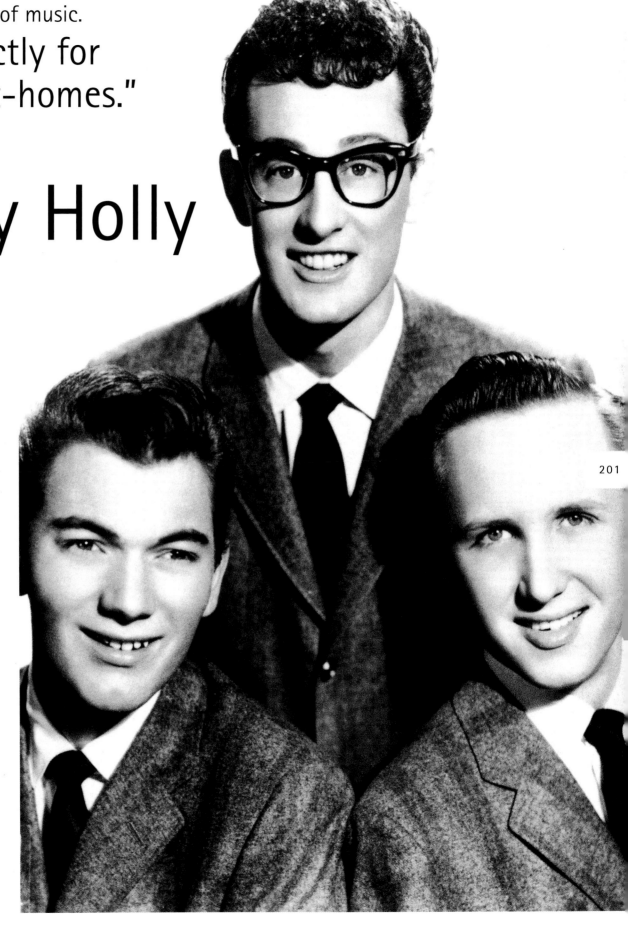

It is possible to put too much emphasis on 'the day the music died', but there is no doubt that when the plane ferrying Buddy Holly (not forgetting the Big Bopper and Ritchie Valens) to Fargo, North Dakota crashed shortly after take-off, a massive, pioneering talent was lost at the age of 22. The two guitar, bass and drums line-up, that was Holly's; he was also one of the first to exploit overdubbing and double-tracking technology. The bespectacled Holly ("he made it easy to wear glasses," said John Lennon), sometimes backed by the Crickets, sometimes solo, created a resilient canon of classics - 'That'll Be The Day', 'Oh Boy!', 'Peggy Sue'. They were songs of simple emotions, sung by the boy next door: "Buddy just seemed to be a little bit more genuine," recalled Cricket Niki Sullivan. After a falling-out in late 1958 with the producer Norman Petty, Holly was investigating a new string-led direction (those inspired *pizzicato* violins on 'Raining In My Heart') before ebbing finances forced him to sign up for that ill-fated tour.

201

Born: Charles Holley 7/9/36 (died 3/2/59) • Recording career: 1956 - 1958 • Sounds: The 'Chirping' Crickets 1957, Buddy Holly 1958

And he just kept rolling along: the Ol' Man River of the blues was going as strong as ever in his seventies, when 'Boom Boom' charted in 1992 courtesy of the sales power of global advertising. Three years earlier he'd released *The Healer*, not really a comeback as, unlike many other bluesmen, he'd managed to dodge oblivion, but a triumphant confirmation of his stature. Bonnie Raitt, Robert Cray and Carlos Santana were queueing up to play alongside Hooker, who'd similarly worked with Canned Heat and Van Morrison in the early 1970s. By then, though a late starter in recording terms (over thirty at the time of his first release, 'Boogie Chillun'), he'd released lavish quantities of R'n'B and blues - dozens of singles for a score of labels under many pseudonyms - bringing a native Delta sensibility and some gospel passion to the Detroit blues, and often recording with nothing more than a few bottletops attached to his shoes to supply accompaniment to his distinctively shifting rhythms.

202

John Lee Hooker

"I'm a man, I love women,
but I don't put nothin' ahead of my music. That's my life.
I am the blues.
I'll never get out of them alive."

Born: Chester Burnett 16/9/20 • Recording career: 1948 - present • Sounds: The Folk Blues Of John Lee Hooker 1959, Hooker'n'Heat 1971, The Healer 1989

Hot Tuna

In the late 1950s, Washington DC pals Jorma Kaukonen and Jack Casady shared an avid interest in the blues - and when guitarist Kaukonen joined a nascent Jefferson Airplane, he suggested Casady for the bass spot. The pair continued their exploration of rural blues in parallel, and formalised the arrangement in 1970 by releasing a live album including numbers by Mississippi John Hurt and the Rev. Gary Davis. Hot Tuna - their publishing company, Fish-Scent Music, confirmed the lubricious intentions of the name - then added electricity, drums and the scratchy fiddle of Papa John Creach to the sound, while Kaukonen supplied original material, including the durable 'Water Song' and 'Ode To Billy Dean', alongside the cover versions. Tuna substantially tanked up the volume, and the distortion, on *America's Choice* - and got increasingly louder until a split in 1978. There ended an experiment in charming purism or excessive self-indulgence, depending on which critic you believed, until a 1990s re-formation.

"Diehard Tuna fans are great. They'll put up with anything." Jorma Kaukonen

203

Key members: Jack Casady 13/4/44, Jorma Kaukonen 23/12/40 • Recording career: 1970 - 1978 & 1990 - present • Sounds: Hot Tuna 1970, Burgers 1971, Hoppkorv 1976

Hothouse Flowers

A couple of TV appearances helped cultivate the Hothouse Flowers' profile. One slot on Gay Byrne's *Late Show* impressed Bono, who signed them to U2's Mother label. And an appearance during judges' decision time in the Eurovision Song Contest helped break their single 'Don't Go', 1988's hippie summer anthem. The band, led by singer Liam O'Maonlaí - his voice Van Morrison, his stage presence more Jim - and guitarist Fiachna O'Braonáin, were the offspring of the Incomparable Benzini Brothers, an award-winning Dublin busking act. They carried the enthusiasm of their street performances over to the Flowers, yet failed to realise it fully on recordings of their songs, which shifted Celtic folk influences (Liam was a dab hand on the *bodhrán,* the traditional Irish drum) to the Southern USA, with blues and gospel well to the fore. They were, perhaps, at their best when *Rolling Stone* tipped them as "the best unsigned band in the world".

"We always had the sense that our music was going to reach beyond Dublin. But the Dublin people are always the first to let us know **if we get too full of ourselves."**

Fiachna O'Braonáin

Key members: Leo Barnes 5/10/65, Jerry Fehily 29/8/63, Fiachna O'Braonáin 27/11/65, Liam O'Maonlaí 7/11/64, Peter O'Toole 1/4/64 • Recording career: 1987 - present

Sounds: People 1988, Songs From The Rain 1993

The Housemartins

They looked so young, didn't they? The Housemartins were Hull's finest (they used to say, in jest, that they were only the city's fourth best band) and proud of it, as their debut album deliberately made clear: *London 0 Hull 4*. The sunny-side-up feel of their music was deceptive, though, hiding a darker, sarcastic side, as on their first hit, 'Happy Hour', a sideswipe at office life. Yet they managed to remain accessible, sitting sweetly atop the UK charts at Christmas 1986 with 'Caravan Of Love'. By their second - and final - album, they were back to their vitriolic habits; shortly afterwards they announced a split, claiming the masterplan had only ever foreseen three years' existence. And so before Paul Heaton and Dave Hemmingway migrated to the Beautiful South and future Fatboy Slim, Norman Cook, returned to his turntables, they left behind one final tongue-in-cheek single, 'Always Something There To Remind Me'.

"I thought the Housemartins songs sounded on radio like I was actually singing there at the time, inside the radio." Paul Heaton

Key members: Norman Cook 31/7/63, Stan Cullimore 6/4/62, Paul Heaton 9/5/62, Dave Hemmingway 20/9/60, Hugh Whitaker • Recording career: 1985 - 1988

Sounds: London 0 Hull 4 1986, The People Who Grinned Themselves To Death 1987

Howlin' Wolf

"When I met Wolf I was afraid of him,
just like you would be of some kind of beast.
It wasn't his size,
it was the sound
he was giving off."

Blues musician Jimmy Shines

Big man, big voice. Over six foot tall and 300 and some pounds, Howlin' Wolf, born Chester Arthur Burnett, cut an imposing figure on stage and amid the blues - a natural showman, his vocal style was as howlin' as the nickname suggested. Born in the Mississippi delta, he learnt to love the blues from harmonica legend Sonny Boy Williamson (married to his half-sister) and vocalist Charley Patton. After the end of World War II, Wolf relocated to Memphis, DJ'ing on local station KWEM and reaching the ears of Ike Turner and Sam Phillips, both scouting for Sun Records - he subsequently moved to Chess in Chicago, where Willie Dixon provided him with a string of songs that became staple fare for 1960s rock acts: 'Little Red Rooster', 'Smokestack Lightnin'', 'I Ain't Superstitious'. The proof of his influence came when Jimi Hendrix, about to de-construct the electric guitar at the Monterey festival in 1967, ripped into his set with Wolf's 'Killin' Floor'.

Born: Chester Burnett 10/6/10 (died 10/1/76) • Recording career: 1951 - 1975 • Sounds: Moaning In The Moonlight 1959, Howlin' Wolf 1962, The Back Door Wolf 1973

"Our aim was to prove you could do it with synthesizers,
and we thought that might be the task of a lifetime." Phil Oakey

The Human League

The electro-pop edition of the Human League was Phil Oakey's re-working of the band that he'd joined when it was run by the Kraftwerk-ish Ian Marsh and Martyn Ware - the version that got a namecheck by the Undertones on 'My Perfect Cousin'. But after a seismic rift, the founders left Oakey to his own devices. They formed Heaven 17, while he improvised a new line-up including a couple of teenage waitresses he met, in a cocktail bar of course, in Sheffield.

But hey, it worked. Synth-led but sympathetic, 'Don't You Want Me', with Oakey and Jo Catherall acting out a fragmenting relationship as The Beautiful South would do on 'A Little Time' a decade later, was a stone-dead Number One. After 1986's *Crash*, Oakey and the girls carried on alone, returning to form in 1995 with *Octopus*, by when they could reflect that they had gone some way to achieving their stated ambition of providing the soundtrack for a generation.

Key members: Ian Burden 24/12/57, Jo Callis 2/5/55, Joanne Catherall 18/9/62, Phil Oakey 2/10/55, Susanne Sulley 22/3/63, Adrian Wright 30/6/56

Recording career: 1978 - present • **Sounds:** Travelogue 1980, Dare! 1981, Octopus 1995

Humble Pie

Replacement 'Clem' Clempson continued the 'hot'n'nasty' trend, but it was quite noticeable that they missed the influence of Frampton's restraint - industry rumours of a rapprochement and re-formation were snuffed out when Marriott died in a fire at his beloved cottage.

It was very nearly a supergroup, though Humble Pie hated the term: Steve Marriott was fresh from the mod pop of the Small Faces, Peter Frampton had been the pin-up guitarist of the Herd, bassist Greg Ridley was ex-Spooky Tooth. They convened at Marriott's 16th-century cottage in Essex and thrashed out a sound that was part blues shouting from Marriott, part smooth guitar, the Frampton influence. 'Natural Born Bugie' was an early UK chart single a little at odds with their then passion for The Band, but presaged a move towards a later heavier sound - very 'eavy, very 'umble, as it were - that also saw Frampton jump overboard (his solo success was capped by 'Show Me The Way').

"We wanted to come in the back door, but the media wouldn't let us - **you're supposed to be amazing the day you come out,** but you need time."

Steve Marriott

Key members: Peter Frampton 22/4/50, Steve Marriott 30/1/47 (died 20/4/91), Greg Ridley 23/10/47, Jerry Shirley 4/2/52 • Recording career: 1969 - 1975 & 1980 - 1981

Sounds: As Safe As Yesterday Is 1969, Performance - Rockin' At The Fillmore 1971, Smokin' 1971

208

Hüsker Dü

"Back in '79 there were a lot of bands picking really punky and power pop names. We wanted to grab hold of something that was timeless, ambiguous **and would not label us."** Bob Mould

Just as the differences between Peter Frampton and Steve Marriott created healthy, then destructive tensions at the heart of Humble Pie, Hüsker Dü first benefited and later lost out to a growing divergence between drummer Grant Hart and guitarist Bob Mould. The sum of their parts - gathered together in Minneapolis - had formed a forceful whole in the 1980s, when the power trio added a turbo-charge of melody to their thousand-mile-an-hour hardcore punk: *Land Speed Record*, their debut album, rocketed through a blistering 17 songs in 26 minutes. However, wider horizons emerged on their covers of the Byrds' 'Eight Miles High' and Donovan's 'Sunshine Superman'. They even got away with a 2-CD concept album (*Zen Arcade*), but after signing to Warners, *Candy Apple Grey* overtly polarised Hart's angry young man and Mould's reflective thinker, and in January 1988 'twas all over. And if you're wondering about the name, it's Swedish for 'Do you remember?'

Key members: Grant Hart 18/3/61, Bob Mould 12/10/60, Greg Norton 13/3/59 • Recording career: 1979 - 1987 • Sounds: Zen Arcade 1984, Flip Your Wig 1985, Warehouse: Songs And Stories 1987

Billy Idol

Give yourself a moniker like that and you've got a lot to live up to. There were times when William Broad did pull it off - in his prime, the 'White Wedding' period - yet most often all that leather, macho and sneering come-on was rather embarrassing. The stage name dated back to his punk days in the UK, first with the band Chelsea, then fathering Generation X. Going solo, Idol flew to New York (he'd lived in Long Island as a child), hooked up with former Kiss manger Bill Aucoin and found a niche on MTV for his looks and cartoonish poses. A motorbike smash in 1990 nearly earned him an obituary, an escape acknowledged in his album *Charmed Life*, but gave him more news coverage than he had had for a while. By the mid-1990s the Internet let him play at being a cyber-Idol: detractors said he'd been a virtual star all along.

"My lyrics support love and beauty and gorgeousness."

Born: William Broad 30/1/55 • Recording career (solo): 1981 - present • Sounds: Billy Idol 1982, Rebel Yell 1983, Charmed Life 1990

With founder member and fellow Scot Clive Palmer, the String Band of Mike Heron and Robin Williamson came into being at (and took its name from) Palmer's Incredible Folk Club in Glasgow. Although their roots were firmly in folk, by the time the group were recording their third album, 1968's *The Hangman's Beautiful Daughter* (having parted company with Palmer), they had amassed a wide array of instruments - sitar, cello, xylophone, harmonica - and undertaken a Cook's tour of world music. Traditional folk, North African native music, raga, a dash of Dylan and Calypso rhythms were matched, or mis-matched, with medieval robes and mysticism. They were time/space travellers in search of the lost chord. Very much of the moment, ISB picked up critical approval and underground plaudits. They should probably have stopped there and then, but carried on regardless, bringing in ever more instruments and trying to create ambitious stage shows, and their aspirations eventually proved top-heavy.

"One of the reasons for the decline was that they stopped hating each other."

Producer Joe Boyd

The Incredible String Band

Key members: Mike Heron 12/12/42, Robin Williamson 24/11/43 • Recording career: 1966 - 1974

Sounds: The 5000 Spirits, Or The Layers Of The Onion 1967, The Hangman's Beautiful Daughter 1968, Wee Tam And The Big Huge 1968

The fulsome memorial service for Michael Hutchence in his native Sydney came a couple of months after the funeral of Diana, Princess of Wales - both deaths were ridden with unanswered questions and tales of souls slain by hidden forces and fears. By that time, Hutchence was the dominant presence in INXS, his liaisons with Kylie Minogue, Helena Christensen and Paula Yates taking him deep into *Hello!* country and making the rest of the band seem anonymous in comparison. Yet the Farriss siblings had been the driving force when the outfit first formed (as the Farriss Brothers) in 1977, experimented as INXS with elements of ska, soul, punk and rock, and toured heavily in Australia before deciding to try and crack the US. They did just that, unleashing Hutchence's stage potency yet further, and by the time of *Kick* and *X* they could move ten million units off the racks - whatever came later, they always knew how to rock.

"Getting stroked by thousands of people every night.

When you're left on your own you feel really alone."

Michael Hutchence

INXS

Key members: Garry Beers 22/6/57, Andrew Farriss 27/3/59, Jon Farriss 18/8/61, Tim Farriss 16/8/57, Michael Hutchence 22/1/60 (died 22/11/97), Kirk Pengilly 4/7/58

Recording career: 1980 - 1997 • **Sounds:** The Swing 1984, Kick 1987, Welcome To Wherever You Are 1992

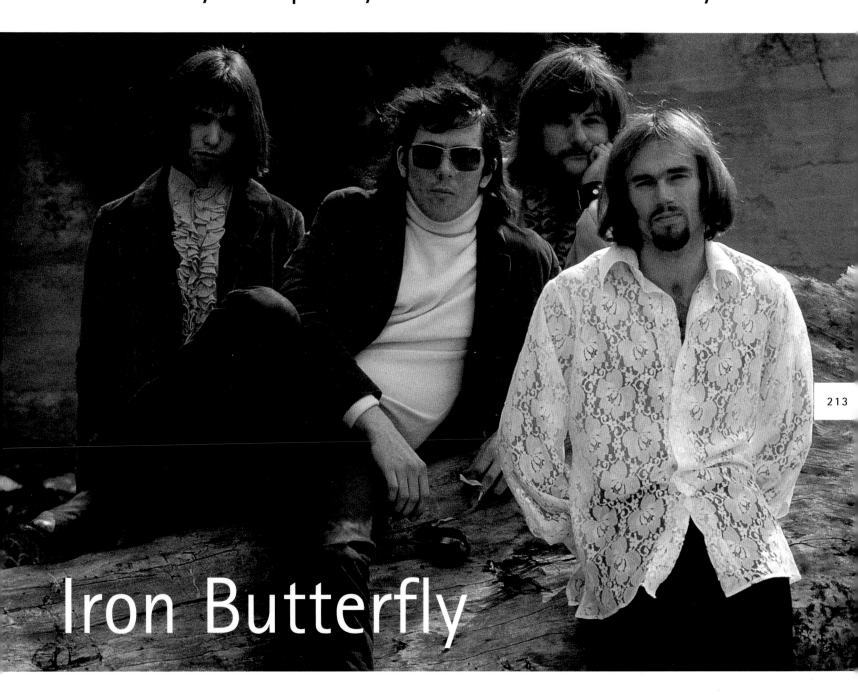

"We wanted to be heavy, tight, together, not only musically but as people.
Heavy and pretty... like an Iron Butterfly." Doug Ingle

Iron Butterfly

If nothing else, Iron Butterfly brought us the 17-minute track, the title number of their 1968 release *In-A-Gadda-Da-Vida* (an adenoidal interpretation of 'In the garden of Eden' was most people's guess at its elliptical meaning) which also contained a two-and-a-half minute drum solo. Yep, the guys had a lot to answer for. These acid-rock precursors of heavy metal sold phenomenal quantities of the said album - at the time it was Atlantic's biggest-ever seller, and by many accounts it was the first rock record to go platinum. Thus it was insidiously plugged into a million drummers' heads that such rhythmic self-gratification was acceptable. Iron Butterfly, who were led by organist Doug Ingle, had previously indulged in rather more predictable Summer of Love fare - 'Flowers & Beads' providing the appropriate hippie feel - before, alongside fellow heavy rock pioneers Blue Cheer, they cleared the way for acts like Journey and Styx.

Key members: Erik Braunn 11/8/50, Ron Bushy 23/9/45, Lee Dorman 19/9/45, Doug Ingle 9/9/46 • Recording career: 1968 -1970 & 1975 - 1976
Sounds: In-A-Gadda-Da-Vida 1968, Ball 1969, Metamorphosis 1970

"It's almost like we'd get worried if we got a good review. My daughter's homework reports are better than our reviews." Steve Harris

NWBHM was the clumsy acronym chosen to define Iron Maiden and Def Leppard. Their New Wave of British Heavy Metal was the preserved heritage of Led Zeppelin and Black Sabbath, nurtured through the punk years, and emerging with a residue of punk's snarl. In fact Maiden's original vocalist Paul Di'Anno sported a kind of Billy Idol look, but by 1981 he had been replaced by Bruce Dickinson, short on genuine cred - he was a public schoolboy, history graduate and national-level fencer -

but long on the requisite tumbling locks. Maiden even had their very own mascot, a cadaverous automaton who answered to the name of Eddie. The formula was a doddle, and like Def Leppard they survived with little alteration, an entry point for any kid getting into metal. On they galloped through Monsters Of Rock festivals, racking up a consistent run of UK Top Three albums - and reaching the top of the singles charts with 'Bring Your Daughter... To the Slaughter' in 1991.

214

Iron Maiden

Key members: Clive Burr 8/3/58, Paul Di'Anno 17/5/59, Bruce Dickinson 7/8/58, Steve Harris 12/3/57, Nicko McBrain 5/6/54, Dave Murray 23/12/58, Adrian Smith 27/2/57, Denis Stratton 9/11/54

Recording career: 1979 - present • Sounds: Iron Maiden 1980, The Number Of The Beast 1982, No Prayer For The Dying 1990

Chris Isaak

"Somebody told me that in this business
you've got to have talent and flashy clothes -
so I thought I'd start by getting the flashy clothes!"

Listening to Chris Isaak was usually a journey to another time, another place. His crooner's voice frequently evoked Roy Orbison, while on *Baja Sessions* he transported the album's listeners to the unhurried beaches of Baja California. Isaak even looked anachronistic, with a 1950s pompadour that could have secured him an audition with the Stray Cats - a rockabilly influence picked up from his parents and later exposure to Elvis's *Sun Sessions* while on a student exchange in Japan. Returning to the USA, he formed Silvertone, including James Calvin Wilsey (master of 1950s guitar sounds), bassist Rowland Salley and drummer Kenney Dale Johnson, all associates in his subsequent solo career. They soldiered on with Isaak's moody songs, garnering little notice - apart from critics complaining that his albums were too samey - until David Lynch (with whom Isaak later worked during one of his acting appearances) selected 'Wicked Game' for the *Wild At Heart* soundtrack, and from there a cult following grew up.

Born: 26/6/56 • Recording career: 1985 - present • Sounds: Silvertone 1985, Heart-Shaped World 1989, Baja Sessions 1996

The Isley Brothers

The sound of the Isleys changed radically when the three original brothers invited younger siblings Ernie and Marvin to join in 1969, especially when Ernie purchased a fuzzbox and started sounding like Hendrix might have done if he'd stayed with them... Jimi was in the Isleys' backing band in 1964 (his contribution captured on 'Testify') as they moved from gospel and R'n'B - 'Shout' was typical of their sound at the time - towards a period with Tamla-Motown, which was generally uninspired apart from 'This Old Heart Of Mine'. But with Ernie's fuzz guitar upfront they enjoyed a glorious mid-1970s, from 'That Lady (Part I)', a number they'd first recorded in 1964, to the heady 'Summer Breeze', a Seals and Croft composition. In the 1980s, the younger Isleys split off, and the sailing was no longer so smooth, but R. Kelly featured Ronald on 'Down Low' in 1996 and their music continued blowing through the jasmine of our minds.

216

"When I think about our legacy I'm amazed at what we've accomplished. Sometimes I gotta sing to believe it..." Ronald Isley

Key members: Ernie Isley 7/3/52, Marvin Isley 18/8/53, O'Kelly Isley 25/12/37 (died 31/3/86), Ronald Isley 21/5/41, Rudolph Isley 1/4/39 • Recording career: 1957 - present

Sounds: Twist And Shout 1962, 3+3 1973, The Heat Is On 1975

The shoes on the front cover of his debut album *Look Sharp* were exquisitely pointed, the footwear of a spiv, but there was nothing fly-by-night about Joe Jackson's songwriting. From day one it was absolutely razor sharp - especially the pained 'Is She Really Going Out With Him?' However, although *I'm The Man* followed in the same vein, Jackson's other musical interests (he'd studied at the Royal College of Music and played in the National Youth Jazz Orchestra) soon took over. First he went all Cab Calloway and Louis Jordan on *Jumpin' Jive*. Next he took up residence in Manhattan, steeping himself in NYC's jazz and Latin vibe for *Night And Day* and the crystalline hit 'Steppin' Out'. By 1991's *Laughter And Lust* a sense that pop was just too predictable was overt in tracks like 'Obvious Song' and 'Hit Single'. This later Joe Jackson was mature, but the spiky youngster had been more original.

217

Joe Jackson

"What I did was take a very long detour through the pop world, and had a great time and hits. But that was never all there was."

Born: 11/4/55 • Recording career: 1978 - present • Sounds: Look Sharp! 1979, Night And Day 1982, Blaze Of Glory 1989

He drove himself away to a new reality and built himself a Never Neverland. Yet behind the weirdness, this was the same Michael Jackson who, barely in his teens, had helped the Jackson Five get four US Number Ones in 1970. Even then he had the James Brown routines down pat and an overweening stage confidence, which masked acute shyness, of course. This was also the same Michael Jackson who, with producer Quincy Jones, had invented a new brand of soul-rock-pop on *Off The Wall* and who had revolutionised perceptions of the music video with the epic 'Thriller' (not forgetting *The Making of 'Thriller'*). Twelve years later, on the far side of Lisa Marie Presley, Bubbles and much speculation, Jarvis Cocker was interrupting Jackson's Messianic Brit Awards performance. By that time it was increasingly difficult to make sense of the tangled web of allegation and disinformation. But who cares? Just re-play 'Billie Jean' and moonwalk the memories.

"I love ET 'cos it reminds me of me. This person is like 800 years old and he's filling you with all kinds of wisdom."

Michael Jackson

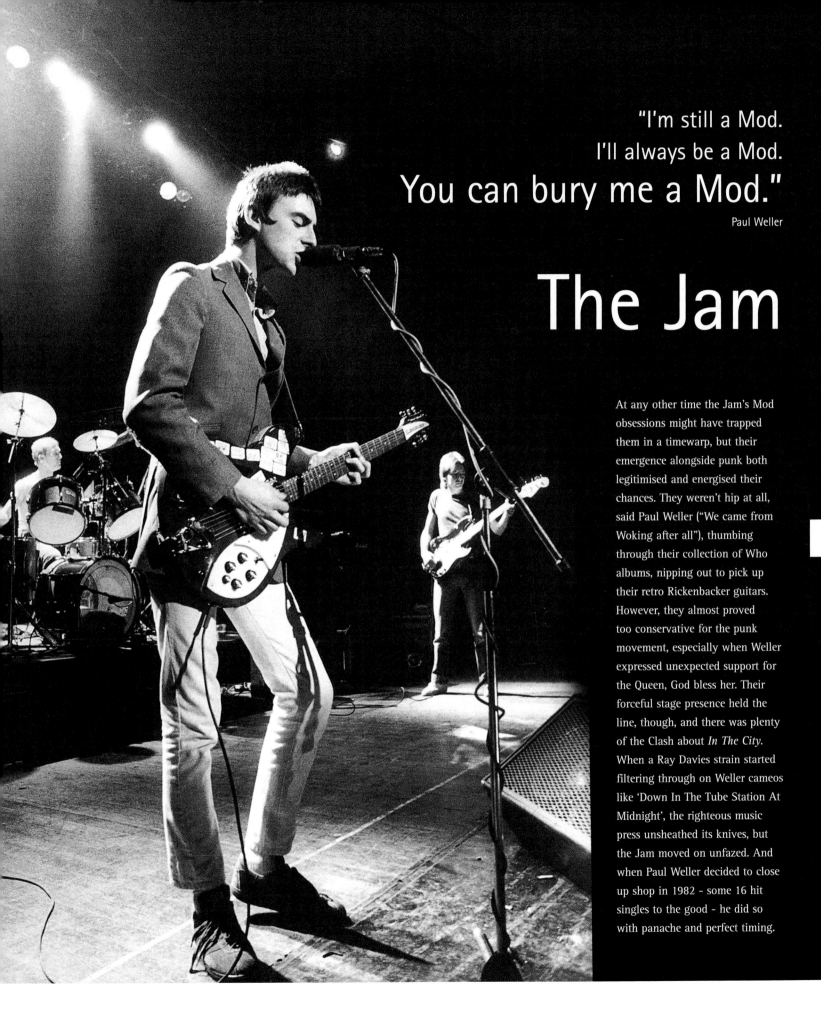

"I'm still a Mod.
I'll always be a Mod.
You can bury me a Mod."
Paul Weller

The Jam

At any other time the Jam's Mod obsessions might have trapped them in a timewarp, but their emergence alongside punk both legitimised and energised their chances. They weren't hip at all, said Paul Weller ("We came from Woking after all"), thumbing through their collection of Who albums, nipping out to pick up their retro Rickenbacker guitars. However, they almost proved too conservative for the punk movement, especially when Weller expressed unexpected support for the Queen, God bless her. Their forceful stage presence held the line, though, and there was plenty of the Clash about *In The City*. When a Ray Davies strain started filtering through on Weller cameos like 'Down In The Tube Station At Midnight', the righteous music press unsheathed its knives, but the Jam moved on unfazed. And when Paul Weller decided to close up shop in 1982 - some 16 hit singles to the good - he did so with panache and perfect timing.

Key members: Rick Buckler 6/12/55, Bruce Foxton 1/9/55, Paul Weller 25/5/58 • Recording career: 1977 - 1982 • Sounds: All Mod Cons 1978, Setting Sons 1979, Sound Affects 1980

"We didn't get along well, the five of us, so it ended up being a three-piece group." Joe Walsh

James Gang

220

It really *was* James' Gang - drummer Jim Fox put the band together in Cleveland in 1966, trying to blend the energy of the Who and the Yardbirds with the Motown sounds playing on radio stations over in Detroit. The problem was that Fox couldn't find a guitarist able to emulate Jeff Beck until he ran into Glenn Schwartz, who helped focus the sound before handing over guitar duties to none other than Joe Walsh. For Walsh - later to find major success with the Eagles - the trio format proved an ideal showcase for his guitar virtuosity. Heavy, funky grooves supplied the basis of signature tunes like 'Funk #49' and 'Walk Away' - the Who's Pete Townshend was a big Walsh fan (as apparently was Bill Clinton!). When Joe departed in 1971, the band never quite found a guitarist to match him. Tommy Bolin, in his pre-Deep Purple days, added plenty of kick for a while, but the Walsh era proved to be the Gang's most adventurous.

Key members: Jim Fox 24/8/47, Dale Peters 9/47, Joe Walsh 20/11/47 • Recording career: 1969 - 1976 • Sounds: Yer Album 1969, James Gang Rides Again 1970, Live In Concert 1971

"I've been hearing live music since before I was born. There I was in my mother's womb and she was gigging." Jay Kay

The son of a jazz singer, Jay Kay's huge hats, buffalo-horned for the band's trademark mascot, hid a talent which was at the very forefront of the Acid Jazz movement. Just as Lenny Kravitz found, conscious similarities to a past hero - in Kay's case, the Stevie Wonder of *Innervisions* - tended to obscure what else was going on. Jamiroquai's tribe of influences embraced the jazz of Lonnie Liston Smith, the fluidity of Gil Scott-Heron, the brass breaks of Becker & Fagen... and a love of the didgeridoo. On the basis of their first single 'When You Gonna Learn', Kay showed he'd learnt very fast, landing an eight-album deal with Sony. The song, an open letter to the world's politicians, also announced the eco-global social concerns which came to the fore on Jamiroquai's firmly funky debut, *Emergency On Planet Earth* (a UK Number One), but which sat a little uneasily with Jay Kay's self-confessed fondness for high-octane cars.

221

Jamiroquai

Key member: Jay Kay 30/12/69 • Recording career: 1992 - present • Sounds: Emergency On Planet Earth 1993, The Return Of The Space Cowboy 1994, Synkronized 1999

Jane's Addiction

To celebrate the band's final gig in Honolulu late in September 1991, Jane's Addiction's singer Perry Farrell stripped buck naked - a symbolic break with a past which had generally seen him modelling a tasteful combination of eye shadow, dreadlocks and girdle. From his first band, the goth-style Psi-Com, Farrell brought a Robert Smith deadpan delivery to the Led Zep metal played by the rest of Addiction, a collection of Los Angeles' finest alternative musicians. Their reputation in the late 1980s was as an extrovert, perverse, sometimes terrifying carnival, a show freeze-framed on their first album, recorded live at Hollywood's Roxy. By the time they were finding some commercial success, Farrell's attention was increasingly focused on the organisation of Lollopalooza, his alternative caravanserai, and after that Hawaiian farewell, Farrell and Stephen Perkins pitched up in Porno For Pyros, while guitarist Dave Navarro transferred his talents to the Red Hot Chili Peppers.

"Nobody can tell me I suck, because I simply don't believe it."

Perry Farrell

Key members: Eric Avery 25/4/65, Perry Farrell 29/3/59, Dave Navarro 7/6/67, Steve Perkins 13/9/67 • Recording career: 1987 - 1991 (reformed 1997 - present)

Sounds: Jane's Addiction 1987, Nothing's Shocking 1988, Ritual De Lo Habitual 1990

Jefferson Airplane

The addition of Grace Slick was Jefferson Airplane's master stroke. Under the leadership of Marty Balin, a folkie inspired by the Beatles to go electric, the Airplane - named after blues guitarist Blind Lemon Jefferson or a spliff, depending on your preference - first featured Signe Toly Anderson on vocals. When she became pregnant, they requisitioned Grace from another band, The Great Society, and along with her powerful, muezzin-like vocals received a bonus: the song 'White Rabbit'.

This Alice Through The Acid Trip number, which spun them to the heart of the Summer of Love, appeared on *Surrealistic Pillow* - along with *Sgt Pepper*, the quintessential album of 1967. By 1970's *Volunteers*, Balin was being overshadowed by the musical and emotional relationship between Slick and Paul Kantner (the only native San Franciscan). He left the couple to pilot the Airplane onwards, but later relented and returned to join their Starship enterprise, supplying the magnificent 'Miracles'.

> "In the 1960s they all treated us like we were great philosopher gods that knew all the answers...
> ## We were the flying saucers." Paul Kantner

223

Key members: Marty Balin 30/1/42, Jack Casady 13/4/44, Spencer Dryden 7/4/38, Paul Kantner 17/3/41, Jorma Kaukonen 23/12/40, Grace Slick 30/10/39

Recording career: 1966 - 1973 (reformed as Airplane 1989 - 1990) • Sounds: Surrealistic Pillow 1967, After Bathing At Baxter's 1967, Volunteers 1969

The Jesus And Mary Chain

The Reid boys initially disguised their pop sensibilities behind a resolute wall of feedback, but between the bricks lay a glimpse of those melodic instincts: on their early single 'Just Like Honey' they were almost syrupy. The brothers from East Kilbride had stormed the citadels of Sassenach press approval with their 1984 debut 'Upside Down' (b/w Syd Barrett's 'Vegetable Man') and - at a time when Bobby Gillespie was simultaneously running Primal Scream and supplying the Chain with his drumming technique - they delivered the landmark album *Psychocandy*, a perfect summation of their dark-lyric-meets-tuneful-noise approach. You either loved or loathed it, and if they pulled off their stunt of only playing an amphetamine-blast fifteen minute set when you went to see them live, the frustration could lead to violence. They later mellowed, notably on the mainly acoustic *Stoned & Dethroned*, but were always better with the feedback at full blast.

"We knew that what we were doing **was going to cause controversy.**"

William Reid

Key members: Jim Reid 29/12/61, William Reid 28/10/58 • Recording career: 1984 - 1998 • Sounds: Psychocandy 1985, Darklands 1987, Honey's Dead 1992

Jethro Tull

"There was a school of thought that Mick Abrahams should be the front man and I should just shuffle off to the back of the stage... **I wasn't having that, obviously.**" Ian Anderson

Flute, codpiece and Catweazle coiffure to the fore, Ian Anderson stood out - often on one leg - as the principal visual attraction of Jethro Tull. But when the band started out in the late 1960s they were really a down-the-line blues outfit, driven by Mick Abrahams' guitar. After Abrahams left to set up Blodwyn Pig, Anderson was able to lead the band - named after an 18th-century agriculturalist, as any fule kno - towards a series of heavy but lyrical songs on *Stand Up* and *Aqualung.* Their folk-enhanced, camp-medieval prog rock was dangerously early 1970s, but when a new order threatened, the Tull niftily dodged the slings and arrows of punk's outrage, carrying on strong and loud into the 80s, even winning a Grammy in 1988 for Best Hard Rock Album (*Crest Of A Knave*). After this excursion, they returned to safer ground, and Anderson to his native Scotland, where he lairded it over a salmon fishing enterprise.

225

Key members: Mick Abrahams 7/4/43, Ian Anderson 10/8/47, Barriemore Barlow 10/9/49, Martin Barre 17/11/46, Clive Bunker 12/12/46, John Evan 28/3/48, Jeffrey Hammond-Hammond 30/7/46

Recording career: 1968 - 1995 • Sounds: This Was 1968, Aqualung 1971, Songs From The Wood 1977

Billy Joel

He was and always would be the Piano Man. Billy Joel was a craftsman songwriter who seemed to annoy the critics; they dismissed the one-time boxer as lightweight, but nonetheless could not deny the immediacy of his hooklines. Lennon and McCartney were early inspirations for Joel, who, after a stint in a hard rock duo called Attila, began to catch notice with 1977's 'Just The Way You Are', a tribute to his first wife Elizabeth ('Uptown Girl' was likewise written for his second wife Christie Brinkley). It was a trademark of his early songs to be inspired by direct emotion, on 'My Life' and 'Tell Her About It', but the later Joel learnt to touch on wider concerns, including his pocket history lesson 'We Didn't Start The Fire'. And if anyone doubted his songwriting skills, they need look no further than *Glass Houses*, an album of brilliant pastiches of the sounds of the 1950s and 60s.

"You're always in the desert looking for an oasis, and all that's out there with you is the piano, this big black beast with 88 teeth."

Born: 9/5/49 • Recording career: 1972 - present • Sounds: Piano Man 1973, The Stranger 1977, River Of Dreams 1993

For nearly a decade no artist had played the Dodger Stadium in Los Angeles; in fact, the last act to perform there had been the Beatles. That Elton John could pack the place was a tribute to the acclaim he'd enjoyed at a career-launching gig at LA's Troubadour Club in 1970, five years earlier - drummer Nigel Olsson remembered that Elton had been subdued before the Troubadour gig, then "all of a sudden he started wearing Mickey Mouse ears and jumping up and down". Stadium shows were ideal for his larger than life theatrics ("I'm 5' 8". I hate being short"); for the Dodgers gig he sported a sequinned baseball uniform. But a matter of days earlier, there were rumours that Elton had taken 60 Valium tablets and/or attempted to drown himself. Even at this major league peak in his working life, a darker side lay not far away.

"The sun was going down, the lights were coming on. I thought 'This shot's going to be like a Hockney – and we're in LA. The perfect moment in the perfect place'."

Terry O'Neill

227

Elton John

Born: Reginald Dwight 25/3/47 • **Recording career:** 1968 - present • **Sounds:** Tumbleweed Connection 1970, Goodbye Yellow Brick Road 1973, Made In England 1995

Janis Joplin

Shortly before the accidental overdose that killed her, Janis Joplin returned to her hometown, Port Arthur in Texas, for a high school reunion. It was payback time for the insults she'd suffered as a teenager, acne-scarred and and treated as a freak ("I want those motherfuckers to see what a fine feathered bird I turned into"), but also a sign of the craving for approval that, by all accounts, marked much of her life. Janis's legend, a rush to oblivion fuelled by sex, drugs and Southern Comfort, was preserved by her death, but at the time she seemed to be on the up, enthusiastic about her new recording sessions (*Pearl* was issued posthumously). Yet there remained a primitive, vulnerable soul whose howl of pain gave her voice extraordinary power and genuine believability. Her father Seth understood: "She was a wild woman and a wilful child," he later recalled. "That was her act, but it was mostly act."

"On stage, I make love to 250,000 people, then I go home alone."

Born: 19/1/43 (died 4/10/70) • Recording career: 1967 - 1970 • Sounds: Cheap Thrills (with Big Brother & The Holding Company) 1968, Pearl 1971, In Concert 1972

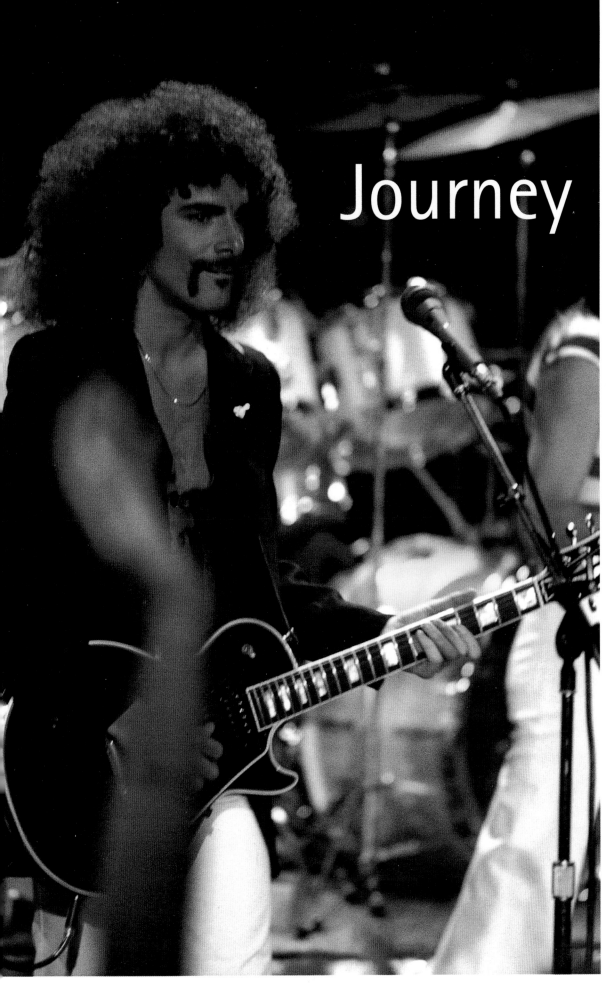

Journey

Neal Schon, a protégé of Carlos Santana, was the guitar mainstay of the Journey sound, supporting vocalist Steve Perry, who was once described as having the vocal qualities of both Ozzy Osbourne and Sam Cooke. This was the combination that fuelled Journey's AOR progress in the late 1970s and early 80s on a series of simply titled, regularly charting albums: *Infinity*, *Departure*, *Frontiers*, the last only kept off US Number One by Michael Jackson's *Thriller*. Before Perry joined the band, Journey had been a jazz-rock band hand-selected by manager Walter Hubert, including Schon, Gregg Rolie - also ex-Santana, the lead singer on 'Black Magic Woman' - and the much-travelled drummer Aynsley Dunbar. Of the original line-up only Schon lasted all the way to their glory days, when they rolled out a carpet for Bon Jovi and co. In 1996, as the band reformed, Mariah Carey, perhaps surprisingly, paid them tribute by recording a cover of their 1982 hit 'Open Arms'.

"There's nothing wrong with being commercial. It's just another way of saying you're successful."

Neal Schon

Key members: Jonathan Cain 26/2/50, Steve Perry 221/1/53, Gregg Rolie 17/6/47, Neal Schon 27/2/54, Steve Smith 21/8/54, Ross Valory 2/2/49 • Recording career: 1975 - 1987 & 1996 - present

Sounds: Infinity 1978, Escape 1981, Trial By Fire 1996

Joy Division

It was, as bassist Peter Hook pointed out, the cruellest of timings that Ian Curtis's death came just weeks before Joy Division achieved the breakthrough that Curtis had so wanted. His suicide in May 1980 was the culmination of a number of attempts (the reasons remain contentious). By June the single 'Love Will Tear Us Apart' set the tone for much of the sound of the 1980s and heralded a success the band could not enjoy without their frontman. The Manchester quartet, inspired like many others by the Sex Pistols, had been launched by Factory Records' Tony Wilson, who famously spent his life savings on pressing their first album, *Unknown Pleasures*; its deeply introspective, romantically gloomy world view was sketched out further on *Closer*. The survivors reformed as New Order, and Bernard Albrecht (now called Sumner) credited Curtis posthumously as the one who had pointed the way forward towards their Kraftwerk-inspired electronics.

> "I was the first to know that Ian had died. It was like a void, **like someone had taken a bridge out from under us.**"
>
> Peter Hook

Key members: Bernard Albrecht 4/1/56, Ian Curtis 15/7/56 (died 18/5/80), Peter Hook 13/2/56, Steven Morris 28/10/57 • Recording career: 1978 - 1980

Sounds: Unknown Pleasures 1979, Closer 1980, Still (Rare And Live) 1981

Judas Priest

Swathed in leather and S&M imagery (singer Rob Halford had a whip for extra stage impact), Brummie band Judas Priest continued the hard rock heritage of Black Sabbath and Deep Purple through the late 1970s and on into the 80s. Priest's version was snappier than their forefathers, crisply packaged heavy metal with lyrics that were guaranteed to upset the self-appointed moral majority. The twin guitars and high-octane aggression that had characterised *British Steel* and *Screaming For Vengeance* were nearly silenced, though, in December 1985, when two teenagers from Reno, Nevada shot themselves (one died at the time, one after an overdose three years later), allegedly after listening to the band's album *Stained Class*. A high-profile lawsuit was ultimately thrown out of court, but five years of tension had taken its toll, and though the success of 1990's *Painkiller* dulled some of the trauma, Rob Halford quit in 1993 - the parting of the ways was acrimonious.

"We were always proud to be known as a metal band. There is no greater form of rock'n'roll." Rob Halford

231

Key members: Ken 'K.K.' Downing 27/10/51, Rob Halford 25/8/51, Ian Hill 20/1/52, Dave Holland, Glenn Tipton 25/10/48 • **Recording career:** 1974 - present

Sounds: Stained Class 1978, British Steel 1980, Painkiller 1990

Johnny Kidd and the Pirates

The piratical costumes that pre-dated Adam Ant by two decades were not the only claim to fame of Johnny Kidd and his swashbuckling band. The Pirates included members of the skiffle group Freddie Heath (Kidd's given name) and the Five Nutters. Ditching the washboards, they came over all Gene Vincent, putting out 'Please Don't Touch', swiftly followed by rock classic 'Shakin' All Over' - covered by the Who, Guess Who and doubtless Who-named bands around the world. In the vacuum before the Beatles, they were a rare, if not the only, example of genuine British rock'n'roll. Though the guitar break on 'Shakin'' had been played by session musician Joe Moretti, it was the arrival of the fine guitarist Mick Green in 1962 which added extra bite. However, as Merseybeat snapped at the Pirates' heels, Kidd split the band in 1966; he quickly formed the New Pirates, but perished in a car crash later that year.

"I strode on stage wearing an eye patch after being struck in the eye by a guitar string... and never looked back!" Johnny Kidd

Key member: Johnny Kidd 23/12/29 (died 7/10/66) • Recording career: 1959 - 1966 • Sounds: Shakin' All Over 1971

Killing Joke

"The feeling of a guy in the First World War **who's just about to run out in the trenches.** That's the feeling we're trying to project, the Killing Joke."

Jaz Coleman

There was always tangible energy on stage when Killing Joke performed, with or without the addition of warpaint - one of their earliest singles was the pounding 'Wardance', and Jaz Coleman applied the appropriate daubs to his elastic features. An almost tribal savagery affected equally the lacerations of their dark humour or the relentless, virtually disco, rhythm section which propped up their heavy punk and FX-laden vocals. John Peel purred when he heard 'Warpaint', and in return for his supportive airplay the band delivered one of the DJ's most requested radio sessions. But concerns about an imminent apocalypse convinced Coleman to head north to Iceland in 1982, putting something of a dent in the band's progress as various other members followed him there. The apocalypse having been postponed, Coleman returned unabashed, and despite Killing Joke's constant falling-outs and reformations, they were fêted by the new generation of Ministry, Soundgarden and Nirvana.

233

Key members: Jaz Coleman 26/2/60, Paul Ferguson 31/3/58, Martin 'Youth' Glover 31/3/58, 'Geordie' Walker 18/12/58 • **Recording career:** 1979 - 1988 & 1990 - present

Sounds: Killing Joke 1980, Night Time 1985, Extremities, Dirt & Various Repressed Emotions 1990

B.B. King

Riley B. King (B.B. was short for Blues Boy, a Memphis nickname) had real Delta blues credibility: his second cousin was guitarist Bukka White. King replicated White's slide guitar style with expressive vibrato and a feel for the jazz of Charlie Christian and Django Reinhardt. After acquiring his cherished guitar 'Lucille' (a Gibson 335), he was ready to strike forth, finding success with Lowell Fulson's 'Three O'Clock Blues', an R'n'B Number One, and initiating a crunching schedule of work: some 300 gigs year in year out. In the late 1960s his talents were given a wider airing to white audiences, playing rock festivals, opening for the Stones, working with Eagles producer Bill Szymczyk - including the hit single 'The Thrill Is Gone' - and later recording with U2 on *Rattle & Hum*. A towering figure, the blues' great ambassador left his most enduring mark on the *Live At The Regal* album, recorded in 1964 - majestically definitive.

"I won't retire until the people retire me."

Born: 16/9/25 • Recording career: 1949 - present • Sounds: Live At The Regal 1965, Completely Well 1969, Deuces Wild 1997

Carole King

"She was 15, and I saw this confident little broad. **She thought everything she wrote was great.** And she was right, ninety percent of it was." Barry Mann

A decade before weaving the magic of 1971's mega-selling *Tapestry*, Carole King was producing some of the great pop songs ever, period. Early friends included Neil Sedaka (sometime sweethearts, his hit 'Oh! Carol' was dedicated to her) and Paul Simon, but her own songwriting failed to take off until she met her first husband Gerry Goffin. He needed music, she needed words - the couple became part of the Brill Building group of young songwriters producing, under intense pressure to deliver from Tin Pan Alley's fat cats, timeless teenage pop. A fraction of their writing credits includes 'The Loco-Motion', 'Up On The Roof', 'Take Good Care Of My Baby', 'Natural Woman' and 'I'm Into Something Good'. And although King had a solo hit in 1962 with 'It Might As Well Rain Until September', she submerged her own performing (she suffered from stage fright anyway) until the latter part of the decade.

235

Born: 2/9/42 • Recording career: 1959 - present • Sounds: Writer 1970, Tapestry 1971, Thoroughbred 1976

"It was the only band where, as a rock drummer,
you could play in 17/16 time
and still stay in decent hotels." Bill Bruford

A slot on the Stones' Hyde Park bill of July 1969 introduced King Crimson to a ready-made retinue who would be genuflecting to their debut album *In The Court Of The Crimson King*. Extensive use of the tremulous string-effect Mellotron could have put them in Moody Blues territory, but Fripp's experimental chordings and techniques marked this as cutting-edge progressive rock. The band promptly imploded and starting auditioning for new members - one of Crimson's great legacies

was its diaspora of past members: Greg Lake, Bill Bruford, John Wetton and Boz Burrell (taught bass by Fripp, Burrell paid enough attention to become Bad Company's bassist). By 1973 only Robert Fripp remained, but swept back in fine style with *Lark's Tongues In Aspic*, as ever oscillating between mystical folk, jazzy noodlings and heavy rock. The following year Fripp firmly announced that King Crimson was over "for ever and ever". The band reformed in 1981, and again in 1993.

King Crimson

Key members: Bill Bruford 17/5/48, Boz Burrell 1/8/46, David Cross 23/4/49, Robert Fripp 16/5/46, Greg Lake 10/11/48, John Wetton 12/7/49

Recording career: 1969 -1974, 1981 - 1984 & 1995 - present • **Sounds:** In The Court Of The Crimson King 1969, Lark's Tongues In Aspic 1973, Thrak 1995

The Kinks

Given Ray Davies' later dominance, it's worth recalling that it was the Kinks' guitarist Dave Davies, his frenetic younger brother, who gave the group's first singles their substantial mettle: he ripped up the speakers in his practice amp and hooked them with a couple of his Vox amps for the raw sound of 'You Really Got Me'. Dave and Ray fought constantly, like all good brotherly bands, but Ray's songwriting skills held sway. By 'Dedicated Follower Of Fashion' and 'Waterloo Sunset' the Kinks had segued to the very model of an English band, with their neatly observed cameos of life in Blighty, always serious but blessed with a twinkling, crinkled smile. From there on it was but a sprightly stroll towards some concept albums, success in America following 'Lola' ('Celluloid Heroes' was the Hollywood parallel of 'Waterloo') and obeisance from Paul Weller, Supergrass and Blur - whose single 'Country House' was an undisguised tribute to the Kinks' 1966 'House In The Country'.

"Playing gives a great sense of self-expression, the energy you create by playing. I used to get mad, and I suppose I'm sort of schizophrenic at heart as well." Dave Davies

Key members: Mick Avory 15/2/44, Dave Davies 3/2/47, Ray Davies 21/6/44, Peter Quaife 31/12/43 • Recording career: 1964 - present

Sounds: Face To Face 1966, Something Else By The Kinks 1967, Arthur (Or The Decline And Fall Of The British Empire) 1969

From their very first gig in 1973 Kiss knew exactly where they were heading: to infinity and beyond, with make-up. They had a minimal audience in the Coventry Club, Queens that night, but they already possessed a press kit, and a vision. Armed with indefatigable confidence and shrewd business nous, Kiss powered onwards in their cartoon character guises. Simmons was a tonguetastic demon, Stanley the star child, Frehley a space cadet and drummer Criss a slightly startled cat - after one of their blood-spitting, pyromaniac gigs, said the official press release, he "finds a quiet corner to curl up in". They inspired immense loyalty from the massed ranks of the Kiss Army who even forgave their heroes that awful moment in 1983 when they appeared in public stripped of the cosmetics (they just looked unprepossessing) and though their sales hardly suffered, it was a huge relief to see the original quartet back in all their true colours in 1996.

Kiss

"The one thing we'll never be accused of **is being a Kiss copy band."** Paul Stanley

Key members: Peter Criss 27/12/45, Ace Frehley 22/4/51, Gene Simmons 25/8/49, Paul Stanley 20/1/50 • Recording career: 1974 - present • Sounds: Alive! 1975, Destroyer 1976, Love Gun 1977

The KLF

"We don't have a manager or a record company. **There's nobody to tell us what to do and what not to do."**

Bill Drummond

When the KLF received the 1992 Brit Award for Best Band it sadly marked the failure of their avowed intent to undermine the institution of the music industry. So, sure enough, they shortly announced, in a full page ad in the *NME*, the end of their "wild and wounded, glum and glorious, shit but shining path". The terrorists of the Kopyright Liberation Front had set out on their mission in the late 1980s, exhuming the sounds of Led Zep and Abba (who sued) in a sampling bonanza, then, as the Timelords, timewarping the *Dr Who* theme for 'Doctorin' The Tardis'. Under the KLF banner they created at least two of the rave scene's essential anthems with '3 a.m. Eternal' and 'Last Train To Transcentral', and their inspirational choice of Tammy Wynette to front 'Justified And Ancient' was a last hurl in the wind before the finale. It was time for the dastardly duo to find new targets for their mischief-making.

239

Key members: Jim Cauty 1954, Bill Drummond 29/4/53 • Recording career: 1988 - 1992 • Sounds: Chill Out 1990, The White Room 1991

"I was chopping up dead bodies at the Bakersfield coroner's office... You need an outlet to let the shit flow." Jonathan Davis

Dissection became a way of life for Korn's Jonathan Davis. His time working in an autopsy room exposed him to the often extremely messy downside of the human condition. When he grafted that on to his own troubled adolescence (broken family, severe bullying) Davis had an endless source of raw material for the angry lyrics that had no qualms about offending anyone or anything. After joining forces with his fellow Kornballs they took their hardcore funk-metal out on the road, creating enough momentum (with some heavy promotional support from their label Epic) to drive *Follow The Leader* to the top of the US charts - the first hardcore act to reach those heights. *Follow* showed signs that this was a maturing band, who were definitely going to be more than a flash in the pan; by the release of *Issues*, they were reducing the amount of rap in the mix, and returning to purer metal, with Davis plaintively declaiming, "All I want in life is to be happy."

Korn

Key members: Reggie 'Fieldy Snuts' Arvizu 2/11/69, Jonathan 'HIV' Davis 18/1/71, James 'Munky' Shaffer 6/6/70, David Silveria 21/7/72, Brian 'Head' Welch 19/6/70 • **Recording career:** 1994 - present

Sounds: Korn 1994, Life Is Peachy 1996, Follow The Leader 1998

Leo Kottke

'Geese farts on a muggy day'... The analogy became the bane of Leo Kottke's life, and featured - almost *had* to feature, like some saintly relic - in every article about the guitarist. It was Kottke's own liner-note description of his deep baritone voice and, though typical of his wry lyrics, was a rare opening up from a self-confessed recluse who compared his low-key performance style to Kabuki drama: huge emotion conveyed by the raising of a single eyebrow. Kottke's communication was best transmitted through his acoustic guitars, on which he was a hugely influential master, fingerpicking his way through a style inspired by veteran blues players Son House and Mississippi John Hurt. Brought to wider attention by the equally reclusive guitarist John Fahey, Kottke recorded the template *6- And 12-String Guitar* and continued quietly releasing quality albums. Though the Shamen sampled a snatch of Kottke on 'Comin' On', he was otherwise an exquisite secret to stumble across.

"I've sold a few records, but I don't think I've made the right one yet."

Born: 11/9/45 • Recording career: 1968 - present • Sounds: 6- And 12-String Guitar 1969, My Feet Are Smiling 1973, A Shout Towards Noon 1986

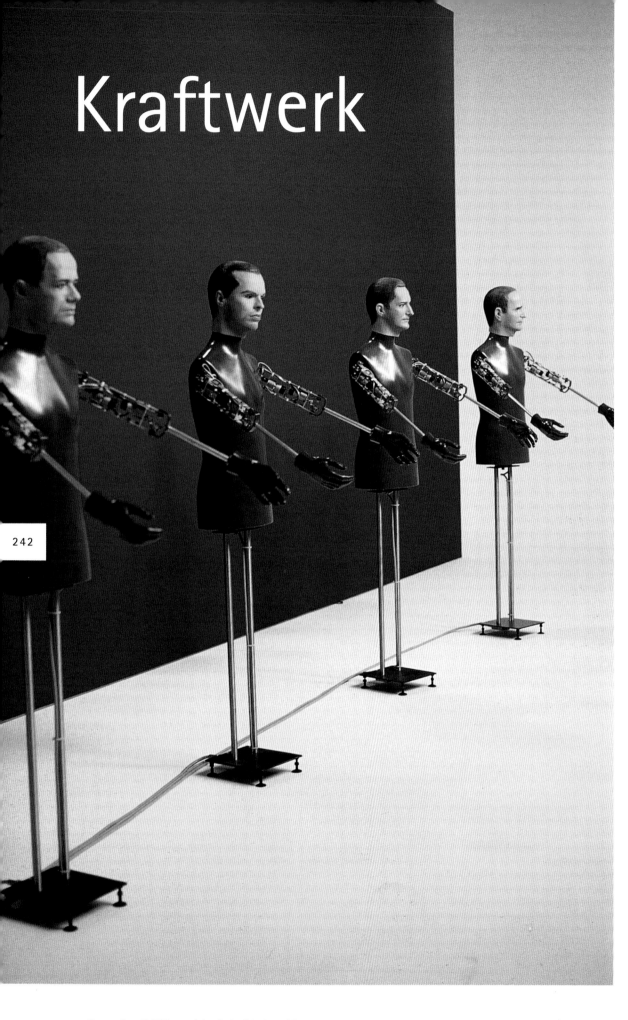

Kraftwerk

"We play the machines, **but the machines also play us."** Ralf Hütter

The mechanistic pioneers of Kraftwerk were led by Ralf Hütter and Florian Schneider, both of whom had studied at Düsseldorf Conservatory: they started recording in one of the city's industrial power plants which gave them their name. The original Kraftwerk had a strong tint of Tangerine Dream and Pink Floyd, but they increasingly turned to the possibilities of electronic and computer-driven sounds, reaching the outside world through the single-friendly, shortened version of 'Autobahn', their musical interpretation of driving down an endless German highway. These muso-technicians had stumbled on a way of creating music which could be background muzak, softly whiling away those late 20th-century industrial blues, or make you get up and dance. At first seen as oddities, they opened up new horizons for Gary Numan, the Human League and OMD, and helped lay the foundations of hip hop and rap: Afrika Bambataa's seminal *Planet Rock* sampled 'Trans-Europe Express' - nuff said.

Key members: Ralf Hütter 20/8/46, Florian Schneider 7/4/47 • Recording career: 1971 - 1991 & 2000 - present • Sounds: Autobahn 1974, Trans-Europe Express 1977, The Man-Machine 1978

Lenny Kravitz

'Rock And Roll Is Dead', declared Lenny Kravitz on the opening track of his 1995 album *Circus*. Hmmm, rather churlish, mused his castigators (and they were legion), since he'd built an entire career on a retrospective celebration of rock music. When Kravitz, who was a showbiz kid - his father a TV news producer, his mother the actress Roxie Roker - attended Beverly Hills High, it was Prince who started his musical juices flowing. Later Kravitz began working with his co-conspirator Henry Hirsch on a kaleidoscope of psychedelia, soul, R'n'B and, well, rather a lot of Hendrix. But despite the brickbats, he could produce a groove, and emitted a musky attraction for the laydeez (he produced Madonna's 'Justify My Love'). Although his insistence on using nothing but unsampled instruments seemed slightly precious, it proved he knew how to play - but by the album *5* he had accepted the inevitable, and at last entered the digital future.

243

"When you're famous people always stare at you. **Sunglasses are a way of keeping your eyes to yourself.**"

Born: 26/5/64 • Recording career: 1989 - present • Sounds: Mama Said 1991, Are You Gonna Go My Way 1993, 5 1998

L7

You messed with L7 at your peril. They had absolutely no compunction about giving not only as good as they got, but better. When the audience at the 1992 Reading Festival gave the band a resoundingly British welcome of lobbed beer glasses, lead singer Donita Sparks riposted by hurling back her own missile, a freshly extracted tampon. The late 1980s offspring of a West Coast posse of forceful female musicians (which also spawned Babes In Toyland and Courtney Love), L7 - their name was from a 1950s sign for 'square' made with the thumb and forefinger of each hand - started off by taking the mickey out of macho metal. But by 1992's *Bricks Are Heavy*, co-produced by Butch Vig (who had just delivered Nirvana's *Nevermind)*, they had forged their own uncompromising in-your-face sound, attacking any targets foolish enough to risk their wrath. Suffice to say that during the rest of the 1990s L7 did not mellow.

"We attract groupies of both sexes. The girls are far more forward in their suggestiveness."

Donita Sparks

Key members: Suzi Gardner 1/8/60, Jennifer Finch 5/8/66, Dee Plakas 9/11/60, Donita Sparks 8/4/63 • Recording career: 1988 - present

Sounds: L7 1988, Bricks Are Heavy 1992, The Beauty Process: Triple Platinum 1997

k.d. lang

Even seriously talented cowgirls get the blues. Kathryn Dawn Lang might have been lower case from an early age, but with 1992's *Ingénue* she announced her arrival in capital letters, moving away from the country sounds she had been raised on in Alberta and had celebrated with her Western swing tribute to Patsy Cline, the Reclines. Her 'torch and twang' approach could certainly cut it in the country world - Shadowland included guest appearances by Loretta Lynn and Brenda Lee - but the Nashville establishment found her a little bit weird, and she outraged the cattle farmers of her homeland by declaring herself pro-animal rights. Then came the change of direction: from the very first track on *Ingénue*, the seductively hypnotic 'Save Me', k.d. put the lang in languorous, and found herself at the forefront of lesbian chic, being shaved by Cindy Crawford on the cover of *Vanity Fair*, and prompting Madonna to remark "Elvis is alive, and she's beautiful".

"I sometimes worry about using my lesbianism as a marketing tool. Let's get over it; it's my art now."

Born: 2/11/61 • Recording career: 1984 - present • Sounds: Shadowland 1988, Ingénue 1992, Drag 1997

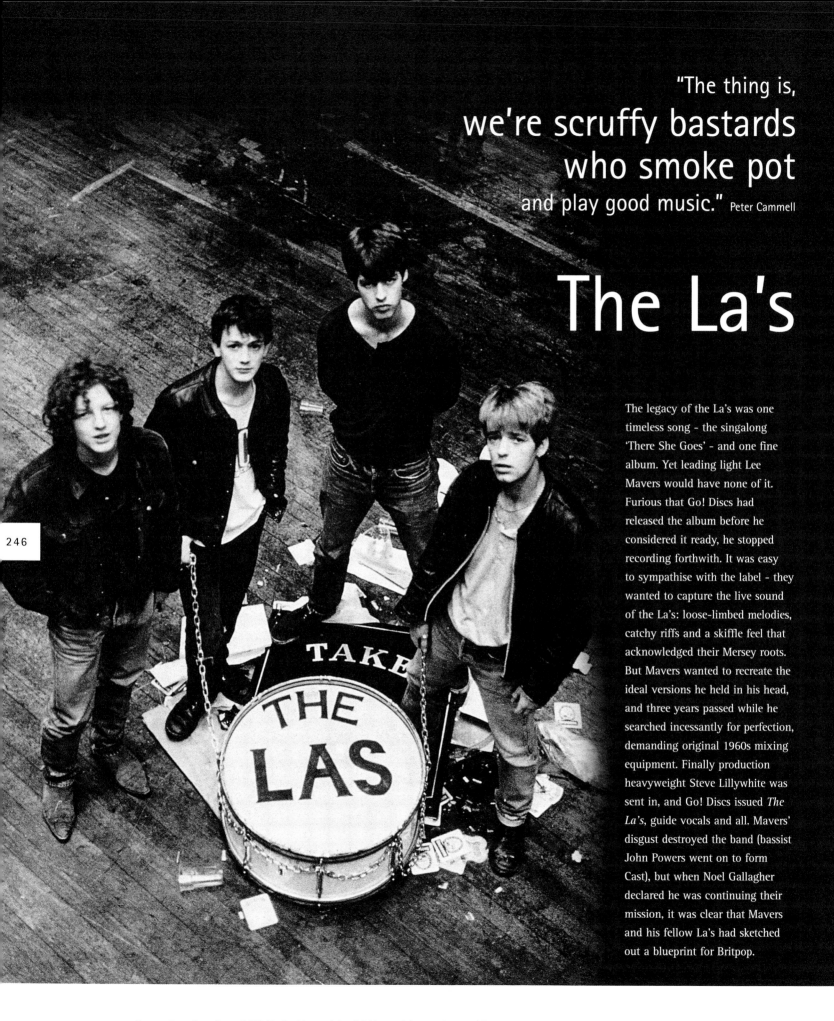

"The thing is,
**we're scruffy bastards
who smoke pot**
and play good music." Peter Cammell

The La's

The legacy of the La's was one timeless song - the singalong 'There She Goes' - and one fine album. Yet leading light Lee Mavers would have none of it. Furious that Go! Discs had released the album before he considered it ready, he stopped recording forthwith. It was easy to sympathise with the label - they wanted to capture the live sound of the La's: loose-limbed melodies, catchy riffs and a skiffle feel that acknowledged their Mersey roots. But Mavers wanted to recreate the ideal versions he held in his head, and three years passed while he searched incessantly for perfection, demanding original 1960s mixing equipment. Finally production heavyweight Steve Lillywhite was sent in, and Go! Discs issued *The La's*, guide vocals and all. Mavers' disgust destroyed the band (bassist John Powers went on to form Cast), but when Noel Gallagher declared he was continuing their mission, it was clear that Mavers and his fellow La's had sketched out a blueprint for Britpop.

Key members: Peter Cammell 30/6/67, Lee Mavers 2/8/62, Neil Mavers 8/7/71, John Power 14/9/67 • Recording career: 1987 - 1990 • Sounds: The La's 1990

"There's only one way a band can function, and that's on the bloody stage." Robert Plant

Led Zeppelin

247

The picture says it all. Led Zeppelin defined once and for all The Rock Band. The late, great John Bonham beating his drums into submission, armed with timpani in case his metronomic, now much sampled, attack was not loud enough ("I like our act to be like a thunderstorm"). John Paul Jones lurking at the back, the master arranger, flitting between bass and his keyboards. Jimmy Page, dubbed "the Paganini of the 70s", squeezing out the bluesiness of the riffs he'd brought to the Yardbirds -

his violin bow trick only an occasional party piece. And Robert Plant, chest puffed, leonine locks flapping, cocksure. They even had the quintessential promoter-eating manager, Peter Grant. Throw in some salacious tour tales involving groupies and members of the fish family, and the image is complete. And yet, never forget the other side: their gentle, mystical, pastoral moments. As Plant declared, "I still enjoy Fairport Convention. The only heavy band I really dig is the Zeppelin".

Key members: John Bonham 31/5/48 (died 25/9/80), John Paul Jones 3/6/46, Jimmy Page 9/1/44, Robert Plant 20/8/48 • Recording career: 1969 - 1979

Sounds: Led Zeppelin II 1969, Led Zeppelin IV (Untitled) 1971, Physical Graffiti 1975

Leftfield

"In England it's possible to sell a lot of records and maintain your credibility. You just have to make music that **keeps you credible.**"

Neil Barnes

Both founders of Leftfield had been drummers, so it is little surprise that their music was an intoxicating rhythm machine. But this was not inhuman mechanical house, rather a new variant with room for a slower dub bass, and the spacey effects that suggested Bleep and Booster had decided to go clubbing. Leftfield were never prolific, but their down time was well spent, selecting a catholic selection of vocalists to override their beats. 'Original' featured indie icon Toni Halliday, Earl Sixteen appeared on 'Release The Pressure' and acquaintance John Lydon added some bite to 1993's inflammatory 'Open Up'. Lydon's snarling chant of 'Burn Hollywood burn!' coincided uncannily with fires sweeping through LA's luxury suburbs. Turning down most offers for re-mixing - other than 'Jump They Say' for David Bowie - the duo left their mark instead on the classic Guinness 'surfing horses' ad and some cult-to-mainstream movies, including *Shallow Grave*, *Trainspotting*, *Go* and *The Beach*.

Key members: Neil Barnes, Paul Daley • Recording career: 1990 - present • Sounds: Leftism 1995, Rhythm And Stealth 1999

It was a shame about Evan. When the chief Lemonhead bounced out on stage in a natty floral dress at Glastonbury 1995 - just the ten hours late - the audience were not best pleased. Seasoned Evan-watchers were also concerned, not because of the cross-dressing, but because he seemed on the verge of losing it big time. A decade earlier, he'd formed Lemonheads with Ben Deily as a punk band with a dark side (they recorded a Charles Manson song) but a later cover of Suzanne Vega's 'Luka' indicated a move towards melody. A rollicking 'Mrs Robinson' - reworked for a 25th anniversary release of *The Graduate* - propelled the band and Dando to major media coverage, and 1992's *It's A Shame About Ray*, full of propulsive two-minute nuggets, duly benefited. Yet Dando was now the only constant, Deily long gone, and the slacker's pin-up felt the pressure. Mixed-up, narcotically challenged, by 1996 the Lemonheads were in limbo.

"Therapy is an American affliction.

It doesn't even work. I already knew what I needed - a cleaning lady."

Evan Dando

Lemonheads

Key member: Evan Dando 4/2/67 • Recording career: 1986 - 1996 • Sounds: Lick 1989, It's A Shame About Ray 1992, Come On Feel The Lemonheads 1993

John Lennon

"I hate the thought of being famous forever."

When John Lennon was felled by Mark Chapman, he was clutching a tape in his hand - Yoko Ono's 'Walking On Thin Ice'. For the last twelve years of his life she had been a constant companion (apart from one brief split when he went AWOL in LA), despite being reviled as the Oriental demon who broke up the beloved Fab Four - "I was a scapegoat for other things," was her view. An established performance artist when they first met - she handed him a card that simply said "Breathe" - she stuck by him as he stripped away the Scouse banter to reveal a complex Everyman: sad anger towards Paul on 'How Do You Sleep?', the visceral pain of 'Mother', the parental love of 'Beautiful Boy'. Although many of his 1970s songs seemed like simplistic sloganeering, their power has grown with time. Lennon was once asked what he and Yoko would be doing 'When They Were 64'. "We're a nice old couple," he replied, "living off the coast of Ireland, looking at our scrapbook of madness." Just imagine.

Born: 9/10/40 (died 8/12/80) • Recording career (solo): 1968 - 1980 • Sounds: Plastic Ono Band 1970, Imagine 1971, Rock'n'Roll 1975

Levellers

If the Levellers didn't choose to be the figureheads of a raggle-taggle collection of eco-warriors, travellers, crusties and the generally disaffected, they found themselves quickly thrust into the role. They were not the only act to drum up folk-punk - the Pogues had been there, done that - or even revive the spirit of Puritan radicals - the New Model Army got there first - but they emerged at a time when the Pogues were in a decline and the music media's attention was concentrating on Manchester. The Brighton band were able, on their own terms, to build a loyal live following that later translated into both album and single sales. This was due not least to the support of those wannabe radicals (aka students) who found the band's anti-establishment call to arms attractive, but could also bop to their music, played at a rattling pace, with layers of violin, mandolin and the occasional didgeridoo.

"We're not preachers, and we're not leaders. Our fans see us as people who are saying exactly what they'd like to say in our position." Simon Friend

Key members: Mark Chadwick 23/6/63, Jeremy Cunningham 2/6/65, Simon Friend 17/5/67, Charlie Heather 2/2/64, Jon Sevink 15/5/65 • Recording career: 1989 - present

Sounds: Levelling The Land 1991, Zeitgeist 1995, Mouth To Mouth 1997

You can't keep a good dog down. Jerry Lee Lewis survived his self-destructive rock'n'roll lifestyle longer than anyone dared hope, creating along the way a persona larger than life, part preacher, part madman (his high school nickname was 'Killer') and part Liberace. A cousin of Jimmy Swaggart, Lewis carried a touch of religious fervour to the stage, breaking on the scene in his early twenties with two monster hits that remain the basis of his success and his reputation. 'Whole Lotta Shakin' Goin' On' and 'Great Balls Of Fire' featured his rowdy piano style, left hand driving the boogie, right hand hammering like a train. Almost immediately, Jerry Lee hit the buffers hard, with revelations that he'd married his 13-year-old cousin. For a decade or more Bible Belt disapproval put him in the sidings, but he kept on going despite the untimely deaths of two wives and two sons. Throughout everything that fate threw at him the Killer's spirit remained undimmed.

252

Jerry Lee Lewis

"I was a kid.

I didn't really know what was going on.

Probably I still don't."

Born: 29/9/35 • Recording career: 1956 - present • Sounds: Jerry Lee Lewis 1957, Great Balls Of Fire! 1964, Live At The Star Club, Hamburg 1965

Since the 1980s rap acts like Public Enemy and Run-D.M.C. had absorbed the backbeats and back catalogue of Led Zeppelin and Aerosmith. Limp Bizkit just let the influences flow the other way, creating their own rapcore hybrid of metal guitar (from Wes Borland) and phat turntable scratching (D.J. Lethal). From Jacksonville, Florida, they owed little to the town's Southern rock tradition of .38 Special and Lynyrd Skynyrd. It was Korn, a band much more to their liking, who took a shine to them and passed a Bizkit demo back to their own producer: bingo. Frontman Fred Durst knew how to act the obnoxious, lippy, dumb brat, but - of course - he was way smarter than that, and extremely funny, especially on the brilliant 'Nookie'. By 2000, they were landing mainstream gigs like the theme for the *M:I-2* movie and their vision of "a fucked-up world" on the smirkingly-titled *Chocolate St*rfish* album was shifting a million copies in one week - yes, sirree.

253

Limp Bizkit

You're seeing black people at metal shows and white people at hip-hop shows.
Everything's starting to melt together." Fred Durst

Key members: Wes Borland, Fred Durst, D.J. Lethal (Leor DiMant), John Otto, Sam Rivers

Recording career: 1997 - present • **Sounds:** Three Dollar Bill, Yall$ 1997, Significant Other 1999, Chocolate St*rfish And The Hot Dog Flavored Water 2000

When Lowell George's death, from a heart attack aged 34, effectively marked the end of Little Feat, it seemed reasonable to conclude that without him the band was nothing. Yet one reason they had become such a critical favourite was the way George's bluesy voice and mellow licks meshed seamlessly with the skills of the other musicians. They mixed a rack of Southern music influences - from blues to rockabilly, gospel to Memphis funk - into a tasty *Dixie Chicken* stew.

In the early 1970s their albums garnered good reviews though low sales, but some serious touring turned things round by the release of their 1974 classic *Feats Don't Fail Me Now*. Guitarist Paul Barrère and keyboardist Bill Payne's influence subsequently grew, causing tensions with Lowell George - and they split just before his death. The band did reform, but they sorely missed George, his divine slide guitar and the exquisitely yearning vocals of 'Long Distance Love'.

Little Feat

"I think of all those **pop groups** making money every night, and I couldn't do that. **I wouldn't last a week."** Lowell George

Key members: Paul Barrère 3/7/48, Sam Clayton, Lowell George 13/4/45 (died 29/6/79), Ken Gradney, Richie Hayward, Bill Payne 12/3/48
Recording career: 1970 - 1979 & 1988 - present • Sounds: Dixie Chicken 1973, Feats Don't Fail Me Now 1974, The Last Record Album 1975

Little Richard

"I'm the innovator.
I'm the emancipator.
I'm the originator.
I'm the architect
of rock'n'roll."

On 14th September 1955 a not
particularly successful singer,
Richard Penniman, was sent to
New Orleans by his new label
Specialty Records. Working
with producer Robert 'Bumps'
Blackwell, Richard was just not
delivering, the magic wasn't
happening. During a break, he
suggested trying a raunchy
number called 'Tutti Frutti', and -
with the lyrics bowdlerised by
local writer Dorothy La Bostie -
just went bonkers: whooping,
hollering, boogie woogie gone
mad. And the world was exposed
to the full-on peacock persona of
Little Richard, the Madame
Pompadour of rock'n'roll, camp
before it became fashionable.
Cavorting on through 'Rip It Up',
'Long Tall Sally' and 'Good Golly,
Miss Molly', the bandwagon
screeched to a halt in 1957 when
Little Richard decided to enrol in
theological college. Returning after
some gospel-only years, he toured
with the Beatles, but now seemed
quaintly dated, and he had to
settle for a long-running role as
a slightly self-parodying icon.

Born: Richard Penniman 5/12/32 • **Recording career:** 1951 - present • **Sounds:** Here's Little Richard 1957, The Fabulous Little Richard 1958, Lifetime Friend 1986

Living Colour

Maybe in the end the politics got in the way. Living Colour used their music to articulate the concerns of the Black Rock Coalition, which guitarist Vernon Reid co-founded. But the music, with or without a message, was storming, able to compete with any hard rock band - Reid's guitar always imaginatively scintillating - but happy to P-Funk it up as well. Mick Jagger was impressed enough with their crossover energy to invite them to participate on his 1987 solo album *Primitive Cool*, and then to oversee demos that helped them sign to Epic. *Vivid* was a confident debut, including the Jagger-produced, velvet-gloved 'Glamour Boys'. Guests on the follow-up included Little Richard (who rapped over 'Elvis Is Dead'), Santana and Queen Latifah, and 1993's *Stain* was powerful and heavy - but then the band lost their way between too many ideas, styles and intentions. As they folded in 1995, Reid simply observed it was "not fun anymore".

"I think that what we're trying to be is individuals in a system that doesn't promote individuality. So in that respect, yes, we're subversive.

Corey Glover

Key members: William Calhoun 22/7/64, Corey Glover 6/11/64, Vernon Reid 22/8/58, Muzz Skillings 6/1/60 • Recording career: 1988 - 1994 • Sounds: Vivid 1988, Time's Up 1990, Stain 1993

He had a fabulous guitar technique, but Nils Lofgren never quite made it in his own right, or under his own steam. Lofgren's band Grin was playing in the Washington DC area when Neil Young came across him, and at 17 there was Nils playing piano - and guitar, though he was uncredited - on Young's *After The Goldrush*. Grin faded as commercial success eluded them, and Lofgren was touted as a possible replacement for Mick Taylor in the Stones (though the same was true of virtually every guitarist of note). His 1975 solo album, *Nils Lofgren*, was well received, but the problem was that his facility to play in any style didn't create an identifiable musical personality, and his light voice just didn't excite. He was the perfect sideman, joining Bruce Springsteen's E Street Band in 1984 for an eight-year stint. A solo breakthrough remained elusive; in 1999 he was back on tour with the Boss.

"Live audiences don't care what position your record is on the charts. **I'm not a hot young band,** but I shine in that environment."

Nils Lofgren

257

Born: 21/6/52 • Recording career: 1970 – present • Sounds: Nils Lofgren 1975, Cry Tough 1976, Acoustic Live 1997

Los Lobos

The success of 'La Bamba' was a double-edged sword. Taken from the soundtrack of the Ritchie Valens bio-pic, the single, which sprang Los Lobos into the limelight, suggested they might be just another club covers band. They had been, way back when, but had decided to investigate their Chicano heritage, developing a new genre of Tex-Mex music: if they didn't invent it, they were its most high-profile providers. An early acoustic set, opening - bizarrely - for John Lydon's PiL ended up with the audience pelting them with bottles, but they persevered, garnering rave reviews for 1984's *How Will The Wolf Survive?*, a seductive conjunto fusion of zydeco, norteño, ballads and down-the-line rock'n'roll. Once 'La Bamba' had charted Los Lobos felt the need to send out a clear message to their compadres that they had not sold out; their next album turned out to be a Hispanic folk exploration entitled *La Pistola Y El Corazón*. Home was definitely where their heart was.

"We hung out at Cesar's house or my mother's house and we'd play Mexican songs all day long, just for the fun of it." Luis Perez

Key members: Steve Berlin 14/9/55, David Hidalgo 6/10/54, Conrad Lozano 21/3/51, Luis Perez 29/1/53, Cesar Rosas 26/9/54 • Recording career: 1978 – present

Sounds: How Will The Wolf Survive? 1984, La Pistola Y El Corazón 1988, Kiko 1992

Every self-respecting rock cognoscente should own Love's *Forever Changes*, so the music gurus tell us incessantly. Nonetheless the album, released in 1967, remains a cult classic, representing Arthur Lee's Love as the hippie band *par excellence*. The opening is all string and brass orchestration, very Herb Alpert, but as the tracks progress you realise this is a serious trip. By the time 'Live And Let Live' delivers the immortal lyric "Oh, the snot has caked against my pants", you know you've arrived, somewhere. Love were unable to build on *Forever Changes* though, since Arthur Lee broke up the band, reforming it unsuccessfully around himself before becoming a legendary recluse (a surfeit of acid was the rumour). In the 1980s he found himself acclaimed by the Damned, Echo And The Bunnymen and Teardrop Explodes, and in the 90s by the High Llamas and New York punksters Das Damen, both of whom backed him on a romp through the classics.

"I've always been in a group, everyone on earth is in a group." Arthur Lee

Love

Key members: John Echols 1945, Ken Forssi 1943 (died 5/1/98), Arthur Lee 7/3/45, Bryan MacLean 25/9/46 (died 25/12/98), Michael Stuart

Recording career: 1966 - 1971 & 1975 • Sounds: Da Capo 1967, Forever Changes 1967, False Start 1970

"No record company was interested because we didn't sound like anything that had come before, nor did we sing with Liverpudlian accents." John Sebastian

Originally a duo formed by John Sebastian and Zal Yanovsky after both had been in the Mugwumps alongside Cass Elliot and Denny Doherty (of the future Mamas and The Papas), Manhattan's Lovin' Spoonful drew on the same strains of jug band, folk and blues - which they called 'good time music' - that had engendered Jefferson Airplane on the West Coast. Sebastian's autoharp introduced their first single 'Do You Believe In Magic.' and the spell was cast, fans and critics entranced as they

accumulated seven US Top Ten singles in 1965-67, sparkling through 'Daydream', 'Rain On The Roof' and their chart-topper 'Summer In The City'. The bubble eventually burst, when Canadian-born Yanovsky was apparently forced to inform after a drug bust or risk deportation; the unpleasantness spoiled the party. After they dispersed John Sebastian enjoyed the highest profile, appearing suitably stoned in the *Woodstock* movie, but never quite matching his songwriting feats with the Spoonful.

The Lovin' Spoonful

Key members: Steve Boone 23/9/43, Joe Butler 19/1/43, John Sebastian 17/3/44, Zal Yanovsky 19/12/46 • Recording career: 1965 - 1969

Sounds: Do You Believe In Magic 1965, Daydream 1966, Hums Of The Lovin' Spoonful 1966

Nick Lowe

Older and wiser, Nick Lowe could look back on a career of variety and craftsmanship, but it was Curtis Stigers' cover of '(What's So Funny 'Bout) Love, Peace And Understanding' on the movie soundtrack of *The Bodyguard* that belatedly brought him major financial rewards. Lowe originally popped up in Brinsley Schwarz, the country/pub rock outfit over-hyped by backers who flew a pack of journalists to see their 1970 US debut at Fillmore East, a monumental PR disaster. Lowe, and the band, survived, and after the Brinsleys split in 1975, he honed his production skills with the Kursaal Flyers, Dr Feelgood and Elvis Costello. His own musical activities continued with Dave Edmunds in Rockpile, and solo hits including '(I Love The Sound Of) Breaking Glass' and 'Cruel To Be Kind'. But a troubled decade in the 1980s, including alcohol problems, depression and an eventual split with wife Carlene Carter, strained even this most laconic observer of life's foibles.

"I only started playing bass so I could get into a group.

I couldn't play drums, I couldn't dance, I wasn't a lead singer."

Born: 25/3/49 • Recording career: 1976 - present • Sounds: Jesus Of Cool (US title: Pure Pop For Now People) 1978, Labour Of Lust 1979, The Impossible Bird 1994

"I plan to stick around and watch my baby girl grow up.
I also plan to collect
for the last ten years of self-abuse." Ronnie Van Zant

Lynyrd Skynyrd

Hey teacher, leave those kids alone... Lynyrd Skynyrd's name immortalised high school sports master Leonard Skinner, notorious for his objections to long hair. He would scarcely have approved of the band's later reputation for boozy punch-ups at live shows which featured a three guitar line-up and two classic Southern boogie songs: 'Sweet Home Alabama' and 'Free Bird', the latter a tribute to Duane Allman, their much-missed Confederate confrère. Yet, like the Allmans,

Skynyrd's progress was cruelly halted by a fatal accident, when a plane crash in October 1977 killed singer Ronnie Van Zant, guitarist Steve Gaines and Gaines' sister Cassie (a backing vocalist). Portentous signs were retrospectively read into the artwork of *Street Survivors*, the album released days earlier, which had a cover image showing fire flickering around the group's heads. Bereft, the remaining members disbanded, but reunited ten years later to preserve the memories.

Key members: Allen Collins 19/7/52 (died 23/1/90), Steve Gaines 14/9/49 (died 20/10/77), Billy Powell 3/6/52, Artimus Pyke 15/7/48, Gary Rossington 4/12/51, Ronnie Van Zant 15/1/48 (died 20/10/77), Leon Wilkeson 2/4/52 • Recording career: 1971 - 1977 & 1988 - present • Sounds: Pronounced Leh-Nerd Skin-Nerd 1973, Second Helping 1974, Street Survivors 1977

"Jumping up and down and the Nutty Dance

is what got us where we are today." Suggs

263

Madness

At the frontline of fun, Madness was an exuberant breath of fresh air in the early 1980s, with breezy singles featuring infectious sax and Suggs' affable vocals. The septet's roots and intentions were clear from their debut single - 'The Prince', dedicated to ska pioneer Prince Buster, whose 1960s hit 'Madness' provided their name - but it was the next release, 'One Step Beyond', that contained the formula which would keep the UK cheerfully amused through 'Baggy Trousers' and 'It Must Be Love'.

Subsequently, with 'Our House' and 'House Of Fun', they proved they could write narrative songs about ordinary people comparable to anything by Ray Davies. Though the 1983 departure of Mike Barson - a significant source of Madness's musical ideas - marked the decline of their lunar glory, a rapturously received greatest hits release in 1992 instigated a string of Madstock events in London's Finsbury Park, which demonstrated the deep and durable affection the group had inspired.

Key members: Mike Barson 21/4/58, Mark Bedford 24/8/61, Chris Foreman 8/8/58, Graham 'Suggs' McPherson 13/1/61, Chas Smash 14/1/59, Lee Thompson 5/10/57, Dan Woodgate 19/10/60

Recording career: 1979 - present • **Sounds:** One Step Beyond 1979, Madness Present The Rise And Fall 1982, Madstock! 1992

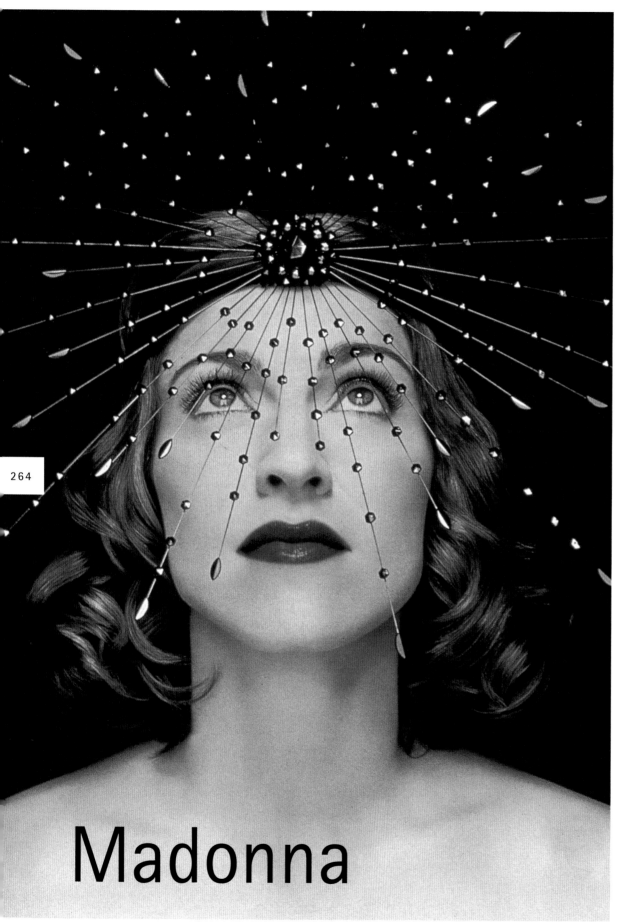

Madonna

"I'm tough and I'm ambitious and I know exactly what I want. If that makes me a bitch – okay."

Ms Ciccone's physical appearance was ever-changing - *'Madonna è mobile'* - but her desire for success remained constant and rigorous: "I think most people who meet me know that's the kind of person I am". Yet when she was still just another wannabe, her first singles were seen as too calculated. It took 1984's 'Like A Virgin' and its communion-slut imagery - equally calculated, but causing the desired controversy - for Madonna's sorcery to begin bewitching the media. She had good back-up, but the instincts - and importantly the songs - were all hers: as William Orbit later described it, "she pushes all the buttons". By the end of the 1980s, she was outshining even Michael Jackson, but her surefooted routine stuttered slightly around 1992 when the blonde ambition started showing its roots. Though *Erotica* and her *Sex* book sold massively, there was previous little mystique to reveal. Madge, ever alert and adaptable, realised the danger and summoned up her new persona - mature, maternal and married... and even sexier.

Born: Madonna Ciccone 16/8/58 • Recording career: 1982 - present • Sounds: Like A Virgin 1984, Like A Prayer 1989, Ray Of Light 1998

"Very, very few musicians have the courage and conviction to play from their hearts."

Christian Vander

Magma

From the French underground there bubbled up Magma, the brainchild of Christian Vander, a drummer/vocalist deeply influenced by the music of John Coltrane and possessed with a vision of a planet where earthly problems had been solved. He called this planet 'Kobaïa' - its language, invented by Vander, supplied the 'words' for Magma's trancelike tracks, which used repetitive rhythms underlying jazz fusion brass and Fender Rhodes piano. Magma's early albums described a flight to Kobaïa. The original plan was that, *Star Wars* style, there should be multiple episodes, but the project foundered through constant personnel changes; at times Vander's cohorts included violinist Didier Lockwood and, for one US tour, the Brecker Brothers. Into the 1980s Magma hunkered down and survived through bootleg tapes and loyal Magmoid fans (British snooker legend Steve Davis was one - he promoted the band at a London performance in 1988). Over thirty years after its launch Magma's interstellar voyage was still ongoing...

Key member: Christian Vander • Recording career: 1970 - 1984 & 1996 - present • Sounds: Magma 1970, Mekanïk Destructïw Kommandöh 1973, Live 1975

The Mahavishnu Orchestra

"The joy of music is like the joy a runner gets from running - **and musically, I'm running."** John McLaughlin

Jazz and rock were often uneasy bedfellows, four-square rock musicians unable to cope with the shifting time signatures of jazz, and PA system volumes squeezing out its subtlety. That was the theory: John McLaughlin went some way to getting the balance right with his Mahavishnu Orchestra. After an R'n'B apprenticeship with Georgie Fame and Gary Bond, McLaughlin was introduced, via jazz drummer Tony Williams, to Miles Davis, who used McLaughlin's blues guitar on his influential 1970 fusion album *Bitches Brew*. Out of that experience McLaughlin founded the Orchestra, blending not only jazz and rock but the traditions of orient and occident. He was a follower of Sri Chimnoy, who had given him the name Mahavishnu, and there was a unfussy approach to their presentation - McLaughlin in white, with trademark double-necked guitar, backed by top-flight technicians, including drummer Billy Cobham, violinist Jean-Luc Ponty and organist Jan Hammer (the *Miami Vice* theme man).

Key members: Billy Cobham 16/5/44, Jan Hammer 17/4/48, Mike Laird 5/2/41, John McLaughlin 4/1/42, Jean-Luc Ponty 29/9/42, Narada Michael Walden 23/4/52

Recording career: 1972 - 1976 & 1984 - 1987 • Sounds: The Inner Mounting Flame 1972, Birds Of Fire 1973, Between Nothingness And Eternity 1973

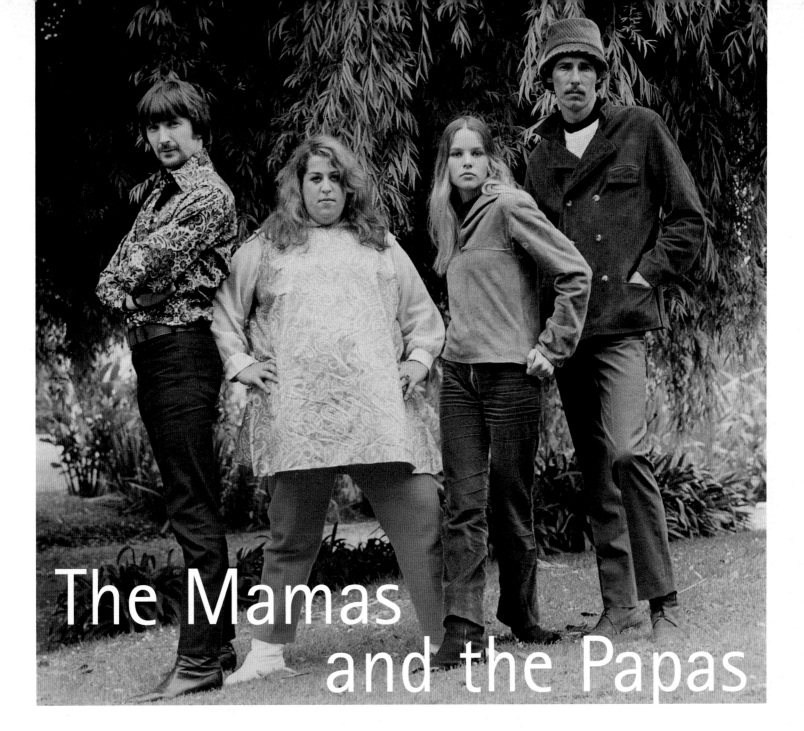

The Mamas and the Papas

For a potted history of the Mamas and the Papas, look and listen no further than 'Creeque Alley', their gently self-deprecating biographical song ("and no one's getting fat - except Mama Cass!"). The four met in the Virgin Islands, where Cass Elliot and Denny Doherty joined forces with John Phillips and his wife Michelle. The lanky John was the songwriting force behind their success, creating, with producer Lou Adler, tight-harmonied advertisements for the appeal of the West Coast:

'California Dreamin'' was their quintessential evocation of sunshine and escape. Phillips also composed the hippie theme tune 'San Francisco' for Scott McKenzie, but the peace and love vibe did not apply to the group. The Phillips' marriage foundered (daughter Chynna later surfaced as one third of Wilson Phillips), and the group split in 1968: after a tired reunion, which failed to revive the old spark, the most promising solo career, Mama Cass's, was cut short by her early death in 1974.

"As rock stars we witnessed the flowering of a new consciousness founded on sex, drugs, rock and the renunciation of Americana." John Phillips

Key members: Denny Doherty 29/11/41, Cass Elliot 19/9/41 (died 29/7/74), Michelle Gilliam Phillips 6/4/44, John Phillips 30/8/35 (died 18/3/01) • Recording career: 1965 - 1968 & 1971

Sounds: If You Can Believe Your Eyes And Ears 1966, Deliver 1967, The Papas And The Mamas 1968

Man

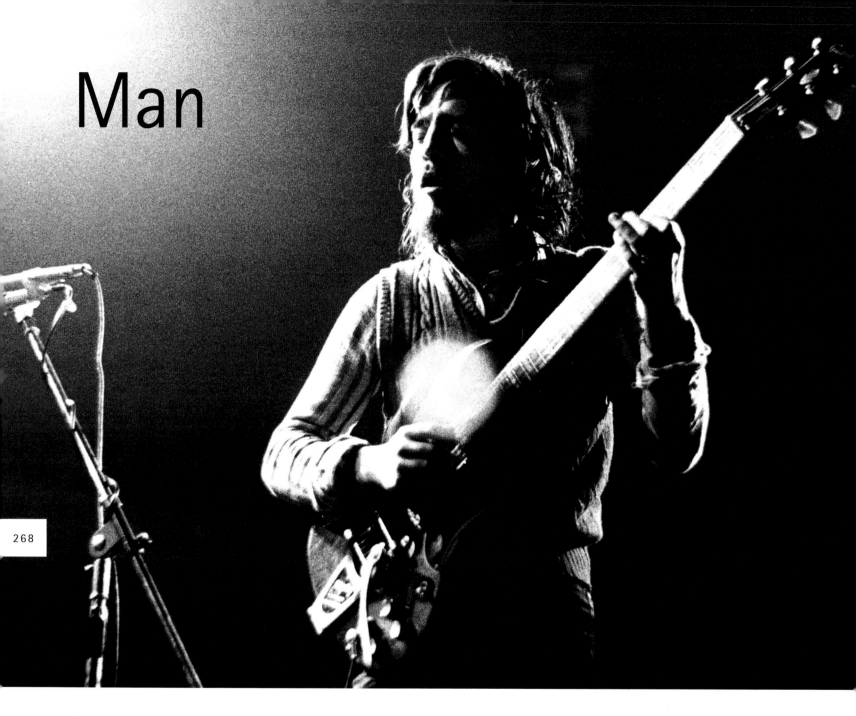

Many were called and many indeed got up to perform with Man: their labyrinthine family tree was of the monkey puzzle variety. Like the West Coast bands they so admired, Man was a free-form fraternity of like-minded musicians, bonded by copious amounts of dope... but also their Welsh nationality. Forget the Fillmore, Man were most at home in the Padget Rooms, Penarth, the venue for a once rare live album. On this and 1972's *Be Good To Yourself* the band provided music for dopeheads

everywhere - 'C'Mon', driven by Micky Jones' choogling guitar riff, and 'Bananas', its succinct opening verse ("I like to eat bananas, 'cos they got no bones. I like marijuana, 'cos it gets me stoned") introducing yet another lengthy guitar work-out. Chops and changes continued - Quicksilver Messenger Service's guitarist John Cippolina joined for a brief, though disappointing, collaboration and drummer Terry Williams left for Dire Straits - but the Manband happily kept on crinting.

"Throughout our set our audience handed us joint after joint.
They rarely applauded -
they were too stoned to move their arms." Deke Leonard

Key members: Martin Ace 31/12/45, Mickey Jones 7/6/46, Deke Leonard 18/12/44, Terry Williams 11/1/48 • **Recording career:** 1968 - 1976 & 1992 - present

Sounds: Live At The Padget Rooms Penarth 1972, Be Good To Yourself At Least Once A Day 1972, Slow Motion 1976

When Richey Edwards disappeared, in February 1995, fans worried for his safety. When his car was found abandoned near the Severn road bridge, they feared the worst, both for him and the future of the Manic Street Preachers - at the time, pretty much the first band to make a mark out of Wales since the days of Man. After all, Edwards had been the one who, challenged by a doubting journalist to prove the sincerity of their punk attitudes, had responded by carving the slogan '4 REAL' into his forearm (although he later described the gesture as "sad"). And yet the remaining trio - there was no question of replacing Edwards - not only continued, but drew fresh strength from his memory, turning the commercial appeal they had always managed - 'You Love Us', 'Suicide Is Painless' - into massive mainstream success, from 'A Design For Life' to 'If You Tolerate This...', adult gems of chart genuineness.

"We always set out to make records about ideas and attitudes that are important and real: the band we never had when we were growing up." Richey Edwards

Manic Street Preachers

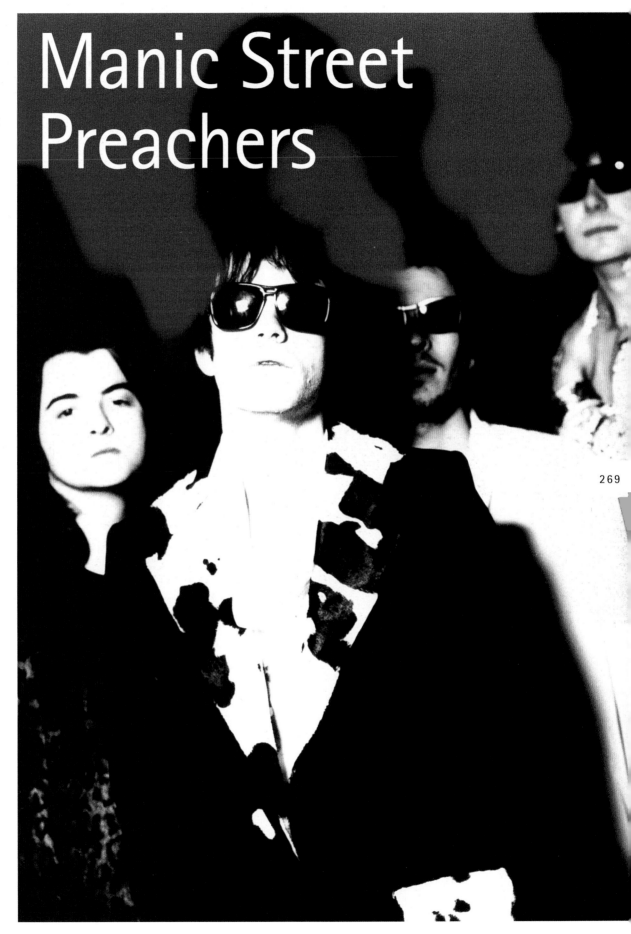

269

Key members: James Dean Bradfield 21/2/69, Richey Edwards 22/12/67, Sean Moore 30/7/70, Nicky Wire 20/1/69 • Recording career: 1989 - present

Sounds: Generation Terrorists 1992, The Holy Bible 1994, Everything Must Go 1996

Aimee Mann

Her solo debut was stunning: from the world-weary 'I Should've Known' onwards, it unveiled a batch of wickedly crafted songs with literate lyrics, black humour and punch in the delivery. Aimee Mann's previous incarnation had been as the lead vocalist in 'Til Tuesday, tipped to follow Cars as a Boston new-wave success after their 1985 single 'Voices Carry'. But label wrangles caused a five-year delay before her first solo album, *Whatever* (the catchphrase of the 1990s, according to Mann). With echoes of Squeeze, Badfinger and the Byrds - Roger McGuinn added his distinctive 12-string to 'Fifty Years After The Fair' - its critical bouquets were flourishing until record company Imago went belly-up. The title of the follow-up release, *I'm With Stupid*, was a typically sardonic comment on failed romantic and commercial relationships. Yet more business hassles followed, and it was film director Paul Thomas Anderson who eventually provided her with an outlet as her songs peppered his 1999 movie *Magnolia*.

"I don't think songwriters listen to themselves talk. They fall into rock clichés. That's what I try to avoid."

Born: 9/8/60 • Recording career: 1993 - present • Sounds: Whatever 1993, I'm With Stupid 1995

Manfred Mann

The band Manfred Mann, which was named after its keyboard-playing leader, seemed set for a pole position in the British beat boom after '5-4-3-2-1' became the theme for *Ready Steady Go!*, the pioneering UK TV chart show. But their two biggest hits that year, 1964, were more out of the doo-wop drawer: 'Doo Wah Diddy Diddy' and 'Sha La La', previously recorded by the Exciters and the Shirelles respectively. Manfred Mann were also fond of Bob Dylan covers, and following some personnel upheavals - harmonica-playing vocalist Paul Jones departed to be replaced by Mike D'Abo, and Jack Bruce briefly held down the bass slot - it was the great man's 'The Mighty Quinn' that provided this edition of the band with a final UK Number One in 1968. Manfred (the man) later returned to create the prog-rock Manfred Mann's Earth Band, best known for yet another cover, this time of Bruce Springsteen's theatrical 'Blinded By The Light'.

"I was trapped in a pop band, and then I was trapped in a kind of jazz thing. The principle here is not to be trapped." Manfred Mann

Key members: Mike Hugg 11/8/42, Paul Jones 24/2/42, Manfred Mann 21/10/40, Tom McGuinness 2/11/41, Mike Vickers 18/4/41 • Recording career: 1963 - 1969

Sounds: The Manfred Mann Album 1964, Soul Of Mann 1967, The Mighty Garvey 1968

"Marilyn Manson is a nightmare made real. We're utterly desensitised to the point where violence is irrelevant."

Marilyn Manson

The deliberate conjunction of a sex symbol's forename and the surname of one of America's most notorious murderers was sufficient warning of the tactics conceived by Brian Warner - Marilyn Manson's alter ego - when he signed to Nothing Records, the label of his influential mentor, Nine Inch Nails' Trent Reznor. Manson's backing band adopted similar pseudonyms, including Madonna Wayne Gacy and Twiggy Ramirez. This was shock rock with a masters degree in marketing: mechanical alternative metal with carefully measured-out doses of provocative behaviour (ripping up the *Book Of Mormon* during a Salt Lake City gig) and album and song titles (*Antichrist Superstar*, 'Cake And Sodomy'). The sound, as a result, was cold and formulaic, but found fertile ground in the adolescent swathes of Middle America and rattled the moral majority. When Manson did try a change of style it failed to work, and for 2000's *Holy Wood* he returned to the trusty formula.

Key member: Brian Warner 5/1/69 • Recording career: 1992 - present • Sounds: Antichrist Superstar 1996, Mechanical Animals 1998, Holy Wood (In The Shadow Of The Valley Of Death) 2000

Bob
Marley

When they flew Bob Marley's
body back to Kingston from
Miami, the boy from Trenchtown
("I've just brought the ghetto
uptown") was about to be given
a state funeral, and his legend
sanctified - a vehicle for many
other people's aspirations.
Producer Coxsone Dodd had first
spotted how Marley and fellow
Wailers Bunny Livingston and
Peter Tosh could convey rude boy
ska to Jamaica's disaffected
youth. Later, after Lee Perry
re-moulded his sound, Island
Records' Chris Blackwell found
what he'd been looking for: a
"rebel-type" reggae artist able to
deliver rock-size sales. 1973's
Catch A Fire, with its Zippo
lighter packaging, intrigued the
music media, and by the time of
'No Woman, No Cry' the other
Wailers were being sidelined,
while Marley headed for global
fame, although he continued to
insist "I'm not a rock star. I'm a
Rastaman". Sad, then, that at the
very time Marley was helping to
introduce reggae to a worldwide
audience, some of the sound
systems back home stopped
playing his music, claiming he
just wasn't tuff enough any more.

273

"Me not of the world, y'know.
Me live in the world but I'm not of the world."

Born: 6/2/45 (died 11/5/81) • Recording career: 1962 - 1980 • Sounds: Catch A Fire 1973, Natty Dread 1974, Exodus 1977

John Martyn

A powerful, effective vocalist - his delivery was cool, but hoarsely emotional - John Martyn was even better noted for his guitar-playing: the use of echo and the attack he brought to his acoustic technique. The Scot began his career as a folk artist, but even on his late-1967 debut, *London Conversation*, there was a jazz lilt - and from the follow-up *The Tumbler* onwards, sax riffs would frequently punctuate his songs of life's bitter-sweet moments. Martyn's own life had its own downs including a drink problem that contributed to the break-up of his marriage, but, with the help of Phil Collins he was able to use music as catharsis on *Grace And Danger*. Eric Clapton was also a supporter - he covered 'May You Never' on *Slowhand* - and Steve Winwood's influence was significant on what some consider to be Martyn's finest set, 1978's *One World*. Certainly it contains some of his most renowned songs, not least the beautiful 'Couldn't Love You More'.

"I love tender players. I just like things tender."

274

Born: 11/9/48 • Recording career: 1967 - present • Sounds: Solid Air 1973, Grace And Danger 1980, And 1996

Massive Attack

"We'd like to balance commercial success with the vibe that we can do what we want." 3-D

In the early 1990s hip hop's obsession with beats per minute was threatening to accelerate out of control. Enter Massive Attack to slow the whole thing down. 3-D, Mushroom and Daddy-G had been core members of Bristol's famed Wild Bunch, the sound system collective which included Nellee Hooper, later of Soul II Soul. With their 1991 debut *Blue Lines*, Massive Attack re-drew the groundplan of dance music: a leisurely, dub-based, pace that got called trip hop, but was more like the groove of summer in the inner city. Vocals were courtesy of Shara Nelson - a long-time associate, her voice was soulfully intense on the richly orchestrated 'Unfinished Sympathy' - reggae artist Horace Andy and a youthful Tricky; Everything But The Girl's Tracey Thorn was a welcome addition on *Protection*. Despite some accusations of stagnation, Massive Attack proved with 1998's chart-topping, award-winning *Mezzanine* that they were still a force to be reckoned with.

Key members: Robert '3-D' Del Naja 1966, Grant 'Daddy-G' Marshall 1959, Andrew 'Mushroom' Vowles 1968, • Recording career: 1988 - present

Sounds: Blue Lines 1991, Protection 1994, Mezzanine 1998

"I came down to London at the beginning of 1963
and we were all blues freaks,
totally obsessive and totally oblivious to whatever else was going on."

John Mayall

Though a versatile performer on guitar, keyboards and harmonica, John Mayall found himself - uncomplainingly - overshadowed by the musicians who passed through his band, the Bluesbreakers. Just as Alexis Korner had nurtured the nascent Stones amongst others, Mayall was like a benevolent housemaster proudly watching his charges head off to conquer the world. In the 1960s his class of protégés were awesome. On guitar: Eric Clapton, Peter Green and Mick Taylor. On bass: Jack Bruce, John McVie and Free's Andy Fraser. Behind the drums: Mick Fleetwood, Aynsley Dunbar and Jon Hiseman. The inclusion of Hiseman, a founder of Colosseum, marked Mayall's shift towards jazz; he later moved geographically to the US, where he went into quiescence. However, 1993's *Wake Up Call* was a proclamation that his roots remained intact, with a hall-of-fame support team including Mavis Staples, Albert Collins and Buddy Guy. But it was a nostalgic retrospective - the heady days of discovery were long gone.

Born: 29/11/33 • Recording career: 1964 - present • Sounds: Bluesbreakers With Eric Clapton 1966, Bare Wires 1968, Wake Up Call 1993

Curtis Mayfield

Already possessing an impressive CV as the songwriting lynch-pin of the Impressions - including 'It's All Right' and 'People Get Ready' - Curtis Mayfield's solo career was launched in 1970. His first album contained the funk classic 'Move On Up', and almost immediately he was approached to score *Superfly*, a film by the son of the director of original blaxploitation movie *Shaft*. The 1972 soundtrack album stood easily in its own right - both the title track and 'Freddie's Dead' were influential masterpieces featuring street-funk grooves, gritty lyrics, scratchy guitar, horns and strings, and Curtis's distinctive falsetto, like a hipper Pop Staples. He only infrequently scaled these towering heights again, but his Buddha-like status was guaranteed. In 1990, Mayfield's life was abruptly changed when a lighting rig collapsed on him, paralysing him from the neck down, and though he produced an album despite this disability, he succumbed to its effects nine years later.

"You had to cross over -

get the white business as well as the black business."

Born: 3/6/42 (died 26/12/99) • Recording career (solo): 1970 - 1996 • Sounds: Curtis 1970, Superfly 1972, Honesty 1982

Mazzy Star

Listening to Mazzy Star was the aural equivalent of a winter's afternoon getting stoned: long, dark and agreeably fuzzy. The doe-eyed waif called Hope Sandoval sang-spoke distinctly indistinct lyrics with the echo unit turned up to full. David Roback finger-picked away, with an occasional flourish of ominous organ. This was 1960s psychedelia re-visited - one of its gloomier inglenooks, where the Doors and the Velvets languished. Roback had emerged from his own Underground, the LA-based Paisley

version, in which his groups Rain Parade and later Opal had formed part of a loose confederation alongside acts like the Bangles and Dream Syndicate; Sandoval meantime had been half of a folk duo. As Mazzy Star they produced a trio of trance-like albums (1993's *So Tonight That I Might See* the most compelling) but gave little away other than obfuscatory answers in rare interviews. After *Among My Swan* in 1996, it was unclear whether another album would emerge from the mists.

"You know, we do spend a lot of time indoors. We appreciate a foggy morning or a rainy day." David Roback

Key members: David Roback, Hope Sandoval • Recording career: 1990 - present • Sounds: She Hangs Brightly 1990, So Tonight That I Might See 1993, Among My Swan 1996

In 1968, when it seemed as if the entire music business was preaching peace, love and harmony, the Motor City Five brought an alternative message: of dope and revolution. Their political bent came from manager John Sinclair, who introduced the band to the radical White Panther Party - and took them to Chicago to perform amid the troubles at the 1968 Democratic Convention. Sinclair also familiarised them with experimental jazz, which they added to high-energy, power-assisted rock to create a brash, chaotic, sound. The 1969 album, *Kick Out The Jams*, recorded live at Detroit's Grande Ballroom, caught MC5 roaring forth, and included an exultant cry of 'motherfuckers', which led to distribution and record label bust-ups. Sales of this and the Jon Landau-produced follow-up *Back In The USA* suggested, however, that the revolution was a little way off.

The next generation more widely appreciated their pre-punk direction - Fred 'Sonic' Smith later married the new-wave icon, his namesake Patti.

"If you take everything in the universe and break it down to a common denominator, all you've got is energy. That's the essence of the urban sound." Wayne Kramer

MC5

Key members: Michael Davis, Wayne Kramer 30/4/48, Fred 'Sonic' Smith 11/4/48 (died 4/11/94), Dennis Thompson Rob Tyner 12/12/44 (died 17/9/91)

Recording career: 1966 - 1971 • **Sounds:** Kick Out The Jams 1969, Back In The USA 1970, High Time 1971

Paul McCartney

A fortnight before the release of *Let It Be*, Paul McCartney's first solo recording was on sale. It seemed indecently hasty, and Macca suffered his share of brickbats, John Lennon remarking "I think he wanted to show he *was* the Beatles". Early albums - with a lo-fi, unpolished feel - were slammed, but revisionism has given them a second chance, and granted McCartney some credit for being the only Beatle to front a regular, working band. Wings gelled under difficult circumstances while recording 1973's *Band On The Run* in Lagos, as Paul, wife Linda and former Moody Blue Denny Laine pulled out all the stops, especially on the heady 'Jet'. If later sentimental releases like 'Mull Of Kintyre' and the duets with Stevie Wonder and Michael Jackson highlighted the absence of Lennon's acerbic input, McCartney survived the flops with his melodic invention, and his humanity, intact. "I don't mind falling in the middle," was his stance. "My dad's advice: 'Moderation, son'."

"I'm surprised at how many ambitions I've got.
And I still want to write one really good song."

Born: 18/6/42 • Recording career (solo): 1970 - present • Sounds: Ram 1971, Band On The Run 1973, Flowers In The Dirt 1989

Meat Loaf

A rock-operatic setting was the perfect backdrop for the Pavarotti-and-then-some physical presence of Marvin Lee Aday, known as Meat Loaf since his schooldays. After appearing in productions of *Hair* and *The Rocky Horror Show*, he met Jim Steinman, a composer who had stage musical aspirations, and for Steinman the singer proved to be an ideal muse. Together they conceived the grandiose package of 1977's *Bat Out Of Hell*, including the verbose, melodramatic but very singable 'You Took The Words Right Out Of My Mouth', and the album lumbered laboriously but relentlessly towards massive long-term sales. When the creative pair parted company in the mid-1980s, most people assumed that *Bat* was a time capsule of pomp, but in 1993 Meat Loaf (who'd maintained a healthy live following) rejoined forces with Steinman to produce the shamelessly, proudly cloned *Bat Out Of Hell II*. They'd do anything for our lucre, it seemed. But guess what? It worked.

"There's images I adopt for the live show - King Kong, Godzilla, the Incredible Hulk. I always said if I took the person off stage he would kill somebody!"

281

Born: Marvin Aday 27/9/51 • Recording career: 1971 - present • Sounds: Bat Out Of Hell 1977, Meat Loaf Live 1987, Bat Out Of Hell II 1993

Mekons

"We were more visible on a major label, but unhappier. Now we're free from that situation." Jon Langford

Like fellow Leeds art students the Gang of Four, Jon Langford and Tom Greenhalgh emerged in the wake of the Sex Pistols - whose gig in the city had inspired them to have a bash - and with a committed left-wing agenda. However, 'Never Been In A Riot', their debut single, gave a strong clue that idealism would be offset by ironic humour. This first phase ended in the early 1980s, but by 1984 the Mekons were back with a new line-up, including former Graham Parker and the Rumour drummer Steve Goulding, and an eclectic sound. *Fear And Whiskey* was full of folk and country (and Susie Honeyman's fiddle playing), but new musical influences never diluted their commitment to political causes - 1989's back-to-basics *Rock N' Roll* was still feisty, still passionate, still radical. Many of the Mekons re-located to Chicago in the early 1990s, but these most indestructible of punk survivors refused to disintegrate.

Key members: Steve Goulding 16/6/54, Tom Greenhalgh 4/11/56, Susie Honeyman, Jon Langford 11/10/57, Sally Timms • Recording career: 1978 - present

Sounds: Fear And Whiskey 1985, Mekons Rock N' Roll 1989, I Love Mekons 1993

The Indiana farmlands of John Mellencamp's birth remained close to his heart: in 1985 he co-organised Farm Aid, and that year's album *Scarecrow* was a direct response to the Midwest's economic crisis. A new, serious Mellencamp was finally ridding himself of the 'Johnny Cougar' tag with which he had been (unwittingly) branded when Bowie's manager Tony DeFries took the singer-songwriter into his stable. Parting company with DeFries but still saddled with the name, he re-established himself when Pat Benatar covered his 'I Need A Lover'; then in 1982 'Jack and Diane', a story-song of kids from the heartland, reached US Number One, as did its parent album *American Fool*. The sound was still hard rock, not a million miles from Bruce Springsteen, but later that decade Mellencamp revisited his Americana folk roots on *The Lonesome Jubilee*. This album instigated a period of dogged introspection before he bounded back with *Dance Naked* and *Mr Happy Go Lucky*.

"We were farmers, basically of Dutch stock. I'm the runt of the litter; everybody else has big muscles."

283

John Mellencamp

Born: 7/10/51 • Recording career: 1976 - present • Sounds: American Fool 1982, Scarecrow 1985, Mr Happy Go Lucky 1996

Mercury Rev

Yerself Is Steam, the album that Mercury Rev first dropped on the world, was so downright left-field that reviewers were forced to lunge for catch-all adjectives: 'reckless', 'sprawling' and 'wayward' - this was like nothing they'd heard before. The band, a collection of media studies students from the University of Buffalo, NY, seemed equally surprised. The project had gestated over three years or more as a piece of musical improv, with members arguing over, even fighting over, the creative ideas. This sonic soda-stream of consciousness - a flood of feedback, flute, time shifts and unidentified noises - bewildered the American market, but found a ready audience in the UK. When founder David Baker left (he formed Shady), Mercury Rev, now led by Jonathan Donahue, lost the white noise syndrome of their formative years to create textures that were melodic, Mellotronic... but still remorselessly reckless, sprawling and wayward.

"As time goes on you realise that **not everything needs to be a free-flowing flood of ideas** all the time."

Jonathan Donahue

Key members: David Baker, Jimmy Chambers, Jonathan Donahue, David Fridmann, Sean Mackowiak, Suzanne Thorpe • Recording career: 1991 - present

Sounds: Yerself Is Steam 1991, See You On The Other Side 1995, Deserter's Songs 1998

Metallica

"It's not about money any more.

It's about egos." Lars Ulrich

The music that united Messrs Hetfield and Ulrich was the kind of British heavy rock - Budgie, remember them? - that by the early 1980s was marooned in the doldrums. However, Lars Ulrich had toured with NWBHM pioneers Diamond Head, and Metallica applied their punk-flavoured energy to metal's ailing, blubbery body. The decibel attack was full-frontal ("Bang that head that doesn't bang" was the motto of their 1983 album *Kill 'Em All*), but there were ideas a-plenty beneath

the aural assault. By *Master Of Puppets* the arrangements were complex and the lyrics investigating the waste of war, drugs and urban violence. Bassist Cliff Burton died in a tour bus crash in 1986, but the band's bass-fuelled sound lived on, each album a carefully prepared and diverse showcase for their instrumental skills. Ten years later, shorn of hair but the fire in their belly undimmed, Metallica could still send *Load* direct to Number One on both sides of the Atlantic.

Key members: Cliff Burton 10/2/62 (died 27/9/86), Kirk Hammett 18/11/62, James Hetfield 3/8/63, Lars Ulrich 26/12/63 • Recording career: 1981 - present

Sounds: Kill 'Em All 1983, Master Of Puppets 1986, Metallica 1991

George Michael

By 1998, George Michael was certainly *Older* - his convoluted battle with Sony still a raw memory - but, as the unfortunate incident in Will Rogers Park proved, not necessarily Wiser. Yet Michael had the grace to rib himself about the 'lewd act' charge, titling his next, compilation, album *Ladies And Gentlemen*. When you recall Wham! in their prime, shorts and all, it's to Michael's credit that he emerged with his credibility virtually intact - where Andrew Ridgeley's was permanently pranged - to put away the childish things of 'Wake Me Up' and 'Young Guns', although his songwriting flair was already clearly evident even in their perky pop. The adult artist was launched on 1987's *Faith*, as Michael, still in his early twenties, was embraced by the music industry's aristocracy, duetting with Elton on 'Don't Let the Sun Go Down' and Aretha on 'I Knew You Were Waiting (For Me)'. By the end of the century he had effortlessly joined their ranks.

"I'm not an arrogant person. But I have a real inner confidence."

Born: Georgios Panayiotou 25/6/63 • Recording career (solo): 1984 - present • Sounds: Faith 1987, Listen Without Prejudice Vol. 1 1990, Older 1996

"If you're looking for a band which is into wearing Lurex bicycle pants and making absolutely forgettable, seamless pop, then we're not your band." Peter Garrett

Peter Garrett was by no means the only musician to run for political office - Sonny Bono made it to the House of Representatives, and Screaming Lord Sutch was a by-election fixture - but for both Garrett and his band Midnight Oil, the campaign was a direct extension of their music; his candidature, on a Nuclear Disarmament ticket in a 1984 Australian Senate election, was very nearly successful. *Diesel And Dust*, an album highlighting the plight of aborigines (particularly on 'Beds

Are Burning'), showed how well Midnight Oil were able to marry political messages and commercial guitar-led rock. From their very early days in the 1970s, they had made their intentions plain, playing right-on fund-raisers and setting up a concert promotion company to ensure low ticket prices. Whether Greenpeace or ex-miners afflicted with blue asbestos cancer (the subject of 1990's *Blue Sky Mining*), Midnight Oil gave voice to the cause - and had significant effect.

Midnight Oil

Key members: Peter Garrett, Peter Gifford, Rob Hirst, Jim Moginie, Martin Rotsey • Recording career: 1979 - present

Sounds: 10, 9, 8, 7, 6, 5, 4, 3, 2,1 1983, Diesel And Dust 1987, Earth And Sun And Moon 1993

From an early age, Steve Miller was blessed with excellent musical acquaintances. His father knew T-Bone Walker and Les Paul, and the young Steve was friends with Boz Scaggs and pianist Ben Sidran. Both later played in the Steve Miller Band, a blues-based outfit which backed Chuck Berry at the Fillmore, appeared at Monterey, and gave Miller the platform to negotiate a lucrative, precedent-setting, contract with Capitol. Albums like *Sailor* and *Brave New World*, which featured guest Paul McCartney (Miller returned the favour 28 years later on *Flaming Pie*), dispensed powerful West Coast rock, but then Miller transformed himself into a slick FM act with 1973's *The Joker*. The title track was a US Number One, as were the later 'Rock 'n Me' and 'Abracadabra'. With these in the bank, Miller only needed to work when he chose to: *Born 2 B Blue* from 1988 marked a low-profile return to his roots.

Steve Miller

"I usually listen to my stuff for six months before I release it. It's music to live with, **like a good old pair of slippers.**"

Born: 5/10/43 • Recording career: 1968 - present • Sounds: Sailor 1968, Brave New World 1969, Fly Like An Eagle 1976

Minutemen

After D. Boon, the Minutemen's goateed guitarist, vocalist and wordsmith, was killed in a van crash in December 1985, critic Robert Christgau compared the waste of his potential to the loss of Lennon and Hendrix. Certainly Boon and his old friend Mike Watt still had much to give. In the housing projects of San Pedro, an LA harbour community, they'd taught themselves rudimentary guitar and bass and, while local bands performed cover versions of rock standards, they wrote their own material. Their name was double-edged: a reference to the War of Independence militia, but equally a description of the brevity of their songs, which made the Ramones seem leisurely. Joining Black Flag on the SST label, they hated being pigeonholed, and introduced touches of funk, jazz and blues - though never diminishing their political edge - until it was all cut short. In the wake of Boon's death Watt and drummer George Hurley considered calling it all a day, but re-emerged, saddened yet defiant, as fIREHOSE.

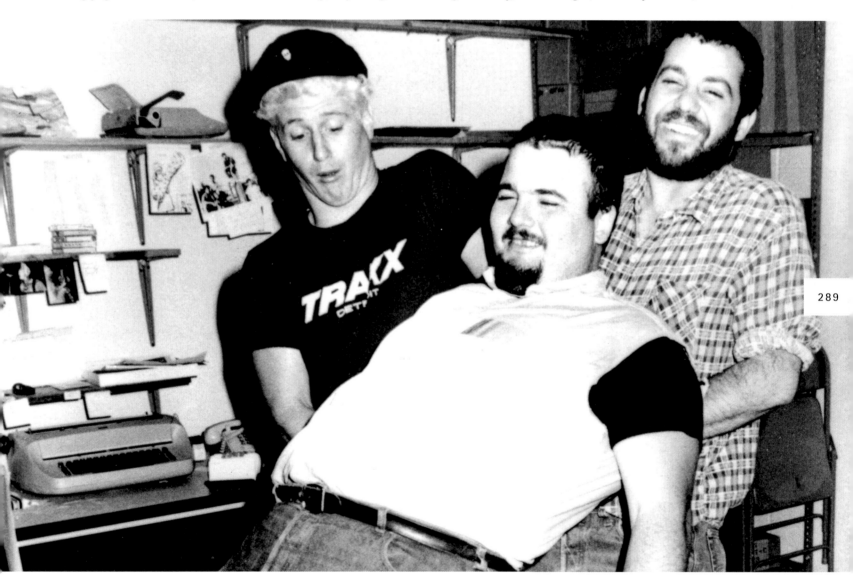

"We didn't really understand punk as a musical style or a way to cut your hair or play your guitar. We thought it was more of an empowerment thing." Mike Watt

Key members: D. Boon 1/4/58 (died 23/12/85), George Hurley 4/9/58, Mike Watt 20/12/57 • Recording career: 1980 - 1985

Sounds: Buzz Or Howl Under The Influence Of Heat 1983, Double Nickels On The Dime 1984, 3-way Tie (For Last) 1985

The Mission

The quality of mercy was exceeding strain'd when Wayne Hussey and Craig Adams parted company with former Sisters of Mercy compadre Andrew Eldritch. There was bad blood - not least a wrangle over names: they wanted to use the Sisterhood, but Eldritch got there first (later, having settled on The Mission, Hussey and Adams were obliged to tour the US as The Mission UK to avoid confusion with the post-punk band Mission of Burma). Opening up immediately with two indie Number Ones - 'Serpent's Kiss' and 'Garden of Delight' - they began a pattern of mainstream chart success, particularly with their second album *Children*, produced by Led Zeppelin's John Paul Jones and revealing the Mission's stronger rock influences (they were into dance by 1992's *Masque*). And there was also an undertow of distinctly un-Gothlike humour: under the pseudonym of the Metal Gurus, they covered Slade's 'Merry Xmas Everybody' in 1990, aided and abetted by Noddy Holder and Jim Lea.

"I always denied I was a Goth.
Then again, looking back on titles like 'Sacrilege' and 'Serpent's Kiss', I guess the weight of evidence is against me." Wayne Hussey

Key members: Craig Adams 4/4/62, Mick Brown, Simon Hinkler, Wayne Hussey 26/5/58 • **Recording career:** 1986 - present • **Sounds:** The First Chapter 1988, Carved In Sand 1990, Masque 1992

"David Geffen used to tell me I was the only star he ever met **who wanted to be ordinary."**

Joni Mitchell

The advice and patronage given to Joni Mitchell by Graham Nash and David Crosby - both romantic involvements - was an obvious bonus in her early years, although she needed little help. Joni was fragile in looks, but never frail. After leaving Canada with her first husband (she retained their married name), her lyrical and melodic versatility was given an airing by Judy Collins' cover of 'Both Sides Now', and CSN&Y's version of 'Woodstock'. From then on she was in charge of her own career. After *Ladies Of The Canyon*, the confessional love songs of *Blue* marked a farewell to folk, and an increasing involvement with Tom Scott's L.A. Express indicated a move towards jazz that by 1979's *Mingus* led to accusations of self-indulgence. Even *The Hissing Of Summer Lawns* - studded with diamond-sharp vignettes and rich in innovative textures - was called the worst album of 1975 by *Rolling Stone*. But with the passing of time, the quality of her work would speak for itself.

291

Born: 7/11/43 • Recording career: 1968 - present • Sounds: Blue 1971, The Hissing Of Summer Lawns 1975, Night Ride Home 1992

"I want to sell a lot of records...

Techno is faceless 'cause most of the artists are afraid to put themselves forward."

The diminutive powerhouse that was Moby eventually outgrew the strictures of techno. Richard Melville Hall, a distant relation of the author of 'Moby Dick' - hence the nickname - was a punk and thrash fan who moved into the New York dance scene in the mid-1980s and discovered that techno merged the best of house and punk. His early releases were righteous: 'Go', a twist on the *Twin Peaks* theme, and 1993's 'I Feel It/Thousand', clocking in at a frenetic 1000-plus bpm.

By his major-label debut *Everything Is Wrong* two years later, he was already spreading his wings, and eventually Moby incurred the wrath of techno purists for selling out (he'd once re-mixed a Michael Jackson track, for Chrissake). Self-confident in his strongly-held beliefs - Christian, vegan, non-drink, non-drug, anti-car - he ignored the naysayers, and delivered a brace of lush anthems for the turn of the century with the ubiquitous 'Porcelain' and 'Natural Blues'.

292

Moby

Born: Richard Melville Hall 11/9/65 • Recording career: 1991 - present • Sounds: Everything Is Wrong 1995, Animal Rights 1996, Play 1999

Moby Grape

"Skip was the maniacal core of the band,
the idiot savant who could see through to the truth of what was going on." Producer David Rubinson

The legend that is Moby Grape rests primarily on one album, their first self-titled release. The Grape were compiled from luminaries of various minor San Francisco and LA bands - the only high-profile member was the brilliant but disturbed Skip Spence, the first drummer with Jefferson Airplane. The group's record label, CBS, were so convinced that their neatly packaged psychedelic blues - far removed from the rambling jams of the Grateful Dead - would be huge that they over-hyped the whole affair. Five singles were released simultaneously, but none charted higher than Number 88 in the US - that was 'Omaha', an upbeat distillation of the band's bouncing, three-guitar, tight-harmonied sound. After this marketing fiasco, it was always going to be an uphill struggle, and *Wow*, the follow-up album, was too hazy, too erratic. Spence, showing signs of paranoid schizophrenia, left and without his fractured vision and energy, the Grape withered.

Key members: Peter Lewis 15/7/45, Jerry Miller 10/7/43, Bob Mosley 4/12/42, Alexander 'Skip' Spence 18/4/44 (died 16/4/99), Don Stevenson 15/10/44

Recording career: 1967 – 1969, 1971, 1978, 1983 & 1990 • Sounds: Moby Grape 1967, Wow 1967, Moby Grape '69 1969

294

The Moody Blues

The arrival of new boys Justin Hayward and John Lodge into the existing Moody Blues initiated a significant new phase for the group. From 1963 to 1967 they had been yet another R'n'B outfit, although they enjoyed a UK Number One with an obscure Bessie Banks song 'Go Now'. When that first line-up - Denny Laine, later of Wings, was a member - broke up, Hayward and Lodge were recruited on guitar and bass respectively, and quickly helped the group develop an 'orchestral' feel (in other words, lots

and lots of layers) reproduced by the quavering tones of that loop-tape marvel, the Mellotron. Hayward also supplied their trademark song, 'Nights In White Satin', which featured on the concept album *Days Of Future Passed*, the first of a sequence of gold-disc earning releases. This was exactly the kind of arty rock that had rougher, tougher bands and hipper-than-thou critics cussing, spluttering and spitting for years to come, while the Moody Blues calmly counted their royalty cheques.

"I look at 'Nights In White Satin'

and see a lot of wisdom in there." Justin Hayward

Key members: Graeme Edge 30/3/41, Justin Hayward 14/10/46, Denny Laine 29/10/44, John Lodge 20/7/45, Mike Pinder 12/12/41, Ray Thomas 29/12/42

Recording career: 1964 - present • Sounds: Days Of Future Passed 1967, Seventh Sojourn 1972, Long Distance Voyager 1981

Alanis Morissette

The trademark of an Alanis Morissette performance was always that hair, a tumbling mass of locks in permanent motion, shaking, tossing, flying about her. But she wouldn't want such cosmetic details to distract the audience from her lyrics and music. Besides, it might just remind people of her earlier manifestation as a teen dance artist, long before she became the Poster Girl of Rage. The success of her debut album *Jagged Little Pill* was by no means overnight. Morissette was a hard-working songwriter, whose parents had released her first single when she was eleven and who'd landed a publishing deal with RCA at 14. Her late teen releases were in the vein of Paula Abdul, and so at odds with the personal, forthright anger of songs like 'You Oughta Know', that she later ensured her juvenilia could not be re-released.

"My whole philosophy on life is that **I'm not about my external appearance.** What I have to say is far more important than how long my eyelashes are."

Born: 1/6/74 • Recording career: 1985 - present • Sounds: Jagged Little Pill 1995, Supposed Former Infatuation Junkie 1998

Morphine

"Why two strings rather than one?

Mark would always say it was so he could play **power chords...**"

Dana Colley

Low-fi but high-brow, Marc Sandman's outfit was obstinately oddball. Here was a band into blues and rock with no electric guitar. Instead, the three-man line-up sported a drummer, Sandman on a bass with only two strings, both tuned to the same note, and Dana Colley on meaty baritone sax. Underpinning the leader's world-weary vocals, often put through a distortion unit, Morphine packed an appropriately addictive punch on numbers like 'Honey White' and 'Cure For Pain', a sound they dubbed 'implied grunge'. The band preferred to play smaller clubs, and remained loyal to the Boston-Cambridge area, even when they signed to DreamWorks. Marc Sandman was a graduate of UMass Boston who only launched a music career in his mid-thirties with the punk-blues group Treat Her Right before forming Morphine. Their fiercely devoted fans were deeply shocked when Sandman died after suffering a heart attack while on stage in Rome in July 1999.

Key members: Dana Colley, Billy Conway, Mark Sandman 24/9/52 (died 3/7/99) • **Recording career:** 1992 - 1999 • **Sounds:** Good 1992, Yes 1995, The Night 2000

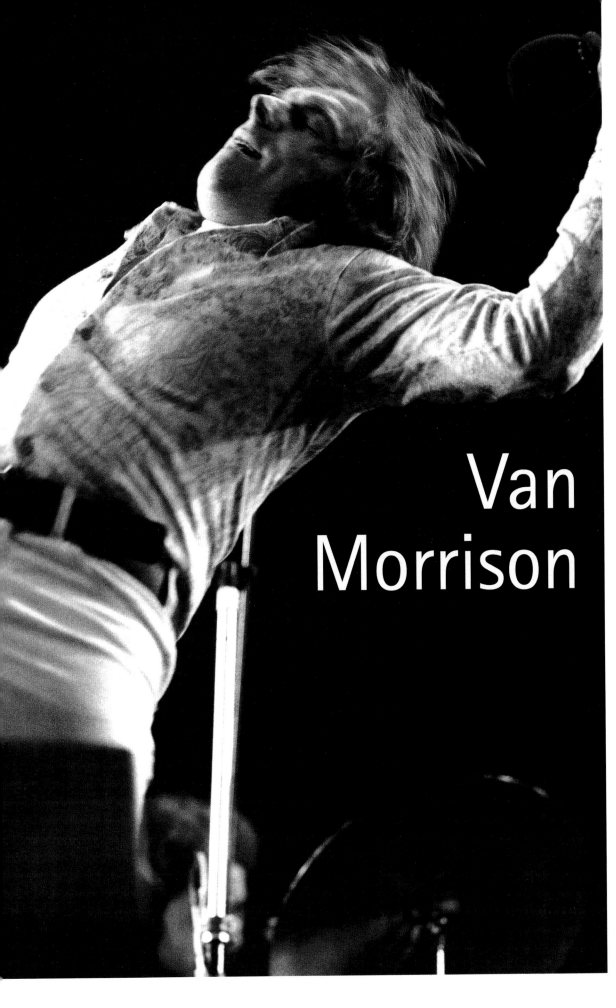

"From 1964 right through to about 1974 it was nothing but work. I'd finish a record, come back from a tour **and walk right back into the studio."**

Van Morrison

The years 1973/74 were a turning point for Van the Man. He took his Caledonia Soul Orchestra out on the road and finally and very firmly established a reputation for powerful stage performances. The Orchestra featured a horn section and string players, and their support reflated Morrison's confidence, after a period when - despite the album strengths of *Moondance*, *Tupelo Honey* and *Hard Nose The Highway* - he'd often fought against stage fright. The tour produced a splendid live album, but by its release the Orchestra had been disbanded, and a decade of non-stop music had produced creative exhaustion. The 1974 Celtic-tinged *Veedon Fleece* album was somewhat opaque, and subsequently Morrison went into the wilderness for three years. He returned, of course, but it took the best part of two decades to recapture the onstage vigour he'd been able to display in those Caledonia Soul Orchestra shows.

Born: 31/8/45 • Recording career: 1964 - present • Sounds: Astral Weeks 1968, Moondance 1970, Hymns To The Silence 1991

"We're all from the same street,
and every member of this band has been in and out of jail,
yet everybody thinks we're a bunch of prissies."

Nikki Sixx

Testosterone warning: the salty dogs of Mötley Crüe are on the loose. Not content with fuelling the wet-dreams of hormonally rampant adolescents with albums like 1987's *Girls, Girls, Girls*, the band went one stage further and gave their fans' fantasies vicarious reality. Mick Mars married ex-Prince girlfriend Vanity, Nikki Sixx wed centrefold Brandi Brandt and drummer Tommy Lee not only famously persuaded both Heather Lockyear and Pamela Anderson to tie the knot, but also inadvertently provided video evidence of his and Pammy's deep love. And they lived up to their bad boy image. Vocalist Vince Neil served time for his involvement in a car crash which killed Hanoi Rocks

drummer Nick Dingley, and Nikki Sixx was announced clinically dead for two minutes during one massive bender. The crueller commentators said that their music, a Kiss-Aerosmith mongrel, had been lifeless much longer, but the Crüe could care less - their albums invariably went platinum. As for their lasting musical heritage, well, the jüry's still öut.

Mötley Crüe

Key members: Tommy Lee 3/10/62, Mick Mars (Bob Deal) 3/4/56, Vince Neil 8/2/61, Nicki Sixx (Frank Ferranno) 11/12/58 • Recording career: 1981 - present

Sounds: Shout At The Devil 1983, Girls, Girls, Girls 1987, Dr Feelgood 1989

Motörhead

Before there was Lemmy, there was Ian Kilmister, a vicar's son from Stoke-on-Trent, and before he created Motörhead, he was Hawkwind's bassist - until a drugs bust in Canada saw him summarily ejected from that group in 1975. Back in the UK, Lemmy test-drove a few musicians and chose as his compadres guitarist 'Fast Eddie' Clarke and drummer Phil 'Philthy Animal' Taylor. This, the classic Motörhead line-up, produced a bombardment of sound that all later speed metal merchants would, unwitting or not, owe a major debt to - the trio also enjoyed chart success, not least with 'Ace Of Spades' in 1980. Yet, despite the

Hell's Angels imagery and aggressive attitude - Lemmy once said that if they moved next door, your lawn would die - Motörhead possessed a sardonic sense of humour, on 'Deaf Forever', for example. And the title track of their album *1916*, which was a touching tale of WWI soldiery, even revealed Lemmy's softer side. But don't tell him I said so.

"Does anybody call me Ian? My mum.
She's the only one who bothers. Everyone else knows me as fuckin' Lemmy." Lemmy

Key members: Eddie Clarke 5/10/50, Lemmy (Ian Kilmister) 24/12/45, Phil Taylor 21/9/54 • Recording career: 1976 - present • Sounds: Ace Of Spades 1980, No Sleep 'Til Hammersmith 1981, 1916 1991

299

> "I write as I talk. I don't exercise in words. I didn't get an Oxford accent just because I happened to make a few bob." Ian Hunter

Mott The Hoople

He was the author of *Diary Of A Rock'n'Roll Star*, after all: Mott The Hoople's Ian Hunter required perma-shades to keep innumerable bleary-eyed mornings at bay. Hunter did a fine approximation of Bob Dylan's singing voice, but even with solid songs supplied by guitarist Mick Ralphs, and production by Guy Stevens (later to oversee the Clash's *London Calling*), Mott's live reputation failed to convert to record sales. Then David Bowie intervened, offering them one of his songs - they turned down 'Suffragette City', but accepted 'All The Young Dudes'. Hunter now sounded distinctly Bowie-ish, yet despite the 1972 chart success of 'Dudes', the band's attempt to straddle progressive rock and pop was uneasy. Mick Ralphs left to join Bad Company - taking 'Can't Get Enough', which he'd originally written for Mott - while Hunter continued glam-rocking, complete with sax and sha-la-la-la vocals, on 'Roll Away The Stone'. This time there was no miraculous resurrection.

Key members: Verden Allen 26/5/44, Ariel Bender (Luther Grosvenor) 23/12/49, Dale Griffin 24/10/48, Ian Hunter 3/6/46, Mick Ralphs 31/5/44, Peter 'Overend' Watts 13/5/47

Recording career: 1969 - 1974 • **Sounds:** Mott The Hoople 1969, All The Young Dudes 1972, Mott 1973

"Mountain is my symphony.
I'm doing the same thing the great classical conductors did in their day.
I'm conducting the music of my own time." Felix Pappalardi

Mountain

Mountain represented the coming together of a virtually irresistible force - the ambition of Felix Pappalardi - and a damn near immovable object - Leslie West. Pappalardi was a one-time Greenwich Village folkie who had acquired some nifty production credits working with Tim Hardin, the Lovin' Spoonful and on Cream's *Disraeli Gears*. Asked to shape up a Long Island group called the Vagrants, Pappalardi simply winkled out Leslie West, the band's guitarist, and conceived Mountain as a vehicle for both of them. The resultant sound was definitely not the Lovin' Spoonful, but Cream and then some. 'Nantucket Sleighride' became familiar to British TV viewers as the *World In Action* theme, but otherwise Mountain were primarily a Stateside success, including the single 'Mississippi Queen'. Even their homeland, though, tired of heavy riffs and over-extended solos, and by the time Pappalardi was shot dead (by his wife) in 1983, his principal keepsake was the deafness caused by Mountain's Himalayan on-stage volume.

Key members: Steve Knight, Corky Laing 28/4/48, Felix Pappalardi 1939 (died 17/4/83), Leslie West 22/10/45 • Recording career: 1970 - 1974 & 1985
Sounds: Mountain Climbing! 1970, Nantucket Sleighride 1971, Live: The Road Goes Ever On 1972

The Move

"I wanted us to sound as original as possible.
Having said that, we wanted to be as powerful as the Who, and vocally like the Beach Boys." Roy Wood

With arch-publicist Tony Secunda behind them, The Move caught attention at every turn. Having hustled 'Flowers In The Rain' into history as the first-ever single broadcast on the new-born BBC Radio One in 1967, Secunda promoted it with a flyer that featured the then Prime Minister Harold Wilson in bed with his secretary. A lawsuit, and much publicity, ensued. And yet the Move were better than mere hype. Roy Wood was an ingenious songwriter able, on demand, to fashion a classical caricature ('Night Of Fear' included a burst of Tchaikovsky's *1812 Overture*) or a psychedelic pastiche ('I Can Hear The Grass Grow'). Seen primarily as a singles band in the UK, where 'Blackberry Way' was a Number One, the Move's albums merited further investigation. Winding down in 1971, Wood then conceived the Electric Light Orchestra with Jeff Lynne, but left Lynne to oversee ELO's activities and concentrated instead on the fun-packed 1950s revivalism of Wizzard.

Key members: Bev Bevan 24/11/44, Trevor Burton 9/3/44, Rick Price 10/6/44, Carl Wayne 18/8/44, Roy Wood 8/11/46 • Recording career: 1967 - 1972

Sounds: The Move 1968, Shazam 1970, Message From The Country 1971

"To get a name, you had to get a record. People lived right up under me, they didn't know who I was until I get a record out. Then they say, 'He live right here!'"

The influence of Muddy Waters still runs deep. Almost single-handedly he brought Chicago blues to the UK, touring in 1958 at the invitation of jazzman Chris Barber. His performances inspired Alexis Korner and Cyril Davies to quit skiffle and form an R'n'B community that spawned a whole school of British bands, not least the Stones, who took their name from Muddy's 'Rollin' Stone Blues'. That was just one of the enduring blues classics he had recorded for Chess in the 1950s, including 'Mannish Boy', 'I've Got My Mojo Working', 'Hoochie Coochie Man' and 'I Just Wanna Make Love To You'. Waters attempted, perhaps unwisely, to introduce elements of rock into his own work (*Electric Mud* in 1968 included a Stones cover) - but under the guidance of the guitarist Johnny Winter, he made a strong return to form in his sixties with *Hard Again*, his own graphic description of exactly how the blues affected him.

303

Muddy Waters

Born: McKinley Morganfield 4/4/15 (died 30/4/83) • Recording career: 1948 - 1980 • Sounds: Muddy Waters At Newport 1960, Fathers And Sons 1969, Hard Again 1977

Mudhoney

Before Nirvana acceded to the throne, Mudhoney were the crown princes of grunge, the biggest act on the Sub Pop roster. Their Seattle pedigree was irreproachable: bassist Matt Lukin was from the locally lionised Melvins, while Mark Arm and Steve Turner both emerged out of Green River, alongside Pearl Jam's Jeff Ament. The problem was that Mudhoney peaked too early - their first single, the insanitary and scorching 'Touch Me I'm Sick', was near-perfect, and a debut EP *Superfuzz Bigmuff* (named after one of Steve Turner's beloved array of effects pedals) was a foundation stone of the grunge sound. But despite all these pluses, they didn't, or didn't seem to, give a superfuzz about riding the Nirvana bandwagon, and their full-length albums were by their own admission patchy - of these, *Every Good Boy Deserves Fudge* was the best. A decade further on, they were pretty well unchanged, a glob of genuine grunge stuck quite happily in the mudflats.

"There are a lot more bands that are relevant to music today than Mudhoney. Just forget us, okay?"

Steve Turner

304

Key members: Mark Arm 21/2/62, Matt Lukin 16/8/64, Dan Peters 18/8/67, Steve Turner 28/3/65 • **Recording career:** 1988 - present

Sounds: *Superfuzz Bigmuff* 1989, *Every Good Boy Deserves Fudge* 1991, *My Brother The Cow* 1995

The Muffs

Like their Californian labelmates Green Day, the Muffs were loud and proud to play classic three-chord punk: fast, boisterous, infectious, no messing. Queen of the Muffs was Kim Shattuck, a product of Orange County, who first came to notice with cult LA garage band the Pandoras, led by the late Paula Pierce. Striking out on her own, Shattuck recruited former boyfriend Ronnie Barnett on bass, fellow Pandora Melanie Vammen, and tried a couple of drummers before Roy McDonald settled in. Then Ms Vammen departed ('musical differences'), leaving the trio to their own devices on *Blonder And Blonder*: the title was allegedly a Courtney Love aside, suggesting that the Muffs and Shattuck in particular were modelling themselves on Hole. In fact, the Kinks and the Buzzcocks were more of a model, and Kim Shattuck's vocals harked back to the Runaways' Joan Jett or early Debbie Harry. And the band's name? Shattuck always maintained that people leapt to totally the wrong conclusions, once memorably remarking, "We're a band, not genitals".

"What's that weird noise?
I guess that's our band." Kim Shattuck

Key members: Ronnie Barnett, Roy McDonald, Kim Shattuck 17/7/67 • Recording career: 1991 - present • Sounds: The Muffs 1993, Blonder And Blonder 1995, Alert Today Alive Tomorrow 1999

Loveless, My Bloody Valentine's 1991 album, arrived like a galactic message beamed in from outer space to make contact with this world. A number of earthlings - including Eno, Butch Vig and Bob Mould - deciphered with wonder its aural hieroglyphs, a hallucinatory concoction of indistinct vocals merged with phased, warped, layered and generally monkeyed-about-with guitar. This was the same MBV who had been a Dublin-based indie band peddling lame imitations of Nick Cave, before

re-thinking their strategy completely in the late 1980s. The shifting swirl of their music and their on-stage inertia were shadowed by a cluster of other 'shoegazing' bands, including Ride and Slowdive, but everyone was waiting for a new recording from the masters. Yet, due mainly to Kevin Shields' notorious perfectionism - *Loveless* took three years and a reported £200,000 to produce - and despite many rumours and promises, the follow-up album had still not turned up by the end of the century.

"You're expected to make this great new record and you're sitting there thinking, well my guitar doesn't even work properly... We just went into slow motion." Kevin Shields

My Bloody Valentine

Key members: Bilinda Butcher 16/9/61, Debbie Googe 24/10/62, Colm O'Ciosoig 31/10/64, Kevin Shields 21/5/63 • Recording career: 1984 - present • Sounds: Isn't Anything 1988, Loveless 1991

"Country rock has always been the most natural thing for me, a lot simpler
than all those arranged things I'd got into."

Rick Nelson came into existence in 1961 - previously he'd been Ricky, but on his 21st birthday he shortened his forename to mark the end of his life as a teen pop idol. Starring in his family's television show, *The Adventures Of Ozzie And Harriet*, had given him a springboard to try and emulate Elvis, and a ready-made fan base who lapped up singles like 'I'm Walkin'' and 'Poor Little Fool'. This wasn't pure merchandising: Nelson had some raw talent, plus a cracking band, including rockabilly genius James Burton on guitar. The mature Rick moved towards a country sound, and in the late 1960s compiled the Stone Canyon Band,

featuring future Eagle Randy Meisner. Some former fans pooh-poohed this change of direction, but he persevered down the country road until New's Year Eve 1985, when a plane carrying Nelson, his fiancée and members of his promising new band crashed in Texas, killing them all.

Rick Nelson

Born: 8/5/40 (died 31/12/85) • Recording career: 1956 - 1985 • Sounds: Ricky 1957, Garden Party 1972, Memphis Sessions 1986

Nelson

Like Rick Nelson, Willie - no relation - had a significant change of gear as the 1960s ended. He had previously carved out a niche as a respected Nashville songwriter, supplying Patsy Cline with 'Crazy' and Roy Orbison with 'Pretty Paper'. But Nelson was keen to perform more, and in 1970 moved to Jerry Wexler's Atlantic Records. Atlantic were not noted for their country roster (labelmates included Aretha Franklin, Yes and Led Zep) but Nelson moved towards a rock/country hybrid on albums like 1973's *Shotgun Willie*, creating a sound, and a look, which became known as 'outlaw' country and appealed to hardcore rednecks as well as fringe-jacketed rockers. Forming the Highwaymen with Kris Kristofferson, Waylon Jennings and Johnny Cash added another lease of life to his career and in 1993, like some venerable blues legend, Nelson, a giant in his own right, could invite Bonnie Raitt, Paul Simon and Dylan to perform on *Across The Borderline*.

"I am what they used to call a troubadour.
What I do for a living is to get people to feeling good."

Born: 30/4/33 • Recording career: 1955 - present • Sounds: Yesterday's Wine 1971, Red Headed Stranger 1975, Across The Borderline 1993

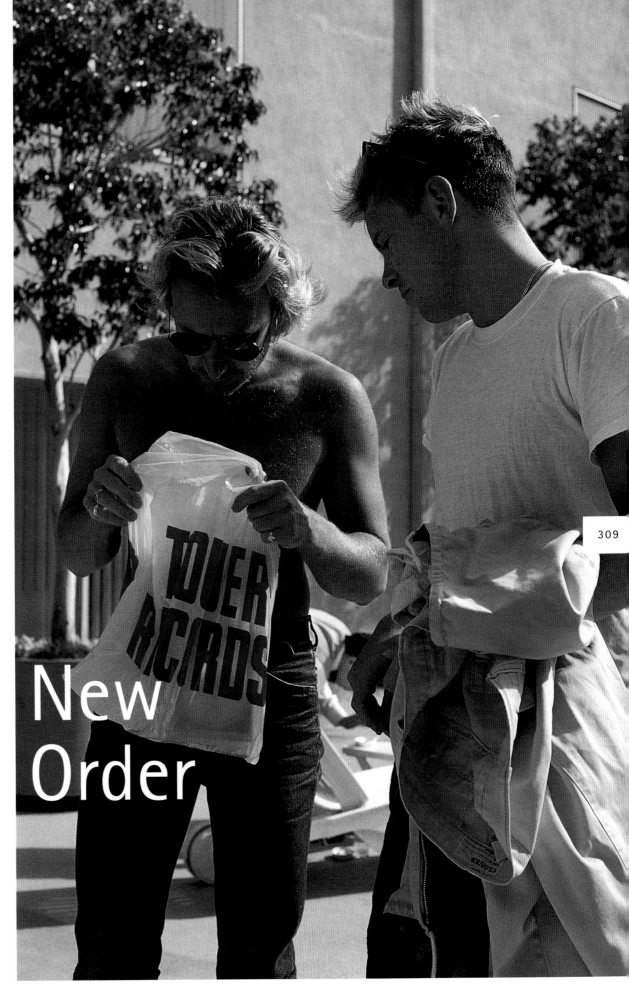

"People copying us doesn't bother me at all. Some of them probably do it better than we do." Peter Hook

The transition from Joy Division to New Order following Ian Curtis's suicide was a gradual process. Gillian Gilbert, drummer Steven Morris's girlfriend, was drafted in on keyboards and Bernard Sumner took over vocal duties, with an initial lack of confidence that meant bass and drums prevailed on their early releases. And the Kraftwerk influence which Curtis himself had wanted to pursue emerged in an addictive pulse that - quite unexpectedly - propelled New Order to a dominant role in disco, their breakthrough coming in 1983 with 'Blue Monday', the best-selling 12-inch single ever. New Order, now with a distinctive voice, let the music speak on their behalf, shunning interviews and excessive publicity. By the end of the 1980s, internal disagreements penetrated the veil of secrecy, but before they took a brief time out they scored a UK Number One with the 1990 England World Cup single, 'World In Motion', which featured John Barnes' rapping and buried for ever excruciating mullet-haired team singalongs...

New Order

Key members: Gillian Gilbert 27/1/61, Peter Hook 13/2/56, Steven Morris 28/10/57, Bernard Sumner 4/1/65 • Recording career: 1981 - present

Sounds: Power, Corruption And Lies 1983, Low-life 1985, Technique 1989

New York Dolls

They were only around for a couple of years, but the New York Dolls left an indelible impression - of lowlife trash. Even in photos they smelt sleazy. Guitarist Johnny Thunders knew some cool R'n'B riffs and singer David Johansen sported Jagger's pout, but the Dolls were not simply ersatz Stones. They had their very own screw-you attitude and a splendid lack of polish. Not surprisingly, punk followed hot on their (platform) heels. Todd Rundgren was the name producer of their self-titled 1973 debut, with tracks like 'Trash' and 'Bad Girl' setting the tone, but the following year a flawed decision was made to bring on board George 'Shadow' Morton, the Shangri-Las' innovative producer. Whoever selected the title *Too Much Too Soon* for the album that resulted was scarily prescient. As the Dolls spilled well over the top, Malcolm McLaren tried to rescue them, but his makeover - featuring a Communist flag backdrop - only hastened terminal meltdown.

"The Dolls were like a street gang who turned over to instruments instead of guns."

Jerry Nolan

Key members: David Johansen 9/1/50, Arthur Kane 3/2/51, Jerry Nolan 7/5/46 (died 14/1/92), Sylvain Sylvain (Syl Mizrahi), Johnny Thunders (John Genzale Jnr) 15/7/52 (died 23/4/91)

Recording career: 1973 - 1974 • Sounds: New York Dolls 1973, Too Much Too Soon 1974

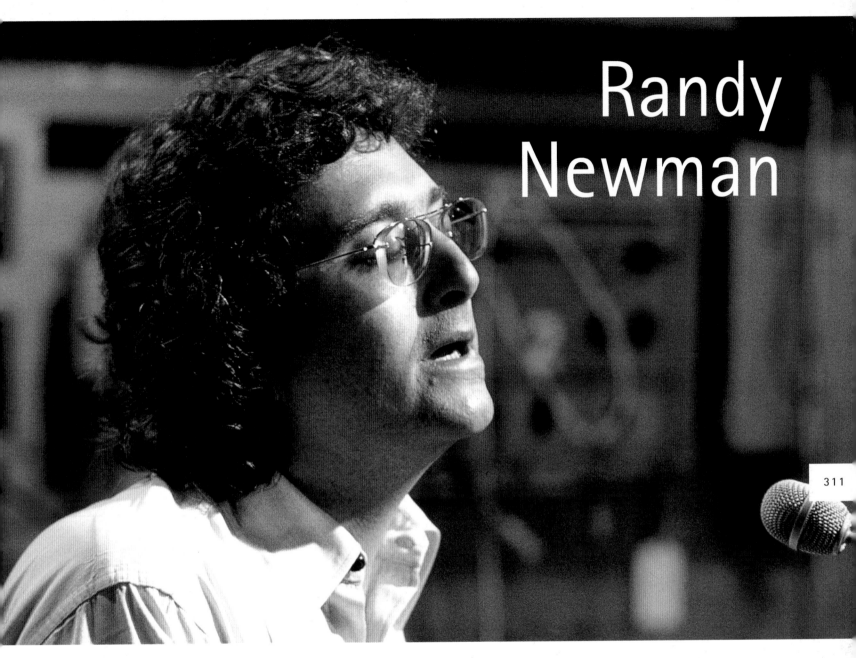

Randy Newman

Satire and irony are dangerous commodities in the wonderful world of popular music. Ask Randy Newman. He promoted both throughout his career, and upset plenty of people along the way. A song like 'Rednecks', written from the viewpoint of a Southern white criticising Yankee liberals, could be interpreted as attacking both sides, neatly upsetting everybody. And 'Short People', from his best-known album *Little Criminals* and another biting dig at bigotry, caused further kneejerk offence. Newman's songwriting skills were immaculate - he wrote for Gene Pitney, Judy Collins and Three Dog Night (their US Number One 'Mama Told Me Not To Come') - but as a performer he proved an acquired taste, and as a human being he remained reclusive. Concentrating on movie scores, Newman enjoyed a resurgence - and reached his biggest audience yet - in the late 1990s, when *Ally McBeal* featured 'Short People' in a glorious gospel version, and his songs punctuated the animation of *Toy Story* and *Antz*.

"I never come down on the side of commerciality when I think the other way is better. That's not particularly heroic, because I don't have a great sense of commerciality."

Born: 28/11/43 • Recording career: 1966 - present • Sounds: 12 Songs 1970, Good Old Boys 1974, Bad Love 1999

The Nice

The keyboard showmanship of Emerson Lake & Palmer was conceived within the Nice, at the heart of which Keith Emerson employed his Hammond organ as an object of power and abuse, dry-humping the innocent instrument and, on occasion, flinging knives at it. The roots of the band lay in straightforward R'n'B - they had originally formed as the backing band for former Ikette P.P. Arnold, but *The Thoughts Of Emerlist Davjack*, the Nice's debut album, although not especially profound, included a variation on Bach and Brubeck in 'Rondo' which indicated a route ahead towards both classical and jazz allusions. They also covered numbers by Bob Dylan, Tim Hardin and Leonard Bernstein: their version of 'America' from *West Side Story* charted but caused controversy when they burnt a Stars and Stripes on stage in the Royal Albert Hall. After guitarist Davy O'List left, the Nice continued as a trio, until a chance encounter between Emerson and Greg Lake...

"You could call us a psychedelic group, but I'd rather you didn't.

It's not a weak or pretty sound, it's very hard-hitting and powerful." Lee Jackson

Key members: Brian Davison 25/5/42, Keith Emerson 1/11/44, Lee Jackson 8/1/43, David O'List 13/12/48 • Recording career: 1967 - 1971

Sounds: Ars Longa Vita Brevis 1968, The Nice 1969, Five Bridges 1970

Christa Päffgen first emerged as Nico in the late 1950s, a covergirl who was in the *La Dolce Vita* set: she had a brief cameo in the Fellini film. Andrew Oldham produced her first single 'I'm Not Sayin'', which had Brian Jones on guitar, but when it flopped she swanned off to Manhattan and became a fixture, now dark and brooding, in Andy Warhol's Factory. Warhol persuaded the Velvet Underground to join forces with her on their first album, with equal billing, but she wanted more. Her own album, *Chelsea Girl*, featured songs by a 16-year-old Jackson Browne (alleged to be a lover along with Bob Dylan and Jim Morrison) and the support of John Cale - he produced Nico's subsequent trio of starkly chilling albums, where her flat drone counterpointed wintry strings or her reedy harmonium. In the 1970s, she went walkabout, an ethereal influence on punks and Goths until her death from a cerebral haemorrhage on holiday in Ibiza.

Nico

"People described her voice as everything from eerie to bland and smooth, to wind in a drainpipe, to an IBM computer with a Garbo accent." Andy Warhol

Born: Christa Päffgen 16/10/38 (died 18/7/88) • Recording career: 1965 - 1974 & 1981 - 1985 • Sounds: Chelsea Girl 1967, The Marble Index 1969, The End 1974

Unlike Tim Hardin, who was best known via other people's versions of his material, Harry Nilsson, an undoubted talent as a songwriter, enjoyed his greatest success covering other people's songs: Fred Neil's 'Everybody's Talking', the *Midnight Cowboy* theme, and 'Without You', the Badfinger song which Nilsson took to Number One in the UK and US in 1972. His own material had previously made some headway, with the Monkees recording 'Cuddly Toy', the Yardbirds tackling 'Ten Little Indians' and Three Dog Night selling a million copies of 'One'. But his own recordings took a while to emerge, despite attracting the attention of John Lennon early on (Nilsson was later a posse member during Lennon's 'lost weekend', and added backing vocals to Ringo's 'You're Sixteen'). In the end his idiosyncratic ways - 1974's *Pussy Cats* was a self-indulgent tribute to rock classics compared to Lennon's crisp *Rock'n'Roll* - and a paucity of public performances hampered further progress.

"We went through a bunch of Beatles albums and couldn't find 'Without You'. Finally I said 'No! It wasn't the Beatles. It was Grapefruit, or something'..."

Harry Nilsson

Born: Harry Nelson III 15/6/41 (died 15/1/94) • **Recording career:** 1966 – 1993 • **Sounds:** Pandemonium Shadow Show 1967, Nilsson Schmilsson 1972, Pussy Cats 1974

314

"There has to be danger, we have to instil a sense of fear in the audience and in ourselves."

Trent Reznor

"Only pain is real," sang Trent Reznor, the main Nine Inch Nail. Or was it? Reznor pushed shock rock to its extremes, smudging distinctions between what might or might not be reality. The video for 'Happiness in Slavery', which featured a masochist performance artist, troubled the censors. Another was impounded by the police on suspicion it included out-takes from a snuff movie. This was the confusion of the establishment that Nine Inch Nails sought, but Reznor found to his surprise it sold mainstream quantities: after MTV had rotated 'Head Like A Hole', *Pretty Hate Machine* shifted over a million copies. Reznor constructed a touring band in 1993 - synths replaced by a massed guitar attack - which widened the audience further. The following year *The Downward Spiral* hit US Number Two, and Oliver Stone invited Reznor - now becoming the doyen of his chosen musical field - to produce the soundtrack for *Natural Born Killers*. Pain, even if you faked it, could pay.

315

Nine Inch Nails

Key member: Trent Reznor 17/5/65 • Recording career: 1989 - present • Sounds: Pretty Hate Machine 1989, The Downward Spiral 1994, The Fragile 1999

"I wish I could have taken a class on becoming a rock star. It might have prepared me for this..."

Kurt Cobain

Why did Kurt Cobain come to represent the 1990s in rock? There was his talent, evidenced by songwriting that merged punk, hard rock and hooklines to create a grunge anthem in 'Smells Like Teen Spirit', a song "as intense as hell," in producer Butch Vig's phrase. There was his attitude, which hated the fact that *Nevermind* was adopted by every unhip thirty-something with a CD player. There was a public private life with Courtney Love (Cobain described their relationship as "like Evian water and battery acid") fanning press interest that at its peak was the slacker equivalent of Posh and Becks. And there was his death in April 1994, the final twist in a spiral of pressures, drugs and near-overdoses - the note near his body quoted Neil Young: "It's better to burn out than fade away". The legend would last, but threatened to overshadow Nirvana's music. Play it again, and remember them both.

Nirvana

Key members: Kurt Cobain 20/2/67 (died 5/4/94), Dave Grohl 14/1/69, Chris Novoselic 16/5/65 • Recording career: 1988 - 1993

Sounds: Nevermind 1991, In Utero 1993, MTV Unplugged In New York 1994

"Do you realise the craving for rock'n'roll you get after having been in the woods with a bow and arrow for three months?"

Ted Nugent

The Motor City Madman was self-styled. When a career with Detroit garage band the Amboy Dukes started to stutter in the early 1970s, Ted Nugent invented a cartoon personality for himself, as a wild outdoorsman with guitar chops. He challenged other axe heroes - Wayne Kramer of MC5, Frank Marino of Mahogany - to go *mano a mano* in electric sparring contests. The caricature, though a gimmick to boost his profile, masked a man of sincerely held beliefs. Most of the rest of the music industry might not have shared them - Nugent was a member of the National Rifle Association, he hunted, and disdained drugs and drink - but he wavered not in his convictions: in 1995 he released 'I Shoot Back', still defiantly pro-firearms. The music that he captured and skinned was pure-bred heavy metal; he was a proponent of the "If it's too loud, you're too old" philosophy. At 50 years and rising, Nugent was still cranking up the volume.

Born: 13/12/49 • Recording career (solo): 1975 - present • Sounds: Cat Scratch Fever 1977, Double Live Gonzo 1978, Spirit Of The Wild 1995

Laura Nyro

"If you look at the different arts, they take a whole lifetime. There are certain times that are very prolific, and other times when they're planting seeds."

At the Monterey Festival in 1967, a 19-year-old Laura Nyro badly misjudged the mood of the hippy audience. Her decision to present something akin to a soul revue proved to be a mistake, especially as her uncategorisable fusion of social consciousness, poetic lyrics, doo-wop and jazz required quality listening time. The crowd booed heartily, leaving Nyro with a bad case of stage fright - she was rescued by David Geffen, who stepped in as her manager. *Eli And The Thirteenth Confession*, her subsequent, critically lauded, album marked the start of a burst of intense and intensive recording. Although 1971's *Gonna Take A Miracle* was a collection of R'n'B/Motown favourites with Labelle on backing vocals, her other releases were polished but deeply introspective, and hence destined to remain cult items. Nyro's output faltered after the 1970s: she produced only the strongly feminist *Mother's Spiritual* in 1984, and a final, still socially aware, album in 1993 before succumbing to cancer.

Born: 18/10/47 (died 9/4/97) • Recording career: 1966 - 1993 • Sounds: Eli And The Thirteenth Confession 1968, New York Tendaberry 1969, Gonna Take A Miracle 1971

"I think life's just a load of questions.
If I don't find the answers now, I'm sure they'll turn up later on.
Our kid wants to know all the answers right now."

Noel Gallagher

In May 1993, Oasis were performing at King Tut's Wah Wah Club in Glasgow. They weren't meant to be playing, but had employed their aggressive *chutzpah* - "We like annoying people; it's a Manchester thing" - to hustle a five-song set. In the audience Creation Records' Alan McGee picked up on Noel's retro songs and Liam's sex appeal. After protracted negotiations he signed them - and the honeymoon began with a string of cocky singles, from 'Supersonic' to 'Whatever'.

Noel, the songsmith who appreciated Burt Bacharach and the Bee Gees ("a phenomenal band"), had a masterplan: to produce three albums and then review the situation. Sure enough, after *Be Here Now* and many sibling squabbles, there was a notable hiatus while the Gallaghers were forced to reassess. The new millennium would retrospectively mark a fresh start, or the beginning of the end. "What we've learnt," noted Liam, "is that we're still the greatest rock'n'roll band in the world."

Oasis

319

Key members: Paul 'Bonehead' Arthurs 23/6/65, Liam Gallagher 21/9/72, Noel Gallagher 29/5/67, Paul 'Guigsy' McGuigan 9/5/71, Alan White 26/5/72 • Recording career: 1994 - present

Sounds: Definitely Maybe 1994, (What's The Story) Morning Glory? 1995, Be Here Now 1997

Ocean Colour Scene

The story of Ocean Colour Scene was one of the triumph of self-belief over the vicissitudes of the music business. The Birmingham quartet had been plying their wares, not terribly successfully, as a guitar-led indie band, and eventually secured - or so it seemed - their ambition of a major deal with Fontana. Then everything went despair-shaped. Two producers came and went, including Jimmy Miller of *Beggars Banquet* fame, and although a third managed to supply the goods, band and label shortly parted company. Through some lean times, Paul Weller gave members of the band gainful employment on *Wild Wood* and *Stanley Road*; Noel Gallagher was equally supportive. The strengths of their live performances and songwriting were once more recognised, and in 1996 a second album, *Moseley Shoals*, was released. At last OCS found some commercial success, but self-belief was still required, as their music was often dismissed as a mish-mash of influences.

"We don't take from a period or style,
we take from our influences and write our own songs." Steve Cradock

Key members: Steve Cradock 22/8/69, Simon Fowler 25/5/65, Oscar Harrison 15/4/65, Damon Minchella 1/6/69 • **Recording career:** 1990 - present

Sounds: Moseley Shoals 1996, Marchin' Already 1997

"I don't do anything in order to cause trouble.
It just so happens that what I do naturally causes trouble."

The tears on the video of the single that launched Sinéad O'Connor as a global star - the dignified Nellee Hooper production of Prince's 'Nothing Compares 2 U' - were apparently real. Sinéad rarely faked it. And paid the price. Behind the anger lay, in her own words, a tender, sweet person. Out of inherent shyness she would flare like a firework whenever she believed passionately in a cause. Ensuing headlines portrayed O'Connor in her early days as nothing but a shaven-headed demon; the press were probably also upset that she did not choose to adopt a standard girlie singer look. Yet when she did try out some big band Broadway standards, on *Am I Not Your Girl?*, her versions (of 'Bewitched, Bothered And Bewildered', for example) were generally ignored. She tried to come to terms with the baggage of her past, of which she had a serious excess, on 1994's *Universal Mother*, but would remain ever vulnerable, perennially fascinating and puzzling.

Sinéad O'Connor

Born: 12/12/66 • Recording career: 1987 - present • Sounds: The Lion And The Cobra 1987, I Do Not Want What I Haven't Got 1990, Faith And Courage 2000

Mike Oldfield

"When I put the Tubular Bells symbol on a record, **it's like the Stones regrouping** and making an album. It's like the rest of the albums I do are solo albums."

Tubular Bells has become such an integral part of rock history that we need reminding Mike Oldfield was still a teenager when it came out; he had already recorded an album with sister Sally and worked with Kevin Ayers. Yet initially no one wanted to touch what would become some 50 minutes of *magnum opus*, constructed around the repeated motifs nearly, but not all, over-dubbed by the multi-instrumental Oldfield. Finally, Richard Branson took a punt: Virgin Records' first release laid the financial foundations for Branson's subsequent empire. Oldfield did remarkably well following up *Tubular Bells'* spectacular success, with the creditable *Hergest Ridge* and *Ommadawn*, the latter imbued with world music influences. But by the punk era, he seemed too much of a virtuoso, and did himself few favours re-working 'In Dulce Jubilo' and the theme to BBC TV children's classic *Blue Peter*. By the 1990s, instructively, he was back to issuing *Tubular Bells II* and *III*.

Born: 15/5/53 • Recording career: 1968 - present • Sounds: Tubular Bells 1973, Ommadawn 1975, Tubular Bells II 1992

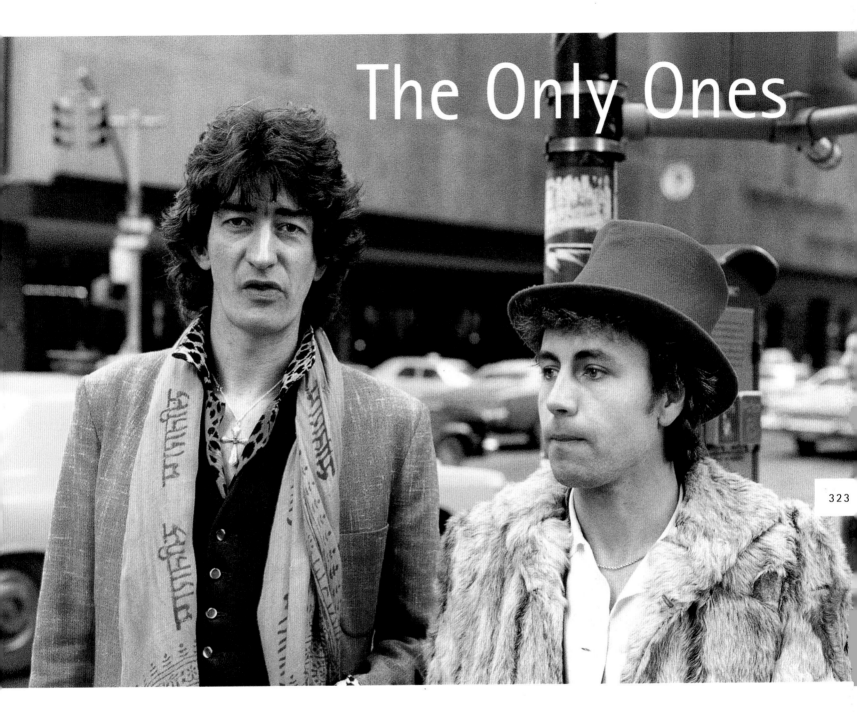

The Only Ones

The band could have been called the Nearly Ones, since they almost managed, through the efforts of singer Peter Perrett, to import the decadence of the New York Dolls into Britain's post-punk New Wave. The connection was not purely imitation: Perrett, blond and emaciated with a strained Lou Reed vocal style, was an acquaintance of Johnny Thunders, the Dolls' guitarist, whom Perrett backed on Johnny's 1978 solo album *So Alone*. However, the Only Ones didn't quite pull it off.

One theory was that, for the era, the band could play far too well - drummer Mike Kellie had worked with Spooky Tooth and Peter Frampton, and John Perry favoured fluid lead solos. The reality was more mundane. Their best single 'Another Girl, Another Planet' just did not get enough airplay, and a combination of drugs and arguments with their record company sapped the band's energies. By the 1980s it was Peter Perrett, as he later admitted, who was on another planet.

"It's a great story, isn't it? Loads of potential and, er, screwed up dramatically!" John Perry

Key members: Mike Kellie 24/3/47, Alan Mair, Peter Perrett 8/4/52, John Perry • Recording career: 1977 - 1980 • Sounds: The Only Ones 1978, Even Serpents Shine 1979, Live 1989

"We had a very Luddite approach to technology, scoffing at groups like Depeche Mode who made 'Metal Mickey music for morons'." Edwyn Collins

Orange Juice

Like most young musicians in 1979, the members of Orange Juice had been trying their hand at punk, but their choice of name was a signal that they were heading for a softer direction. Initially sponsored by Postcard Records - run by Edwyn Collins' friend Alan Horne, and home for a while to a promising crop of Scottish bands that included Aztec Camera - Orange Juice were in the business of light, bright romantic pop, typified by singles like 'Falling And Laughing' and 'Simply Thrilled

Honey'. Their aspirations musically were hindered somewhat by a lack of proficiency, but they learnt fast and the arrival of Zimbabwean Zeke Manyika on drums added a welcome rhythmic discipline. However, despite the resulting funkiness of 1984's *Texas Fever*, sales were rarely exciting (apart from a UK Top Ten hit with 'Rip It Up'). Collins felt he'd squeezed the last goodness from the outfit and set off on a solo career that only finally came good with 'A Girl Like You' ten years later.

Key member: Edwyn Collins 23/8/59 • **Recording career:** 1980 - 1984 • **Sounds:** You Can't Hide Your Love Forever 1982, Rip It Up 1982, The Orange Juice 1984

"What we're doing is taking things that are so obvious and putting them against a House backdrop. People stare it in the face and love it." Alex Paterson

Orb

Steve Hillage, a visitor from the planet Gong, performed with the Orb when Alex Paterson put together a live show in 1991 - establishing a direct link back over two decades to the hippie bands that everyone assumed had disappeared into the ether. Paterson, an A&R man for the EG label, conceived the Orb's ambient sound as a post-rave chill-out with Jim Cauty - later one half of KLF - as they married the textures of Tangerine Dream, Eno, and Gong of course, with the Chicago House of Larry Heard. Their landmark release was (and you *had* to be chilled out just to read the title) 'A Huge Ever Growing Pulsating Brain That Rules From The Centre of the Ultraworld', spiced up by samples taken from the late, great Minnie Riperton's delightful 1975 hit 'Loving You', once a few knotty little copyright problems had been sorted out. More and more ambience followed, including 'The Blue Room', a 40-minute single - a hyper-hypnotic groove to take you straight to Orblivion.

Key member: Alex Paterson 1960 • Recording career: 1989 - present • Sounds: The Orb's Adventures Beyond The Ultraworld 1991, UFOrb 1992, Orblivion 1997

Roy Orbison

"I started using sunglasses in Alabama.

I was doing a show with Patsy Cline and Bobby Vee and left my clear glasses on the plane."

There was melodrama in Roy Orbison's voice, and genuine tragedy in his private life. In 1966 he had re-married his first wife Claudette, the subject of a song he wrote for the Everly Brothers; a few weeks after the wedding she died in a motorbike accident. Two years later, he lost his two eldest sons in a house fire. Orbison stopped writing almost immediately, marking the end of a prolific phase, and putting on hold the Big O's trademark falsetto and near-operatic production style of 'In Dreams' and 'Oh, Pretty Woman'. Sun Records' Sam Phillips had originally tried to turn him into a rockabilly act. "But I'm a ballad singer," protested Orbison, and indeed he broke through with 'Only The Lonely' in 1960 (a song he'd offered to Elvis and the Everlys - both acts turned it down). Sadly a fatal heart attack cut short a promising late 1980s comeback, including a platinum solo album, *Mystery Girl*, and his work with the Traveling Wilburys.

Born: 23/4/36 (died 6/12/88) • Recording career: 1955 – 1988 • Sounds: In Dreams 1963, Oh, Pretty Woman 1964, Mystery Girl 1989

Orchestral Manœuvres In The Dark

The Bunnymen had their drum machine Echo. Orchestral Manœuvres In The Dark had Winston - a four-track TEAC tape deck who provided loops and backing tracks, and was an additional band member in their live shows. Like Echo, Winston was eventually replaced by flesh and blood. His owners, Andy McCluskey and Paul Humphreys, had been listening to a lot of Kraftwerk when they started out in 1978, and from the debut single 'Electricity' onwards, their métier was synth-powered electro-pop, deep and crisp and even. The production skills became tighter through 'Enola Gay' and 'Locomotion' - the pair even added a horn section on their 1985 album *Crush*. Teen movie *Pretty In Pink* provided a platform for their 1986 US hit with 'If You Leave' but it was something of a final flourish for the partnership, as Humphreys was preparing to move on. After a three-year hiatus, McCluskey revived OMD with 'Sailing On The Seven Seas' and looped onwards.

"Some people still complain about the tape recorder.

They say it's a cheat." Paul Humphreys

Key members: Paul Humphreys 27/2/60, Andy McCluskey 24/6/59 • Recording career: 1979 - 1988 & 1991 - present • Sounds: Orchestral Manœuvres In The Dark 1980, Dazzle Ships 1983, Crush 1985

Joan Osborne

After plugging away for years in New York blues clubs, Joan Osborne was suddenly turning up at the Grammy Awards in February 1996 with a clutch of nominations. A decade earlier, persuaded by friends to perform at the Abilene bar in Manhattan, she and the accompanist had but one song in common, Billie Holiday's 'God Bless The Child'. It went down well, and Osborne began a love affair with the blues, her voice capable of Janis Joplin belters or Bonnie Raitt heartbreakers. Rick Chertoff at Polygram signed her up and introduced her to Eric Bazilian, late of 1980s pop group the Hooters: it was Bazilian who provided her with the US Number One single 'One Of Us' ("What if God were..."). The album *Relish* also contained a touch of erotic charged (on 'Let's Just Get Naked'), and included Osborne's neat visual observations - she had been a film student - but strangely, after all the critical hullabaloo, it took her five years to produce a follow-up.

"Most of my friends ended up staying in Kentucky, getting married and having kids. I wanted to do something different, **so I was considered a bit of a freak.**"

Born: 8/7/63 • Recording career: 1992 - present • Sounds: Soul Show 1992, Relish 1995, Righteous Love 2000

Robert Palmer

Those who encountered Robert Palmer in his crooning 'She Makes My Day' moments would be forgiven for thinking that the man had come hotfoot from Caesar's Palace, but this was just another phase in a career that had already covered substantial stylistic mileage. Palmer first made his presence felt in Vinegar Joe, a much cherished UK R'n'B group in which he shared vocals with Elkie Brooks. He was sent into solo orbit by Island's Chris Blackwell: the debut album, 1974's *Sneakin' Sally Through*

The Alley, was blessed with a mellow sheen provided by Little Feat's Lowell George, the Meters and ace session drummer Bernard Purdie. Palmer then continued shifting ground, including collaborations with Gary Numan (on the electro-pop 'Johnny And Mary') and Duran Duran's Andy and John Taylor in the band Power Station, which led to the slick, raunchy and ballsy 'Addicted To Love'. By 1999 Palmer completed his musical circumnavigation with an album called *Rhythm & Blues*.

"I won't be doing the Las Vegas lounges. I can't handle those crowds."

Born: 19/1/49 • Recording career (solo): 1974 - present • Sounds: Sneakin' Sally Through The Alley 1974, Double Fun 1978, Riptide 1985

Graham Parker and the Rumour

The Rumour were a London pub-rock supergroup, with members culled from Brinsley Schwarz (including Brinsley himself), Ducks Deluxe and Bontemps Roulez. They were already gigging when Stiff Records founder, Dave Robinson, paired them with Graham Parker, who'd been hustling his own material. Both parties benefited: Parker's edgy vocals needed the band's tight framework, and the Rumour gained a spiky frontman. The combination worked well, especially on tracks like 'White Honey' or their cover of the Trammps' 'Hold Back The Night'. However, Parker was never a relaxed singer, and his bitter tone was a touch unrelenting - a rare leavening of (sardonic) humour came in the song 'Mercury Poisoning', his jibe at Mercury Records following a dispute. By then he had also, gallingly, found himself overtaken by Stiff Records' rising star Elvis Costello. Parker struck back with the excellent album *Squeezing Out Sparks* in 1979, but further incandescence proved to be intermittent.

"By the time we got to Squeezing Out Sparks we were doing a whole different thing, something that only an idiot would describe as pub rock... I think." Graham Parker

Key member: Graham Parker 18/11/50 • Recording career: 1976 – 1980 • Sounds: Howlin' Wind 1976, Heat Treatment 1976, Squeezing Out Sparks 1979

Gram Parsons

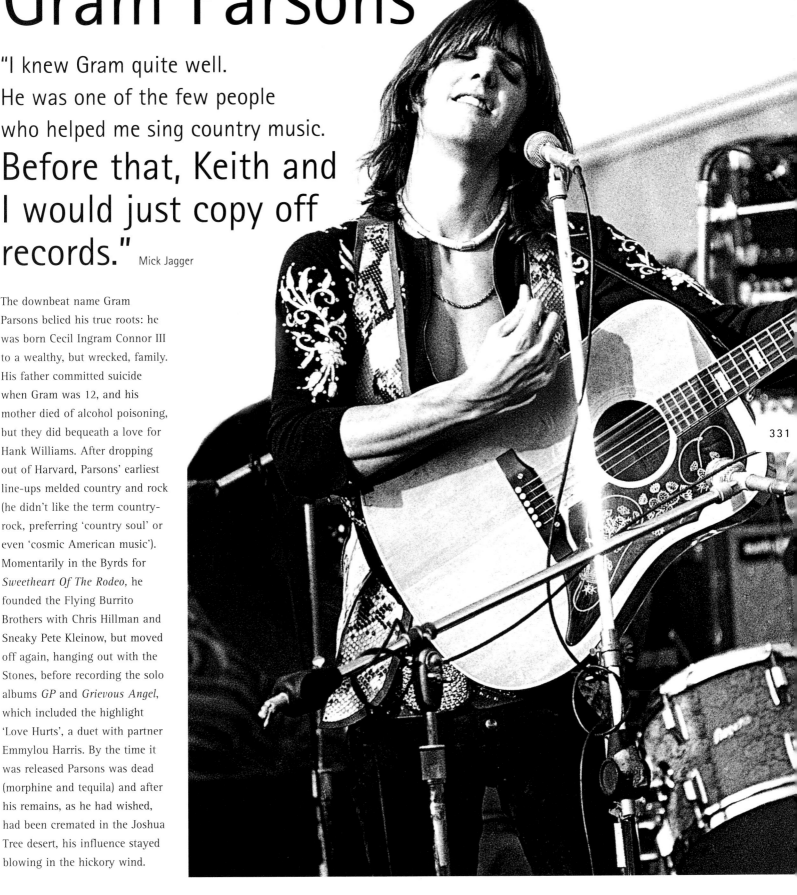

"I knew Gram quite well.
He was one of the few people
who helped me sing country music.
**Before that, Keith and
I would just copy off
records."** Mick Jagger

The downbeat name Gram
Parsons belied his true roots: he
was born Cecil Ingram Connor III
to a wealthy, but wrecked, family.
His father committed suicide
when Gram was 12, and his
mother died of alcohol poisoning,
but they did bequeath a love for
Hank Williams. After dropping
out of Harvard, Parsons' earliest
line-ups melded country and rock
(he didn't like the term country-
rock, preferring 'country soul' or
even 'cosmic American music').
Momentarily in the Byrds for
Sweetheart Of The Rodeo, he
founded the Flying Burrito
Brothers with Chris Hillman and
Sneaky Pete Kleinow, but moved
off again, hanging out with the
Stones, before recording the solo
albums *GP* and *Grievous Angel*,
which included the highlight
'Love Hurts', a duet with partner
Emmylou Harris. By the time it
was released Parsons was dead
(morphine and tequila) and after
his remains, as he had wished,
had been cremated in the Joshua
Tree desert, his influence stayed
blowing in the hickory wind.

331

Born: Cecil Connor III 5/11/46 (died 19/9/73) • Recording career: 1967 - 1973 • Sounds: GP 1972, Grievous Angel 1974

Geographically, the members of Pavement were scattered variously on the East and West Coasts, making regular rehearsals something of a problem. However, it was a perfect example of the loose, low-fi approach of the band. They could certainly never be accused of suffering from over-production, and their live shows were notoriously unpredictable, especially when original, erratic drummer Gary Young was behind the kit (he was eventually, amicably, fired). But such was Pavement's amateur,

slacker charm, encapsulated on 1992's *Slanted And Enchanted*, where feedback and distortion rubbed shoulders with Stephen Malkmus's laconic delivery of near-melodies and actual hooks on 'Trigger Cut' and 'Here'. Theirs was a campus-friendly sound, and one which worked even better in the UK, where 1995's *Wowee Zowee* charted while loitering way down in the States, suffering from criticism that the album was too diffuse and too fractured. What did people expect? That was Pavement's art.

Pavement

"We're not the next R.E.M., we're the next Barclay James Harvest!"

Stephen Malkmus

Key members: Mark Ibold 30/10/66, Scott Kannberg 30/8/66, Stephen Malkmus 30/5/66, Bob Nastanovich 27/8/67, Steve West 8/12/66 • Recording career: 1989 - 1999

Sounds: Slanted And Enchanted 1991, Crooked Rain, Crooked Rain 1994, Terror Twilight 1999

Pearl Jam

"Some people might say that I have a death-wish. That's wrong. **I have a total life-wish.**" Eddie Vedder

One of Seattle's most promising bands was Mother Love Bone, but its potential was abruptly halted by the death of vocalist Andrew Wood in 1990. Pearl Jam emerged from its ashes, when Eddie Vedder became involved, boiling up an intoxicating recipe of grunge meets classic hard rock: Hendrix, Led Zeppelin and the Doors were all noted as influences. It is an indication of the band's swift acceptance that less than six months after their debut album *Ten* (named after the shirt number of the New Jersey Nets' Mookie Blaylock) reached US Number Two, Eddie Vedder was inducting Jim Morrison posthumously into the Hall of Fame. Despite some media hype, there was never really a Blur/Oasis-style grudge match with Nirvana, but in 1993 *Vs.* went straight to the top of the US charts, outselling *Nevermind*, just as *Ten* had. Yet, despite their subsequent consistently high sales, a loyal fanbase and Vedder's real star quality Pearl Jam could never quite eclipse the Cobain myth.

Key members: Dave Abbruzzese 17/5/64, Jeff Ament 10/3/63, Stone Gossard 20/7/66, Mike McCready 5/4/65, Eddie Vedder 23/12/64 • **Recording career:** 1992 – present

Sounds: Ten 1992, Vs. 1993, Yield 1998

"If a person keeps living, he'll run into himself."

On the verge of potential greatness, Carl Perkins was dealt a bad hand by the cosmic cardsharp. He had just recorded 'Blue Suede Shoes' for Sam Phillips in December 1955 - an instant rockabilly anthem. Then, on tour in 1956, a car accident seriously injured Carl and brother Jay. By the time Carl recovered, the impetus had been lost, and when Jay died two years later from a brain tumour related to the crash, Carl turned to booze to salve his wounds. He ended up, undeservedly, a one-hit wonder, although he was pleasantly surprised to find the Beatles were fans: they recorded a number of his songs, including 'Matchbox'. 'Blue Suede Shoes' survives him, as well as the so-called *Million Dollar Quartet*, a 1956 jam session at Sun Records involving Perkins, Elvis, Jerry Lee Lewis and Johnny Cash (who popped in while shopping, but didn't sing). Now that was one hell of a band.

Carl Perkins

Born: 9/4/32 (died 19/1/98) • Recording career: 1955 - 1996 • Sounds: The Dance Album Of Carl Perkins 1957, Ol' Blue Suede Shoes Is Back 1977, Go Cat Go! 1996

In his own understated, shrinking violet way (not), Lee 'Scratch' Perry has been a pioneer of reggae, dub and dancehall. Originally a deejay on Coxsone Dodd's sound system in Kingston, he split with Dodd in 1966, the grudge inspiring a song called 'The Upsetter'. It gave Perry one of his many nicknames, but also the freedom to develop his own style, notably with the Wailers - whose sound he beefed up and slowed down, using the Barrett brothers rhythm section out of his own group, the Upsetters. For a five-year period from 1969 Perry issued dozens of singles and began exploring the technological constraints and possibilities of his tiny, homely studio Black Ark, his own *Revolution Dub* and Max Romeo's *War Ina Babylon* both benchmarks. Perry's decidedly offbeat humour and ideas - and his weird but very wonderful stream-of-consciousness interviews - grew wilder over the years, but his guiding hand was always totally sane.

"It was only four tracks written on the machine, but I was picking up twenty from the extra-terrestrial squad. I am the dub shepherd."

Lee 'Scratch' Perry

Born: 28/3/36 • Recording career: 1963 - present • **Sounds:** The Upsetter 1969, Blackboard Jungle 1973, Super Ape 1976

Pet Shop Boys

"Because everything we do is supposed to be cynical, clever, ironic and all that, **people often miss the emotional side."** Neil Tennant

On the cover of *Actually*, Neil Tennant, natty in a tux, was yawning widely like a languid synth-era Noel Coward, a feigned boredom that declared "all this is just too too much, dear boy". But behind the digital programming was an acute sense of melody, humanity, care and attention that said otherwise. Tennant was a *Smash Hits* journalist when he encountered Chris Lowe, and on a business trip to New York he met disco producer Bobby 'O' Orlando, who oversaw the Pet Shop Boys' debut 'West End Girls'. On its first release in 1984 little happened, but re-styled by Stephen Hague it went to UK and US Number One, setting up a run of extremely palatable hits, from 'It's A Sin' to camped-up Elvis ('Always On My Mind') and the wicked mix of U2's 'Where The Streets Have No Name' with Andy Williams on 'Can't Take My Eyes Off You'. Hummable? Definitely. Boring? Never.

Key members: Chris Lowe 4/10/59, Neil Tennant 10/7/54 • Recording career: 1984 - present • Sounds: Please 1986, Actually 1987, Very 1993

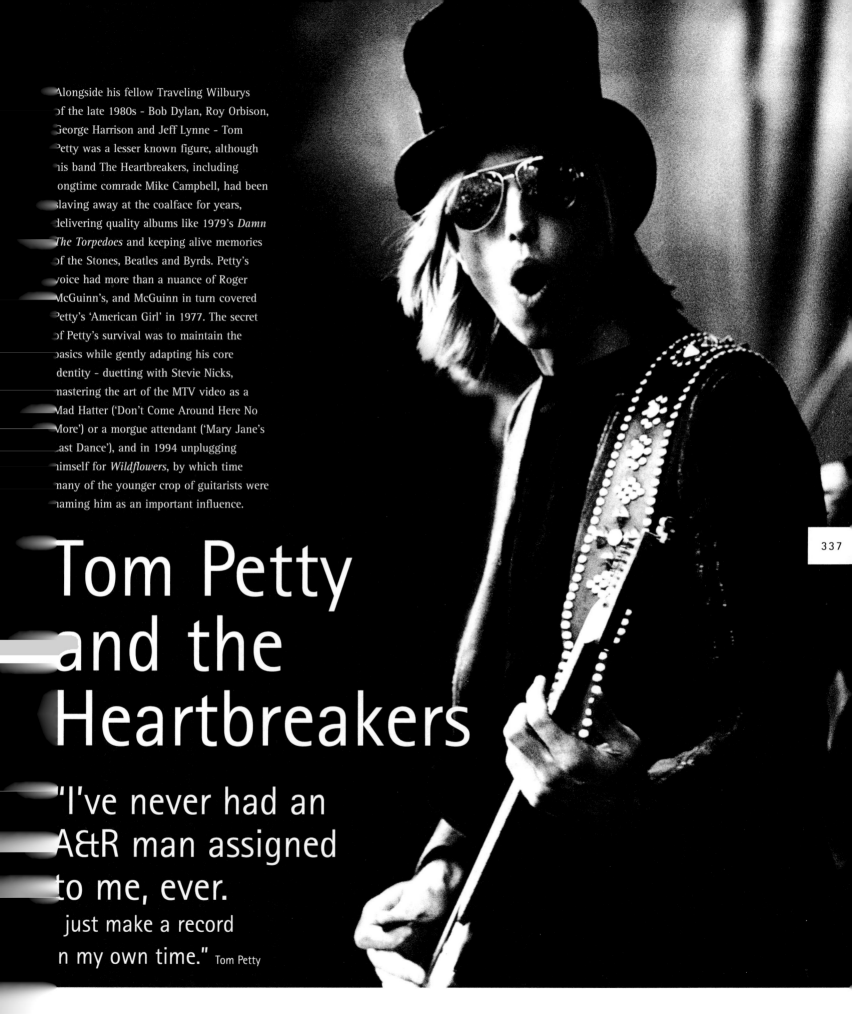

Alongside his fellow Traveling Wilburys of the late 1980s - Bob Dylan, Roy Orbison, George Harrison and Jeff Lynne - Tom Petty was a lesser known figure, although his band The Heartbreakers, including longtime comrade Mike Campbell, had been slaving away at the coalface for years, delivering quality albums like 1979's *Damn The Torpedoes* and keeping alive memories of the Stones, Beatles and Byrds. Petty's voice had more than a nuance of Roger McGuinn's, and McGuinn in turn covered Petty's 'American Girl' in 1977. The secret of Petty's survival was to maintain the basics while gently adapting his core identity - duetting with Stevie Nicks, mastering the art of the MTV video as a Mad Hatter ('Don't Come Around Here No More') or a morgue attendant ('Mary Jane's Last Dance'), and in 1994 unplugging himself for *Wildflowers*, by which time many of the younger crop of guitarists were naming him as an important influence.

Tom Petty and the Heartbreakers

"I've never had an A&R man assigned to me, ever. I just make a record in my own time." Tom Petty

Key member: Tom Petty 20/10/52 • Recording career: 1976 - present • Sounds: Damn The Torpedoes 1979, Southern Accents 1985, Wildflowers 1994

Liz Phair

'Guyville' was not Liz Phair's invention - the term came from a song by the Chicago band Urge Overkill - but she knew exactly where its male-dominated, testosterone-flooded city limits were and promptly ramraided its downtown. Her first album *Exile In Guyville* (a pointed response to the Stones' *Main Street* equivalent) titillated but more often terrified most men, who blushed to their uptight roots at her unvarnished sexual lyrics. Though it was OK for a bloke, a woman just shouldn't be singing about these things, they thought. But Phair had simply set to music the kind of intimate discussions women had "in the harem pit", as she put it, which coincided with a mood of upfront female frankness. Predictably she found herself typecast - and tried hard on the follow-ups *Whip-Smart* and *whitechocolatespaceegg* to convince the world she wasn't just a nice suburban girl who talked dirty by emphasising her songwriting and guitar work.

"So many women have said the very things I'm saying, just in different ways. I hit a chord and suddenly people heard it."

Born: 17/4/67 • Recording career: 1993 - present • Sounds: Exile In Guyville 1993, Whip-Smart 1995, whitechocolatespaceegg 1998

339

Pink
Fairies

Think pink, think Twink. John 'Twink' Alder worked with the Pretty Things on their rock opera/concept album *S.F. Sorrow* before joining the Deviants, a Notting Hill underground band who had three releases under their belt. The Deviants' frontman Mick Farren had decided to concentrate on being a noted music journalist. Twink was appointed second drummer and promptly renamed the band, who continued the underground tradition of free gigs à la Hawkwind - with whom they shared a few members - and conceived 1971's *Never Never Land*, which was, in summary, as far out as far out could and should ever be. Unable to top that, Twink left and the band eventually recruited UFO guitarist Larry Wallis - a heavier sound inevitably ensued. However, after Wallis had departed for an early version of Motörhead (who later covered the Fairies' 'City Kids') the band were declared DOA in the late 1970s. The Fairies came back to life in 1987 but vital signs were non-existent.

Key members: Russell Hunter, Paul Rudolph, Duncan Sanderson, Twink (John Alder) • Recording career: 1971 - 1973 & 1987
Sounds: Never Never Land 1971, What A Bunch Of Sweeties 1972, Kings Of Oblivion 1973

Pink Floyd

"Our music is about neuroses, but that doesn't mean we are neurotic.

We are able to see it, and discuss it." Dave Gilmour

As Syd Barrett's contribution to Pink Floyd faltered, Dave Gilmour was brought in on guitar. The idea was that Barrett would still write songs *in absentia*, like a Brian Wilson figure, but when it became clear this was unlikely, the rest of the band were obliged to pick up the baton. Of them all, Roger Waters responded best to the challenge, and it was his commitment that produced a commercial breakthrough - "we were underground until *Dark Side Of The Moon*," according to Nick Mason.

Dark Side was the timely confluence of a loose but coherent concept, accessible lyrics, great sound effects, Gilmour's guitar soaring on 'Time' and 'Money', the polish of sax and female vocals (Clare Torry's orgasmic 'Great Gig In The Sky') and Alan Parsons' hi-fi engineering. The final icing was Storm Thorgerson's iconic packaging, forecasting that this was the high point of the band's pyramid; Waters typically observed that the album "finished the Pink Floyd off once and for all".

Key members: Syd Barrett 6/1/46, Dave Gilmour 6/3/46, Nick Mason 27/1/45, Roger Waters 9/9/44, Rick Wright 28/7/45 • Recording career: 1967 - present

Sounds: The Piper At The Gates Of Dawn 1967, Dark Side Of The Moon 1973, The Wall 1979

Pixies

"I did buy a little instruction book.

I was trying to read music, but after a while it was going over my head." Joey Santiago

The archives of rock history owe a great deal to the small ads sections. Founding Pixies Black Francis and Joey Santiago set out their agenda with one such request for musicians into 'Hüsker Dü and Peter, Paul and Mary' (Kim Deal was the only respondent!), and the conflation of hard rock and pop was the beauty and the beast at the heart of their recordings, once astutely described as like 'Beach Boys on acid'. They were press favourites in the UK, where their albums went Top Ten (their homeland turned out to be more resistant) including *Doolittle* and *Bossanova*, which both had producer Gil Norton tightening up the sound for the marketplace, but not diffusing its impact. Francis and Kim Deal's variant vocal approaches added additional interest, but Deal's increasing desire to write herself - she set up the Breeders with Tanya Donelly as a sideline - created growing tensions, and by 1993 Black Francis was announcing that they'd hung up their Pixie hats.

Key members: Black Francis (Charles Thompson) 1965, Kim Deal 10/6/61, David Lovering 6/12/61, Joey Santiago 10/6/65 • Recording career: 1987 - 1992

Sounds: Surfer Rosa 1988, Doolittle 1989, Bossanova 1990

P J Harvey

Like Manfred Mann, P J Harvey was the name of the group, but whereas Manfred Mann was fronted by Paul Jones, Polly Jean Harvey was clearly the magnetic force at the heart of her band. It also meant, she said, that when she decided to move on from her first line-up she would be less constrained. In the event it only took two albums before she spread her wings. After the release of her debut *Dry* in 1992, an uncompromisingly punkish set of songs that touched on the same lyrical territory as Liz Phair (only more introvertedly), and the follow-up *Rid Of Me*, she abandoned the severe, black-clad look that she'd sported when the band first came out of the West Country. The new Polly Harvey, scarlet lipsticked and looking like she'd dressed up in her mum's best clothes, was liberated at a single bound - now she was free to be whatever she wanted.

"I don't want to do anything that's just straight glamorous. It has to have some element of uneasiness or humour."

Polly Harvey

Key member: Polly Harvey 9/10/69 • Recording career: 1991 - present • Sounds: Dry 1992, To Bring You My Love 1995, Stories From the City, Stories From The Sea 2000

The Pogues

The history of the Pogues was the musical equivalent of a trawl round the bars of Ennis, County Clare: you couldn't quite remember all the details but you were pretty sure you'd had a very good time. Shane MacGowan actually hailed from Tunbridge Wells (though he grew up in Tipperary) and it was in the UK that he found his comrades-in-arms for the Pogues' Irish folk-punk. Legend has it when they signed to Stiff Records as Pogue Mahone - a transcription of *póg mo thóin*, the Irish for 'kiss my arse' - their signing fee was a crate of Guinness. Although the band's main aura was one of riotous chaos, the songwriting, particularly by MacGowan and Jem Finer, was subtle, with a love of melody evident in their Christmas 1987 hit 'Fairytale of New York', recorded with Kirsty MacColl. By then MacGowan was having problems keeping it all together and he was fired in 1991 for, guess what, inebriation on tour. It had been a rollicking ride.

"I'm sick of performing live. You have to do it, but it's a bit like screwing for a living."

Shane MacGowan

Key members: Philip Chevron 17/6/57, James Fearnley 9/10/54, Jem Finer 20/7/55, Shane MacGowan 25/12/57, Andrew Ranken 13/11/53, Spider Stacy 14/12/58

Recording career: 1984 - 1996 • Sounds: Rum Sodomy & The Lash 1985, If I Should Fall From Grace With God 1988, Hell's Ditch 1990

The Police

By the time of the Police's final album, *Synchronicity*, it was clear that of the trio, Sting's songwriting was (blond) head and (stripy) shoulders above the other two. But initially Sting, a sometime teacher, sometime jazzer, was the junior member. Stewart Copeland had drummed for prog-rockers Curved Air, while Andy Summers had seen action with the Animals, Soft Machine and Zoot Money. None were spring chickens - Summers was in his late thirties - but they managed to connect with

the post-punk scene courtesy of energy and bleached hair. 'Roxanne' was an arresting (no pun etc.) single in the summer of 1979, setting the scene for their 'white reggae' mix of Sting's jazz instincts, Copeland's crisp drumming and Summers' spare flange-echo guitar. Some found the songs superficial, even pompous, but the hits kept on coming - 'Walking On The Moon', 'Every Little Thing She Does Is Magic', 'Every Breath You Take' - until, with impeccable timing, they pulled the plug.

"I had to talk Sting out of leaving in 1977, by saying

'Look, it's just around the corner'.

I had to keep his morale up." Stewart Copeland

Key members: Stewart Copeland 16/7/52, Sting (Gordon Sumner) 2/10/51, Andy Summers 31/12/42 • Recording career: 1977 - 1983 & 1986

Sounds: Reggatta De Blanc 1979, Ghost In The Machine 1981, Synchronicity 1983

"I think I am a little different upstairs, yeah...
but so are a lot of people."

Iggy Pop made it to fifty, which surprised many people, not least himself, since he'd tried hard to avoid ageing. Drugs, of course. Self-mutilation on stage: where Alice Cooper employed props, Iggy used his own body. And on stage in Detroit, inciting local gang the Scorpions to finish him off. He was a truly mixed-up kid: part the bespectacled James Osterberg (from a very straight background in Ann Arbor, Michigan) part his stone-crazy alter ego Iggy - Jim Morrison imbued with real malevolence. His band, the Stooges, arrived like a jet of Agent Orange to strip flower power bare, and explored the outer reaches of excess in Stooge Mansions, the *Fun House* of their best album. After Iggy checked into a mental institution, David Bowie nurtured him back to some kind of health to see punk follow Iggy's lead (and Stooge Ron Asheton's guitar). He survived: it was time for golf and a little light gardening.

Iggy Pop

Born: James Osterberg 21/4/47 • Recording career: 1969 - present • Sounds: Fun House (with the Stooges) 1970, Lust For Life 1977, American Caesar 1993

Portishead

Take the M5 south past Bristol and there's the slip-road to Portishead, the suburb where Geoff Barrow grew up and which he introduced to the world - though he dashed the tourist board's hopes by describing it as "pretty and twee, actually quite horrible". Shaping his musical vision through tape op work on Massive Attack's *Blue Lines*, Barrow found his voice in Beth Gibbons, and *what* a voice, capable of ice-cold angst, tremulous emotion or a chanteuse's smoky breathiness over the musical soundtrack of their award-winning album *Dummy*. This was not just trip-hop - they spurned the term anyway - it was a Todd A-O wide pan across

the band's interest in mood music and 1960s spy movies: 'Sour Times' ("Nobody loves me") the perfect sampler. After three years, the follow-up album, uninventively titled *Portishead*, at least stopped everyone wearing out their CDs of *Dummy*, but it was, in essence, more of the same.

"Just because our music sounds quite mellow at first, people seem to think
'Ah, we'll play that when we're having friends round for a fondue party'." Geoff Barrow

346

Key members: Geoff Barrow 9/12/71, Beth Gibbons 4/1/65, Dave McDonald 1964, Adrian Utley 1958 • Recording career: 1994 - present • Sounds: Dummy 1994, Portishead 1997, PNYC 1998

Prefab Sprout

Carefully crafted pop runs the risk of becoming an all-too-easy target for accusations of frailty and lack of depth. Paddy McAloon skated over that thin ice with great elegance for a while with his band Prefab Sprout. What the Sprouts offered was the kind of music perfect for a wet winter Wednesday - jazzy and tasteful fare, what one American commentator pointedly dubbed 'Steely Dan Lite', and they could have benefited from a touch of the Dan's sardonic steel. *Steve McQueen,*

the album (renamed *Two Wheels Good* in the US after McQueen's daughter complained) was classy enough, and *From Langley Park To Memphis* attracted contributions from Stevie Wonder and Pete Townshend. The Who were early heroes of McAloon, along with Elvis Presley: 'The King Of Rock'n'Roll' was Prefab's biggest hit, and 1990's *Jordan: The Comeback* included a four-song set charting Presley's life. Literate songwriter he was, but Paddy McAloon was no Elvis...

"I'm notoriously bad at remembering my own lyrics." Paddy McAloon

Key members: Neil Conti 12/2/59, Martin McAloon 4/1/62, Paddy McAloon 7/6/57, Wendy Smith 31/5/63 • **Recording career:** 1982 - 1990 & 1997 - present

Sounds: Steve McQueen (US title: Two Wheels Good) 1985, From Langley Park To Memphis 1988, Jordan: The Comeback 1990

Elvis Presley

"Rock'n'roll has been in for about five years.
I'm not going to sit here and say that it's gonna last because I don't know."

At the start of 1958, recording the soundtrack for *King Creole*, Elvis Presley was on the cusp of a major life change. In August that year his beloved mother Gladys died; two months later Private Elvis set sail for Germany. It was the end of Elvis Part One: the shy, lonely boy with a lust for music discovered by Sam Phillips, who was looking for a white boy who could sing black ("All he did was sit with his guitar on the side of his bed at home," recalled Sam). With Scotty Moore and Bill Black, Presley recorded 'That's All Right Mama' at Phillips' studio in July 1954. It was, in a genre full of 'seminal moments', one of the truly great ones - and as Little Richard exclaimed, "I thank God for Elvis Presley". Four years later, the shadowy figure of Colonel Tom Parker had taken a grip, and out of the army, Elvis's life would be far less clear-cut, submerged in fantasy, slander and myth.

Born: 8/1/35 (died 16/8/77) • Recording career: 1954 - 1977 • Sounds: Elvis Presley 1956, Elvis Is Back! 1960, From Elvis In Memphis 1969

Pretenders

'Stop Your Sobbing' was a Ray Davies song from the first Kinks album which the Pretenders choose as their debut single at the end of 1978. Their leading light Chrissie Hynde met her idol Davies in 1980, leading to a relationship, but it didn't last: Hynde married Simple Mind's Jim Kerr in 1984. By then, the original Pretenders line-up - the one that produced 'Brass In Pocket' and 'Talk Of The Town', when Hynde's quavering voice

and ineffable cool were at their peak - had been ravaged by the drug-related deaths of guitarist James Honeyman-Scott and the recently fired bassist Pete Farndon. Even Hynde's tough-talking exterior and thick skin couldn't hide the hurt. She re-grouped, a single like 'Don't Get Me Wrong' proving she hadn't lost her grip, and though she began to concentrate on eco causes, she could still thrill on 1995's acoustic *The Isle Of View*.

"No one has ever seen my legs, my ass, my tits. Even my fucking face I've hidden beneath my fringe. I'm the original yashmak rocker!" Chrissie Hynde

Key members: Martin Chambers 4/9/51, Pete Farndon 12/6/52 (died 14/4/83), James Honeyman-Scott 4/11/56 (died 16/6/82), Chrissie Hynde 17/9/51

Recording career: 1978 - 1987 & 1990 - present • Sounds: Pretenders 1980, Learning To Crawl 1984, The Isle Of View 1995

Pretty Things

"I don't think we could have played a pop song if we tried.

In fact I know we couldn't - when we did try it wasn't very good." Dick Taylor

Other than their name - taken from a Bo Diddley number - there was little pretty about the Pretty Things: their behaviour was deliberately outré, and their R'n'B down and distinctly dirty. At one point they almost threatened to out-Stone the Stones: Dick Taylor and Phil May had attended art college with Keith Richards, and Taylor was briefly the bass-player in a nascent Stones line-up. But, as is the way of the music business, the Pretty

Things had a few bad breaks and, after 'Honey I Need' in 1965, failed to chart again. They moved into psychedelia by composing an acid-rock opera, *S.F. Sorrow*, which was rumoured to have given Pete Townshend a kickstart for Tommy. However, it didn't do the trick, although they were respected enough for Bowie to cover two of their songs on *Pin-Ups* and for Led Zep's Swan Song label to try and rescue their flagging career.

Key members: Phil May 9/11/44, Brian Pendleton 13/4/44, Viv Prince 9/8/44, John Stax 6/4/44, Dick Taylor 28/1/43 • Recording career: 1964 -1976 & 1980, 1984 - 1989, 1995 - present

Sounds: Pretty Things 1965, S.F. Sorrow 1968, Parachute 1970

"At the risk of sounding pretentious, I think Primal Scream always tried to make something beautiful." Bobby Gillespie

The constants of Primal Scream have been Bobby Gillespie and his out-and-out admiration for 1960s rock'n'roll. When he started the band in the 1980s, simultaneously drumming for the Jesus And Mary Chain, the influence of the Stooges and the Stones was pretty obvious, and the music was not going anywhere particularly fast. It was the vibrant club scene that changed Primal Scream's fortunes, allowing master alchemist Andy Weatherall to create a rocking-funk-dance amalgam that gave a glimpse of the future on *Screamadelica*. But although the follow-up *Give Out But Don't Give Up* boasted the considerable presence of the Memphis Horns and George Clinton, the album, for all its soulful R'n'B funk, was slated for being too retro. The criticisms stung, and the band lost their shape. 1997's *Vanishing Point* threatened to be self-fulfilling, but three years later *Xtrmntr* (with My Bloody Valentine's Kevin Shields on board) was a splendidly splenetic, clangorous piece of retaliation.

Primal Scream

Key members: Bobby Gillespie 22/6/64, Andrew Innes, Robert Young • **Recording career:** 1985 - present • **Sounds:** Screamadelica 1991, Give Out But Don't Give Up 1994, Xtrmntr 2000

Prince

Howard Stern called him "The Artist People Formerly Cared About", but Prince was unfazed. "The people who really know the music don't joke about it. I know exactly who I am." Perhaps the most unexpected aspect of his identity was that Prince was actually his real name, after the Prince Rogers Trio, his father's jazz group. At 20 he was already prolific, his horny impishness straddling a funk-rock groove on *Dirty Mind*. Although songs like 'Head' and 'Sister' (with its incest theme) limited his airplay, less overt songs let his melodic skills shine through: '1999', 'Little Red Corvette' and the *Purple Rain* soundtrack, which made up for the dire movie. But he could never leave the controversial stuff alone - his unreleased *Black Album* was the hottest bootleg of 1988 - and he almost dropped out of the mainstream until the *Batman* movie gave him a route back in. If only TAFKAP could stop being so damn weird...

"I try not to repeat myself.

It's the hardest thing in the world. There's only so many notes a human being can muster."

352

Born: Prince Nelson 7/6/58 • Recording career: 1978 - present • Sounds: Dirty Mind 1980, Sign O' The Times 1987, Diamonds And Pearls 1991

Procol Harum

Where would we have been without the R'n'B school for budding British bands that existed in the 1960s? Procol Harum were yet more old boys, pianist/singer Gary Brooker having formerly been part of the Paramounts, who had released a few singles before reaching a dead end. He was put in touch with lyricist Keith Reid and together they cooked up Procol's surreal debut release 'A Whiter Shade Of Pale', with lyrical fandango farrago courtesy of Reid and a dash of

Air On The G String courtesy of Bach. It was a dream start, going straight to Number One in the UK, but became something of a stone around Procol's communal neck, even though the follow-up single 'Homburg' charted. They drafted in the ex-Paramounts guitarist Robin Trower (later the living embodiment of Jimi Hendrix), who added oomph on excellent, though generally ignored, albums like *A Salty Dog* - but frustratingly 'Whiter Shade' overshadowed their best efforts.

"Some of Keith's lyrics were five or six lines, but 'Whiter Shade' was a mammoth thing, a full-up A4 masterpiece." Gary Brooker

353

Key members: Gary Brooker 29/5/45, Matthew Fisher 7/3/46, Bobby Harrison 28/6/43, Dave Knights 28/6/45, Ray Royer 8/10/45 • **Recording career:** 1967 - 1977 & 1991

Sounds: Procol Harum 1967, A Salty Dog 1969, Broken Barricades 1971

Prodigy

While a large slice of the UK's youth was immersing itself in rave culture, the rest of the nation wasn't sure what was going on there (which was, of course, part of its appeal). It was left to the Prodigy to lift a corner of the tent flap when their hard dance singles began getting mainstream chart action - 1991's 'Charly' and 'Everybody In The Place' turning a trickle into a deluge. Liam Howlett, mastermind and master mixer, had undergone a conversion to rave from hip hop somewhere in Essex, where else, in the late 1980s. When he encountered Keith Flint's energy and Leeroy Thornhill's flexibility, he constructed a genuine band, which was one of the outfit's great strengths. After 'Firestarter' got everybody jumping in 1996 and made Keith Flint's hair a national treasure, 'Smack My Bitch Up' landed the Prodigy in trouble - a sure sign they'd arrived.

"If the Prodigy were the Wu-Tang Clan, nobody would say anything about the title 'Smack My Bitch Up.'" Saffron of Republica

Key members: Keith Flint 17/9/69, Liam Howlett 21/8/71, Maxim Reality (Keeti Palmer) 21/3/67, Leeroy Thornhill 8/10/68 • Recording career: 1991 - present

Sounds: Experience 1992, Music For The Jilted Generation 1994, The Fat Of The Land 1997

The Psychedelic Furs

When screenwriter John Hughes based his script for *Pretty In Pink* on a 1981 Psychedelic Furs single, the band were unprepared for the knock-on effect. A re-recorded version featured in the teen comedy and suddenly Furs gigs were full of screaming girls. Strange times for a UK band who'd revelled in the chaos of punk, whilst kicking against its strictures by drawing on a raft of earlier influences - not least the Velvets, whose 'Venus In Furs' inspired the group's name. Early albums, produced by Steve Lillywhite and Todd Rundgren, captured Richard Butler's hoarse vocals wrapped in noise, but voguish commercial pressures to follow up 'Pretty In Pink' and crack the American AM market left the Furs feeling they'd turned into the very bands they originally hated. A return to basics revived their spirit but not their sales and constant members guitarist John Ashton, vocalist Richard Butler and his brother Tim moulted into various East Coast projects.

"I was listening to the Velvet Underground and Bob Dylan, and the two seemed to fit."
Richard Butler

Key members: John Ashton 30/11/57, Richard Butler 5/6/56, Tim Butler 7/12/58 • **Recording career:** 1980 - 1991 • **Sounds:** Psychedelic Furs 1980, Talk Talk Talk 1981, Mirror Moves 1984

"The word is what gets people riled and spiked. But if you spark them up and don't give them no directions **people will lose it."** Chuck D

The production team behind Public Enemy was called the Bomb Squad: they planted an explosive mixture. Self-styled 'prophets of rage', Public Enemy were articulate fighters for black rights, their college background automatically putting them on a different footing from gangsta rap. WBAU, the radio station at Adelphi University, Long Island, was where the individual elements came together: Chuck D's oratorical voice and committed ideals offset by the looning about of Flavor Flav, with Terminator X at the turntables, Professor Griff running their Ministry of Information, and Hank Shocklee and Bill Stephney overseeing operations. Public Enemy was a finely drilled team, working as a unit to deliver hard-edged political education lessons for black and white alike from 'Bring The Noise' and 'Don't Believe The Hype' onwards. Courted by the rock world, they toured with U2 and the Sisters Of Mercy, but were nobody's stooges - and more than any other act they made hip hop a credible cultural force.

Public Enemy

Key members: Chuck D (Carlton Ridenhour) 1/8/60, Flavor Flav (Willian Drayton) 16/3/59, Terminator X (Norman Rogers) 25/8/66 • Recording career: 1985 - present

Sounds: It Takes A Nation Of Millions To Hold Us Back 1988, Fear Of A Black Planet 1990, Muse Sick-n-hour Mess Age 1994

"If somebody had told me in 1981 that it would take 13 years to get recognised, **I would have been horrified."** Jarvis Cocker

Pulp

It did take an exceptionally long time for Pulp to find their moment. Way back when, in the early 1980s, they were playing canteen gigs in the lunchbreaks at Jarvis Cocker's school in Sheffield. John Peel showed enough interest to invite them to record a session - but their college commitments cut progress short. The next line-up was interrupted by an importune defenestration which put Cocker in a wheelchair for a year. This slow, erratic progress continued until 1993, when Island signed an at-last-settled formation. As Britpop flourished, Cocker's very English, very funny observations of mundane sexual adventure transformed him into the thinking girl's gangling sex object - and into a fully fledged hero for his admirers following that Brit Awards fracas with Michael Jackson. 'Common People' and 'Disco 2000' were an aloof cut above the laddishness of many of their contemporaries, so much so that you knew Britpop was going to be just one staging post on Pulp's nomadic travels.

Key members: Nicholas Banks 1966, Jarvis Cocker 10/9/63, Candida Doyle 1964, Stephen Mackey 1967, Russell Senior 1962 • **Recording career:** 1981 - present
Sounds: His'n'Hers 1994, Different Class 1995, This is Hardcore 1998

"For my headstone I'll have a nice big bass guitar
in white marble with black strings."

Suzi Quatro

However cartoonish the image, there weren't too many leather-jumpsuited ballsy chicks on the charts in the early 1970s, and Suzi Quatro, her bass slung low, was the precursor of Joan Jett and a host of other runaways. One of five musical kids (sister Patti cropped up in Fanny), Suzi formed various groups with her siblings, including a band called Cradle which, fresh from some R&R gigs in Vietnam, was spotted by British starmaker Mickie Most. He snatched Suzi from Cradle and brought her back to the UK, where the Chinn and Chapman songwriting team churned out 'Can The Can', 'Daytona Demon' and 'Devil Gate Drive', the kind of formulaic singles that made Most's RAK Records, also home to Mud, the bubblegum label of the day. Suzi mellowed, a little, in her later life; by the 1990s she was writing and starring in a musical based on the life of the Etonian-devouring Tallulah Bankhead.

358

Born: 3/6/50 • Recording career: 1973 - present • Sounds: Suzi Quatro 1973, Your Mama Won't Like Me 1975

Queen

"We were adamant that 'Bohemian Rhapsody' could be a hit in its entirety. We have been forced to make compromises, **but cutting up a song will never be one of them.**"

Freddie Mercury

When Wayne, Garth and the guys headbanged in their car to Brian May's thundering guitar riff on 'Bohemian Rhapsody', we laughed because we'd all been there. The song was Queen's crowning glory, not only in its regal extent (seven minutes in the original), but because it captured the essence of Freddie Mercury's operatic posturing, May's ultra-precise fretwork, and the group's fierce obsession with detail - according to May, the tape for 'Bohemian Rhapsody' kept wearing out "every time Fred decided to add a few more 'Galileos'". Remarkably, having delivered 'Rhapsody' so early on in their career - 1975 - they managed to maintain the pace, stealing the limelight at Live Aid ten years later. Bob Geldof said that Mercury had loved it, able to "ponce about in front of the whole world"; another ten years on and he was still holding centre stage from beyond the grave.

Key members: John Deacon 19/8/51, Brian May 19/7/47, Freddie Mercury (Farok Bulsara) 5/9/46 (died 24/11/91), Roger Taylor 26/7/49 • **Recording career:** 1973 - 1991 & 1995 - 1997

Sounds: Sheer Heart Attack 1974, A Night At The Opera 1975, A Kind Of Magic 1986

Quicksilver Messenger Service

"Dino and I have a perfect arrangement: when Dino's in the band, I'm not." John Cipollina

Though they never achieved the recognition factor of a Jefferson Airplane or a Grateful Dead, the Quicksilver Messenger Service rode right through the heart of late 1960s San Francisco. But they didn't have a Grace Slick or a Jerry Garcia upfront, especially once original vocalist Dino Valenti, a Greenwich Village folksinger, disappeared to serve a prison sentence. After some variations, QMS's central quartet established itself - all four of them were Virgos, hence the Quicksilver reference to Mercury, their ruling planet. Lengthy instrumental jams allowed John Cipollina and Gary Duncan's twin guitars to fence each other, a duel best captured on *Happy Trails* (worth buying just to enjoy its evocative cover artwork by George Hunter) with its 25-minute workout based on Bo Diddley's 'Who Do You Love'. Valenti returned from his stint in jail, but his return and increasing domination fractured the band, with members departing and rejoining, seemingly at random - bassist David Freiberg most notably became a regular crew member of Jefferson Starship.

Key members: John Cipollina 24/8/43 (died 29/5/89), Gary Duncan 4/9/46, Greg Elmore 4/9/46, David Freiberg 24/8/38, Dino Valenti 7/11/43 (died 16/11/94) • Recording career: 1968 - 1975 & 1987

Sounds: Quicksilver Messenger Service 1968, Happy Trails 1969, Shady Grove 1969

"Ed invited us to come over to his house and jam.
Dave and I figured we'd play a couple of blues tunes. Instead we jammed for five hours straight, then all quit our old bands the next day." Reggie Scanlan

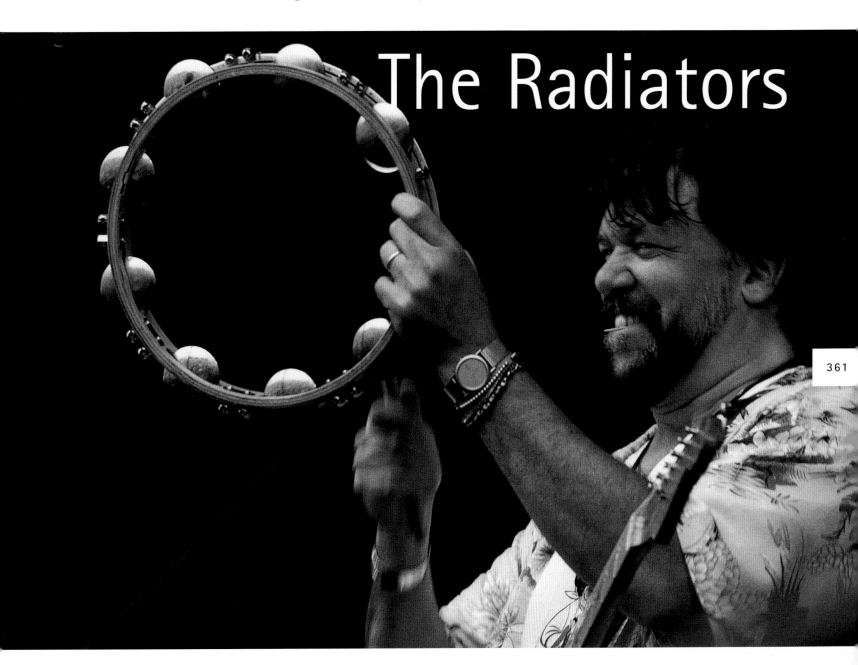

The Radiators

They called it 'Fish-head music': a feisty concoction of rock'n'roll, soul, country, jazz and swing that could only, according to Big Easy aficionados, have been brewed up within the city limits of New Orleans. The five members of the Radiators, staying together and playing together for over twenty years since they first joined forces in 1978, found a steadily growing market for their live shows across the States, eventually able to pack out New York's Roseland Ballroom each time they hit Manhattan. This was an act who were best sampled live, where they could gauge the mood of an audience and draw on a repertoire of something more than 300 numbers to find exactly the right response. Just as foodies might circulate word-of-mouth recommendation for an exquisite, unknown restaurant, Radiators fans would pass on the buzz about tracks like 'Papaya', 'Doctor Doctor' and the band's paean to the delights of eating crawfish, 'Suck The Head'.

Key members: Camile Baudoin, Frank Bua, Dave Malone, Reggie Scanlan, Ed Volker

Recording career: 1980 - present • **Sounds:** Law Of The Fish 1987, New Dark Ages 1995, Songs From The Ancient Furnace 1997

Radiohead

"As soon as you get any success **you disappear up your own arse** and lose it forever." Thom Yorke

Thom Yorke and his fellow Radioheads took one good, early piece of advice - changing their name from On A Friday, a moniker which would doubtless have limited their chances. The band, who formed while schoolboys at Abingdon School (a public-school education that unfairly rendered them open to rock credibility jibes), regrouped in Oxford after various college careers and through an early demo landed themselves a deal with EMI. However, one of their first singles, 'Creep', featuring Yorke's typically anguished lyrics and Jonny Greenwood's howling guitar, was initially viewed as too depressing and got little airplay. Yet while the band licked their wounds, the single burrowed its way around the world's markets, exploding in the US and finally charting in the UK. Sessions for a second album proved fraught, but producer John Leckie eventually extracted *The Bends*, and out of its three-guitar textures Yorke's aching vocals surfaced to produce their first mini-masterpiece... Readers of *Q* magazine later voted *OK Computer* the greatest album of all time.

Key members: Colin Greenwood 26/6/69, Jonny Greenwood 5/11/71, Ed O'Brien 15/4/68, Phil Selway 23/5/67, Thom E. Yorke 7/10/68 • Recording career: 1992 - present

Sounds: The Bends 1995, OK Computer 1997, Kid A 2000

"Silencing artists like us that have a dissenting voice is very appealing to those in power."

Tom Morello

Rage Against The Machine

When Rage Against The Machine signed to Epic, part of the Sony megalith, they left themselves wide open to snide side-swipes about collaborating with the very corporate, capitalist machine that the band had been attacking. RATM ignored the barbs: they had entered the belly of the beast and an album like *Evil Empire*, hitting Number One, could bring their message to the masses. Political animals by heritage - guitarist Tom Morello was a nephew of Jomo Kenyatta - they mounted the soapbox, grabbed a mike and turned their anger and scorn on abuse and exploitation. These were not Ben Harper's crafted songs of injustice. This was ranting sloganeering, with Zack de la Rocha - whose skinny frame belied his vocal power - rapping over Morello's thick, heavy riffs. Nor was it just hot air: the band donated fees from opening U2's *Pop* tour to radical causes and joined in direct action on the streets. And by *The Battle Of Los Angeles*, their sonic blast - previously there just to ram home the message - had developed a personality all of its own.

Key members: Tim Commerford, Zack de La Rocha 1970, Tom Morello 30/5/65, Brad Wilk 5/9/68 • **Recording career: 1993 - present**

Sounds: Rage Against The Machine 1993, Evil Empire 1996, The Battle Of Los Angeles 1999

The Raincoats

We all love our secret bands. Kurt Cobain came across a Raincoats album, and found there a bunch of soulmates whose honest emotions affected him so much that he tracked down founder member Ana da Silva somewhere in Notting Hill, persuaded DGC (Nirvana's record label) to re-issue the Raincoats' back catalogue and encouraged the band to re-form briefly. In 1976 da Silva and Gina Birch, inspired by the example of the Pistols and the Clash, of course, but also by the women of the Slits and X-Ray Spex, had responded to punk's DIY call to arms and eventually convinced the Slits' drummer Palmolive to join their ranks. With the addition of the classically trained violinist Vicky Aspinall, the Raincoats were an all-female band who owed nothing to male-fantasy outfits like the Runaways, and produced a primeval punk-folk sound on original songs like 'Fairytale In The Supermarket' or de-constructing the Kinks' 'Lola' with cheek, fun and a pinch of salt.

"Punk was a very asexual time, a time to stand on your own two feet, and I wasn't very aware of being a girl." Gina Birch

364

Key members: Gina Birch 1956, Ana da Silva 1949 • Recording career: 1979 - 1984 & 1996 • Sounds: The Raincoats 1979, Odyshape 1981, Moving 1984

Bonnie Raitt

After two decades' graft, Bonnie Raitt had Don Was to thank for her comeback, 1989's Grammy award-winning album *Nick Of Time*. His production skills brought commercial success with this and its follow-up *Luck Of The Draw*, but there were carpers who deemed it all too slick. The musicianship was exemplary, yet it was Bonnie's voice that hit the right buttons: a ballad like 'I Can't Make You Love Me' could, on the right (or wrong) night, move you to tears. Her first, constant love - as vocalist and guitarist - was the blues: Son House was a major influence on her trademark slide technique. Raitt's first release contained unadulterated down-the-line blues, but subsequent albums included material by Jackson Browne, Randy Newman and J.D. Souther. She needed the 1980s to regain her breath and undergo some rehab, but never stopped playing; a long overdue live album, *Road Tested*, demonstrated how those dues had honed her sound to perfection.

"Every time I see her live,

I wish we could make the original records over again."

Producer Don Was

Born: 8/11/49 • Recording career: 1971 - present • **Sounds:** Give It Up 1972, Nick Of Time 1989, Road Tested 1995

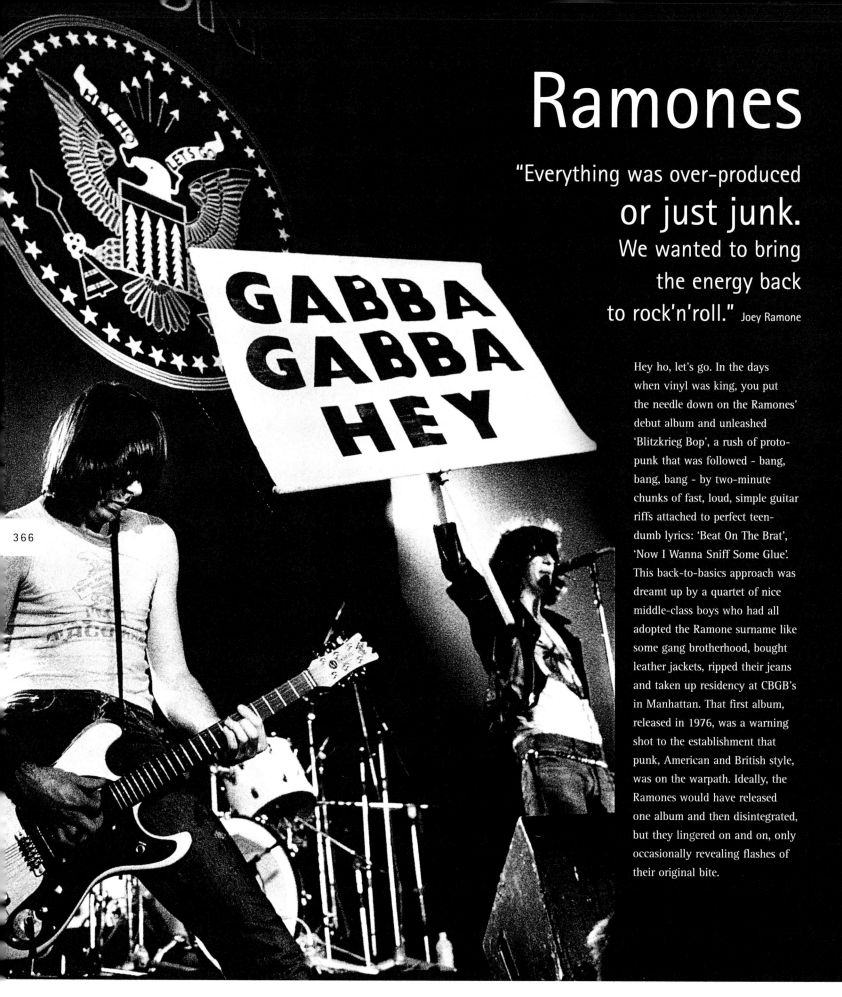

Ramones

"Everything was over-produced **or just junk.** We wanted to bring the energy back to rock'n'roll." Joey Ramone

Hey ho, let's go. In the days when vinyl was king, you put the needle down on the Ramones' debut album and unleashed 'Blitzkrieg Bop', a rush of proto-punk that was followed - bang, bang, bang - by two-minute chunks of fast, loud, simple guitar riffs attached to perfect teen-dumb lyrics: 'Beat On The Brat', 'Now I Wanna Sniff Some Glue'. This back-to-basics approach was dreamt up by a quartet of nice middle-class boys who had all adopted the Ramone surname like some gang brotherhood, bought leather jackets, ripped their jeans and taken up residency at CBGB's in Manhattan. That first album, released in 1976, was a warning shot to the establishment that punk, American and British style, was on the warpath. Ideally, the Ramones would have released one album and then disintegrated, but they lingered on and on, only occasionally revealing flashes of their original bite.

GABBA GABBA HEY

366

Key members: Dee Dee Ramone 18/9/52, Joey Ramone 19/5/51 (died 15/4/01), Johnny Ramone 8/10/51, Tommy Ramone 29/1/52 • Recording career: 1976 - present

Sounds: Ramones 1976, Rocket To Russia 1977, It's Alive 1979

"Democratic foursomes don't work in the 70s

like they did in the 60s when there were fewer musical directions." Eric Carmen

As all around them in 1972 the big boys of rock were getting grandiose ideas, compiling concept albums and generally forgetting their roots, Eric Carmen and the Raspberries stood firm in their respect for the recent past: specifically the inspiration of the Beatles, the Beach Boys and the Hollies. Pop-rock with hooklines and harmonies was already sounding dated, but they appeared oblivious. On 'Don't Wanna Say Goodbye' and 'Go All The Way' Carmen's vocals could be reminiscent

of Paul McCartney, although guitarist Wally Bryson could echo Paul Kossoff as much as George Harrison. Capitol Records exhausted the full gamut of Raspberry-related packaging ideas (punnet-shaped album covers, scratch'n'sniff stickers et al.) though the ripple was shortlived. The first line-up split up and Eric Carmen put together another version, but after 1975's *Starting Over* proved a false dawn, he admitted defeat, went solo and charted with the big ballad sound of 'All By Myself'.

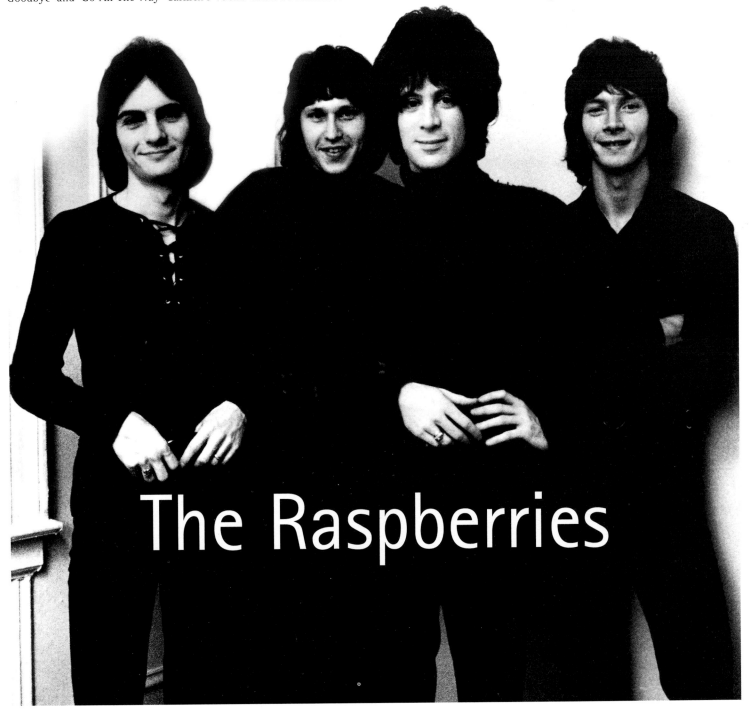

The Raspberries

Key members: Jim Bonfanti 17/12/48, Wally Bryson 18/7/47, Eric Carmen 11/8/49, Dave Smalley 10/7/49 • **Recording career:** 1972 - 1974 • **Sounds:** Raspberries 1972, Side 3 1973, Starting Over 1974

"He was a freak and I was a freak, so we decided to freak together."

Flea on Anthony Kiedis

In many ways the Red Hot Chili Peppers drew on the same influences as Primal Scream - 1960s rock and George Clinton's P-Funk - but they ran it through a different set of filters. Bassist Michael 'Flea' Balzary and vocalist Anthony Kiedis (the Chilis' very own Glimmer Twins) also stirred in some punk, metal and a strong sense of the visual. Though they were pretty much the first to serve up this concoction, they still took a while to get the balance right, despite the input of George Clinton himself on 1985's *Freaky Styley*. They also needed time to rid themselves of a rather annoying frat boy humour, including the encore routine where they'd appear naked, bar jock socks on cocks, and even in 1987 they were still smirking away with 'Party On Your Pussy'. Things changed when guitarist Hillel Slovak OD'd in 1988, and a more serious band emerged, given discipline by Def Jam founder Rick Rubin, who produced *BloodSugarSexMagik*: the perfect sum of their parts.

Red Hot Chili Peppers

Key members: Flea (Michael Balzary) 16/10/62, John Frusciante 5/3/70, Jack Irons 18/7/62, Anthony Kiedis 1/11/62, Dave Navarro 7/6/67, Hillel Slovak 13/4/62 (died 25/6/88), Chad Smith 25/10/62

Recording career: 1984 - present • Sounds: Freaky Styley 1985, BloodSugarSexMagik 1991, Californication 1999

The second night of the Monterey Festival in June 1967 closed
from Otis Redding, backed by Booker T. and The MG's, whose g
Steve Cropper was Redding's main songwriting partner. The ma
audience's enthusiastic response confirmed that Redding was s
over from the soul market where his talents had been nurtured
initially emulated fellow Georgia boy Little Richard, but when
up his ballad 'These Arms Of Mine' in 1962 he changed direct
grainy soul voice was ideal for communicating intimate emot
dubbed 'Mr Pitiful'), though it didn't damp the fire of uptemp
like 'Respect' or 'I Can't Turn You Loose'. New opportunities b
the Monterey appearance, but Redding could not capitalise c
December that year, four days after recording 'Dock Of The I
a plane crash, and the possibilities drifted away like a whist

"One day I drove
a friend to a
recording session.
They had 30
minutes left and
I asked if I could
do a song.
I've been
singing ever
since."

Otis Re

Born: 9/9/41 (died 10/12/67) • Recording career: 1959 - 1967 • Sounds: Otis Blue 1965, The Dictionary Of Soul 1966, King And Qu

Lou Reed

In 1982, on *The Blue Mask*, Lou Reed sang that he was just an average guy. Depends what you call average. Like an impressionist, Reed had the ability to explore a host of musical personalities while giving away very little about himself ("I've hidden behind the myth of Lou Reed for years"). Only David Bowie was quite as chameleon-like, and it was Bowie who gave shape and glam to *Transformer*, Reed's second post-Velvets album, which contained 'Walk On The Wild Side', his thumbnail sketch of Andy Warhol's coterie. Then the transformations continued: middle-European moroseness on *Berlin*, live and heavy metal on *Rock'n'Roll Animal*, the white noise tedium of *Metal Machine Music* - of the latter he said "Nobody is supposed to be able to do a thing like that and survive". But survive he did and, never quiet for long, Reed continued to challenge and change over the next quarter of a century, at the end of which he emerged with his integrity remarkably intact.

"I've never been interested in writing pop songs.
I don't consider myself part of pop music at all."

Born: Louis Firbank 2/3/42 • Recording career (solo): 1972 - present • Sounds: Transformer 1972, Coney Island Baby 1976, New York 1989

"I do think we touch on a wider range of music than just about anyone right now. I don't think we get enough credit for doing it." Peter Buck

The success of R.E.M.'s *Out Of Time* took guitarist Peter Buck aback: "Good Lord, it's selling - that's the weird thing". During the previous ten years the Athens, Georgia band had exerted considerable influence over the US alternative music scene. Early releases featured Buck's

R.E.M.

ringing guitar work and Michael Stipe's obtuse and mumbled lyrics ("I don't know what the *fuck* he's singing about", revealed Bill Berry). This was great for the college circuit, but it looked like they might stay rooted there, even after Stipe's vocals became clearer. Exhausted, R.E.M. took a sabbatical in 1989, and by the time they returned, the world at large was finally ready for them. 'Shiny Happy People' and 'Losing My Religion' seemed to be playing just about everywhere, and follow-ups *Automatic For The People* and, to a lesser extent, *Monster* consolidated their position as arguably the most important rock band of the decade.

Key members: Bill Berry 31/7/58, Peter Buck 6/12/56, Mike Mills 17/12/58, Michael Stipe 4/1/60 • Recording career: 1981 - present

Sounds: Murmur 1983, Out Of Time 1991, Automatic For The People 1992

The Replacements

"I like the idea of us being losers - not the guy who has nothing, **but the guy who has nothing to lose."**

Paul Westerberg

There was a lot of musical activity in Minneapolis circa 1979. Prince was releasing his sexed-up debut album; Hüsker Dü were gathering their forces. Across town the Replacements drew on the same punk energy, only with more recklessness and more desperation. Their first songs were full of a very teenage disaffection - 'Fuck School', 'Dope Smokin' Moron' and 'Gary's Got A Boner' - and on stage they were often completely out of it, best caught on their 1984 album *The Shit Hits The Fans.* But though they claimed in an early song to hate music, Paul Westerberg, the Replacements' vocalist, revealed his skills on *Let It Be*, where their garage songs were interspersed with his ballads of Midwestern dissatisfaction. When guitarist Bob Stinson was fired, they lost energy, and were further diluted after accepting a major label deal - the last couple of albums were less about the Replacements, and more a preparation for Westerberg's solo career.

Key members: Chris Mars 6/4/61, Bob Stinson 17/12/59 (died 18/2/95), Tommy Stinson 6/10/66, Paul Westerberg 31/12/60 • Recording career: 1981 - 1990

Sounds: Sorry Ma, Forgot To Take Out The Trash 1981, Let It Be 1984, Pleased To Meet Me 1987

The Residents

A rock historian's nightmare, the Residents never revealed their names nor any biographical details and gave no interviews, communicating with the outside world only via intermediaries. On rare performance outings, the group appeared in huge eyeball masks, with jaunty top hats. What information did emerge was that the four Residents had come together in Shreveport, Louisiana in the mid-1960s, since when Zappa, Captain Beefheart and Sun Ra had been amongst their influences... Beyond that there was little to go on other than their albums (the whole point, presumably). The first, *Meet The Residents*, ran into legal problems through its cover, a savage parody of *Meet The Beatles. Not Available* was produced on the condition that it would be sealed in a vault for four years. A trio of 1980s albums related a titanic struggle between the Moles and the Chebs. It was all terribly avant-garde. For the brave of heart only.

"The first audition tape didn't have a name on it.

When it was returned it was just addressed to 'the Residents' at that address. They said 'It must be us.'"

Manager Hardy Fox

373

Key members: Answers on a postcard, please • Recording career: 1972 - present • Sounds: Meet The Residents 1974, The Residents Commercial Album 1980, Freak Show 1990

"I got my goody two shoes image **through being completely normal,** which goes to show how perverse our society is."

Cliff Richard

The Shadows were much more than Cliff Richard's puppets, as they proved when they branched out on their own with Hank Marvin's Fender Strat twanging out 'Apache', 'FBI' and 'Kon Tiki' - and inspiring the likes of Jeff Beck and Brian May to take up the electric guitar. Cliff, a rock'n'roller at heart, had been encouraged by his musical advisers to work with an orchestra, but insisted that he wanted a real band. His first backing group were called the Drifters, but to avoid clashing with Clyde McPhatter's group a name change was required as 'Move It' took off in 1958. It's amazing to recall that the *NME* called Cliff's act 'vulgar' - he was Britain's contender for the homegrown Elvis slot. Then he cleaned up his act, and after 'Living Doll' (written by *Oliver!*'s Lionel Bart), there came the sappy teenage films and chirpy banter atop a summer holiday bus... as Cliff started hogging the middle of the road.

Cliff Richard and the Shadows

374

Key members: Jet Harris 6/7/39, Hank B. Marvin 28/10/41, Tony Meehan 2/3/43, Cliff Richard 14/10/40, Bruce Welch 2/11/41 • Recording career: 1958 – present

Sounds: Cliff Sings 1959, Me And My Shadows 1960, The Young Ones 1961

"I sing to certain people in the audience and I ignore the rest of them."

Jonathan Richman

As Jonathan Richman proved, even geeky suburbanites could play rock'n'roll. Inspired by the Velvet Underground, his first band of Modern Lovers were no slouches: drummer David Robinson and organists Jerry Harrison moved on to the Cars and Talking Heads respectively. In 1972, after landing a deal with Warners, the Lovers recorded an album with John Cale as producer - including the two-chord anthem 'Roadrunner', later covered by the Sex Pistols - but disputes delayed its release until 1976. By then Richman had returned to Boston and stripped the sound back to an acoustic rockabilly, so the next album *Rock'n'Roll With The Modern Lovers* appeared to be a radical jump: rough, ready, adenoidally offkey and whimsical ('Rockin' Rockin' Leprechauns' was typical of his lyrics). Richman pursued this naive, adolescent seam both with and without the Lovers, and in 1998 his cult status was reinforced by onscreen appearances as a troubadour in *There's Something About Mary*, commenting in song on the movie's storyline.

375

Jonathan Richman and the Modern Lovers

Key member: Jonathan Richman 16/5/51 • Recording career: 1975 - 1978 & 1985 - 1988 (solo 1988 - present) • Sounds: Modern Lovers 1976, Rock'n'Roll With The Modern Lovers 1977

Smokey Robinson

It was Tamla Motown founder Berry Gordy who spotted potential in a young Smokey Robinson, then applying his frail falsetto to R'n'B standards with the Miracles. Gordy took the Miracles under his wing; they in turn provided Tamla with its first significant hit, 'Shop Around'. Robinson blossomed under Gordy's tutelage. He sang on the Miracles' finest moments: 'You Really Got A Hold On Me' and 'The Tracks Of My Tears'. He produced the Supremes and the Temptations. As a writer he created fine melodies like 'My Guy' and 'Get Ready' and accessible lyrics that shed some light on love's curious paradoxes - "I've got sunshine on a cloudy day". Bob Dylan famously rated him 'America's greatest living poet'. A Motown executive, Robinson took his corporate duties seriously, his children rejoicing in the names Berry and Tamla! And still he kept his own career rolling, working either with ('Tears Of A Clown') or without ('Being With You') the Miracles. One of the greats.

"Berry Gordy taught me how to make my songs be a story
with a beginning, a middle, an end and a theme."

Born: 19/2/40 • Recording career: 1958 - present • Sounds: Going To A Go-Go 1965, Time Out For... 1969, A Quiet Storm 1975

Tom Robinson

'The Artist Formerly Known As Gay' was a tag Tom Robinson applied to himself in the 1990s when it became known he was in a straight relationship and had a child. It was typical of his ironic take on a role as one of the first overtly gay performers. Robinson didn't just out himself, he sang it loud, proud and clear on '(Sing If You're) Glad To Be Gay', a stomping chant of a single that would raise few eyebrows now, but was a forceful, challenging message in 1977. Though no punks, the Tom Robinson Band fitted in quite easily with their repertoire of uncomplicated, four-square anthems - '2-4-6-8 Motorway' their best known - over the top of which Robinson could add the agit-prop messages of his choice. The TRB folded, surprisingly swiftly, and though Robinson carried on, he found subsequent chart success hard to come by, other than 1982's simple, moving 'War Baby'.

"The essence of great performance is **energy, passion** and total commitment."

Born: 1/7/50 • Recording career: 1978 - present • Sounds: Power In The Darkness 1978, North By Northwest 1982, Love Over Rage 1994

"It's weird talking to younger guys.
The Stones have been there throughout their whole lives." _{Keith Richards}

The Rolling Stones

The music that first united Mick Jagger and Keith Richards was the blues; Keef remembered that "we just listened to the blues and played all day and slept all night". They'd known each other since primary school, but met again in their teens, in a train carriage in Deptford, and discovered their common interest. Gravitating to the R'n'B scene being cultivated by Alexis Korner, they became part of a floating community which included Brian Jones, Paul Jones, John Baldry and Charlie Watts.

With luck rather than judgment a band coalesced. The pair worked their charms on Charlie ("I couldn't stand rock'n'roll") Watts. Bill Wyman, they said, only got in because of his amp. Ian Stewart, boogie woogie pianist and the sixth Stone, was involved from the beginning. And as the buzz emanated from their residency at the Crawdaddy Club in Richmond, enter the bright hustler Andrew Oldham, and... well, the rest was a summation of every side - good and bad - of rock'n'roll history.

Key members: Mick Jagger 26/7/43, Brian Jones 28/2/42 (died 3/7/69), Keith Richards 18/12/43, Mick Taylor 17/1/48, Charlie Watts 2/6/41, Ron Wood 1/6/47, Bill Wyman 24/10/36

Recording career: 1963 - present • Sounds: Aftermath 1966, Let It Bleed 1969, Sticky Fingers 1971

One of contemporary music's great interpreters, Linda Ronstadt left her birthplace of Tucson, Arizona to frequent the heart of late 1960s Californian country-rock: LA's Troubadour Club. Her first band, the folkish Stone Poneys, released a couple of albums, but her own solo efforts found her being squeezed reluctantly into a country gal image - the cover of *Silk Purse* featured her mud-spattered amid a herd of hogs. David Geffen, and later Peter Asher, helped her re-invent a soft, sexy image covering songs by J.D. Souther, Warren Zevon and Anna McGarrigle - the beautiful 'Heart Like A Wheel' - as well as Buddy Holly and Smokey Robinson. Accused sometimes of slickness, it was more that the choice of backing musicians was impeccable: the band on her eponymous 1971 album later became the Eagles. Ronstadt continued alighting on and promoting class material, from Broadway standards to Hispanic folk songs - she was half Mexican, half German - and producing *Suspending Disbelief*, the 1993 comeback album of master songwriter Jimmy Webb.

Linda Ronstadt

"It was hard singing my style of country
because kids were afraid it was uncool."

Born: 15/7/46 • Recording career: 1969 - present • Sounds: Linda Ronstadt 1971, Heart Like A Wheel 1974, Winter Light 1993

Roxy Music

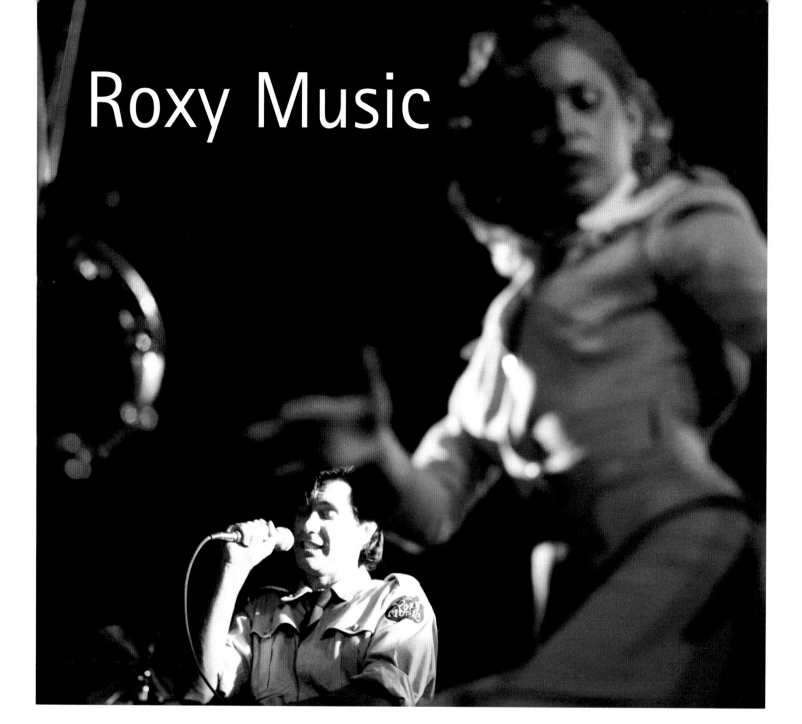

"From the beginning,
I didn't want Roxy to be any old rock'n'roll band.

I wanted it to be able to do anything." Bryan Ferry

The stripped-down GI look that Bryan Ferry adopted in the mid-1970s coincided with some of Roxy Music's least studied, toughest music. The band's image had always been carefully considered from its first unveiling: 50s kitsch alongside Brian Eno's peacock spaceman. Eno left when Ferry's central role proved too powerful - it *was* Ferry's band after all - but Roxy was never again as imaginative as in the days of 'Virginia Plain' and 'Do The Strand'. Mind you, Eddie Jobson was no mean replacement for Eno, and the contributions of the musicians behind Ferry's croon were essential - Paul Thompson providing solid, powerful drumming to pull it all together, Phil Manzanera supplying diamantine guitar breaks (both evident on Roxy's under-rated 1974 single 'All I Want Is You'). Their album artworks were equally vital, but the mannerism was in danger of becoming mannered by 1982's *Avalon*. The stylist Ferry sussed it, and closed the show for a couple of decades.

Key members: Brian Eno 15/5/48, Bryan Ferry 26/9/45, Eddie Jobson 28/4/55, Andy Mackay 23/7/46, Phil Manzanera 31/1/51, Paul Thompson 13/5/51 • Recording career: 1972 - 1982

Sounds: For Your Pleasure 1973, Country Life 1974, Avalon 1982

Run-D.M.C.

'Walk This Way' was Run-D.M.C.'s sign of the times: Joe Perry and Steve Tyler of Aerosmith receiving a welcome career boost courtesy of the smart, happening black kids whose sound was on the way up. It wasn't quite as street as the image suggested - Run-D.M.C came from the comparatively middle-class area Hollis, Queens, and had a headstart in the music business since Run's brother Russell Simmons was MD of Def Jam Records. But they did re-invent rap. 'It's Like That' pared the sound back to the quick: drum machine, no bass, overlapping vocals. 'Rock Box' added the metal guitar that made 'Walk This Way' the big rap crossover hit. Then, behind the Cazal glasses, they took their eye off the ball, while the next wave led by Public Enemy did it tougher, harder. Run-D.M.C. came back - born again on 1993's *Down With The King* - but the torch had passed.

"Us inner-city kids couldn't afford to go to Studio 54. We wanted to be harder and more raw." Darryl McDaniels

381

Key members: Jason 'Jam Master Jay' Mizell 21/1/65, Darryl 'D.M.C.' McDaniels 31/5/64, Joey 'Run' Simmons 14/11/64 • Recording career: 1984 - present

Sounds: Run-D.M.C. 1984, King Of Rock 1985, Raising Hell 1986

The Runaways

Sometime around 1975 Kim Fowley, the LA-based producer who had once created B. Bumble And The Stingers, had a vision of a female Ramones. More of a wet dream, possibly, since it involved recruiting horny high school girls hovering on the border of jailbait country. He found some willing volunteers - the kind of girls who looked like they'd get freaky with you, then trash your house - as well as a precocious lyricist, the 13-year-old Kari Krome, to supply authentic verbals. But the masterplan backfired as the group, more like Sweet than the Ramones, got overhyped, and their onstage *déshabillé* made the whole thing seem too tacky. They left behind one classic song - 'Cherry Bomb' - and headed elsewhere, early member Micki Steele joining the Bangles, Joan Jett forming the Blackhearts, Cherie Currie into film work. Bassist Jackie Fox joined a San Francisco law firm: the Runaways later used her knowledge to sue Fowley for unpaid royalties.

"In the end, Kim Fowley wanted to sell us to somebody else, so we said goodbye. We weren't going to be sold." Joan Jett

Key members: Cherie Currie 30/11/59, Lita Ford 19/9/58, Jackie Fox 20/12/59, Joan Jett 22/9/58 • Recording career: 1976 - 1978 & 1987

Sounds: The Runaways 1976, Queens Of Noise 1977, Live In Japan 1977

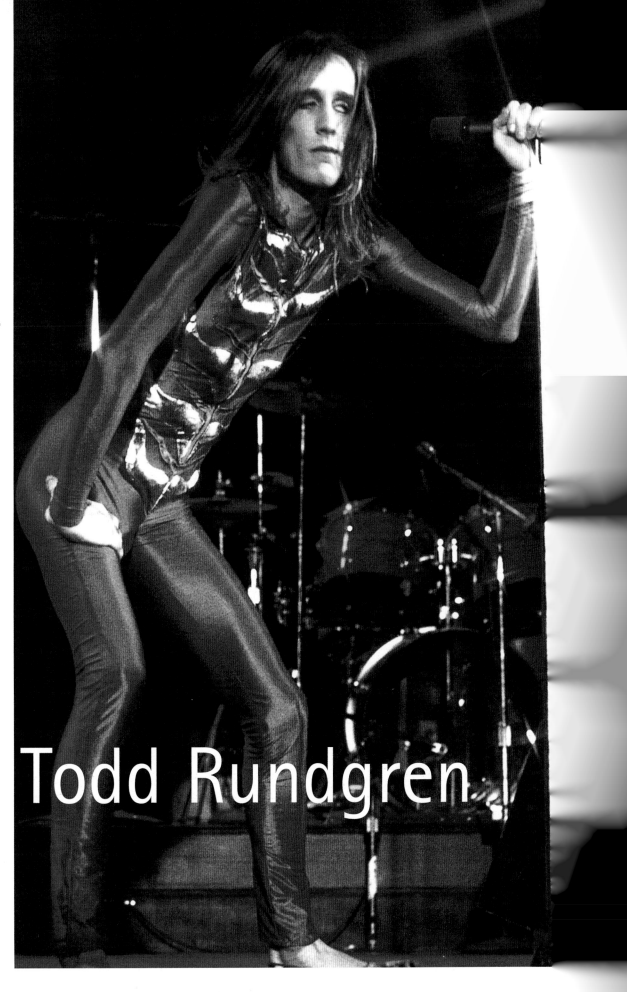

"I don't have an aversion to any music, but I do bring to it the realisation that **95% of everything is mediocre-to-crap.**"

A wizard? A true star? An alien visitor? Todd Rundgren was the original curate's egg-beater: spectacularly talented at all kinds of everything. His devoted fans knew he was a genius, the rest of the world couldn't quite get a fix on him. He wrote gorgeous pop tunes like the Bread-ish 'Hello It's Me' from his time in the 1960s with the Nazz. Solo, he showed that he could effortlessly handle all the instrumental duties for three out of four sides of *Something/Anything?* on a tour from Hendrix to soul and back. His production skills were sought after and delightfully eclectic, including Meatloaf's *Bat Out Of Hell*, Grand Funk and Fanny, Badfinger and the New York Dolls. With his band on the side, Utopia, Rundgren offered hard rock or mysticism, and in the 1990s he explored new cyber-music possibilities, maybe preparing to beam himself back to whence he came: one Utopia album was called *Oops! Wrong Planet...*

Todd Rundgren

Born: 22/6/48 • Recording career (solo): 1970 - present • Sounds: Something/Anything? 1972, A Wizard, A True Star 1973, Hermit Of Mink Hollow 1978

Rush

"As much as our fans think they know all about us, they don't and never have." Neil Peart

The literary preferences of Rush's principal songwriter Neil Peart lay firmly in the section marked Sci-fi and Fantasy. When he replaced original drummer John Rutsey, his lyrics gave a distinctive identity to what had previously been a fairly straightforward Led Zep/Cream copy band. Peart's influence revealed itself fully on *2112*, a futuristic concept album from 1976, which married his storylines with the rest of the Toronto trio's always excellent musicianship. Over the decades the three built up great live empathy and an extremely loyal following - although Peart trimmed back some of his penchant for lengthy, complex songs (they even started having singles hits after 'The Spirit Of Radio' in 1981) the formula changed very little. Whenever it did, with a diversion into synths, techno or AOR, they lost momentum, but a return to basics in the early 1990s produced US Top Five albums like *Roll The Bones* and *Test For Echo* - doing what they did best.

Key members: Geddy Lee 29/7/53, Alex Lifeson 27/8/53, Neil Peart 12/9/52 • **Recording career:** 1973 - present • **Sounds:** 2112 1976, Moving Pictures 1981, Test For Echo 1996

Leon Russell

Here, there and everywhere, Leon Russell has cropped up as a master craftsman helping to fashion some of popular music's finest hours. A classical pianist and trumpeter who had the bonus of guitar lessons from James Burton (the legendary Elvis/Rick Nelson sideman), Russell spent much of the 1960s as a session musician: working with Phil Spector on the 'Wall Of Sound', appearing on the Byrds' 'Mr Tambourine Man', the Righteous Brothers 'You've Lost That Lovin' Feeling', even Herb Alpert's 'A Taste Of Honey'. The moving force behind Joe Cocker's ramshackle *Mad Dogs And Englishmen* tour of 1970, he supplied Cocker with the song 'Delta Lady', the Carpenters with 'Superstar' and George Benson used 'This Masquerade' as his breakthrough number. Russell's solo career also had its moments: his countrified drawl at its strongest on *Carney*, a US Number Two album from 1972, and the vaudeville bar-room single 'Tight Rope'. Some CV.

"The songs are the songs: the stories are for me and the songs are for everyone."

Born: 2/4/41 • Recording career (solo): 1968 – present • Sounds: Leon Russell 1970, Leon Russell And The Shelter People 1971, Carney 1973

Santana

The fluid musical boundaries of the San Francisco scene provided ideal ground for Carlos Santana to cross-fertilise the blues with the Latin rhythms of his Tijuana childhood. Mike Carabello and Jose Areas added a percussive flourish to the drumming of Mike Shrieve as Santana's appearance at Woodstock went down a storm, 'Soul Sacrifice' a highlight of the movie. It proved to be the springboard for a trio of exciting albums (the fusion was genuinely new). Best of all was *Abraxas* with its covers of Fleetwood Mac's 'Black Magic Woman' and Tito Puente's 'Oye Como Va' plus 'Samba Pa Ti', the vehicle for a quintessential Carlos Santana solo - sexy, sweet and sustained. When Gregg Rolie and Neal Schon left to form Journey, Carlos headed towards jazz, working with Buddy Miles and fellow Sri Chinmoy converts John McLaughlin and Alice Coltrane. Patchy in the 1980s and 90s, he had virtually been written off until a triumphant return with 1999's multi-Grammy winning album *Supernatural*.

"Jazz is an ocean. Rock'n'roll is a swimming pool. **I hang out on a lake."** Carlos Santana

Key member: Carlos Santana 20/7/47 • Recording career: 1969 - present • Sounds: Abraxas 1970, Caravanserai 1972, Supernatural 1999

"I realise that if you're not the one putting the fingertips on the strings it's **nowhere near as fascinating.**"

The technique of the man is dazzling, but where some guitar virtuosi are only into flaunting their party tricks, Joe Satriani had the good taste to know when to stop showing off, and when to apply some more subtle shading. Jimi Hendrix sparked his guitar studies, although Satriani also took piano lessons from be-bop pianist Lennie Tristano, and in turn became a teacher - counting Metallica's Kirk Hammett and the equally, if not more, breathtaking Steve Vai among his pupils. After a first band, Squares, folded, Satriani went back to honing his skills and on 1987's *Surfing With The Alien* blew other guitarists away with an all-instrumental showcase in which he used his guitar like a larynx, vocalising verse and chorus structures over the hard rock of 'Ice 9' or the ballad 'Always With Me, Always With You'. When he broke his personal silence in 1989, though, his own vocal offerings presented very little threat to his playing.

Joe Satriani

Born: 15/7/57 • Recording career: 1984 - present • Sounds: Surfing With The Alien 1987, Flying In A Blue Dream 1989, Joe Satriani 1995

For ten years Boz Scaggs did his own Lido shuffle, from R'n'B towards white soul. He had been at school with Steve Miller, and the two played in various groups together until Scaggs formed R'n'B band The Wigs, headed to Europe, and ended up recording a solo debut album in Stockholm. Returning to the States, he helped out on two Steve Miller Band releases (*Sailor* and *Children Of The Future*) before chancing his solo arm again: *Rolling Stone* founder Jann Wenner produced the album *Boz Scaggs* in 1969, Duane Allman guesting on 'Loan Me A Dime'. Scaggs' soulful mood then gained the upper hand, but commercial success remained elusive until 'Lowdown' and the poppy 'Lido Shuffle' off 1976's *Silk Degrees* did the business. After a quiet phase running a nightclub in San Francisco, Scaggs emerged again in 1991 to perform 'Drowning In The Sea Of Love' for Donald Fagen's *New York Rock And Soul Revue*.

"When you discover an instrument, a way of using your voice - whole worlds open up."

Boz Scaggs

"It's just like a marriage.

Most bands break up because of ego problems,

but we have it under control." Herman Rarebell

Scorpions

389

With 'Rock Like A Hurricane' in 1984 the Scorpions established themselves in the top flight of hard rock (and as Germany's most successful rock act) - but by then they'd been in existence for the best part of 15 years. Rudolf Schenker and his younger brother, guitarist Michael, formed the band in the early 1970s, though Michael shortly left to join UK metal act UFO. That the Scorpions had missed him was evident when he came back and re-energised 1979's *Lovedrive*, but he couldn't handle the pace and departed again to be replaced by Matthias Jabs. This line-up of the Scorpions developed the kind of melodic hard rock that made them huge stars in Europe, and after performing in the USSR in 1988, Klaus Meine was inspired to write their biggest hit, the whistling 'Wind Of Change', which earned them an audience with Mikhail Gorbachev. Although grunge then depleted their fans' massed ranks, the Scorpions gamely scuttled onwards.

Key members: Francis Buchholz 19/2/50, Matthias Jabs 25/10/56, Klaus Meine 25/5/46, Herman Rarebell 18/11/53, Rudolf Schenker 31/8/48 • Recording career: 1972 - present

Sounds: In Trance 1975, Love At First Sting 1984, Crazy World 1990

Gil Scott-Heron

Gil Scott-Heron had a legitimate claim, if he wished, to be the original rapper: in the early 1970s he was proclaiming his political poems over rhythmic music. Scott-Heron (whose father, as a trivia aside, played football for Celtic) already had a couple of novels under his belt when he began collaborating with pianist Brian Jackson at university in Pennsylvania. Though Scott-Heron, a lanky *griot* in Nixonian America, pulled few punches with his words - 'Whitey On The Moon' and 'The Revolution Will Not Be Televised' - he softened the delivery with classy jazz-funk from musicians of the calibre of flautist Hubert Laws and bassist Ron Carter. He also possessed a mellow singing voice, splendid on 'Lady Day And John Coltrane' and jazz radio favourite 'I Think I'll Call It Morning'. Twenty years on, unhappy that rap lacked depth and humour, he sent a warning flare aloft for the new generation with 'Message To The Messengers'.

"The artist who limits himself to one medium has lost a valuable opportunity for further growth."

390

Born: 1/4/49 • Recording career: 1972 - present • Sounds: Winter In America 1973, The Revolution Will Not Be Televised 1974, Reflections 1981

"The single most disorientating thing about success was that it happened so quickly."

Seal

After years frequenting London's club-and-pub scene without a career break, Sealhenry Samuel went travelling in Asia in the late 1980s. When he returned from his adventures, he found the acid house scene was buzzing and met Adamski, with whom he began collaborating. Their sessions bore fruit in the 1990 UK Number One 'Killer', which Seal also sang on. He was now a hot property: the ex-Buggle Trevor Horn's ZTT label signed him up, and his debut album *Seal* produced another major hit in 'Crazy'. A distinctive figure, not least because of the facial scars caused by a bout of the TB-like disease lupus, he returned with a second album, confusingly also called *Seal*, this time attracting the presence of Jeff Beck and Joni Mitchell, plus his old mucker Adamski on 'Kiss From A Rose', used on the soundtrack of *Batman Forever*. Things had come full circle, so much so that Seal now came to a temporary standstill.

Born: Sealhenry Samuel 19/2/63 • Recording career: 1990 - present • Sounds: Seal 1991, Seal 1994, Human Being 1998

The Seeds

Garage bands were the crudely energetic punks of American rock in the 1960s - and the Seeds could be counted among the punkiest, their best music the kind of simple guitar riffs that could have quite easily graced CBGB's ten years later on, their look both deliberately downbeat and faintly sinister. They had one significant hit in 1966 with 'Pushin' Too Hard', which contained the essential Seeds sound: vocalist Sky Saxon running through his full repertoire of snarls, sneers and howls over the band's freakbeat. Where the Seeds really wanted to be, you could tell, was 'Up In Her Room' (a 14-minute number off *A Web Of Sound*), mainly because her parents wouldn't have approved. In 1967 they embraced psychedelia on *Future*, featuring both tabla and tuba, but their own prospects were shortlived. Sky Saxon settled in Hawaii, called himself Sky Sunlight and preached a message of love, fruit and herbs. Guitarist Jan Savage took a different fork - and joined the LAPD.

"They were full of shit,
and so was I. And none of us cared." Critic Lester Bangs

392

Key members: Rick Andridge, Daryl Hooper, Jan Savage, Sky Saxon (Richard Marsh) • **Recording career:** 1965 - 1967
Sounds: The Seeds 1966, Web Of Sound 1966, Raw And Alive At Merlin's Music Box 1968

Bob Seger

When Bruce Springsteen became famous, Bob Seger found himself accused of sounding just like the Boss, which must have been galling since he had been there first. Originally a local hero in Detroit, Seger surfaced in various bands in the area before *Ramblin' Gamblin' Man*, his 1968 Capitol debut, allowed him to start shaping a straightforward Middle American rock'n'roll. Forming the hard-touring Silver Bullet Band in 1975 was a further step forward - a cracking live album (*Live Bullet*) and the rocking single 'Hollywood Nights' preceded *Against The Wind*, his first Number One. Producer Bill Szymczyk had worked with the Eagles, and Glenn Frey, a Seger fan, had sung backing vocals on 'Ramblin' Gamblin' Man'; Seger returned the favour on 'Heartache Tonight'. There would be plenty more of the same fare through the 1980s and beyond, punctuated by the singles 'Shame On The Moon' and 'Shakedown', featured on the soundtrack of *Beverly Hills Cop II*.

"The chance to play rock'n'roll as an adult is a privilege."

Born: 6/5/45 • Recording career: 1966 - present • Sounds: Ramblin' Gamblin' Man 1968, Night Moves 1976, Against The Wind 1980

"The way Alex lived his life, he pushed it to the edge.
He wouldn't do things by half measure."

Ted McKenna

The Sensational
Alex Harvey
Band

Tear Gas were a Glasgow band doing not much of anything until they were joined by Alex Harvey in 1972. Harvey, to put it mildly, had been around the block: he'd been there, done that and probably had a fight with it. Gorbals-born, he had first been a skiffle star ('The Tommy Steele of Scotland'), backed Eddie Cochran and Gene Vincent with his Big Soul Band, and performed in the musical *Hair*. For the Sensational Alex Harvey Band he mugged it up, playing an

ageing street punk alongside clown-faced guitarist Zal Cleminson. Harvey, vocally, was prepared to take on all comers: Jacques Brel ('Next'), Tom Jones (a legendary, storming version of 'Delilah'), even Fred Astaire - 'Cheek To Cheek' was on the 1976 covers album *The Penthouse Tapes*. SAHB had fun, but were too theatrical for the real punk revolution. Harvey, in any case, was not well: he died from a heart attack in 1982 (the band, ghoulishly, reformed in the 1990s).

Key members: Zal Cleminson 4/5/49, Chris Glen 6/11/50, Alex Harvey 5/2/35 (died 4/2/82), Hugh McKenna 28/11/49, Ted McKenna 10/3/50

Recording career: 1972 - 1978 & 1994 - present • Sounds: Next 1973, The Impossible Dream 1974, The Penthouse Tapes 1976

Sepultura

Brazil - a land of great music, home of the samba, bossa nova, Heitor Villa-Lobos and Egberto Gismonti - but generally not noted as a centre of thrash metal... That is, until Sepultura rose up somewhere in Belo Horizonte. The Cavalera brothers, Max on guitar, Igor on drums, had been suckled on a diet of Motörhead, whose 'Dancing On Your Grave' inspired their name, the Portuguese for 'grave'. To a layer of Metallica and Anthrax, they added their own specifically Brazilian anger, fuelled by local conditions of poverty. The channel to wider recognition was via US label Roadrunner who released Sepultura's double guitar onslaught with *Morbid Visions* in 1986, and the internationally successful *Beneath The Remains*. The band continued to strengthen their political emphasis - 'Biotech Is Godzilla' had lyrics by Dead Kennedy Jello Biafra - and the Brazilian content and percussion, but after *Roots* in 1996, vocalist and mainman Max Cavalera unexpectedly quit to form Soulfly.

"You wonder why we sound the way we do? We are born in scum, **we live in filth and we die in dirt."** Max Cavalera

Key members: Igor Cavalera 24/9/70, Max Cavalera 4/8/69, Andreas Kisser 24/8/68, Paulo Jnr 30/4/69 • Recording career: 1985 - 1996

Sounds: Beneath The Remains 1989, Chaos A.D. 1993, Roots 1996

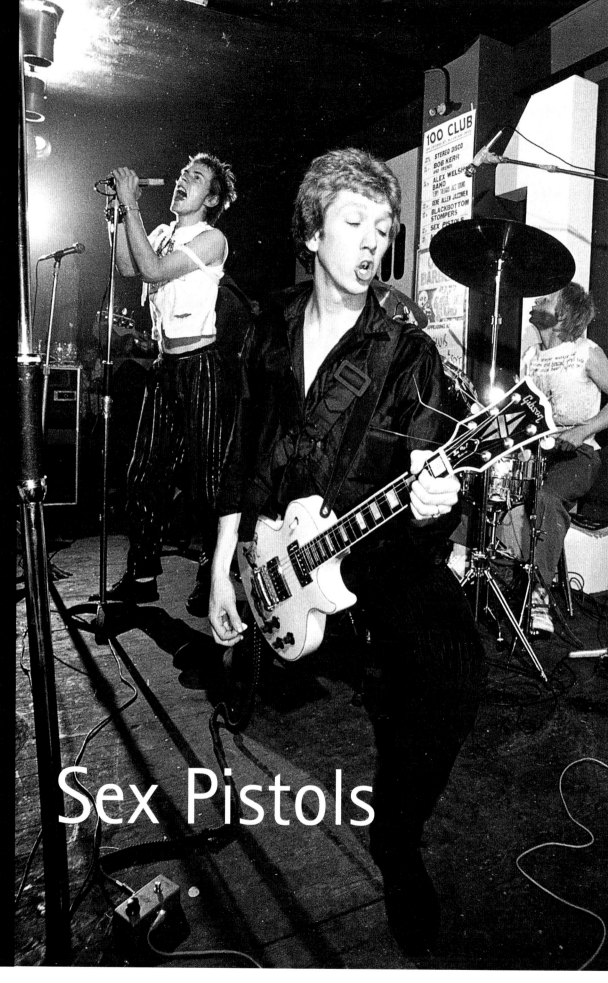

> "Maybe a new generation of kids who are fucking sick of what's going on will listen to the Pistols stuff and realise these songs actually meant something."
>
> Johnny Rotten

It was all a rock'n'roll swindle. "Ever get the feeling you've been cheated?" was Johnny Rotten's sneering *envoi* at the Sex Pistols' final gig. Malcolm McLaren, after unsuccessfully trying to rescue the New York Dolls, had found his new muse when John Lydon strolled into SEX sporting his 'I Hate Pink Floyd' T-shirt. The Pistols sound was not that new - primitive garage wiv a London accent - but a Britain still in transition to the late 20th century was ripe for shocking. Johnny's attitude was perfect: he poured scorn on everyone - other punk bands like the Damned and the Clash ("they make me *cringe*"), even McLaren ("the man was just a collector of ideas"). When it all went wrong and Rotten walked out in January 1978, the sham was revealed - Sid Vicious a pathetic junkie, the Ronnie Biggs episode simply ridiculous. And yet. And yet. The Sex Pistols changed rock music totally, definitively. End of story.

Sex Pistols

Key members: Paul Cook 20/7/56, Steve Jones 3/5/55, Johnny Rotten aka John Lydon 31/1/56, Sid Vicious (John Ritchie) 10/5/57 (died 2/2/79) • Recording career: 1976 - 1979 & 1996

Sounds: Never Mind The Bollocks Here's The Sex Pistols 1977

Not a million Surrey miles from Woking, crucible of the Jam, is Hersham, home of Sham 69's Jimmy Pursey. Like the Jam, and most other punk bands, Sham's forte was the single, in their case repetitive football-style chants which encapsulated Pursey's one-dimensional populist views - "If the kids are united, they will never be defeated". They were easy to chunter along to, none more so that 'Hurry Up Harry' ("we're all going down the pub") which sounded like Chas and Dave Play Punk. Though Pursey's own politics were left-wing, the National Front started following the band and causing trouble, which permanently tainted Sham's reputation. When the rest of the band wanted to try and make it in the States - a pretty improbable proposition - Pursey folded the group, but formed a new line-up in the late 1980s, this time with keyboards and sax, before milking the revival circuit, while true Sham fans quietly headed for the pub.

397

Sham 69

"I do pick on the crowd if they don't wanna know us. I ain't up there singing a bunch of songs **for their approval.**"

Jimmy Pursey

Key members: Mark Cain, Albie Maskall, Dave Parsons, Jimmy Pursey • **Recording career:** 1977 - 1980 & 1988 - present

Sounds: Tell Us The Truth 1978, That's Life 1978, Adventures Of The Hersham Boys 1979

The Shamen

"The best way to be subversive is to go inside and eat it from inside out."

Colin Angus

The Shamen suffered a shattering blow in 1991, when during a trip to the Canary Island La Gomera to shoot a video for 'Progen (Move Any Mountain)', Will Sin drowned in a swimming accident. But Sin's family encouraged Colin Angus to carry on the work they'd started. Angus persevered and later that year saw the culmination of their vision as 'Move Any Mountain - Pro Gen '91' went Top Ten and in 1992 'Ebeenezer Goode' reached Number One, triggering some controversy over DJ Mr C's repeated "E's are good" line. Will Sin had joined forces with Angus when the Shamen was a psychedelic rock band based in Aberdeen; the pair then headed south to London to listen and learn in the capital's acid house clubs. A residency at T&C2, the Town & Country Club's alternative venue, allowed them to mount 'Synergy', a regular multi-media happening - it became the test laboratory for the Shamen's particular branch of hallucinogenic chemistry.

398

Key members: Colin Angus 24/8/61, Will Sin 23/12/60 (died 23/5/91), Richard 'Mr C' West • Recording career: 1986 - 1999 • Sounds: In Gorbachev We Trust 1989, En-Tact 1990, Boss Drum 1992

Simon and Garfunkel

After the release of *Wednesday Morning, 3am*, Simon and Garfunkel's 1964 album, Paul Simon - disappointed with its lack of impact - took time out in Britain; it was the trip when he began writing 'Homeward Bound' at Widnes railway station. In his absence, producer Tom Wilson remixed 'The Sound Of Silence', adding electric guitar and a rhythm section to the original acoustic guitar and voices. Although Simon was not best pleased, when the song reached Number One in the USA, the old schoolfriends re-united. Art's angelic tenor and Paul's increasingly crafted writing felt extremely groovy for some four years or so, benefiting from exposure in *The Graduate*, and building to the magnificent sweep of 'Bridge Over Troubled Water'. But during the 800 hours that 'Bridge' took to record, the duo fell apart - "the only strain," said Simon, "was to maintain a partnership. You gotta work at a partnership." They failed, but what a legacy.

"Art and I came from this Queens childhood to international fame together, so it was more like touching base with who you were." Paul Simon

Born: Art Garfunkel 5/11/41, Paul Simon 13/10/41 • Recording career: 1964 - 1970 (reunited 1975 & 1981)

Sounds: Parsley, Sage, Rosemary & Thyme 1966, Bookends 1968, Bridge Over Troubled Water 1970

"It was strange meeting Mick Jagger, 'cos people had always commented on the resemblance."

A daughter of Richard Simon, co-founder of publishing house Simon & Schuster, Carly's career had a false start when Albert Grossman, Bob Dylan's manager, arranged a recording session for her backed by the Band; but the results were not released. Her debut finally arrived in 1971, and included 'That's The Way I've Always Heard It Should Be', which contained the seeds of Simon's musical personality - vulnerable, but sassy and sexy (as per *Playing Possum*'s cover shot by Norman Seeff). She came good on 'You're So Vain', generating a rash of speculation over whether the song's subject was Warren Beatty or Mick Jagger, who sang the backing vocals. Simon declined to comment, concentrating instead on her marriage to James Taylor: they were the royal couple of singer-songwriters, a relationship detailed in *Hotcakes*. But after the mid-1970s she lost some confidence, and had most success with movie numbers: the Bond theme 'Nobody Does It Better' and the Oscar-winning 'Let The River Run' from *Working Girl*.

400

Carly Simon

Born: 25/6/45 • Recording career: 1971 - present • Sounds: Anticipation 1971, No Secrets 1972, Letters Never Sent 1994

"I'm not sure what I'm searching for.
Is it a theory? Is it a person? Is it a God?
Is it a new pair of shoes?" Jim Kerr

The decision to work with Steve Lillywhite - who'd produced U2's *Boy*, *October* and *War* - signposted the direction that Simple Minds wanted to follow: anthemic rock. Lillywhite duly supplied the goods on 1984's *Sparkle In The Rain* which delivered the stadium-sized 'Waterfront'. The band had previously tried out a variety of sounds - first as punk band Johnny and the Self-Abusers, then art rock in a Magazine-cum-Bowie mould, a brief flirtation with danceable electropop (the single 'I Travel')

and gradually the lusher guitar textures which Steve Lillywhite could manipulate. However, their biggest hit was a song they had originally not wanted to record: a track for the 1985 movie *The Breakfast Club*, 'Don't You (Forget About Me)', which had already been turned down by Billy Idol and Bryan Ferry. Less fleet of foot than U2, Simple Minds found themselves somewhat bogged down, but Jim Kerr and Charlie Burchill, the original Self-Abusers, stayed solid at the heart of the band.

Simple Minds

401

Key members: Charlie Burchill 27/11/59, Jim Kerr 9/7/59 • Recording career: 1979 - present • Sounds: New Gold Dream (81-82-83-84) 1982, Once Upon A Time 1985, Néapolis 1998

Simply Red

Mick Hucknall suffered a fair amount of abuse in his time, much of it brought down on his own red-locked head as the result of a healthy sense of his own talent. Few queried, though, that Hucknall had a fabulous, effortless voice. It was the principal commodity that he and manager Eliot Rashman decided to market after the collapse of the Frantic Elevators, a first attempt to ride up to stardom - one song from the Elevators' repertoire, 'Holding Back The Years', was re-cycled as a showcase for Hucknall's blue-eyed soul skills. Though adept at cover versions, notably a bravura rendition of Philly act Harold Melvin and the Blue Notes' 'If You Don't Know Me By Now', his own songwriting ability was improving all the time: 1991's *Stars* positively sparkled with polished assurance. The album also displayed the contributions of horn player Tim Kellett and keyboardist Fritz McIntyre, long-time sidemen for what had effectively become the long-running Mick Hucknall Show.

"Being a redhead means **you always have problems.**" Mick Hucknall

Key members: Mick Hucknall 8/6/60, Tim Kellett 23/7/64, Fritz McIntyre 2/9/58 • Recording career: 1985 - present • Sounds: Picture Book 1985, A New Flame 1989, Stars 1991

"I'd hate to be extremely approachable. From being very young and wanting to be my own person, I was quite happy if I scared people." Siouxsie Sioux

Siouxsie and the Banshees

As punk stirred itself, Siouxsie Sioux - Susan Dallion - and her muckers from Bromley were there. An early formation included Sid Vicious (on drums) and at the 100 Club's Punk Festival in September 1976 the Banshees performed just one number: an extraordinary recitation of the Lord's Prayer. Later Siouxsie was one of the TV guests who ruined Bill Grundy's career and launched the Pistols'. With her presence as punk's safety pin-up girl, the Banshees perked significant interest in 1978 with their album *Scream* - very Munchian - and the Orientally flavoured, intelligently worded single 'Hong Kong Garden'. Five years later they had their biggest UK hit with the Beatles' 'Dear Prudence' after a period when Robert Smith's influence as a band member had broadened their aspirations. Smith's Cure commitments proved too onerous to stay for long, but Siouxsie carried on, adding a little late 1980s techno and landing a 1991 US hit with 'Kiss Them For Me'.

Key members: Budgie (Peter Clarke) 21/8/57, Steve Severin (Steven Bailey) 25/9/55, Siouxsie Sioux (Susan Dallion) 27/5/57 • Recording career: 1978 - 1995

Sounds: The Scream 1978, Juju 1981, Peepshow 1988

The Sisters Of Mercy

Never were there such devoted Sisters. Well, not quite, as a major bust-up in 1985 proved. It had started so promisingly, when Oxford graduate Andrew Eldritch and his Leeds friend Gary Marx, accompanied by the drum machine Doktor Avalanche, developed their Goth combination of sombre vocals, techno, metal and pallid faces, first emerging from the gloom of 1980 with 'The Damage Done'. The band's most settled line-up, including guitarist Wayne Hussey, only lasted a couple of years before Hussey and bassist Craig Adams triggered severe unpleasantness by splitting to form the Mission. Eldritch led the Sisters onwards - amongst his acolytes were Patricia Morrison from US swamp-rockers Gun Club and Tony James of Generation X and Sigue Sigue Sputnik - as they enjoyed commercial success with 'This Corrosion' and 'Temple Of Love (1992)'. Although the Sisters continued to perform, the world awaited a follow-up to their last original album, 1990's *Vision Thing*.

"I was banned from music classes as a child,

and told I would never, ever be able to understand anything.

I was quite prepared to accept that..." Andrew Eldritch

Key members: Craig Adams 4/4/62, Andrew Eldritch 15/5/59, Wayne Hussey 26/5/58, Gary Marx • Recording career: 1980 - 1985 & 1987 - 1993

Sounds: First And Last And Always 1985, Floodland 1987, Vision Thing 1990

Slade

Dave Hill's haircut was indisputably crazee, and you could certainly feel the noize of Noddy Holder's raucous vocals. Slade, a bunch of self-deprecating Midlanders, had enormous fun with their mis-spelt, energetic singles (which masked some clever songwriting). They could never disappear for long, as every Christmas the classic singalong 'Merry Xmas Everybody' would be wheeled out, and invariably chart. Chas Chandler, ex-Animal and Hendrix manager, came across the group in 1969 performing as Ambrose Slade. He shortened their name and dressed them in skinhead gear, but when that dated, they camped it up and aimed, very successfully, for the teenage glam market. As punk superseded the likes of 'Coz I Luv You', they had the good humour to release *Whatever Happened To Slade?* in 1977. Latterly, however, US metal act Quiet Riot's cover of 'Cum On Feel The Noize' and the Mission's take on 'Merry Xmas Everybody' was a tribute to the affection they inspired.

"I kicked like mad in the womb,
so my mum says,
and was screaming when I hit daylight.
S'pose it was my first spotlight."

Noddy Holder

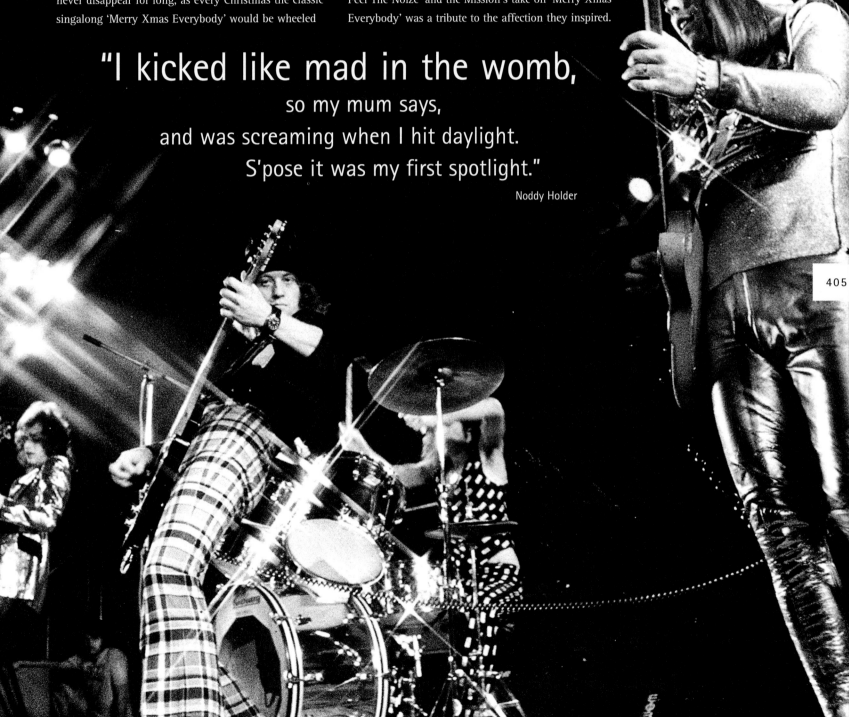

405

Key members: Dave Hill 4/4/52, Noddy Holder 15/6/50, Jimmy Lea 14/6/52, Don Powell 10/9/50 • Recording career: 1969 - 1988 & (as Slade II) 1993 - present

Sounds: Slade Alive 1972, Slayed? 1973, Whatever Happened To Slade? 1977

The Slits

The punk philosophy of not allowing technical ability to get in the way of the message was followed diligently by the Slits, who overcame an almost total lack of proficiency to become an influential all-female act, opening their performance ledger as a support act on the Clash's 'White Riot' tour of 1977. Yet despite the exposure they found it hard to land a deal; by the time they signed with Island Records original drummer Palmolive had left to join the Raincoats.

Island linked them with up with producer Dennis Bovell, previously known for his work with dub poet Linton Kwesi Johnson. Thus their 1979 album *Cut* - renowned in certain quarters for its bare-breasted, mud-smeared tribalistic cover photo - had a dub feel that was not particularly typical of their early pure punk sound (which was best captured on a session recorded for John Peel's radio show), but in compensation, Ari Up's voice remained as quaintly amateur as ever.

"A typical guy wants the woman under his thumb, like his housewife and all that, and we're not having it!" Ari Up

Key members: Viv Albertine, Palmolive, Tessa Pollit, Ari Up (Arianna Foster) • Recording career: 1979 - 1981 • Sounds: Cut 1979

Sly and the Family Stone

Sly Stone's band was all about integration. In true late-1960s San Francisco style, he brought together soul, R'n'B and rock, white and black musicians, and the female members were not merely pretty accoutrements: Sly's sister Rose was on keyboards, Cynthia Robinson on trumpet. This was a fusion of fun and funk - the sound of 'I Want To Take You Higher' - that everybody began to copy, especially Larry Graham's slap bass. Inevitably, but depressingly, it couldn't last, as narcotic and political problems mounted. The Family blew out a third of their gigs in 1970, while Sly came under pressure from black radicals to get more political. By *There's A Riot Goin' On*, despite great singles like 'Family Affair', the funk was masking an edgier, darker, more paranoid feel. Though 1973's *Fresh* temporarily arrested the slither downhill, by the end of the decade Sly's Family were completely dysfunctional. A comeback was eagerly anticipated, but never arrived.

"People have got the right person but the wrong impression about him, and they don't deserve that." Sly Stone

407

Key members: Greg Errico 1/9/46, Larry Graham 14/8/46, Jerry Martini 1/10/43, Cynthia Robinson 12/1/46, Freddie Stone 5/6/46, Rosemary Stone 21/3/45, Sly Stone 15/3/44

Recording career: 1966 - 1983 • **Sounds:** Dance To The Music 1968, Stand! 1969, There's A Riot Goin' On 1971

Small Faces

"It was the Small Faces
that brought me to the Mods
as a source of inspiration.
I bought a Rickenbacker, a Lambretta
and got a haircut
like Steve Marriott." Paul Weller

They were full of surprises, these diminutive Artful Dodgers - developing far beyond their original status as the East End's mod kings. The Small Faces were all natty togs, hip cool and energy, and 'What'cha Gonna Do About It?' was a debut that threw down the gauntlet in 1965. It also featured feedback, a rarity at the time, and on later sessions, with the advantage of extended studio time, they were able to enjoy exploring recording techniques. The tongue-in-cheek psychedelia single 'Itchycoo Park', for example, introduced a cymbal sound which they processed through a phaser. By the 1968 concept album, *Ogdens' Nut Gone Flake*, they'd hired gobbledygook comedian Stanley Unwin to link the songs, and commissioned a circular tobacco tin album sleeve. Then Marriott decided to form Humble Pie, the remaining Faces found Rod Stewart and Ron Wood - and Kenney Jones later had the unenviable job of trying to replace the irreplaceable Keith Moon for their one-time Mod rivals the Who.

408

Key members: Kenney Jones 16/9/48, Ronnie Lane 1/4/46 (died 4/6/97), Steve Marriott 30/1/47 (died 20/4/91), Ian McLagan 12/5/45 • Recording career: 1965 - 1969

Sounds: The Small Faces 1966, Small Faces 1967, Ogden's Nut Gone Flake 1967

Smashing Pumpkins

The release of *Mellon Collie And The Infinite Sadness* in 1995 was a risk for the Smashing Pumpkins: a double CD with 28 songs. Had main mover Billy Corgan overstretched himself? That they more than got away with it - the album was a US Number One, UK Number Four - was testimony to their status within the alternative hierarchy. They had achieved that position through a Moulinex blend of Corgan's musical favourites (the Floyd, Thin Lizzy, Black Sabbath, Depeche Mode) with

timely grunge guitar behind a fondness for strings or the piano ramblings of *Mellon Collie*'s title track. Originally a duo of Corgan - who, yes, did once boast a healthy coiffure along with an outsize ego - with James Iha plus drum machine, the Pumpkins' first single 'I Am One' led to a brief involvement with Sub Pop. But they slyly signed to Virgin America's indie label Caroline, allowing them to segue to the major after *Gish*, which opened them up to criticisms of careerism.

"Believe me, in one week I could write ten songs
that sound like Smashing Pumpkins,
but I don't think that's what people want." Billy Corgan

Key members: Jimmy Chamberlain 10/6/64, Billy Corgan 17/3/67, James Iha 26/3/68, D'Arcy Wretzky 1/5/68 • Recording career: 1989 - 2000

Sounds: Gish 1991, Siamese Dream 1993, Mellon Collie And The Infinite Sadness 1995

"How would I describe my music? Three-chord rock merged with the power of the word."

The men in Patti Smith's life proved supportive. Playwright Sam Shepard encouraged her literary leanings, including her love for William Burroughs and Baudelaire. Blue Öyster Cult stalwart Allen Lanier similarly strengthened her rock sensibilities (she co-wrote songs for the Cult) - just as later Television would inspire her to upgrade the musical backing for her poetry from Lenny Kaye's guitar to a full-scale band. Robert Mapplethorpe supplied her with some iconic cover images, especially for her debut, *Horses*. And Fred 'Sonic' Smith, from MC5 and Television, settled down with her to raise a family: his death in 1994 provoked her return to recording on *Gone Again*. Revered as the shaman of punk - some claimed her 'Hey Joe/Piss Factory' was the first punk rock record - or decried as self-indulgent, Smith had made one earlier comeback after breaking bones in her neck by falling off a stage, resurrecting herself on 1978's *Easter* with 'Because The Night', a song co-written with Bruce Springsteen.

Patti Smith

Born: 30/12/46 • Recording career: 1974 - 1979 & 1988 & 1995 - present • Sounds: Horses 1975, Easter 1978, Gone Again 1996

Morrissey single-handedly did more for gladioli sales than anyone since Dame Edna Everage. A performance trademark, stuffed in his back pocket, the flowers were a symbol of Morrissey hero Oscar Wilde, and typical of the Smiths' singer's fondness for cultural references. Hence his other stage visuals, 1950s singer Johnnie Ray's hearing-aid and Billy Fury's haircut, and the record covers featuring Jean Marais or Joe Dallesandro. But the Smiths would have been as mundane as their name without the contribution of Johnny Marr's guitar. At the lead of the post-synth guitar revival, his layers of chiming guitar were equally, if not more, influential than Morrissey's sensitive but sardonic persona. Each reached their peak on *The Queen Is Dead* - Morrissey's vocals and lyrics soul-searching on 'The Boy With The Thorn In His Side', Marr constructing the wrap-around sound of 'Bigmouth Strikes Again' - shortly before indie's odd couple finally fell out.

"The Smiths' message is that people should discard any notions of in-ness or hipness or coolness.

Morrissey

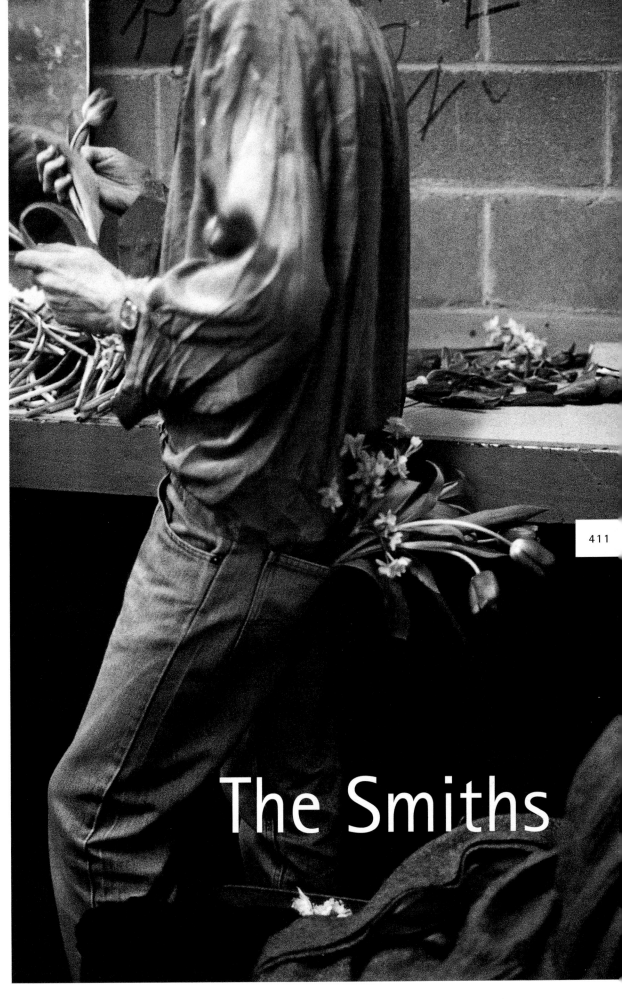

411

The Smiths

Key members: Mike Joyce 1/6/63, Johnny Marr 31/10/63, (Steven) Morrissey 22/5/59, Andy Rourke 1963 • Recording career: 1983 - 1987

Sounds: The Smiths 1984, Meat Is Murder 1985, The Queen Is Dead 1986

Soft Cell

Another musical export from Southport in Lancashire - Gomez would follow some twenty years on - Marc Almond, who was attending Leeds Poly, discovered that he shared a passion for Northern soul with David Ball. Like a slightly (no, make that *supremely*) more camp version of Sparks, Almond did the posing and posturing, loving every minute, while Ball supplied the musical support. After Stevo, boss of Some Bizzare (sic) Records, launched the duo with 'The Girl With The Patent Leather Face' on a 1980 sampler, they struck gold with their next single. This was a delve back into the Northern soul archives: 'Tainted Love', first recorded by Gloria Jones (Marc Bolan's girlfriend, she was unlucky to be at the wheel of the Mini which crashed and killed him). Though Soft Cell tried hard to top the insistent electro-synth of 'Tainted Love', they never quite managed it, and after a while Almond's non-stop cabaret grinding just felt a teeny bit too tacky.

"When Soft Cell finished there was never any animosity.
We were both at a creative high." Marc Almond

412

Key members: Marc Almond 9/7/59, David Ball 3/5/59 • Recording career: 1980 - 1984 • Sounds: Non-Stop Erotic Cabaret 1981

Soft Machine

Soft Machine rumbled forwards along its own underground tracks, unobserved by the vast bulk of 1970s rock fans. Along the way, future Gong luminary Daevid Allen helped kickstart them as a psychedelic band improvising at London's UFO club alongside Pink Floyd. Then bassist Kevin Ayers departed for a solo career, taking away much of their hippie mystique: after his replacement Hugh Hopper joined, they sloped relentlessly towards jazz-rock. By their third LP, helpfully called *Third*, instrumental work-outs were the order of the day - on tour they'd used a full brass section but, unable to pay them all, only saxophonist Elton Dean (the inspiration for Elton John's stage name) remained on the album. At this point another of the founder members, drummer Robert Wyatt, decided to move on. As his wry humour and vocals disappeared over the horizon, Soft Machine - with none of the original group involved after 1976 - was about to start going through the motions.

> "It was the idea **that music could stretch beyond the song format,** the idea of harmonies beyond the Bert Weedon chord shapes." Robert Wyatt

Key members: Kevin Ayers 16/8/45, Hugh Hopper, Mike Ratledge 1943, Robert Wyatt 28/1/45 • Recording career: 1967 - 1991

Sounds: The Soft Machine 1968, Volume Two 1969, Third 1970

"The name came out of the 70s when I was a teenager and the two things I was really into - Sonic Smith from the MC5, and Big Youth, **the reggae toaster.**"

Thurston Moore

Sonic Youth's performance debut was at the 'Noise Festival', a June 1981 New York event they helped organise. Adventures in sound would be their mission, an outgrowth of the No-Wave post-punk scene and the avant-garde influence of their mentor, guitarist Glenn Branca. The twin guitars at their heart, controlled by Thurston Moore and Lee Ranaldo, were not playing Wishbone Ash harmonies or using fancy effects boxes, just seeing what you could wring out of a common or garden electric guitar. From *Bad Moon Rising* onwards, their distortions, discordances and feedback began forming into pieces of music which were quite close to songs. After all, their tongue-in-cheek offshoot Ciccone Youth had lots of fun subverting pop formulas. Though never conventional, Sonic Youth became more accessible through *Daydream Nation* and *Dirty*, and as elder statesmen (and woman) of the alternative scene proved you could sign to a major label - they chose Geffen - and not lose credibility.

414

Sonic Youth

Key members: Kim Gordon 28/4/53, Thurston Moore 25/7/58, Lee Ranaldo 3/2/56, Steve Shelley 23/6/62 • Recording career: 1982 - present

Sounds: Sister 1987, Daydream Nation 1988, Washing Machine 1995

Soul Asylum

Close on the heels of Hüsker Dü and the Replacements, Soul Asylum emerged from the city of Minneapolis in the early 1980s. Their fast and loose metal sound was more in the style of the Replacements, though with a little more country and jazz deep in the mix, but it was Hüsker Dü's Bob Mould who produced their debut. After four years on indie label Twin/Tone, they moved up to the majors with A&M, but things didn't click - maybe, some thought, because their EP *Clam Dip & Other Delights* cheekily parodied the cover of A&M founder Herb Alpert's *Whipped*

> "Neurosis and insecurity goes with being in a rock band. With us, there always seems to be this element where we haven't quite established ourselves yet."
>
> Dave Pirner

Cream equivalent. Whatever the hoodoo, Soul Asylum extracted themselves from the contract at some cost - reportedly $200,000 - and almost broke up under the strain. But Dave Pirner worked on his songs while they were all scattered and came back stronger, though slicker: the 1993 single 'Runaway Train' gave the band significant profile, as did Pirner's romance with Winona Ryder.

Key members: Karl Mueller 27/7/63, Dan Murphy 12/7/62, Dave Pirner 16/4/64, Grant Young 5/1/64 • **Recording career:** 1984 - present

Sounds: Hang Time 1988, Grave Dancers Union 1993, Candy From A Stranger 1998

Soundgarden

Crowds attending Guns N' Roses' mammoth world tour of 1991-92 were treated to Soundgarden as one of the support acts, which helped broaden their profile - as later did a cracking video for 'Black Hole Sun'. They were one of the earliest acts to appear on Seattle's Sub Pop label, not least because Bruce Pavitt, Sub Pop's founder, was a long-time Illinois pal of Kim Thayil and Hiro Yamamoto. More Led Zep and Black Sabbath than anything else, Soundgarden nonetheless were a lot more than pure metal, grafting on elements of punk and psychedelia. Though major labels tried to poach them, they resisted until 1990 before joining A&M, the first Sub Pop band to go to a major. *Badmotorfinger* suffered from being released at the same time as Nirvana's *Nevermind*, but 1994's *Superunknown* went straight to Number One in the USA. However, in April 1997, after some internal problems, Soundgarden announced, quite calmly, that a 'mutually amicable' split had taken place.

"I can tell you, **we don't get a lot of feminists** and we don't get a lot of yuppies in our audience."

Chris Cornell

416

Key members: Matt Cameron 28/11/62, Chris Cornell 20/7/64, Kim Thayil 4/9/60, Hiro Yamamoto 13/4/61 • Recording career: 1987 - 1996

Sounds: Louder Than Love 1989, Badmotorfinger 1991, Superunknown 1994

"We don't stare at our shoes or try to change the world. **We want folks to have a good time."**

Rick Miller

As their song 'Fried Chicken And Gasoline' suggested, Southern Culture On The Skids (SCOTS for short) produced a secret recipe of R'n'B, rockabilly, Tex-Mex and country & western that was lip-licking, high-octane boondocks rock. Songwriter Rick Miller, a lanky sometime Cramps fan, founded the band in Chapel Hill, North Carolina in the mid-1980s. His be-wigged girlfriend, that Spoonerologists' delight Mary Huff, supplied bass guitar and occasional vocals; and the trio was completed by drummer Dave Hartman. Together they cooked up a storm - "deep-fried, blow-dried and electrified" - and delivered an affectionate but sideways look at Southern life through mini-sagas of dirt track racing, moonshine, corn and porn. With the addition of keyboard player Chris 'Cousin Crispy' Bess in 1998, SCOTS entered the new century as they meant to go on: *Liquored Up And Lacquered Down* was as rich and flavoursome as the gravy and grits at Crooks Corner.

417

Southern Culture On The Skids

Key members: Chris Bess, Dave Hartman, Mary Huff, Rick Miller • Recording career: 1986 - present

Sounds: Too Much Pork For Just One Fork 1990, Dirt Track Date 1995, Liquored Up And Lacquered Down 1999

Southside Johnny and the Asbury Jukes

The New Jersey coastal town of Asbury Park had a buzzing music scene in the early 1970s: there was R'n'B nut Southside Johnny Lyon (nicknamed after his passion for Chicago's South Side blues), guitarist Steve Van Zandt and one Bruce Springsteen. When the Boss broke nationally, both Van Zandt - who joined Springsteen's E Street Band - and Southside Johnny benefited. The good-time R'n'B energy of the Asbury Jukes, brass section and all, found itself with a record deal and

a formula: cover some Springsteen songs, and invite guest appearances from Ronnie Spector and Lee Dorsey. After two similar albums, the Jukes produced one containing only their own material... and achieved their highest chart position. But then it was back to where they were most at home - the bar-room intimacy of Asbury Park - and the best of their subsequent albums, 1991's *Better Days*, returned to the tried and tested: some Springsteen songs and a guest slot for Jon Bon Jovi.

"Everything I still do live on-stage is Southside Johnny Lyon.
I told him that it's his fault I can't dance,
because he never learned." Jon Bon Jovi

Key member: Johnny Lyon 4/12/48 • Recording career: 1976 - present • Sounds: I Don't Wanna Go Home 1976, Reach Out And Touch The Sky 1981, Better Days 1991

Europe provided a convenient bolthole for the Mael brothers. After their LA-based band Halfnelson had been spotted by Todd Rundgren, their Rundgren-produced debut saw little commercial action, even when it was re-released under the snappier Sparks name. But on a tour of Europe they'd experienced a good reaction, and so the brothers decided to up sticks to the UK, where they put together a new backing band and joined forces with producer Muff Winwood, brother of Steve, and ex-bassist of the Spencer Davis Group. The interplay between the stage demeanour of keyboardist Ron Mael (deadpan, wired, Hitler moustache) and the exuberance of the falsetto-voiced Russell found a ready market for their left-field 'This Town Ain't Big Enough', one of five UK hits in the two years 1974 and 75. Once Winwood moved on, chart success was harder to come by until Giorgio Moroder gave them a disco makeover in 1979. From then on, cult status awaited them.

"We came to England and **there was a very instant reaction** which was opposite to the States, because we were doing a more European or English thing." Russell Mael

Sparks

Key members: Ron Mael 12/8/50, Russell Mael 5/10/55 • **Recording career:** 1972 - 1988 & 1994 - present • **Sounds:** Kimono My House 1974, Propaganda 1974, Gratuitous Sax And Senseless Violins 1994

The Specials

Forefathers of the 2-Tone movement, the Specials triggered a mini-wave of ska revivalism. The Coventry-based band came out of a punk/reggae background, but veered towards the ska end, poppifying the original JA version. A support slot on a Clash tour offered a way forward, but proved a dead end, so the group re-gathered and set up their own label, 2-Tone, in tribute to the black and white integration of the band and their rude boy look. As well as the Specials' successes -

'A Message To You, Rudy' and 'Too Much Too Young', the public service announcement for contraceptives which provided their first Number One - the 2-Tone label supported a community of like-minded bands: Madness, the Beat, the Selecter. 1981's 'Ghost Town', which coincided with a summer of urban unrest in the UK's inner cities, marked their farewell. Three of the band went on to form Fun Boy Three; founder Jerry Dammers continued, but the special ingredient was missing.

"In the 60s the Rolling Stones based themselves on R'n'B. Then all the heavy bands based themselves on the blues. We just use ska in the same way." Jerry Dammers

420

Key members: John Bradbury, Roddy 'Radiation' Byers, Jerry Dammers 22/5/54, Lynval Golding 7/7/52, Terry Hall 19/3/59, Horace 'Gentleman' Panter, Neville Staples 11/4/56

Recording career: 1979 - 1985 & 1996 - present • Sounds: Specials 1979, More Specials 1980

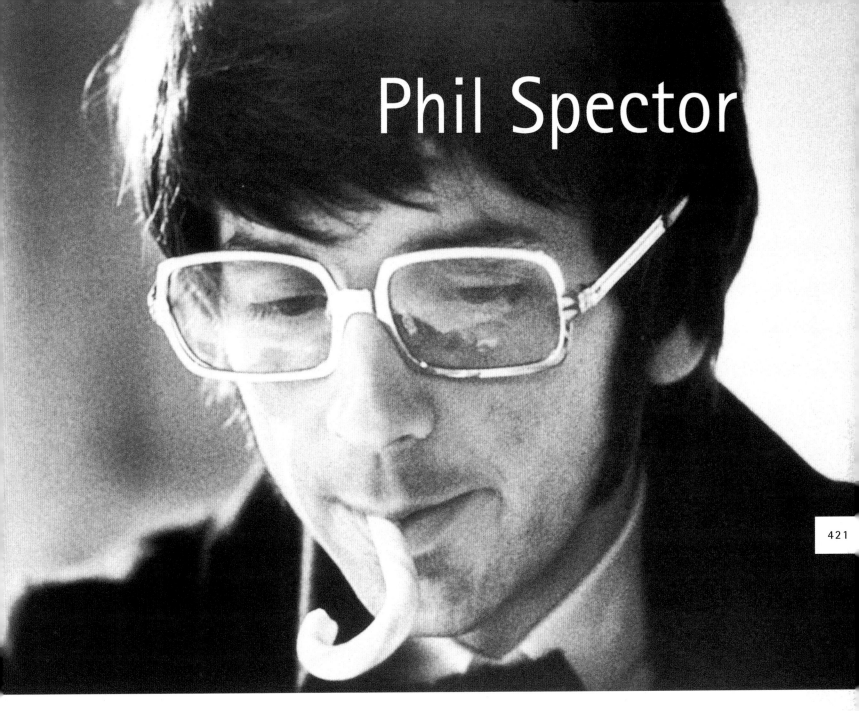

Phil Spector

Although a performer who enjoyed a US Number One in 1958, as one third of the Teddy Bears, Phil Spector's main instrument was the control desk at Hollywood's Gold Star Studios. There his fingers arpeggio'd their genius onto singles like 'Be My Baby' and 'You've Lost That Loving Feeling', each fortifying the remarkable, dense instrumentation of his Wall Of Sound. Spector was a millionaire at 21 - the "first tycoon of teen" in Tom Wolfe's phrase - but his Midas touch was fallible. His *A Christmas Gift For You* album had a release date of 22nd November 1963, but after JFK's assassination few were in the mood. In 1966, his masterpiece, Ike and Tina Turner's 'River Deep, Mountain High', though a hit in the UK, flopped in the States: Spector eventually retreated to eccentric exile in his mansion, occasionally breaking cover to produce John Lennon, Leonard Cohen or the Ramones. However his brief period of intense success had ensured a niche in the rock'n'roll pantheon.

"My records are built like a Wagnerian opera: they start simply and they end with **dynamic force, meaning and purpose."**

Born: 26/12/40 • Recording career: 1958 - 1980 • Sounds: A Christmas Gift To You 1963

Spinal Tap

So close to the truth of rock'n'roll's worst excesses, self-delusions and pomposities, Spinal Tap - the ultimate rock spoofers - earn their rightful place because they went out and performed, brilliantly, on the road. Spun out of an idea that the three comedy-improv performers, with Rob Reiner,

put together for a 1978 ABC-TV show, it took six years to make the full-length feature film (or 'rockumentary', as Reiner in the guise of director Marty DiBergi put it). They had done their homework diligently: the accents were impeccable Estuary English, the music pastiche of the highest order. For anyone who hasn't seen Spinal Tap, fans' mantra-like reciting of classic lines or moments - the 'Stonehenge' debacle, the backstage catering ("a complete catastrophe"), Nigel Tufnel's tribute to Bach and Mozart on 'Lick My Love Pump' - drift meaninglessly through their transom. There's only one cure: go buy the video. This one goes to 11.

"The closer we dared to get to the reality, the closer the real thing dared to get to us." Harry Shearer aka Derek Smalls

Key members: Christopher Guest (aka Nigel Tufnel) 5/2/48, Michael McKean (aka David St Hubbins) 17/10/47, Harry Shearer (aka Derek Smalls) 23/12/43

Recording career: 1961 - present (surreal world) & 1992 (real world) • Sounds: Break Like The Wind 1992

"Jay felt that he and Mark would be better off playing as a straight hard-rock band without the jazz influence. Spirit had too much variety." Randy California

Still one of the better kept secrets of rock history, Spirit featured the unlikely pairing of Randy California (which was not his real name, believe it or not), whose guitar skills had once been included in the Blue Flames alongside J. Hendrix Esq., and his stepfather Ed Cassidy, a 40-something shaven-headed jazz drummer who had worked with Gerry Mulligan, Thelonious Monk and Art Pepper. Spirit was further blessed with the electric piano of John Locke and the lyrics and

vocals of Jay Ferguson. This was a class outfit, and their first three, highly eclectic albums prepared the ground for 1970's *Twelve Dreams Of Dr Sardonicus* - a classic in retrospect, it only managed to reach US Number 63 on release. This also marked the end of the band's best period: Ferguson and Mark Andes split to form Jo Jo Gunne, and in the aftershock the line-up fluctuated alarmingly. Randy California's death in a 1997 drowning accident was a huge loss.

Spirit

423

Key members: Mark Andes 19/2/48, Randy California (Randy Wolfe) 20/2/51 (died 2/1/97), Ed Cassidy 4/5/23, Jay Ferguson 10/5/47, John Locke 25/9/43

Recording career: 1968 - 1972, 1976 - 1981, 1984 & 1990 - present • Sounds: The Family That Plays Together 1968, Twelve Dreams Of Dr Sardonicus 1970, Future Games 1977

Spiritualized

Lie back and think TM - if you could get transcendental and horizontal, Spiritualized could provide all the aural ambience you needed to transport yourself to another plane. The band was one of the children caught in a bitter divorce between the partners in Spacemen 3, the 1980s psychedelic noise outfit. Half the material on their final album was by Peter Kember (who subsequently formed Spectrum), the remainder by Jason Pierce, already exploring a minimalist, symphonic version of the Spacemen sound. For the Spiritualized debut, *Lazer Guided Melodies*, he developed his guitar drones and repetitions into infinitely shimmering mantras - great on CD, even better live. The title of a third album, 1997's *Ladies And Gentlemen, We Are Floating In Space*, suggested more of the same, but Pierce had moved on, tightening up the sound and bringing in guest musicians, including pianists Jim Dickinson - a long-time collaborator of Ry Cooder - and Dr John.

Key member: Jason Pierce 19/11/65 • Recording career: 1990 - present • Sounds: Lazer Guided Melodies 1992, Pure Phase 1995, Ladies And Gentlemen, We Are Floating In Space 1997

Dusty
Springfield

"I don't have any serious regrets,
but there are certain things I'd do differently."

Greatly mourned when cancer finally defeated her, Dusty Springfield had been returned to glory in the 1980s by the Pet Shop Boys: their collaboration on 'What Have I Done To Deserve This' in 1987 was a comeback after far too long in the wilderness. Dusty's zenith had been in the late 1960s, when, after appearing with her brother Tom in the Springfields, she abandoned folk pop for a white soul sound. Always a careful selector of material, she proved an intelligent interpreter of

Bacharach/David and Goffin/King songs, as well as the Italian song 'Io Che Non Vivo (Senzate)' aka 'You Don't Have To Say You Love Me'. Then in 1968 she headed to the epicentre of her spiritual home: Stax Studios in Memphis. With Aretha Franklin's mentor Jerry Wexler and top sessionmen on hand, she revelled in the opportunity - 'Son Of A Preacher Man' was just one of many stand-out tracks on the resulting *Dusty In Memphis*, now a much-revered classic album.

Born: Mary O'Brien 16/4/39 (died 2/3/99) • Recording career (solo): 1963 - 1995 • Sounds: A Girl Called Dusty 1964, Everything's Coming Up Dusty 1965, Dusty In Memphis 1969

Bruce Springsteen

The hype might have sunk another performer. There was Bruce Springsteen on the verge of making it, and Boston journalist Jon Landau - having seen Springsteen in performance - wrote one of the most quoted lines of rock criticism: "I saw rock and roll future, and its name is Bruce Springsteen". Bizarrely, Landau ended up working on *Born To Run* as co-producer, and must have been heartily relieved when the title track, in all its sprawling grandeur ("my songs are supposed to be bigger than life"), went some way to delivering his prediction. As Springsteen the working-class bard emerged - prolific on *The River*, stark on *Nebraska*, stadium-big on *Born In The U.S.A.*, unflinching on *Tunnel Of Love* - he was aided and abetted by the mighty stage presence of Clarence Clemons and the rest of the E Street Band. As Chrissie Hynde said, "He just gets onstage and invites you in... He's like the bar band you never had."

"He's not the Boss.
He works for us. More than a boss, he's the owner, because more than anyone else, Bruce Springsteen owns America's heart." Bono

Born: 23/9/49 • Recording career: 1973 - present • Sounds: Born To Run 1975, Nebraska 1982, Tunnel Of Love 1987

426

Squeeze

The States proved resistant for some time to the charms of Squeeze, not surprisingly, since the band were very, very English. South London likely lads Chris Difford and Glenn Tilbrook developed a nice line in crafty, crafted pop, full of vernacular lyrics that tumbled over each other in 'Up The Junction' or 'Pulling Mussels (From The Shell)'. They were compared to Lennon and McCartney, though there was the strong whiff of a whelk stall that was definitely not Merseyside. Their first album had little to do with the later Squeeze sound - John Cale was an off-beat choice of producer - but they got back on track with 'Cool For Cats'. Boogie woogie maestro Jools Holland supplied gentlemanly keyboards; when he left to start a media career, replacements Paul Carrack - the voice of Ace's pub rock classic 'How Long' - and Don Snow kept his piano seat warm until the original line-up reformed in 1985.

"Glenn and I use the John West theory when it comes to songs.
It's the ones we reject that make ours the best."

Chris Difford

Key members: Chris Difford 4/11/54, Jools Holland 24/1/58, Glenn Tilbrook 31/8/57 • Recording career: 1977 - 1982 & 1985 - present • Sounds: Argy Bargy 1980, East Side Story 1981, Play 1991

Status Quo

As the opening act for the Wembley leg of Live Aid, Status Quo were perfect: heads down, they let rip with a boogie bugle call to a global audience on 'Rockin' All Over The World' - the song written by former Creedence Clearwater Revival frontman John Fogerty. Never critics' favourites, their fans, the Quo Army, didn't care if the barre-chord formula altered little over the years. In fact the Quo sound *had* altered radically since their 1968 hit 'Pictures Of Matchstick Men', when the group were dabbling in psychedelic pop. The change occurred around 1970 as a cover of Steamhammer's 'Junior's Wailing' marked the move to hard-rockin' boogie. After testing the new sound out on tracks like 'Paper Plane' and 'Don't Waste My Time', it reached perfection on

'Caroline' and 'Down Down'. Bassist Alan Lancaster left the band after Live Aid (their original drummer John Coghlan had already gone) and it fell to Parfitt and Rossi to become custodians of the golden riff.

> "We were criticised a lot for supposedly hanging onto a successful formula which we didn't know we had. In retrospect, we would have been called stupid for not sticking to it."
>
> Francis Rossi

Key members: John Coghlan 19/9/46, Alan Lancaster 7/2/49, Francis Rossi 29/4/49, Rick Parfitt 12/10/48 • Recording career: 1968 – present

Sounds: Ma Kelly's Greasy Spoon 1970, Hello 1973, In The Army Now 1986

Steely Dan

"What we try to do is nudge very, very competent musicians into doing something extraordinary." Walter Becker

Nobody ever managed to copy Steely Dan. No one got remotely close. They could try and ape the jazz chordings, grooves and razor-sharp lyrics, but they usually tried too hard, or lacked Walter Becker and Donald Fagen's sense of the *mot* (and note) *juste*. It was just a shame Walt and Don had a better rapport with the misfits and loners of their songs - Charlie Freak, Kid Charlemagne, Cousin Dupree - than a real live flesh-and-blood rock group, parachuting in guest musicians as

early as Elliot Randall's solo on 'Reelin' In The Years' from their already distinctive and assured debut album *Can't Buy A Thrill*. Because when Steely Dan *was* a band, it was a great band: Jeff 'Skunk' Baxter's heartwarming guitar, Denny Dias's jazz chops, Jim Hodder and Jeff Porcaro doubling up on drums. But touring brought Becker and Fagen out in a rash - and after a July 1974 gig in Santa Monica, it was nigh on a 20-year countdown to the ecstasy of the Dan's next live show.

Key members: Jeff 'Skunk' Baxter 13/12/48, Walter Becker 20/2/50, Denny Dias 12/46, Donald Fagen 10/1/48, Jim Hodder 1948 (died 5/6/90), Michael McDonald 12/5/52, Jeff Porcaro 1/4/54 (died 5/8/92)

Recording career: 1972 - 1980 & 1995 - present • Sounds: Can't Buy A Thrill 1972, Pretzel Logic 1974, Aja 1977

Steppenwolf

"I don't care what anyone says. You've got one of the best voices in rock'n'roll. Springsteen ain't got nothin' on you!" Little Richard to John Kay

'Born To Be Wild', the opening track of Dennis Hopper's 1969 movie *Easy Rider*, not only became an instant biker anthem, but included in its lyrics the phrase 'heavy metal thunder', which rock lexicographers believe was the first formal use of the phrase. The song had already charted at US Number Two the year before *Easy Rider* was released (the follow-up 'Magic Carpet Ride' also reached the Top Three) but gave a misleading leading impression of Steppenwolf, who were not merely heavy metal headbangers. Previously a Toronto-based blues line-up called Sparrow, the band were equally interested in politics - anti-war and anti-drugs -

as in their 1970 song 'Snow Blind Friend'. Leader John Kay's shades were less of a Harley pose than the fact he'd been purblind since childhood. In fact it was drummer Jerry Edmonton's brother (who revelled in the name Mars Bonfire) who wrote 'Born' and implied their outlaw image.

430

Key members: Jerry Edmonton 24/10/46 (died 28/11/93), John Kay 12/4/44, Goldy McJohn 2/5/45 • Recording career: 1967 - 1971 & 1974 - 1977 • Sounds: Steppenwolf 1968, Monster 1969, Live 1970

Stereophonics

"You write a song in your bedroom, and a few months later there are people running about beside the River Kwai filming a video for it." Kelly Jones

From their homes in Cwmaman, in the valleys of South Wales, the Stereophonics could sit and watch the bright lights over the hills. All three, including the two unrelated Joneses, came from the close-knit community, and consequently their songs were on a human, small-town scale. The freshness and honesty of their debut, *Word Gets Around*, sprang precisely from the intimacy of events in their vicinity: 'A Thousand Trees' was the story of a neighbourhood environmental dispute, 'Local Boy In The Photograph' dipped behind the headlines of a suicide. And the limitations of performing as a stripped-down trio - Kelly Jones's yearning voice over guitar, bass and drums - kept the music simple and straightforward but capable of power, just like fellow Welshmen the Manics, who latterly had had the same formation. By 1999's *Performance And Cocktails*, the Stereophonics' horizons had widened: now they could observe 'Plastic California' and a whole wide world beyond.

431

Key members: Stuart Cable 19/5/70, Kelly Jones 3/6/74, Richard Jones 23/5/74 • **Recording career:** 1997 - present

Sounds: Word Gets Around 1997, Performance And Cocktails 1999, Just Enough Education To Perform 2001

Cat Stevens

When Cat Stevens relinquished the music industry in 1979, converting to the Muslim faith and changing his name to Yusef Islam, there were those who thought it might be simply a short-term stunt. It soon became abundantly clear that his beliefs ran deep: so much so that his support for the fatwa on Salman Rushdie quashed a burgeoning revival in the late 1980s: 10,000 Maniacs had recorded 'Peace Train' and Maxi Priest had charted with 'Wild World'. His Cat Stevens persona - he was born Steven Georgiou - was the acoustic guitarist and folk singer whose songwriting skills were recognised by the Tremeloes (who covered 'Here Comes My Baby') and Rod Stewart ('The First Cut Is The Deepest'). After a two-year break coping with a bout of tuberculosis, Stevens was wiser and sadder on *Teaser And The Firecat*, which brought us 'Morning Has Broken', and *Tea For The Tillerman*: gentle, introspective, delicate.

"When you get to the top and you find that it is corrupt,
what do you do?
You have to look elsewhere for peace of mind and fulfilment."

Born: Steven Georgiou 21/7/47 • Recording career: 1966 - 1979 • Sounds: Mona Bone Jakon 1970, Tea For The Tillerman 1970, Teaser And The Firecat 1971

I think I started getting wrapped up in believing my own image between 1977 and 1979, **when I did think I was God's gift to women."**

Often throwing a spanner into his own works, Rod Stewart came perilously close to blowing it all. He possessed an unforgettable voice, that Steampacket, Jeff Beck and the Faces had all appreciated. And he was far from a slouch as a songwriter: 'An Old Raincoat Won't Let You Down' off his first solo album and 'Maggie May' easily stood the test of time. But after *Every Picture Tells A Story*, his triumphant 1971 release, his solo career could not co-exist with a role as the Faces' singer, and he began a migration towards Hollywood, Britt, silk jumpsuits, and 'Do Ya Think I'm Sexy'. Although he subsequently recorded plenty of dross,

he never drowned completely, always keeping his head just above the surface. Even when the chips were down, the Stewart larynx could and would deliver something extra special, like his cover of Van Morrison's 'Have I Told You Lately' from a 1993 *MTV Unplugged* special.

Rod Stewart

Born: 10/1/45 • **Recording career:** 1964 - present • **Sounds:** Gasoline Alley 1970, Every Picture Tells A Story 1971, Unplugged And Seated 1993

Sting

"I wrote a happy song once.

Now what the fuck was it called?"

Where Rod Stewart in his post-Faces guise ran the risk of ridicule for his jet-set, blonde-chasing ways, Sting, after the disbanding of the Police, encountered similar problems - not so much for a hedonistic lifestyle but for his overtly cerebral approach. A decision to record with top-flight jazz musicians like saxophonist Branford Marsalis, pianist Kenny Kirkland and drummer Omar Hakim was not the stuff of show-biz aspirations. Sting had played in Newcastle jazz line-ups way back when - now he could afford to work with the best. But the resulting coolness, coupled with Sting's solemn commitment to environmental causes, and the sombre colours of *The Soul Cages*, written following his father's death, made it seem as if he simply took everything too seriously. However, as the 1990s wore on, his songwriting talents shone through, and the craft of 'If I Ever Lose My Faith In You' or 'Fields Of Gold' began to earn deserved recognition.

Born: Gordon Sumner 2/10/51 • **Recording career (solo):** 1982 - present • **Sounds:** The Dream Of The Blue Turtles 1985, Nothing Like The Sun 1987, Ten Summoners Tales 1993

The first coming of the Stone Roses, surfing the crest of Manchester's 'baggy' wave, suggested they could sweep everything before them. No overnight success - the band had previously built up a local reputation through warehouse raves - it was 1988's 'Elephant Stone', produced by New Order bassist Peter Hook, that landed them an eight-album deal with Silvertone Records. The eponymous first album promised much. It was a confident gaggle of breezy 1960s-style tracks, full of self-belief ('I Wanna Be Adored' and 'I Am The Resurrection' said it all and resonant of the Byrds, Love, even Simon and Garfunkel. But then they entered a lengthy legal dispute with Silvertone. By the time a follow-up, *Second Coming*, arrived in 1994, the world had revolved a few too many times - Blur and Oasis were the new boys running the block. Key songwriter John Squire quit in 1996, and Ian Brown declared the Roses dead in October that year.

"I think we're relevant, we're important! I think we're exciting, mind-expanding! I know I'm blowing me own trumpet!" Ian Brown

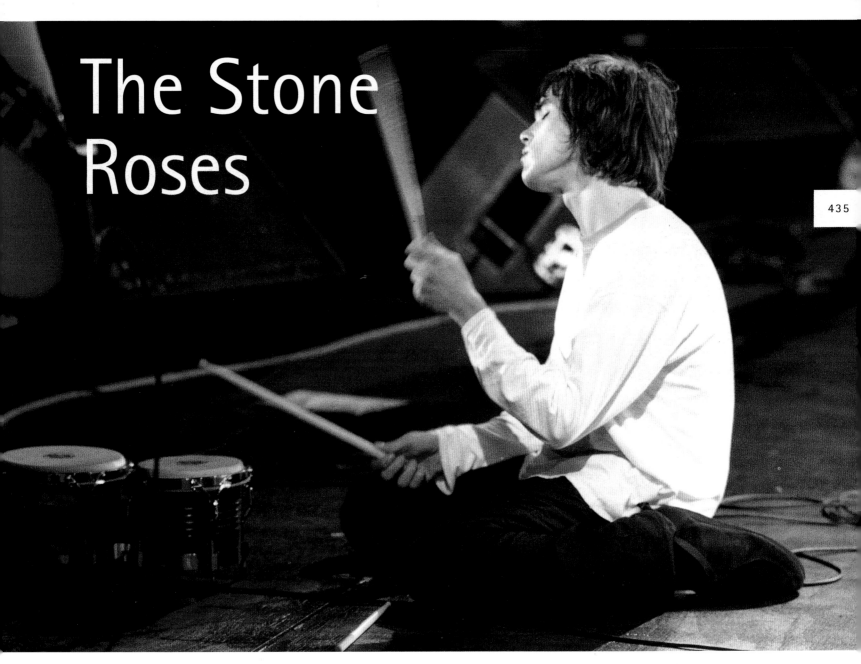

The Stone Roses

435

Key members: Ian Brown 20/2/63, Gary 'Mani' Mounfield 16/11/62, John Squire 24/11/62, Alan 'Reni' Wren 10/4/64 • **Recording career:** 1985 - 1995

Sounds: The Stone Roses 1989, Second Coming 1994

Stone Temple Pilots

Frequently lumped into the same bag as bands like Pearl Jam and Alice in Chains, the Stone Temple Pilots preferred to avoid comparisons with Seattle, staying down the other end of the West Coast in San Diego. They drew primarily on hard rock influences: Led Zeppelin, but also Kiss, whose make-up they emulated on stage for two gigs in August 1993. The Pilots' founders, vocalist Scott Weiland and bassist Robert DeLeo, met at a Black Flag gig, and by chance discovered that they were dating the same girl: a friendship emerged (whether the original relationships survived is not known). DeLeo brought in his older brother Dean on guitar, and the band moved swiftly towards a hit debut with *Core* in 1993, and a Number One, *Purple,* the following year which contained the radio-friendly 'Interstate Love Song'. Their sound was perfect for stadium tours, but Weiland subsequently incurred drug convictions and enforced rehab, which curtailed activities somewhat.

"You have to keep in mind why you're doing this.
Keep it like it was when you'd pick up a tennis racquet **and play air guitar in front of the mirror."**

Scott Weiland

436

Key members: Dean DeLeo 23/8/61, Robert DeLeo 2/2/66, Eric Kretz 7/6/66, Scott Weiland 27/10/67 • Recording career: 1993 – present

Sounds: Core 1992, Purple 1994, Tiny Music... Songs From The Vatican Gift Shop 1996

A couple of years before The Men In Black rode in on the back of punk, the Stranglers were placing small ads as a 'soft rock' band looking for a keyboard player (Dave Greenfield replied). But as disaffected teenagers started picking up guitars and having a go, the Stranglers took notice. They managed to finesse the age difference, up to a point - though the music press always remained unconvinced - and toughened up their act. *Rattus Norvegicus* had the right sound and the right sneer, and there was a mild flurry of controversy over the lyrics of 'Peaches': the word 'clitoris' had to be substituted by 'bikini'. Although 'No More Heroes' was a hit, they started picking up critical backlash for the male (and menopausal) chauvinism of songs like 'Bring On The Nubiles'. After falling out of favour at the end of the 1970s, the Stranglers staged a brief recovery in 1982 via the unlikely waltz-time harpsichord riffs of 'Golden Brown'.

"Black was the nearest thing to a corporate image the band had."

Jean-Jacques Burnel

437

The Stranglers

Key members: Jet Black (Brian Duffy) 26/8/48, Jean-Jacques Burnel 21/2/52, Hugh Cornwell 28/8/49, Dave Greenfield 29/3/49 • Recording career: 1977 - present

Sounds: Rattus Norvegicus 1977, No More Heroes 1977, La Folie 1981

"I think it's the height of arrogance to go on stage and not be extraordinary and brilliant. It's the height of arrogance to make average music." Brett Anderson

Suede

The cover of Suede's debut album was an emblem of the androgynous image that the band liked to project: a tight crop on a kissing couple whose gender was non-specific - in fact they were both women. Justine Frischmann was second guitarist in the band's original line-up but left to form Elastica before Suede secured a *Melody Maker* cover in April 1992, which in turn pre-dated the release of any recorded music. That kind of anticipation could have been disastrous, but they responded in style as the theatrical glam of 'Metal Mickey' and 'Animal Nitrate' drove the album to UK Number One. The follow-up, *Dog Man Star*, was marred by the departure of guitarist Bernard Butler halfway through its creation after a falling-out with singer Brett Anderson, but the songs they wrote survived, continuing the David Bowie vibe, albeit it with a darker, more melancholy feel. After 1996's *Coming Up*, their once-bright star began to fade.

Key members: Brett Anderson 27/9/67, Bernard Butler 1/5/70, Simon Gilbert 23/5/65, Matt Osman 9/10/67 • Recording career: 1992 - present

Sounds: Suede 1993, Dog Man Star 1994, Coming Up 1996

Suicide

"Our music just affects the mind in a certain way... **like some kind of dope,** I suppose." Marty Rev

Suicide was never painless, and their music could never be filed under easy listening. Watching them live was akin to an extreme sport as Alan Vega revelled in goading the audience: when they supported the Clash and Elvis Costello in 1978, violence ensued. This was, of course, all in the name of art. Vega, sculptor, painter, gallery owner, all-round artiste, would act out a kind of Elvis Presley routine - a mumbling, roaring, angry Elvis - over a backdrop of primitive synth and drum patterns provided by his partner-in-crime Martin Rev. Never commercial - even when the Cars' Ric Ocasek, who was a fan, produced their second album in 1980 - Suicide saw the ripples of their influence expand as times changed: first through other voice and synth acts like Soft Cell and Erasure (though there the confrontational element was, let's say, minimal) and later the industrial dance sound of Ministry and Nine Inch Nails.

Key members: Marty Rev, Alan Vega 1948 • **Recording career:** 1977 - 1981, 1988 & 1992 • **Sounds:** Suicide 1977, Alan Vega/Martin Rev - Suicide 1980, The Way Of Life 1988

Supergrass

"All we want to do is make mental music and do mental things.
Whatever else comes along - we'll take it!" Gaz Coombes

Ah, the joys of youth. Choppering in out of the sun, the cheeky monkeys of Supergrass transported the summery August 1995 anthem 'Alright' to a grateful nation. Their Red Cross parcel of blithe good humour and high spirits also continued on the album *I Should Coco*. Depending on which track you listened to, it showed an indiscriminate teenage faddishness (or eclecticism, if you were a po-faced adult) for the Buzzcocks, Elton John, the Kinks, or whoever happened to be that

day's new discovery. Then, as young flibbertigibbets are wont to do, they started growing up. The title of their second album - *In It For The Money* - showed an alarming cynicism taking root, although they could still have fun at breakneck speed on a track like 'Richard III'. By 1999's *Supergrass*, their lack of imagination in coming up with a funky name for the new album was a sure sign of rapidly approaching maturity. Bald patches, middle-age spreads and slippers could not be far behind.

Key members: Gaz Coombes 8/3/76, Danny Goffey 7/2/74, Mickey Quinn 17/12/69 • Recording career: 1994 - present • Sounds: I Should Coco 1995, In It For The Money 1997, Supergrass 1999

Talking Heads were by anybody's definition an art school band - three quarters of its members had attended the Rhode Island School Of Design. The wallflower was Jerry Harrison, who'd attended the school of Jonathan Richman and the Modern Lovers. Despite their roots, they made their debut in a tough testing ground: New York's CBGB's, supporting the Ramones. It gave them a kind of punk thumbs-up, so that David Byrne's clipped vocals and the Heads' off-beat songs - which might have appeared simply affected in another setting - seemed suitably hip and urban on their debut, *Talking Heads: 77*, including the much-emulated 'Psycho Killer'. Brian Eno caught the band performing at London's Rock Garden: his production input from *More Songs About Buildings And Food* through to *Remain In Light* encouraged, but also disciplined, their artier side. The path they then pursued was rarely on the road to nowhere - always something there to intrigue us.

441

Talking Heads

"We decided we wouldn't do guitar solos or drum solos, we wouldn't make any grand gestures. We'd try and be very to the point." David Byrne

Key members: David Byrne 14/5/52, Chris Frantz 8/5/51, Jerry Harrison 21/2/49, Tina Weymouth 22/11/50 • Recording career: 1977 - 1988 & 1992

Sounds: Talking Heads: 77 1977, Remain In Light 1980, Speaking In Tongues 1983

Tangerine Dream

Such a great name: it's almost impossible to imagine anything better for a post-psychedelic, ambient, electronic German band. In fact, Tangerine Dream's first manifestation was as an unter-Grateful Dead/Doors band, but it didn't take long for the Moogs to kick in. Edgar Froese resided as the mainstay of the group when Virgin Records (cock-a-hoop off the back of Mike Oldfield's *Tubular Bells*) signed the band. Their textural washes and sonic canvases seemed best suited for a quasi-religious experience. Indeed, in 1974 they packed out the Cathedral at Reims - 6,000 fans trying to fit into a space normally reserved for 2,000 celebrants - and enjoyed the event so much they expanded the idea into a 'tour' of York Minster, Liverpool and Coventry Cathedrals, with the highlights released on *Ricochet*. When Edgar Froese's son Jerome became involved in the 1990s, it was clear that the Dream could last forever. Tune in, turn on and flop out.

"Salvador Dali showed me that everything was possible." Edgar Froese

442

Key members: Peter Baumann, Chris Franke 6/4/53, Edgar Froese 6/6/44 • Recording career: 1970 - present • Sounds: Phaedra 1974, Ricochet 1976, Exit 1981

"No one had a name like ours. 1978 was all short, dour names. **Ours was far fucking out."** Julian Cope

Julian Cope, the frontispiece of The Teardrop Explodes, was one eccentric dude, as he proved when he moved on from the Liverpool band to his own trip of a solo career. The Teardrop formed part of the acid mists that engulfed Merseyside in the late 1970s (punk, for some reason, never having completely taken root in Liverpool); Cope had worked previously in Crucial 3 with Ian McCulloch, the chief of the Bunnymen, and Pete Wylie, leader of Wah! With cohorts including label manager Bill Drummond, later of the KLF - and obviously a restraining influence - Cope spiked his music with a tab of psychedelia. Though the tightly produced single 'Reward' breached the UK Top Ten, the hallucinations of 'Sleeping Gas' and 'Bouncing Babies' were far more typical. As the personnel around him ebbed, flowed and evaporated, Cope was given a free hand on 1981's *Wilder* to explore his particular paintbox of colour and emotions - it was an exhilarating final fling.

The Teardrop Explodes

Key member: Julian Cope 21/10/57 • Recording career: 1979 - 1983 • Sounds: Kilimanjaro 1980, Wilder 1981

"When the Fanclub are fifty we'll probably be doing covers of Primal Scream songs on the cabaret circuit... such is life." Norman Blake

The wave of 1960s retro that washed up over Sean O'Hagan's High Llamas also rippled through to Scotland and Teenage Fanclub, another band for whom acts like the Beach Boys or Big Star, along with the Beatles, were the moving forces (the Fanclub had a significant role in a long-overdue resurgence of interest in Big Star). Norman Blake had been a member of Duglus Stewart's quirky BMX Bandits before forming the Boy Hairdressers, which contained the nucleus of the Fanclub.

A first album, 1989's *A Catholic Education*, was distinctly grungey, but by the time of the second, *Bandwagonesque*, all those West Coast influences were gaining the upper hand - although ex-Dinosaur Jr. guitarist Don Fleming co-produced and helped retain some nuances of Seattle. Criticised or acclaimed by turns for being a) too retro, b) too cheesy, c) having too much fun, the Fanclub persisted and made sure that their harmonies, melodies and good vibrations remained intact.

444

Teenage Fanclub

Key members: Norman Blake 20/10/65, Gerard Love 31/8/67, Raymond McGinley 3/1/64, Brendan O'Hare 16/1/70 • **Recording career:** 1989 - present

Sounds: Bandwagonesque 1991, Grand Prix 1995, Songs From Northern Britain 1997

"What a load of rubbish it was, the old days.
It was tedium, dreadful tedium..." Tom Verlaine
Television

If you wanted to be cool in Britain in 1977, and didn't own a copy of *Marquee Moon*, you could forget it. Television had been the first new-wave band to perform at the Manhattan club CBGB's in March 1974, ahead even of the Ramones. Tom Verlaine, né Miller, and Richard Hell, né Myers, shared a passion for the Velvet Underground, Moby Grape, the Dead, and Patti Smith's literary learning curve: Verlaine, Tom not Monsieur Paul, collaborated with her on the poetry volume *The Night*.

Hell possessed the right punk antennae - he wrote '(I Belong To The) Blank Generation' - but his bass-playing was just too limited; Fred 'Sonic' Smith, Patti's future husband, replaced him before Television recorded. Hell formed the Voidoids, then the Heartbreakers with New York Doll Johnny Thunders. The new Television line-up cut *Marquee Moon*, a flop in the US though acclaimed in the UK, but by *Adventure*, internal unrest was causing more than temporary interference.

Key members: Billy Ficca, Richard Hell (Richard Myers) 2/10/49, Richard Lloyd, Fred 'Sonic' Smith 10/4/48 (died 4/11/94), Tom Verlaine (Thomas Miller) 13/12/49

Recording career: 1975 - 1978 & 1992 • Sounds: Marquee Moon 1977, Adventure 1978, Television 1992

Clever, beautifully put together, craftsmen at work. But you always wanted 10cc to let rip, or add a piquant dash of Steely Dan's lethal malevolence. A Mancunian supergroup, the members came together from two primary sources. Graham Gouldman had worked alongside Eric Stewart in the Mindbenders and brought a fine songwriting pedigree, including 'For Your Love', the Yardbirds' hit. Godley and Creme were art school pals who, in the 1980s, applied their visual talents to promo videos. As Hotlegs, the group had a hit with 'Neanderthal Man' before joining UK, the irrepressible Jonathan King's label. He suggested the 10cc name - allegedly an average male ejaculate, plus a bit - and from their Strawberry Studios a number of tongue-in-cheek gems emerged: doo-wop spoof 'Donna', the chugging 'Wall Street Shuffle' and the perennial disco snogathon 'I'm Not In Love'. But once Godley and Creme left the songs got too corny, including the cod-reggae 'Dreadlock Holiday'. So nearly, nearly brilliant.

10cc

"Sacred cows are lovingly demolished. It's not really contempt. **It's ridicule.**" Eric Stewart

446

Key members: Lol Creme 19/9/47, Kevin Godley 7/10/45, Graham Gouldman 10/5/46, Eric Stewart 20/1/45 • Recording career: 1972 - 1983 & 1992 - present

Sounds: Sheet Music 1974, The Original Soundtrack 1975, How Dare You! 1976

The sextet that first formed 10,000 Maniacs was actually the cut-down version. At one point the Maniacs, if not myriad in number, could certainly count on at least a dozen members. Their music was a 1980s take on folk-rock, and appropriately they signed to Elektra (the classic folk-rock label), with Joe Boyd, who'd worked with Fairport Convention, producing *The Wishing Chair*. Natalie Merchant was the Maniac mainspring: her lyrics alert, her voice passionate but plaintive, her animated stage persona at odds with an off-stage grace. In certain quarters they later scored points by removing Cat Stevens' 'Peace Train' from *In My Tribe*, after Stevens, as Yusef Islam, had supported the Salman Rushdie fatwa. 1992's *One Time In Eden* marked the start of Natalie Merchant's departure (she said it had been like being in a band with five husbands), whereupon original member J.C. Lombardo returned, with Mary Ramsey, to take up her gentle cudgels.

"The band wanted to know why I wrote miserable songs all the time. I hadn't even noticed."

Natalie Merchant

447

10,000 Maniacs

Key members: Jerome Augustyniak 2/9/58, Rob Buck 3/8/58 (died 19/12/00), Dennis Drew 8/8/57, Steven Gustafson 10/4/57, J.C. Lombardo 30/9/52, Natalie Merchant 26/10/63

Recording career: 1982 - present • Sounds: The Wishing Chair 1985, In My Tribe 1987, Our Time In Eden 1992

The stand-out feature of Ten Years After was Alvin Lee - the hottest guitar-slinger in the (Fillmore) West. Therein lay his, and the band's, problem. Formed in the Nottingham area, they developed a blend of blues, boogie and hard rock that could cut it across the Atlantic, and enjoyed enthusiastic responses in San Francisco and New York - so much so that they were able to land an appearance at Woodstock. The movie of the festival gave them extensive exposure: approximately ten minutes of 'I'm Going Home', featuring Alvin rippling through his repertoire of extremely fast licks. He was never allowed to forget it. Whenever Ten Years After appeared, Alvin was obliged to deliver the same million notes per minute. The predictability and the pressure took their toll in the long run, so it's best to go back to that *Woodstock* film or their earlier album *Undead* to hear what all the fuss was about.

448

"We work jams and remember certain phrases,
but it gets to the point where you're constantly doing old tricks."

Alvin Lee

Ten Years After

Key members: Chick Churchill 2/1/49, Alvin Lee 19/12/44, Ric Lee 20/10/45, Leo Lyons 30/11/43 • Recording career: 1967 - 1974 & 1989

Sounds: Undead 1968, Sssh 1970, Cricklewood Green 1970

Texas

ans, Texas (and Ry Cooder's slide guitar work) was the vibe. Glasgow, Strathclyde was the reality - where, circa 1987, Sharleen Spiteri was introduced to John McElhone. He'd already tasted some success in Altered Images, alongside Clare Grogan, and in Hipsway; she was a sometime hairdresser's assistant with a dark chocolate voice. They began writing together - 'I Don't Want A Lover', their first song, became Texas's debut hit - and found a guitarist, Ally McErlaine, who could emulate the Cooder technique. Yet though Texas carried on comfortably for several years, something happened in 1997. Overnight, it seemed, Spiteri was snapped up as the cover girl of the moment, a sudden increase in profile that did no end of good for their 'modern soul' combination of Prince, Motown, Stax, Roxy Music, the Stones et al. The album *White On Blonde*, including the singles 'Say What You Want' and 'Black Eyed Boy', benefited enormously, as they entered the clone star state of mind.

"We're taking
the soul and blues
influences we've always
had and using 90s beats
and dance rhythms
**to take it up
to today."**

Sharleen Spiteri

Key members: Eddie Campbell 6/6/65, Richard Hynd 17/5/68, Johnny McElhone 21/4/63, Ally McErlaine 31/10/68, Sharleen Spiteri 7/11/67 • **Recording career:** 1989 - present

Sounds: Southside 1989, White On Blonde 1997, The Hush 1999

The The

Swirling around Matt Johnson's distinctive profile, his brainchild The The ran through a number of styles, pinned together by Johnson's serious, though shifting, concerns. Or they seemed shifting because of intermittent releases and lengthy sabbaticals. Emerging as a duo with synth player Keith Laws, the pair released one single before contractual ructions meant the experimental first album, *Burning Blue Soul*, had to be released under Johnson's name (Laws had drifted away in any case). *Soul Mining* bore the hallmarks of Johnson's high pop awareness on the single 'Uncertain Smile' - then, after a lay-off for illness, 1986's *Infected* engendered a dark vision of US military might and sexual apocalypse. But by the end of the 1980s, with something approaching a real band - Johnny Marr and ex-ABC drummer David Palmer were new co-conspirators - Johnson and The The were ready for a new decade, which would involve the accessible acoustics of *Dusk* and a Hank Williams tribute album, *Hanky Panky*.

"I've acquired this tag of 'miserable bastard'.
I have a lot of fun in my life,
but happiness is very, very difficult to write about and describe." Matt Johnson

450

Key member: Matt Johnson 15/8/61 • Recording career: 1980 - present • Sounds: Soul Mining 1983, Infected 1986, Dusk 1993

451

Thin Lizzy

The late Phil Lynott, of Brazilian/Irish heritage, didn't have to try too hard to project himself as an outsider in the Ireland of the 1970s, in a country yet to uncage the Celtic tiger. But he retained a close connection with the national penchant for romanticism: the first line-up of Thin Lizzy recorded both 'Eire', Lynott's reworking of Irish history, and the single 'Whiskey In The Jar', a traditional tale of vagabonds roaming through Cork and Kerry.

But as the band prepared to take on wider horizons, and after original guitarist Eric Bell left, the harder side of Thin Lizzy took the spotlight. With a twin lead guitar set-up, and a live sound honed on US tours (where they once blew Bachman-Turner Overdrive off the stage), Lizzy stomped back in with 'The Boys Are Back In Town', firing the dancehalls of the world alight, and setting the tone for the band's remaining years.

"Sometimes I go out there and go completely berserk...
and it's nothing to do with drugs." Phil Lynott

Key members: Brian Downey 27/1/51, Scott Gorham 17/3/51, Phil Lynott 20/8/51 (died 4/1/86), Brian Robertson 12/9/56 • Recording career: 1971 - 1983

Sounds: Jailbreak 1976, Live And Dangerous 1978, Black Rose (A Rock Legend) 1979

Richard Thompson

By the time he left Fairport Convention in 1971, Richard Thompson had already bequeathed a significant legacy as one of Fairport's founders. Among the musicians on his first solo recording, *Henry The Human Fly*, was singer Linda Peters (a friend of Fairport vocalist Sandy Denny), who became Mrs Thompson. Now billed as Richard and Linda Thompson, the couple released the acclaimed album *I Want To See The Bright Lights Tonight*, its uplifting title track contributing to a rich piece of work. After converting to the Sufi-Moslem religion, their output slowed; by the time of 1982's *Shoot Out The Lights*, the marriage was foundering, and their contributions to tracks like 'Don't Renege On Our Love' and 'Just The Motion' added a poignant, pointed sub-text. Thompson's world-weary voice subsequently wearied some more, but his songwriting and clean guitar work remained as powerful as ever - his credibility high, his profile too low. Maybe his devoted fans preferred it that way.

"I would try to write songs from a woman's viewpoint; that was quite difficult, but rewarding. If I failed, I could always just sing them myself."

Richard Thompson

452

Born: 3/4/49 • Recording career: 1972 - present • Sounds: I Want To See The Bright Lights Tonight 1974, Shoot Out The Lights 1982, Hand Of Kindness 1983

> "You can be out of tune or you can play the wrong note, but if you can put a smile on someone's face then I figure we're successful." George Thorogood

George Thorogood and the Destroyers

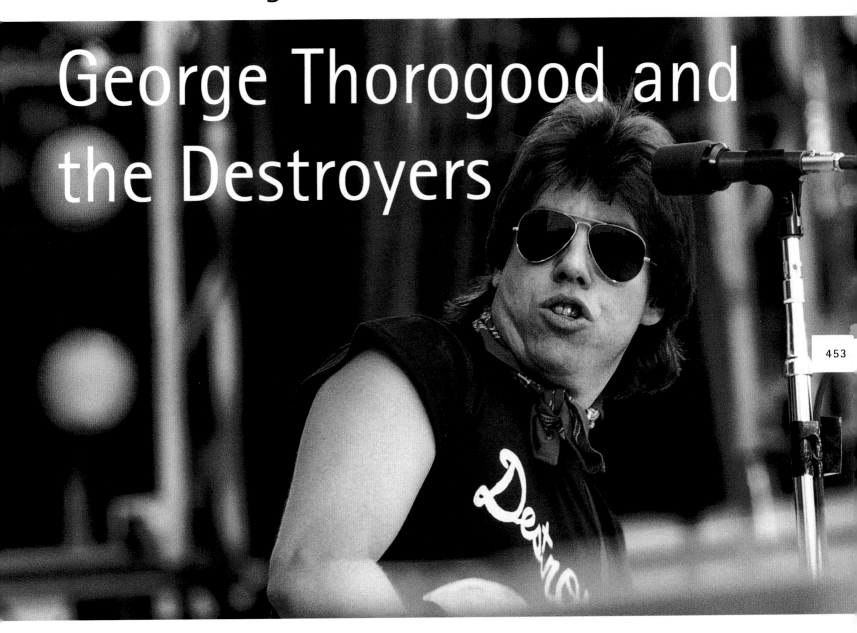

From the moment he saw dedicated bluesman John Paul Hammond performing in 1970, George Thorogood would follow an equally unswerving path, With his backing band the Destroyers, he paid joyful homage to the likes of John Lee Hooker (including a rollicking version of 'One Bourbon, One Scotch, One Beer'), Bo Diddley, Elmore James and Chuck Berry, up to and including the latter's signature duckwalk. This was no-bullshit music, loud and straight down the line, which usually found a welcoming audience - the Destroyers opened for the Stones on their 1981 tour, and Thorogood jammed with Albert Collins on Live Aid's Washington stage. And although the band earned their stripes doing covers, they also created original material that could stand its own ground, especially George's 'Bad To The Bone', featured in *Terminator 2*. As the fickle shooting stars of the musical firmament sparkled above them, the Destroyers set their course and ordered full steam ahead.

Key members: Billy Blough, Hank Carter, Jeff Simon, George Thorogood 31/12/52 • **Recording career:** 1977 - present

Sounds: George Thorogood & The Destroyers 1977, Bad To The Bone 1982, Live 1986

Three Dog Night

Danny Hutton - a session singer with one minor US hit, 'Roses And Rainbows' - had a vision in the late 1960s of a group featuring a three-pronged vocal attack. Gathering the necessary cohorts to form Three Dog Night, his vision materialised better than anyone expected, as a sequence of eleven US Top Ten hits was launched by a version of Harry Nilsson's 'One'. Most comfortable interpreting other people's material, Hutton and co. struck back at accusations that they were too slick and too commercial by pointing out that their success had given wide coverage to previously little-known singer-songwriters. As well as Nilsson, other beneficiaries had been Laura Nyro, Randy Newman, the then unproven team of Elton John and Bernie Taupin, and folk singer Hoyt Axton, whose 'Joy To The World', as performed by Three Dog Night, was the biggest-selling US single of 1971 (and whose mother Mae, trivia fans, was the composer of Elvis's 'Heartbreak Hotel').

"We're not ashamed of being businessmen, because we all love the music, **and that's no hype.**" Mike Allsup

454

Key members: Mike Allsup 8/3/47, Jimmy Greenspoon 7/2/48, Danny Hutton 10/9/42, Chuck Negron 8/6/42, Joe Schermie 12/2/45, Floyd Sneed 22/11/43, Cory Wells 5/2/42

Recording career: 1968 - 1976 & 1993 • Sounds: Three Dog Night 1969, It Ain't Easy 1970, Around The World With Three Dog Night 1973

"Although I made a pretty good job of staying experimental, there were times when I would tour because I needed to pay the rent." Genesis P-Orridge

The cover photo of Throbbing Gristle's 1979 album *20 Jazz Funk Greats* portrayed what seemed to be an MOR quartet posing among the flora of a south-coast cliff-top. Could these be the same four deviants accused by one UK national newspaper of wrecking civilisation as we knew it? Sure was: Throbbing Gristle - led by Genesis P-Orridge - were the masters of shock and confrontation. An early example of their installation art had involved piles of used nappies and tampons: they'd have been guaranteed

a Turner Prize nomination 20 years later. P-Orridge's lover Cosey Fanni Tutti - a bonny Yorkshire lass called Christine Newby - had adorned the pages of *Fiesta*, *Rustler* and the *Journal Of Sex*. And their music was industrial noise, way before it became fashionable, aided and abetted by technician Peter Christopherson's early sampling devices. They subtitled their *Greatest Hits* album (they never had a hit, of course) 'Entertainment Through Pain' - it could equally have been the Gristle's perfect epitaph.

Throbbing Gristle

Key members: Chris Carter 28/1/55, 'Sleazy' Peter Christopherson 27/2/55, Genesis P-Orridge (Neil Megson) 22/2/50, Cosey Fanny Tutti (Christine Newby) 4/11/51 • **Recording career:** 1977 - 1980
Sounds: D.O.A. 1978, 20 Jazz Funk Greats 1979, Mission Of Dead Souls 1981

"I hate people who don't see music as a vehicle for the truth, high and mighty as that sounds."

Kristin Hersh

Stepsisters Tanya Donelly and Kristin Hersh founded the Throwing Muses with high school colleagues from Newport, Rhode Island, but they required the belief and support of a British label, 4AD, to nurture their low-key, campus-friendly career. Much of the press attention about the band focussed around Kristin Hersh, who had suffered from a bipolar disorder as a teenager. Certainly their albums offered a range of mood swings behind the stepsisters' guitars, full of dark ponds, slow swirling waters and shimmering fountains. Hersh dominated the Muses, and Donelly became increasingly frustrated - although she managed to get a song or two on each album (including 'Green' and 'Not Too Soon'), it was not enough. So she formed an offshoot, Breeders, with the Pixies' Kim Deal, before moving on to Belly. One muse down, Hersh nevertheless managed to hold the band together, and on *Red Heaven* and *University* - as a trio - they showed their rockier chops.

Throwing Muses

Key members: Tanya Donelly 14/7/66, Kristin Hersh 7/8/66, Leslie Langston 1/4/64, David Narcizo 6/5/66 • Recording career: 1986 - 1997

Sounds: Throwing Muses 1986, The Real Ramona 1991, University 1995

456

Johnny Thunders

"Rock'n'roll is about attitude. I couldn't care less about technique."

In the New York Dolls' trash-flash cast Johnny Thunders (né John Genzale Jnr) was their Keith Richards, a sneering, fearless, one-riff punk, notoriously sloppy on stage. He and drummer Jerry Nolan then left to form the Heartbreakers with Television's Richard Hell: the first supergroup of punk. Malcolm McLaren brought them over to the UK in 1976 for the Pistols' Anarchy tour, and Thunders stayed on in London, recording the solo album *So Alone* with British admirers including Steve Marriott and the Only Ones' Peter Perrett. After the Heartbreakers broke up in 1984, Thunders released various - mainly live - albums and tried to kick his heroin habit, but was found dead in a New Orleans hotel aged 38. His Italian family buried him in Queens alongside his acoustic guitar - his long-time promoter revealing that despite Thunders' reputation for total unreliability, he always turned up on time. His sister simply said he was "a pain in the ass. But good".

Born: John Genzale Jnr 15/7/52 (died 23/4/91) • Recording career (solo): 1978 - 1990 • Sounds: So Alone 1978

Tindersticks

The Tindersticks' spark was a slow burn, not a blowtorch - music delivered with the unhurried pace and atmosphere of a bar in the wee hours, drenched in a smoke-filled fug. Singer Stuart Staples possessed a deep, deep voice, down there in Lee Marvin country at times, although most comparisons were with Lee Hazlewood, Nancy Sinatra's mentor. Rich and romantic, his voice suited the spare *singspiel* of the 1993 single 'Marbles', the lush arrangements of *tindersticks*, the band's second album, and on 'Travelling Light' interwove with Walkabout Carla Torgeson's vocals in the most delightful way. The material earned critical praise from the music press, but also happily coincided with the mid-1990s championing of easy listening and lounge music - a John Barry vibe lurked constantly beneath the surface. Encouraged, they even dared to tour with a chamber orchestra (a logistical nightmare that had flummoxed many another band in the past) and carried it off with panache.

"If we were the sort of people **that did wear jeans and T-shirts,** we wouldn't make the music that we do." Stuart Staples

458

Key members: Dave Boulter, Mark Colwill, Neil Frazer, Dickon Hinchcliffe, Al McCauley, Stuart Staples • Recording career: 1992 - present • Sounds: TINDERSTICKS 1993, tindersticks 1995, Curtains 1997

Traffic

The first outing of Traffic was a straight left turn into psychedelic pop, as the founder members - Steve Winwood, fresh from the Spencer Davis Group, was the best known - draped a tint of the Summer of Love over 'Paper Sun' and 'Hole In My Shoe', later covered by Neil of the Young Ones. Winwood contributed his distinctive Hammond organ and electric harpsichord, Dave Mason some sitar licks, Chris Wood warbled on flute and sax. When the others got too jazzy, Mason - the keeper of the band's pop flame - left along with his songwriting precision ('Feelin' Alright', a future standard, was one of his). After Winwood's brief

diversion with Blind Faith, a 'solo' album evolved into a loose-limbed, funky Traffic release called *John Barleycorn Must Die* - a Transatlantic success. The group subsequently expanded to include Rick Grech, second drummer Jim Gordon and Ghanaian Reebop Kwaku-Baah on percussion, but they then began to meander like a Sunday afternoon mimser.

"We see movements and roam through the temples of our minds. We get tripped out with the countryside..." Jim Capaldi

Key members: Jim Capaldi 24/8/44, Dave Mason 10/5/45, Steve Winwood 12/5/48, Chris Wood 24/6/44 (died 12/7/83) • Recording career: 1967 - 1974 & 1994

Sounds: Traffic 1968, John Barleycorn Must Die 1970, The Low Spark Of High-Heeled Boys 1971

Travis

"The drummer from the Pretenders, Martin Chambers, described the sound of our music as 'simplicity with weight'. He said we made him remember why he did this in the first place." Fran Healy

Paris, Texas was obviously a popular video rental in the Glasgow area - Sharleen Spiteri and Johnny McElhone took their band name from the last word of the movie's title, Travis from one of its characters (they'd previously been called Glass Onion...). Another key decision - after taking on board some no-bullshit advice from an American music business veteran - was prising away their bassist and keyboard player and bringing in old friend Dougie Payne on bass. Signed to the new

Independiente label set up by Andy McDonald after Go! Discs folded, Travis saw Good Feeling, released in 1997, fare quite well, and 1999's The Man Who reach UK Number Five before drooping. But then an appearance at Glastonbury, when the heavens opportunely opened just as they launched into 'Why Does It Always Rain On Me?', helped boost the album back up to Number One and sent Fran Healy's vocals - a David Gates for the new century - into everybody's consciousness.

Key members: Andy Dunlop 16/3/72, Fran Healy 23/7/73, Dougie Payne 14/11/72, Neil Primrose 20/2/72 • **Recording career:** 1997 - present • **Sounds:** Good Feeling 1997, The Man Who 1999

Meet the Troggs. They were the garage band who hailed not from America's suburban sprawl but the less likely setting of Andover in Hampshire. Their pre-punk simplicity produced three indelible moments. The first was their primitive 'Louie Louie' sound-alike 'Wild Thing', retrieved from the obscurity of its first recording (attributed to Jordan Christopher and the Wild Ones) by Larry Page, the onetime Kinks' manager who was overseeing the Troggs' affairs. The song was a no-frills classic, which Jimi Hendrix selected to round off his momentous Monterey Festival set in 1967. Their second contribution to rock history was the hilarious *Troggs Tapes* - an out-take of the band having a furious and fabulously foul-mouthed studio argument, which became a much-loved and bootlegged collectible amongst fellow musicians. And finally there was 'Love Is All Around', which, courtesy of Wet Wet Wet and *Four Weddings And A Funeral*, gave Troggs frontman and the tune's songwriter Reg Presley a belatedly lucrative feeling in his fingers.

The Troggs

"We had night after night of somebody unplugging the mikes during the first or second number because we were too potent for the main act."

Reg Presley

Key members: Ronnie Bond 4/5/43 (died 13/11/92), Chris Britton 21/6/45, Reg Presley 12/6/43, Pete Staples 3/5/44 • Recording career: 1966 - 1968 & 1975 - 1992

Sounds: From Nowhere The Troggs 1966, Live At Max's Kansas City 1981, Athens Andover 1992

The Tubes

From Phoenix, Arizona by way of San Francisco, the Tubes introduced revue-style theatre into rock'n'roll. In their heyday, the late 1970s, their touring roadshow would blow into town like a wacky *Cirque du Soleil*, with a cast of crazed characters poking fun at most areas of the music business. Johnny Bugger ("I was a punk before you were a punk")

would be followed by the fabulous Quay Lewd, a drugged-out rock star teetering on his two-foot-high platform shoes and squeezed into a eye-watering jockstrap. Most of these characters were played by Fee Waybill (aka John Waldo), whose famed 'Mondo Bondage' S&M routine with Re Styles, the Tubes' dancer, once caused the good burghers of Portsmouth to get seriously apoplectic. The secret ingredient behind all the props was the band's all-round excellent musicianship - their anthem 'White Punks On Dope' a great number in its own right - without which the joke, like an unbalanced Quay Lewd, would have fallen flat on its face.

"We all loved the name because of its many different connotations: inner tubes, TV tubes, laser tubes, fallopian tubes, you couldn't pin it down." Fee Waybill

462

Key members: Rick Anderson 1/8/47, Michael Cotten 25/1/50, Prairie Prince 7/5/50, Bill Spooner 16/4/49, Roger Steen 13/11/49, Re Styles 3/3/50, Fee Waybill (John Waldo) 17/9/50, Vince Welnick 21/2/51 • Recording career: 1975 - 1986 & 1996 - present • Sounds: The Tubes 1975, Young And Rich 1976, What Do You Want From Live? 1978

"Ike was totally dominating.
Everything was done when he wanted and how he wanted. Once I got on stage that was my outlet, that was my freedom."

Tina Turner

Tina Turner firmly commandeered the spotlight in 1984 when 'What's Love Got To Do With It?' launched her on a revitalising solo career, by which time revelations about life with Ike had permanently sullied his reputation ("I've never been what you thought I was," he retorted). Three decades earlier he had been a rock'n'roll pioneer - his 1950 recording of 'Rocket 88' with the Kings Of Rhythm a genuinely seminal release. After meeting and marrying the former Annie Mae Bullock, he constructed the Ike and Tina revue: Tina upfront exuding sensuality, Ike rocking behind, the Ikettes softening the blast. Their bold pairing with Phil Spector on 'River Deep, Mountain High' barely registered in the USA: Spector was seriously crushed by its rejection, but the Turners recovered - their last major hit, 'Nutbush City Limits', coming in 1973. Written by Tina, it marked the stirrings of forthcoming independence: "It felt good to fight back... The door's open, I'm out of here."

Ike and Tina Turner

Born: Ike Turner 5/11/31, Tina Turner 26/11/39 • Recording career: 1960 - 1975 • Sounds: Live! The Ike And Tina Show 1965, River Deep - Mountain High 1966, Workin' Together 1970

U2

"We used to broadcast what we believed in,
now we broadcast what we don't believe in." Bono

Fuelled by the ideals of punk and the zeal of their beliefs, U2 (originally called The Hype, but wisely renamed by their art director Steve Averill) built a similarly earnest following - "there was a decision to stare down the 80s" - through the trilogy of Steve Lillywhite-produced albums: *Boy*, *October* and *War*. While synths threatened to swamp the known music world, U2 combined The Edge's massive guitar textures with driving rhythms and Bono's instinctive showmanship. An inspired performance of 'Sunday Bloody Sunday' at Live Aid transmitted their passion to a global audience; U2 took up the challenge and moved to new levels of spine-tingling and stadium-filling magnificence. In the 1990s they were big enough and confident enough to play the post-modernist game, exploring techno and ambient sounds and, lawks a-mercy, occasionally able to poke fun at themselves - "comedians are the real rebels of the 90s," said Bono. We knew they'd *always* be serious, but it was a start.

Key members: Bono (Paul Hewson) 10/5/60, Adam Clayton 13/3/60, The Edge (David Evans) 8/8/61, Larry Mullen 31/10/61 • Recording career: 1979 - present

Sounds: War 1983, The Joshua Tree 1987, Achtung Baby 1991

UB40

The cover of their debut - an enlarged UB40 unemployment benefit card - was a clever promotional device, but also a symbol of their left-wing convictions. In the years of buoyant Thatcherism and unelectable socialism this could have been an unrewarding occupation, but they plugged on, popularising reggae in the UK as much as Bob Marley had done in the 1970s. Early singles were full of anger - including 'One In Ten', their sarcastic attack on the levels of unemployment - but the

Campbell brothers and their multi-racial Midland posse took a decision to move into more purely commercial ground as the 2-Tone movement led by the Specials faltered. The central policy of New UB40 was the cover version: 'Red Red Wine' (a Neil Diamond song), Elvis Presley's 'Can't Help Falling In Love', and the collaborations with Chrissie Hynde on 'I Got You Babe' and 'Breakfast In Bed'- a return favour for the slot that the band had been given on a Pretenders tour way back in 1978.

"When we first played Bob Marley at home,
Dad said 'Get that gibberish off my turntable!'" Ali Campbell

Key members: Astro (Terence Wilson) 24/6/57, Jim Brown 20/11/57, Ali Campbell 15/2/59, Robin Campbell 25/12/54, Earl Falconer 23/1/57, Norman Hassan 26/1/58, Brian Travers 7/2/59, Mickey Virtue 19/1/57 • **Recording career:** 1980 - present • **Sounds:** Signing Off 1980, Labour Of Love 1983, Promises And Lies 1993

UFO

"I think it's time that people knew. We weren't the blokes that made Michael Schenker mad, **he made us mad!** We were the sensible ones."

Pete Way

The first encounters with UFO, in 1969, were inauspicious: a boogie band with a light space rock lustre, their offerings were largely ignored in their UK homeland. However, they found a much more positive response in France, Japan - where they had a hit with a cover of Eddie Cochran's 'C'mon Everybody' - and Germany. On tour in the latter, they found a replacement for original guitarist Mick Bolton, who had quit in 1973: this was Michael Schenker, currently playing with brother Rudolf in the Scorpions. When Schenker strapped on his Gibson Flying V, UFO found another gear, and - under the production guidance of Ten Years After bassist Leo Lyons - released a run of high-powered hard rock albums. The band lived life on the road to the full. It eventually took its toll on Schenker, who left in 1978 (briefly reuniting with them in 1995) - UFO's starriest moments are collected in the live double album *Strangers In The Night*.

Key members: Phil Mogg 15/4/48, Andy Parker 21/3/52, Michael Schenker 10/1/51, Pete Way 7/8/51 • Recording career: 1970 - 1983, 1985 - 1988 & 1992 - present

Sounds: Phenomenon 1974, Lights Out 1977, Strangers In The Night 1979

"Critics tend to dismiss our music as bland, pompous or over the top. I reckon it's because they don't really listen to it that closely." Midge Ure

Ultravox

Midge Ure was a late import to Ultravox, rescuing it from imminent self-destruction. The original line-up, fronted by John Foxx - and sporting an exclamation mark at the end of the group's name - had developed a Kraftwerk-synth sound behind Foxx's part-Bowie, part-Ferry vocals. Although Brian Eno had produced their first album, they found themselves dropped by Island Records in 1979, whereupon the Foxx-less remnants drafted in Midge. His CV included stints in Visage (alongside Steve Strange and Ultravox's Billy Currie), teenyboppers Slik and Rich Kids, with ex-Pistol Glen Matlock. Ure's arrival added a fresh sheen which permeated the portentous grandeur of 'Vienna', and for a while, with hits like 'The Thin Wall', Ultravox were in the vanguard of new romanticism. But Ure became deeply involved with Bob Geldof's Band Aid, co-writing 'Do They Know It's Christmas?', and while Ultravox performed at Live Aid it was effectively their swan song.

Key members: Warren Cann 20/5/52, Chris Cross 14/7/52, Billy Currie 1/4/52, Midge Ure 10/10/53 • Recording career: 1976 - 1986 (reformed 1993 - present)
Sounds: Ultravox! 1976, Ha! Ha! Ha! 1977, Vienna 1980

The Undertones

In 1978 the Undertones, like a class at the end of a school year, came tumbling out of Derry, buzzing with the energy of punk but with nary a sneer on their faces. The Undertones sang of the heady pleasures of the young male: girls, girls, Subbuteo and summer holidays (on the joyous 'Here Comes The Summer'). John Peel's reaction to their debut, 'Teenage Kicks', was eulogic: he declared it his favourite single of all time. With this credible support, their good-hearted progress scampered on, through 'You've Got My Number' and 'My Perfect Cousin'. And although they later tinkered with the formula, going back to a love of Motown with a cover of the Isleys' 'Got To Have You Back' in 1983, it was only once their fresh-faced approach started to verge on the callow. They realised the danger, and put an end to a career which had been as near-perfect as any of their singles (though they reformed, minus Sharkey, in 1999).

"By the time we recorded 'Teenage Kicks' we were ready to jack it all in. If nothing happened with it we were going to give up." John O'Neill

Key members: Michael Bradley 13/8/59, Billy Doherty 10/7/58, Damian O'Neill 15/1/61, John O'Neill 26/8/57, Feargal Sharkey 13/8/58 • Recording career: 1978 - 1983 & 2000 - present

Sounds: The Undertones 1979, Hypnotized 1980, The Sin Of Pride 1983

> "'La Bamba' probably goes back 200 years. When Ritchie Valens sang it **he didn't know what he was singing about,** because he didn't have the Spanish."
>
> Cesar Rosas of Los Lobos

Ritchie Valens

Sitting alongside Buddy Holly and the Big Bopper on the doomed flight from Mason City, Iowa to Fargo, North Dakota was Ritchie Valens. He'd barely had time to make any kind of mark: after all, he was only 17. However, what few recordings he had made were the stirrings of a Hispanic strain of rock'n'roll, continued after his death by Chris Montez and Chan Romero. Ritchie (born Valenzuela) grew up in Pacoima, California where he became particularly enamoured of Little Richard's unbridled energy. In 1958 his career was launched with 'Come On, Let's Go' - later a UK Top Ten hit for Tommy Steele - followed by the double-header of 'Donna', written for his girlfriend, and 'La Bamba'. This traditional Mexican wedding song, blessed with the same perennial guitar riff that later drove 'Louie Louie' and 'Wild Thing', was a 1987 hit for Los Lobos following the glamorised bio-pic of Valens' brief life.

469

Van Der Graaf Generator

Peter Hammill, the main focus of Van Der Graaf Generator, was once praised by Johnny Rotten. An odd tribute, at face value, since VDGG appeared to be part of those very prog-rock excesses that Mr Rotten would absolutely despise: the heavy organ and sax-based sound, a gargantuan physics lesson of a name, flakily cosmic lyrics. But what did stand out were Hammill's gloomy, doomy vocals - he was likened to a 'male Nico' - which would also be cited by later Goth acts as a formative influence. The band, who been formed by a bunch of Manchester University students, had in fact split up before their first release; Hammill was working on a solo album which just happened to include his former colleagues, and it ended up with the Van Der Graaf branding. Subsequent line-ups ebbed and flowed around him, sax player David Jackson providing some blasts of free-form jazz, and Robert Fripp guesting on a couple of albums. No static at all.

"Somebody says 'Do you want to get Van Der Graaf together?' and you say 'Well, I think **I'll have a lie down** and think about it." Guy Evans

Key members: Hugh Banton, Keith Ellis, Guy Evans, Peter Hammill 5/11/48, Chris Judge Smith • Recording career: 1968 - 1972 & 1975 - 1978

Sounds: H To He, Who Am The Only One 1970, Pawn Hearts 1971, Still Life 1976

David Lee Roth, who provided the gymnastic visual half of the band while Eddie Van Halen performed the guitar pyrotechnics, flexed his last for them in 1985, announcing a solo career with a re-work of 'California Girls', complete with Carl Wilson and a bevy of beach babes. Would the band ever reach the heights of 'Jump' again? The band

survived seamlessly, even prospered, bringing in old warhorse Sammy Hagar, formerly of the 1970s proto-metal outfit Montrose. What this all proved was that, much as Roth had bags of charisma and energy to cover up a not spectacularly good voice, it was Eddie Van H who was their secret weapon. Nobody but nobody had played guitar with such speed and technique, not even Hendrix, and though Eddie was quickly copied and then outdone by Steve Vai and Joe Satriani, his effects - tapping the fretboard with his right hand, arm-wrestling the tremolo bar - were revolutionary... though Hendrix had much, much more soul.

Van Halen

"There is no city on the face of the earth that does not have at least one band whose entire approach is to imitate old-school Van Halen." David Lee Roth

Key members: Michael Anthony 20/1/55, David Lee Roth 10/10/55, Alex Van Halen 8/5/55, Eddie Van Halen 26/1/57 • Recording career: 1978 - present

Sounds: Van Halen 1978, 1984 1984, 5150 1986

The members of Vanilla Fudge were once called the Pigeons, a light pop act in the vein of New York vocal group the Rascals. Later, when Vanilla Fudge dispersed, the rhythm section of Tim Bogert and Carmine Appice formed a power trio with Jeff Beck. In between, the Fudge produced a weird hybrid all of their own: lengthy versions of pop classics with some grandiose production by George 'Shadow' Morton, of Shangri-La's fame. Their first target - the Supremes' 'You Keep Me

Hanging On' - was fully Fudged, a process that involved slowing the song right down to seven minutes plus with dollops of organ, gospel harmonies and maybe some quasi-sitar noodling. The Beatles' 'Ticket To Ride', the Impressions' 'People Get Ready' and the Zombies' 'She's Not There' underwent the same treatment. Their concept album, *The Beat Goes On*, attempted to summarise 25 years of pop music - and that was just the title track. Perhaps predictably, it failed: brave, but doomed.

Vanilla Fudge

472

Stevie Ray Vaughan

"Stevie's only regret was that he was not born black. The worst thing he could say about his own playing when he had a rare off night was **'I sounded really white tonight'.**" Former manager Chelsea Millikin

Stevie Ray Vaughan was equally at home with the blues and rock'n'roll: hence the respectful version of Jimi Hendrix's 'Voodoo Chile' on *Couldn't Stand The Weather*. His interpretation of Jimi's 'Little Wing' later appeared on *The Sky Is Crying*, the posthumous album which was prepared by his brother Johnnie (of the Fabulous Thunderbirds) after Stevie died in a helicopter crash in August 1990. The chopper, also carrying members of Eric Clapton's entourage, crashed on the way back from a Wisconsin gig, at which Stevie had been playing alongside E.C., Buddy Guy and Robert Cray - heady company that proved he'd made it. After years touring the circuit in Austin, Texas, his work with the trio Double Trouble led to an invitation from David Bowie to guest on *Let's Dance*, while John Hammond produced their exuberant debut *Texas Flood*. From then until his death, he played a major role in the revival of interest in the blues.

473

Born: 3/10/54 (died 27/8/90) • Recording career (solo): 1983 - 1990 • Sounds: Couldn't Stand The Weather 1984, In Step 1989, The Sky Is Crying 1991

"I guess in order to keep growing I have to get more involved **and not do the isolationist thing.**"

In 1990 the UK remix outfit D.N.A. sampled Suzanne Vega's 'Tom's Diner' and popped a dance beat underneath it. Vega and her record company A&M were initially less than pleased, but had the nous to let it run, giving her a far broader profile then she might otherwise have enjoyed. The following year, *Tom's Album*, an entire collection of covers of the song (including one by R.E.M.) was released. Her original and addictive *a cappella* version had appeared on 1987's *Solitude Standing* and was essential Vega: an honest, direct, neatly observed slice of life. The following track was 'Luka', a deftly handled song on the hidden shame of domestic abuse, which reached the US Top Three. It was a significant step in the re-emergence of folk from the wilderness of the early 1980s - and Vega's success, not least with the critics, created opportunities for other artists including Tracy Chapman and Michelle Shocked.

474

Suzanne Vega

Born: 12/8/59 • Recording career: 1985 - present • Sounds: Suzanne Vega 1985, Solitude Standing 1987, Nine Objects Of Desire 1996

The Velvet Underground

For a band who later developed such an all-pervasive influence, the Velvet Underground's sales figures were actually microscopic. That they survived at all was due to some managerial finesse and the extra aura bestowed by Andy Warhol. At a time when the mainstream groove was one of peace and bliss, Lou Reed's urban ditties were less about love and dope than S&M ('Venus In Furs') and hard drugs ('Heroin'). The tectonic clash of Reed's passion for rock'n'roll and poetry with John Cale's avant-garde classicism appealed to Warhol, who dreamt up the inspired collaboration with Nico for their first album, and created its iconic banana cover. As his input waned the Velvets retained their diversity and perversity, but under record company pressure to be (please) a little more commercial, were at their most accessible on *Loaded*, with 'Sweet Jane' and 'Rock & Roll'. Tucker and Cale had left, and Lou Reed was about to, but the seeds of the legend had germinated.

"The only reason we wore sunglasses on stage was because we couldn't stand the sight of the audience." John Cale

Key members: John Cale 9/3/42, Sterling Morrison 29/8/42 (died 30/8/95), Lou Reed 2/3/42, Mo Tucker 1945 • Recording career: 1967 – 1973 & 1993

Sounds: The Velvet Underground And Nico 1967, White Light/White Heat 1968, Loaded 1970

The Ventures

'Walk Don't Run', a track they first heard played by country guitarist Chet Atkins, gave the Ventures a break-out single in 1959. Their simplified version reached Number Two in the national charts and, along with its follow-up 'Perfidia', marked the start of a sequence of instrumental hits for their classic combo of lead and rhythm guitar, bass and drums. Like their UK counterparts the Shadows, the group had a penchant for tailored outfits and precise musical arrangements, and survived both shifting musical tastes and personnel changes by adapting their basic formula to the latest fads - the twist, surf, even psychedelia - and by being prepared to experiment with, for example, fuzz guitar techniques. Although the Ventures' last hit of any note was 'Hawaii Five-O' in 1969, the biggest-selling instrumental group ever just carried on and on (they remained immensely popular in Japan), having influenced a whole generation of American musicians, from Blondie and the B-52's to Johnny Thunders.

"No matter what we play, it always sounds like the Ventures." Bob Bogle

Key members: Bob Bogle 16/1/37, Nokie Edwards 9/5/39, Mel Taylor 1934 (died 11/8/96), Don Wilson 10/2/37

Recording career: 1960 - present • Sounds: Walk Don't Run 1960, Ventures In Space 1963, The Ventures on Stage 1965

The Verve

"It's the **power of the music that drew the Verve back together**, not us really. It's the addictive quality of being in the greatest rock'n'roll band in the world." Richard Ashcroft

Wigan: home of George Orwell's Pier, and the Verve, masterly creators of cosmic soundscapes. If only they had been able to maintain the continuity and cohesion of the town's rugby league team. After building up a healthy reputation in the indie charts in the early 1990s - 'She's A Superstar', 'Blue' - they had tightened up their loose and psychedelic song structures by 1995's more robust *A Northern Soul*, after touring alongside Manchester neighbours Oasis, with whom they

shared producer Owen Morris. On the verge of a major breakthrough they split up. And everyone thought that was the end of the Verve (they were originally plain Verve, but had to add the 'The' to avoid confusion with the American jazz label). Two years later they returned, intoning *Urban Hymns*, and constructing - around an Andrew Loog Oldham loop - the anthemic edifice of 'Bitter Sweet Symphony'. Once again, they broke up at the vital moment. A pattern had been set.

Key members: Richard Ashcroft 11/9/71, Simon Jones 29/7/72, Nick McCabe 14/7/71, Peter Salisbury 24/9/74 • Recording career: 1992 - 1998

Sounds: A Storm In Heaven 1993, A Northern Soul 1995, Urban Hymns 1997

Gene Vincent

"Gene was **dragged from the stage in Arizona by the local sheriff** in the middle of doing 'Lotta Lovin''. They had to shoot tear gas into the joint." Backing singer Tommy Facenda

Ian Dury left many legacies, but one of his most moving was 'Sweet Gene Vincent', a tribute to the "sad Virginia whisper" of the rockabilly great. Like Carl Perkins, Vincent's reputation was based on one classic single: 'Be Bop A Lula'. His 1956 recording with backing band the Blue Caps was just the ticket for Capitol Records, looking for the next Elvis (legend has it that Presley's mother Gladys thought it *was* her son's new single). Vincent's image was meaner and moodier than Elvis, and when the music biz started looking for cleaner-cut stars, he found his strongest audience in the UK. Touring there in 1960, he was a passenger in the car crash that killed Eddie Cochran. Badly affected by the incident, Vincent lost his way, and though John Peel's Dandelion label released a comeback (*I'm Back And I'm Proud*) in 1970, he died of a stomach ulcer the following year.

Born: 11/2/35 (died 12/10/71) • Recording career: 1956 - 1970 • Sounds: Bluejean Bop! 1956, Gene Vincent And the Blue Caps 1957

The name was a deliberate contradiction - 'femmes' was the band's local slang for 'wimps' - and the music the Violent Femmes produced had all of the confused awkwardness of a gaggle of teenage boys: rebellious, sarcastic and self-conscious. Out of Milwaukee - *viva Wisconsin!* - the trio hit the ground running with their 1983 self-titled debut, filled with simple punk-folk acoustic songs (especially 'Blister In The Sun' and 'Kiss Off') that were masterful summaries of adolescent emotion. With little promotion, it sold a million copies: there were a lot of mixed-up kids out there. They never achieved that purity again. Singer and guitarist Gordon Gano altered their direction by introducing his Christian beliefs - he was a Baptist minister's son - and on *The Blind Leading The Naked*, there was an extra layer of production values (by Talking Heads' Jerry Harrison). The Femmes continued in the 1990s, but, too old now to have acne or angst, their impact was subdued.

"We figured the Violent Femmes moniker was okay for a couple of gigs, but after eleven years we're getting to an age where it's not exactly as dignified as we'd like." Brian Ritchie

479

Violent Femmes

Key members: Victor De Lorenzo 25/10/54, Gordon Gano 7/6/63, Brian Ritchie 21/11/60 • Recording career: 1983 - present

Sounds: Violent Femmes 1983, The Blind Leading The Naked 1986, Why Do Birds Sing? 1991

"I still keep one foot in the streets.

I get letters from waitresses, truck drivers, fry cooks, people from all different walks of life."

Best known through his film appearances - including Jim Jarmusch's *Down By Law* and Robert Altman's *Short Cuts* - Tom Waits allowed himself to be typecast as a bohemian hobo. It was the persona he had created at Los Angeles' Troubadour Club in the 1970s: goatee beard, battered hat, his long, extraordinarily bendy fingers caressing the piano keys. His profile increased when Troubadour regulars the Eagles covered 'Ol' 55', and for the rest of the decade Waits perfected his low-life, late-night performances - on *Nighthawks At The Diner* recreating a night-club atmosphere with an audience invited into the studio. In 1983 he tried a radical change on *swordfishtrombones*, a ramshackle set that he called "junkyard orchestral deviation", which had horns and marimbas punctuating the familiar bourbon-rich mumble of the Waits voice. His next album, *Rain Dogs*, though still experimental, included 'Downtown Train' (a hit for Rod Stewart), proof that melancholy romanticism was his true forte.

480

Tom Waits

Born: 7/12/49 • Recording career: 1973 - present • Sounds: Closing Time 1973, Rain Dogs 1985, Bone Machine 1992

"The most tragic thing about Scott is that he had every single ingredient needed **to become one of the biggest stars of the '90s** if he'd decided to go down the Rod Stewart/Elton John path." _{Jonathan King}

Scott Walker

The Walker Brothers were a fraternal invention of pop's imagination - in reality Scott Engel, John Maus and Gary Leeds, whose teen pop career was spectacular for a couple of years from 1965, once they had transposed themselves from the States to the UK. 'Make It Easy On Yourself' and 'The Sun Ain't Gonna Shine (Anymore)' - originally a Frankie Valli and the Four Seasons number - gave them, and particularly Scott, a massive following. But when Scott went solo he caught everyone off balance, mixing lush orchestrations and his crooner's voice with challenging material. He raided the canon of Belgian singer Jacques Brel for each of his first three albums, and his own songs entered dark, oblique lyrical territory. Though the albums charted, Walker slipped into reclusiveness, and his cult status - preserved by the likes of Julian Cope, David Bowie and Marc Almond - was only heightened by the once-a-decade appearance of ever more oblique releases.

Born: Scott Engel 9/1/44 • **Recording career (solo):** 1967 - 1984 & 1995 - present • **Sounds:** Scott 2 1968, Scott 4 1969, Tilt 1995

War

A collaboration with Eric Burdon, the former Animals vocalist, gave War its initial profile, but it was actually Burdon's departure that galvanised their finest years. Formerly a high school group called the Creators, and later a West Coast brass-heavy blues act known as Night Shift, the band's membership had ebbed and flowed. Producer Jerry Goldstein teamed the outfit with Burdon, resting in LA after his Animals adventures, who introduced harmonica player Lee Oskar to the ranks, and together they all Declared War on a somewhat unfocused 1970 album. Following a couple of releases and tours, Burdon left, claiming exhaustion ('Spill The Wine' was the highlight of his involvement): War prospered, channelling their fusion of R'n'B, jazz and latino funk into hit singles like 'Slippin' Into Darkness' and 'The World Is A Ghetto'. The 1970s were their prime time, but they enjoyed a mini-revival in the 1990s, re-discovered by the hip-hop/R'n'B scene.

"We were in the middle of the peace movement, and Eric Burdon used to do a lot of weird things. We figured if we called the group War, people would notice it." Producer/manager Jerry Goldstein

Key members: 'Papa' Dee Allen 18/7/31 (died 30/8/88), Harold Brown 17/3/46, Morris 'B.B.' Dickerson 3/8/49, Leroy 'Lonnie' Jordan 21/11/48, Chas Miller 2/6/39 (died 1980), Lee Oskar 24/3/48,

Howard Scott 15/3/46 • Recording career: 1970 - present • Sounds: The Black-Man's Burdon 1970, All Day Music 1971, The World Is A Ghetto 1972

"The name is probably the coolest thing about the band - **it's all been downhill since then."**

Don Was

Don Was was born Donald Fagenson, and there was a shadow of Steely Dan's Donald Fagen in the literate cleverness of Was (Not Was). The two Wases - no relation, naturally - were both products of Detroit. David (Weiss) left to do sax, flute and keyboard sessions in LA, while Don stayed home: they wrote songs by correspondence. Landing a record deal, they populated their first release with members of MC5 and P-Funk - their albums always featured great guest lists, including Ozzy Osbourne, Mel Tormé, Leonard Cohen and Iggy Pop; primary vocal duties were handled by Sir Harry Bowens and Sweet Pea Atkinson. In the late 1980s the pair were still arcane and malevolent, but created a pair of funky hits with 'Spy In The House Of Love' and 'Walk The Dinosaur' alongside the twisted Americana of songs like 'I Blew Up The United States'. Don moved into production - notably overseeing Bonnie Raitt's *Nick Of Time* - and come 1993 Was (Not Was) was not.

Was (Not Was)

Key members: David Was (David Weiss) 26/10/52, Don Was (Donald Fagenson) 13/9/52 • Recording career: 1981 - 1993

Sounds: Born To Laugh At Tornadoes 1983, What Up, Dog? 1988, Are You Okay? 1990

The Waterboys

Mike Scott, leader of the Waterboys, was sitting in the bar of a New York hotel when his girlfriend asked him whether it was difficult to write a song. Without further ado, he jotted down a verse and chorus, which formed the basis of 'The Whole Of The Moon'. The song was released on the Waterboys' 1985 album *This Is The Sea*, at which time they were being tipped as a band with enough sonic sweep to take on U2 or Simple Minds. But then keyboard player Karl Wallinger left to host World Party, and Scott, an Edinburgh native, upped his Celtic quotient by moving to Galway to work with folk-inspired musicians including Steve Wickham of In Tua Nua. A warm Irish influence was evident on the stripped-back *Fisherman's Blues* and *Room To Roam*, but it was a 1991 re-issue of 'The Whole Of The Moon' that created their biggest commercial splash.

"The name conjures up images of us bringing musical water to thirsty people. I like that." Mike Scott

Key members: Mike Scott 14/12/58, Anthony Thistlethwaite 31/8/55, Karl Wallinger 19/10/57 • Recording career: 1983 - 1993 • Sounds: The Waterboys 1983, This Is The Sea 1985, Fisherman's Blues 1988

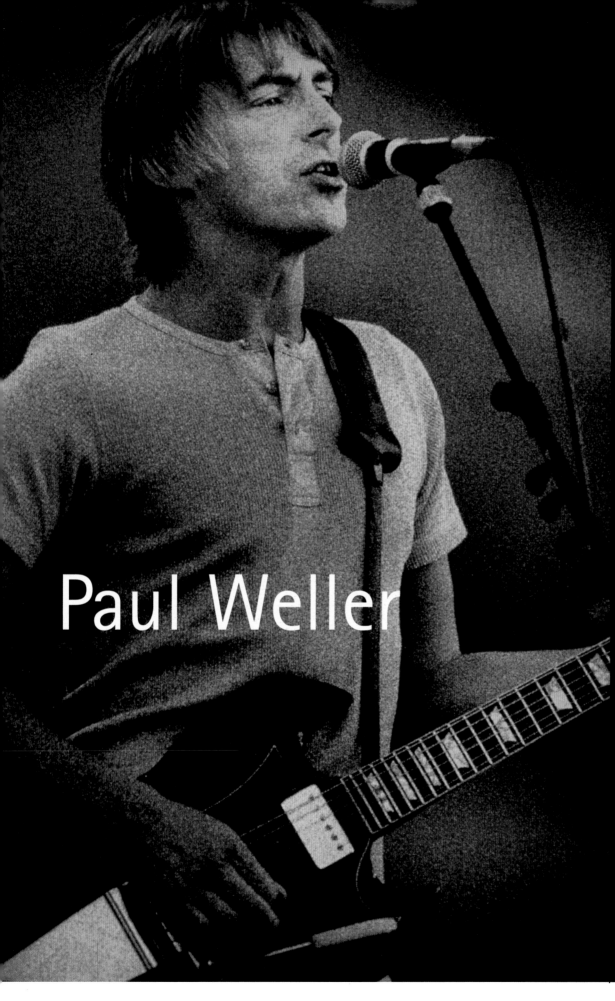

Paul Weller

"I've still got edge in my music, hopefully always will have - and if my music ever got as laid-back and mellow as Eric Clapton's I'd pack it in. **Or shoot myself.**"

'Has My Fire Really Gone Out?' asked Paul Weller on *Wild Wood*. Well might he have asked. When the Jam closed for business in 1982, his stock was riding high, but he managed to fritter it away. His soul quest with the Style Council had its moments, but as time went on opinion was that it was all Style and little content. By 1990 Weller had no record deal and an uncertain future. Yet he did keep the faith, quietly road-testing new material; as he'd once looked to the Who, he now sought inspiration from Traffic and the Small Faces. By *Wild Wood*, a mature Weller was clearly flourishing. As younger bands like Ocean Colour Scene - whose Steve Cradock was a regular sideman - and Kula Shaker tapped the same roots, Weller was greeted as a returning hero by audiences at Glastonbury and Phoenix. He'd come a long way from (and to) *Stanley Road*.

485

Born: 25/5/58 • Recording career (solo): 1991 - present • Sounds: Wild Wood 1993, Stanley Road 1995, Heavy Soul 1997

The Who

"Sometimes I really do believe that **we're the only rock band on the face of this planet that knows what rock'n'roll is all about."** Pete Townshend

It was a question of mod-ulation. If the Who had stayed in their Mod clothing they might well have burnt out after the perfect panache of 'My Generation' and 'Substitute'. A substantial ground shift was required; ignoring the disbelievers ("we've always been pig-headed"), Pete Townshend delivered a radical departure with *Tommy*. And though he found it difficult to follow up the rock opera, when the band emerged with a new original album, 1971's *Who's Next*, it was hard rock of the highest class. Once again the foursome - Townshend windmilling on guitar, Keith Moon manic, Roger Daltrey peacock-proud, John Entwistle unfazed - seemed invincible. Moon was a one-off, "like an old dog that ain't house-broke" according to Lynyrd Skynyrd's Ronnie Van Zant, and when he died, many thought they should have stopped then and there. As it was, they limped on - one limb missing - for five years too long.

Key members: Roger Daltrey 1/3/44, John Entwistle 9/10/44, Keith Moon 23/8/47 (died 7/9/78), Pete Townshend 19/5/45 • Recording career: 1965 - 1982

Sounds: The Who Sings My Generation 1965, Tommy 1969, Who's Next 1971

Wilco

Some people never got over the demise of Uncle Tupelo, the alternative country group whose album *No Depression* provided a generic term for similarly-minded acts who loved the music but not the sentimentality of country. However Tupelo's Jeff Tweedy - following a less than amicable split with his co-founder and childhood friend Jay Farrar - *did* get over it. Gathering the remnants of the band into Wilco, a debut album, *A.M.*, broke little new ground, but 1996's *Being There* proved to be a remarkable *tour* both *de force* and *d'horizon*. A new direction was declared from the opening cut with the grandiose psychedelia of 'Misunderstood', through the cheerful boogieing brass of 'Monday' and the Lennon-like 'Red-Eyed And Blue'. *Mermaid Avenue*, an archival collaboration with Billy Bragg (adding music to un-released Woody Guthrie lyrics) underlined their respect for the past, but did not halt Wilco's development, as the vintage keyboards and pop of *Summer Teeth* kept their options wide open.

"They made us captains of the **alternative country** boat, but they didn't realise we didn't know how to steer... We're landlubbers!"

Jeff Tweedy

Key members: Jay Bennett, Ken Coomer, John Stiratt, Jeff Tweedy 25/8/67 • **Recording career:** 1995 - present • **Sounds:** Being There 1996, Mermaid Avenue (with Billy Bragg) 1998, Summer Teeth 1999

Robbie Williams

You had to hand it to Robbie Williams. When Take That's star-spangled career ended in 1996 - Robbie having parted company with them the previous year - the hot money was on Gary Barlow to become the George Michael for a new generation, and Michael Owen to continue as a cute young charmer. In the post-That stakes Robbie was an also-ran. Initially he seemed to be doing little to help improve the odds, working his way through a succession of managers and high-profile girlfriends, a bit of a media joke - although he nonetheless scored UK Number Twos with 'Freedom' and 'Old Before I Die'. After 1997 he turned everything around. The cheeky chappie pulled himself together and entered an unstoppable phase: sensitive on 'Angels', camping it up on 'Let Me Entertain You', a sexy Mr Millennium. And while Messrs Barlow and Owen struggled, Robbie was the toast of the Glastonbury crowds. As he'd once sung, 'Everything Changes'...

"The worst thing you can do is try to be cool. Honesty is the best policy - just be a dick and people respect you for it!"

Born: 13/2/74 • Recording career (solo): 1996 - present • Sounds: Life Thru A Lens 1997, I've Been Expecting You 1998, Sing When You're Winning 2000

Johnny and Edgar Winter

The brothers Winter were often linked, but in fact only played together intermittently. Of the two Johnny initially gained most attention after *Rolling Stone* magazine singled him out for praise in a 1968 article. A striking figure (he and his brother were both albino), his reputation was based around his blues guitar-playing, which the Stones admired - they opened their Hyde Park gig with his song 'I'm Hers And I'm Yours'. Edgar, on keyboards and sax, joined Johnny on his second album, then scored a 1972 US Number One in his own right with the instrumental 'Frankenstein'. Meantime Johnny was overcoming a drugs problem, but returned to form with *Still Alive And Well*, and played a substantial role in the later years of Muddy Waters' career. After a relatively quiet decade in the 1980s - although Edgar supplied the sax break for Tina Turner's '(Simply) The Best') - the brothers played together again in 1992, the year in which Johnny released *Hey, Where's Your Brother?*

"Edgar was never into blues.
We both have respect for what each other is doing,
but wouldn't really want to be doing it ourselves." Johnny Winter

Born: Edgar Winter 28/12/46, Johnny Winter 23/2/44 • Recording career: (Johnny and Edgar Winter) 1976, (Johnny Winter) 1959 - present, (Edgar Winter) 1970 - present

Sounds: Johnny Winter And... Live 1971, They Only Come Out At Night (Edgar Winter) 1972, Together 1976

Wire

"Every track on Pink Flag is a recycled rock classic. Done at weird angles, maybe, but I can recognise them." Colin Newman

The primary signal sent out by the first Wire album, *Pink Flag*, was the announcement of yet another punk band. The year was 1977; the album, Ramones-style, contained no less than 21 tracks, of which over half lasted no longer than two minutes; the musical skills on parade were rudimentary. But unexpectedly their record label was Harvest, the EMI label which was home to Pink Floyd, and the art school background shared by all four members seeped through. Thus their crudeness was, seen from another angle, pure minimalism; the distorted guitar sounds a deliberately abrasive texture. Two further albums, *Chairs Missing* and *154*, developed the themes. R.E.M. admired them enough to cover 'Strange' on *Document* in 1987, by which time Wire, after several years away, had returned to the fray. Drummer Robert Gotobed left four years later. The remaining trio, with self-conscious and mathematical wit, continued under the name Wir.

Key members: Bruce Gilbert 18/5/46, Robert Gotobed 1951, Graham Lewis 2/2/53, Colin Newman 16/9/54 • Recording career: 1977 - 1980 & 1987 - 1991

Sounds: Pink Flag 1977, 154 1979, The Ideal Copy 1987

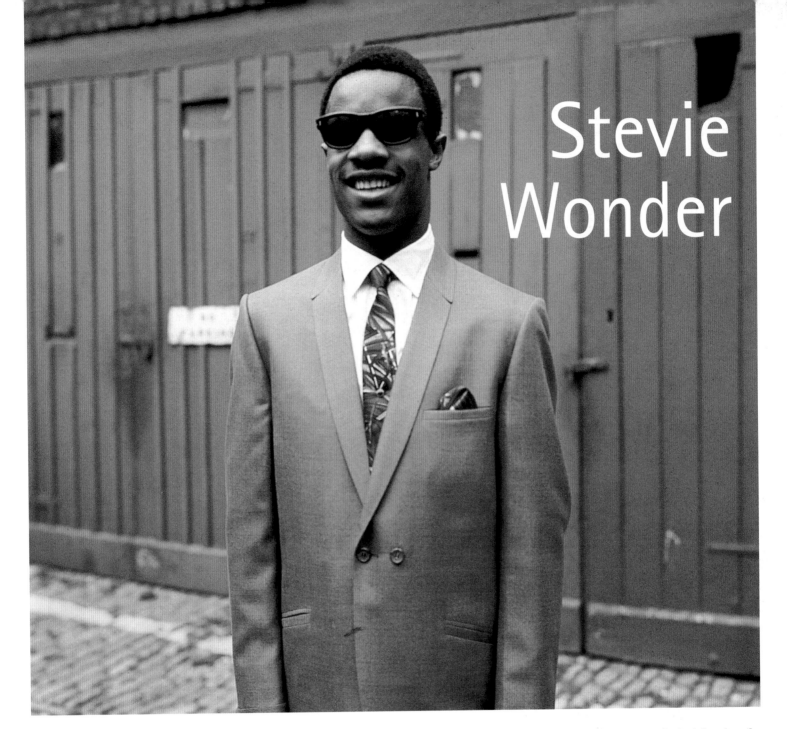

"Music shouldn't be so complicated that it's beyond everyone's capabilities, **nor should it be so simple that you cannot use your mind to think about it."**

Still not fifty at the turn of the century, Stevie Wonder had decades of music left in him. Though his recent output had not been prolific, he'd already produced an enormously innovative body of work. The four years 1972-76 - from *Talking Book* to *Songs In The Key Of Life* - had been the most productive, as Wonder gained complete artistic control after years as Motown's teenage prodigy. The fruits of this freedom included the rich jazziness of 'Sir Duke' and the clavinet-driven funk of 'Superstition' - "funk," he said, "is the soul going deep into itself". Not surprisingly, even Wonder's fertile imagination - "I have an idea of what colours are; purple is a *crazy* colour to me" - eventually took time out: in the 1980s, although still commercially astute, he veered away from the social awareness of 'Living In The City' back towards the greetings card simplicity of 'I Just Called To Say I Love You'.

Born: Steveland Judkins Morris 13/5/50 • Recording career: 1962 - present • Sounds: Talking Book 1972, Innervisions 1973, Songs In The Key Of Life 1976

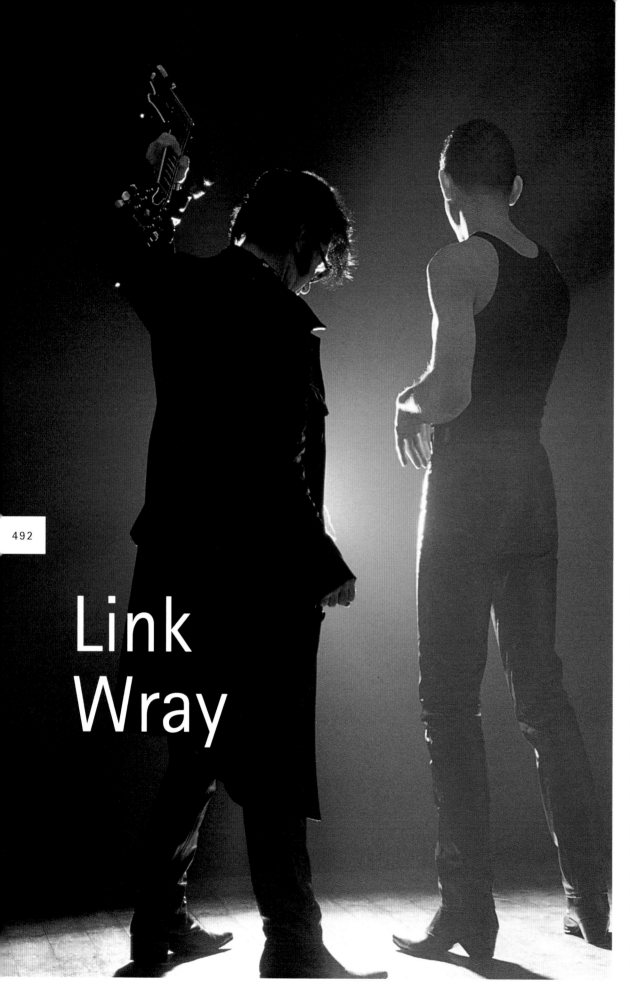

Link Wray

"He is the King.
If it hadn't been for Link Wray and 'Rumble' **I would never have picked up a guitar."**

Pete Townshend

It was odd to see Link Wray back in the spotlight when he joined forces in 1978 with the new wave rockabilly singer Robert Gordon, formerly of the Tuff Darts. In addition to influencing Pete Townshend, Wray's guitar sound had had a direct effect on both Eric Clapton and Jeff Beck - and a thousand later metal bands. But he remained surprising little known outside muso circles. His reputation was based almost entirely on the moody, menacing fuzz-guitar instrumental 'Rumble', released in 1958 and featuring an effect he'd achieved by ramming a pencil into his speaker. After a number of power chord follow-ups - 'Rawhide' and 'Jack The Ripper' - Wray disappeared back to a family farm in Maryland, making music in a primitive studio in one of the outhouses. The results emerged on a series of albums in the early 1970s which blended rustic blues and gospel with Wray's strained vocals.

Born: 2/5/35 • Recording career: 1958 - 1980 & 1986 - present • **Sounds:** Link Wray And The Wraymen 1959, Link Wray 1971, Beans And Fatback 1973

When Soft Machine founder member, drummer and vocalist Robert Wyatt fell from a fourth-story window in June 1973, a broken back confined him to a wheelchair. But the accident failed to dampen his, by then solo, career: the following year *Rock Bottom*, produced by Pink Floyd's Nick Mason, was (sympathy notwithstanding) critically lauded. Wyatt's dry sense of humour had survived intact, apparent in the album's title and his fondness for wordplay: a later release was titled *Ruth Is Stranger Than Richard*, and his first group after Soft Machine was called Matching Mole, a pun on the French for the previous band's name. Surrounding himself with stimulating collaborators, including Ivor Cutler, Mike Oldfield, the late trumpeter Mongezi Feza, and much later Everything But The Girl's Ben Watt, Wyatt eventually concentrated on interpretations of other writers' material - a decision leading to his magnificent and elegant versions of Elvis Costello's 'Shipbuilding' and Peter Gabriel's 'Biko'.

"Technical inadequacies in some of my performances are, of course, **entirely deliberate** and reproduced as evidence of my almost painful sincerity."

Robert Wyatt

493

Born: 28/1/45 • Recording career (solo): 1970 - present • Sounds: Rock Bottom 1974, Nothing Can Stop Us 1982, Shleep 1997

X

At the butt end of the 1970s, Los Angeles had seen New York and London spawn punk. On the West Coast, the music scene was essentially moribund, to most outsiders just the place the Eagles came from. Along with bands like Bags, Plugz and the Weirdos, X led the charge to restore some pride. Under the guidance of the Doors' Ray Manzarek, they released a caustic debut album, *Los Angeles*, and 1981's *Wild Gift*, which *Rolling Stone* magazine voted Album of the Year. Bassist John Doe and his co-vocalist Exene Cervenka (the pair were married for a period) had met at a Venice writing workshop, and Doe turned a poem of Exene's into a song... What the critics loved was how X had taken punk's basic vocabulary and added flourishes of rockabilly - guitarist Billy Zoom once worked with Gene Vincent - and above all humour. But real commercial success eluded them, and though still playing at the turn of the millennium, X remained outsiders to the corporate music machine. They probably preferred it that way.

"**The rage** we had came from bad parenting and the nothingness of suburbia, and that is also where the **lust for life came from.**" John Doe

Key members: D.J. Bonebrake 8/12/55, Exene Cervenka 1/2/56, John Doe (John Nommensen) 25/2/53, Billy Zoom (Tyson Kindale) 20/2/48

Recording career: 1978 - 1988 & 1993 - present • Sounds: Wild Gift 1981, Under The Big Black Sun 1982, Live At The Whiskey A Go-Go On The Fabulous Sunset Strip 1988

X-Ray Spex

Poly Styrene, the unmistakable figurehead of X-Ray Spex, was up there alongside Siouxsie Sue, the Slits and the Raincoats as one of punk's pantheon of female role models. The tragedy was that the Spex released so little material, just one dynamite single ('Oh Bondage Up Yours!') and one studio album in 1978 - *Germ-Free Adolescents* - to broadcast their captivating digs at the consumerist society of the 1970s. Poly wailed, shrieked and screamed over the right-on punk guitar of Jak Airport and the trademark sax breaks that added extra depth to their sound - supplied by Rudi Thompson after the band's original saxophonist Lora Logic left to form Essential Logic. Then, there was silence. Poly had joined the Hare Kṛṣṇa movement and reverted to her born name of Marion Elliot. She went on to release a couple of solo albums, and the Spex briefly re-united in the mid-1990s, but it was all too little, too late.

495

"My lyrics are serious... and yet not serious."

Poly Styrene

Key members: Jak Airport (Jack Stafford), Paul Dean, B.P. Hurding, Poly Styrene (Marion Elliot), Rudi Thompson • **Recording career:** 1978 - 1979 & 1996

Sounds: Germ Free Adolescents 1978, Live At The Roxy 1991, Conscious Consumer 1996

"I like lumps and spiky bits, music that makes you think 'Oh Gosh, what's that?'" Andy Partridge

Home became permanently where XTC's heart was after their guitarist Andy Partridge suffered a severe case of the stage frights in 1982, just after the band had released their biggest chart hit, the presciently titled 'Senses Working Overtime'. A decision to concentrate on studio work followed soon after. Maybe it was inevitable: once they had moved on from their punk beginnings, XTC's intelligent, quirky sensitivities - never run of the mill, but always catchy, viz. 'Making Plans For Nigel' - were perhaps not best suited for a gruelling concert schedule. Relieved from tour duties, their music became lusher, more considered. They even had the time to create a parallel group called the Dukes of Stratosphear, a psychedelia pastiche which at one time outsold XTC's own releases. On 1989's *Oranges & Lemons*, Partridge made his priorities clear with 'Chalkhills And Children' (his local Wiltshire countryside and his kids) - but their fans still pined for some kind of live performance.

496

XTC

Key members: Terry Chambers 18/7/55, Dave Gregory 21/9/52, Colin Moulding 17/8/55, Andy Partridge 11/1//53 • Recording career: 1977 - present

Sounds: Drums And Wires 1979, Skylarking 1986, Oranges & Lemons 1989

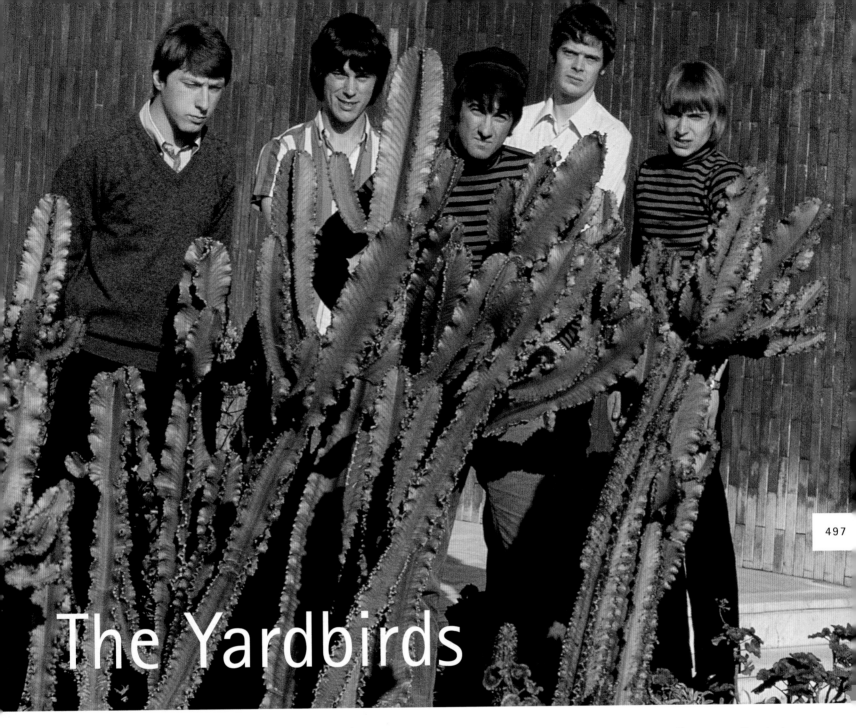

The Yardbirds

The succession of Yardbirds guitarists reads like a mini Hall Of Fame: Clapton, Beck, Page. Spare a thought for original job holder Tony Topham, who stepped down, under pressure from his family, because at 15 he was too young to tour. Eric Clapton joined as the group took over the Crawdaddy club slot which the Stones had recently vacated. Their frenetic R'n'B jams were captured on *Five Live Yardbirds*, but when they moved into studio pop - 'For Your Love', written by

Graham Gouldman, later of 10cc - the purist in Clapton was disturbed. He left, and Jeff Beck burst in, taking the poppier material on to new heights with distortion and feedback, and on 'Shapes Of Things', towards psychedelia. It was left to Jimmy Page to buttress the Yardbirds' final days as they began to fall apart in 1968. To fulfil certain touring obligations he called on vocalist Robert Plant and drummer John Bonham - Led Zeppelin was about to be launched.

"A lot of our music derived from America's own black music so we were, in a way, presenting an acceptable face of their own music - obviously coloured by our interpretation." Chris Dreja

Key members: Jeff Beck 24/6/44, Eric Clapton 30/3/45, Chris Dreja 11/11/45, Jim McCarty 25/7/43, Jimmy Page 9/1/44, Keith Relf 22/3/43 (died 14/5/76), Paul Samwell-Smith 8/5/43

Recording career: 1964 - 1968 • Sounds: Five Live Yardbirds 1964, Yardbirds (Roger The Engineer) 1966

"We have to stick out for what we believe in,
even to the extent of not making it easier on the audience." Steve Howe

The fantasy landscapes, created by illustrator Roger Dean, which adorned Yes covers in the mid-1970s were perfectly of their time, but forever locked the group into an era of patchouli oil, afghan coats, mystical lyrics and top-heavy classical aspirations. They suffered the concerted opprobrium of the music press, yet refused to yield, still going strong at the turn of the century. The technical quality of Yes's music was never in doubt - original drummer Bill Buford later joined King Crimson and Rick Wakeman displayed his keyboard virtuosity on his solo album *The Six Wives Of Henry VIII*. But once *The Yes Album* and *Fragile* had established a market for their carefully constructed, highly textured symphonies, they couldn't resist the indulgence factor. *Tales From Topographic Oceans* consisted of four tracks, each lasting for one side of an LP: it was a US Number One, but an irreversible turning point. For decades thereafter, Yes were a critical no go area.

Yes

Key members: Jon Anderson 25/10/44, Steve Howe 8/4/47, Chris Squire 4/3/48, Rick Wakeman 18/5/49, Alan White 14/6/49 • **Recording career:** 1969 - present

Sounds: The Yes Album 1971, Close To The Edge 1972, Going For The One 1977

Neil Young

"I've got a few demons, but I manage to co-exist with 'em. That's what makes you crazy, that's what makes me play my guitar the way I play it sometimes."

When Neil Young was hailed as the Grandaddy of Grunge in the 1990s, touring with Sonic Youth and recording with Pearl Jam, the younger acts were responding to the garage-style distorted guitar of *Ragged Glory*. But Young was also the mellow folk singer of 'After The Gold Rush' and 'Heart Of Gold'. He veered between those two poles for his entire career, along the wending way producing an emotionally and musically eclectic output. His first solo album, recorded just after leaving Buffalo Springfield and before joining Crosby, Stills & Nash, seemed to lack something. In response he gathered together the backing band, Crazy Horse, that would support many of his future explorations. The deaths of guitarist Denny Whitten and CSN&Y roadie Bruce Berry led to a period of self-doubt, almost self-destruction (1975's famously dark, disturbed *Tonight's The Night*). It took well over a decade for Young to recover fully and reap the harvests once more.

499

Born: 12/11/45 • Recording career (solo): 1969 - present • Sounds: After The Gold Rush 1970, On The Beach 1974, Ragged Glory 1990

Frank Zappa

"Stuff that everybody else does naturally just seems as impossible as shit to me. It's like trying to develop a convincing English accent."

Including compilations and bootlegs, Frank Zappa's discography runs to well over 50 albums. That's a lot of Zappa. Therein you can find all sides of the man: from social satirist (*We're Only In It For The Money*) to under-rated guitarist (*Hot Rats*) or Varèse disciple (*Orchestral Favourites*). You could take your pick, but if you chanced on what was for you the 'wrong' version, it might scare you off for years... Zappa was always challenging, always unorthodox: his daughter Moon Unit longed for "a father who wore tan slacks and mowed the lawn", but as one of the Mothers Of Invention, keyboardist George Duke, observed, "he's really so straight that he's bizarre". It was an incident on a 1971 Mothers tour of Europe, when their equipment burnt down at the Montreux Casino, that inspired Deep Purple's 'Smoke On The Water' - the moment immortalised in Ritchie Blackmore's classic riff. Zappa doubtless appreciated the irony of it all.

Born: 21/12/40 (died 4/12/93) • Recording career: 1966 - 1993 • Sounds: Freak Out! 1966, We're Only In It For The Money 1968, One Size Fits All 1975

Warren Zevon

On *Sentimental Hygiene*, Warren Zevon's 1987 comeback album, his standing amongst the music fraternity was clear from the calibre of his backing band (three quarters of R.E.M.), the arrangements by George Clinton and guest appearances by Bob Dylan, Neil Young and Don Henley. The reason Zevon needed that comeback was fully explained in the song 'Detox Mansion', typical of his self-deprecating satire. A decade earlier he had been poised for great things. Following a disappointing debut in 1969, Zevon had concentrated on writing jingles and arranging, but his friend Jackson Browne persuaded him to return to recording, and *Warren Zevon* was released in 1976. Again the supporting cast was stellar: Browne producing, Bonnie Raitt, Stevie Nicks and Lindsey Buckingham performing. Zevon's songs were already pointedly pushing pins into existence in LA-LA Land - notably 'I'll Sleep When I'm Dead' - but Rehab Mountain soon became a regular destination. After spending much of the 1980s straightening himself out, Zevon continued ploughing his own trenchant furrow.

"Lots of other people had done love songs really well.

But no one was really writing Hunter S. Thompson or Norman Mailer kinds of songs."

Born: 24/1/47 • Recording career: 1969 - present • Sounds: Excitable Boy 1978, Sentimental Hygiene 1987, Life'll Kill Ya 2000

The Zombies

"Our success came too easy; we never had to pay any dues; we didn't work or starve or sleep in the van." Paul Atkinson

The Zombies had all the visual style of the St Albans grammar schoolboys they were - more likely to appear on *Top Of The Form* than *Top Of The Pops* - but their music was far more adventurous. All in their teens, bar bassist Chris White, the group had immediate success with their debut single 'She's Not There', featuring Rod Argent's jazzy electric piano and Colin Blunstone's high-pitched vocal line. It reached US Number Two, but they found it hard to match. A series of classy singles refused to succeed, apart from 'Tell Her No', and the Zombies, in frustration, split up just after recording the psychedelic *Odessey And Oracle* (the mis-spelling courtesy of the album's designer). But their following in the States had not entirely evaporated, and one cut, 'Time Of The Season', reached Number Three there a year after their demise. The five original Zombies would not play together again until 1997.

Key members: Rod Argent 14/6/45, Paul Atkinson 19/3/46, Colin Blunstone 24/6/45, Hugh Grundy 6/3/45, Chris White 7/3/43 • Recording career: 1964 - 1968

Sounds: Begin Here 1965, Odessey & Oracle 1968

ZZ Top

Three things you should know about ZZ Top: they come from Texas, they play unrelenting blues-based boogie, and drummer Frank Beard is, perversely, the only one of the trio without That Beard. His comrades, Billy Gibbons and Dusty Hill, started sprouting their hirsute trademarks somewhere around 1979, after a decade of extremely hard touring. The dues paid off. By 1974 they were already able to headline a gig in Austin with an audience of 80,000, supported by Bad Company and Santana. However, their biggest commercial success came in the 1980s, when they used their visual image to maximum effect on the nascent MTV, making sexy/sexist videos for singles like 'Gimme All Your Lovin'' and 'Legs'. As they freely admitted, the formula was one they'd milk for all it was worth. And in a strange way it was hugely re-assuring to know that ZZ Top would be there, boogying on down, happily after ever.

"You can do a lot with three chords,
and that's all we've needed. It's certainly all we know." Billy Gibbons

503

Key members: Frank Beard 11/6/49, Billy Gibbons 16/12/49, Dusty Hill 19/5/49 • **Recording career:** 1970 - present • **Sounds:** Tres Hombres 1973, Deguello 1979, Eliminator 1983

This is a chronological index organised by the start date of each entry's recording career, as listed in the book. A number represent the beginning of solo careers: John Lennon or Peter Gabriel, for example. Some acts were recording and releasing albums for years before they broke through; others just seem to have been around for ever.

A credit for photographer and/or agency follows each artist entry.

John Lee Hooker
George Zygmund
(Rex Features)

Muddy Waters
John Selby
(Rex Features)

1948

Ray Charles
Lori Stoll
(Retna Pictures)

B.B. King
Frilet
(Rex Features)

1949

Bobby Bland
David Redfern
(Redferns)

1951

Howlin' Wolf
Baron Wolman
(Retna Pictures)

Little Richard
Photofest
(Retna Pictures)

1953

Hank Ballard
Michael Ochs Archives,
(Redferns)

Bill Haley and his Comets
David Redfern
(Rex Features)

Elvis Presley
Photofest
(Retna Pictures)

1954

Chuck Berry
Dezo Hoffman
(Rex Features)

1955

Johnny Cash
Globe Photos
(Rex Features)

Eddie Cochran
Michael Ochs Archives
(Redferns)

Bo Diddley
Robert Altman
(Retna Pictures)

Willie Nelson
Photoreporters
(Rex Features)

Roy Orbison
Dezo Hoffman
(Rex Features)

Carl Perkins
Glenn A. Baker
(Redferns)

1956

James Brown
Make this
Suspense
(Rex Features)

The Coasters
Michael Ochs Archives
(Redferns)

Sam Cooke
Photofest
(Retna Pictures)

Lonnie Donegan
Percy Hatchman
(Rex Features)

The Everly Brothers
Dezo Hoffman
(Rex Features)

Aretha Franklin
Ross Marino
(Retna Pictures)

Buddy Holly
Photofest
(Retna Pictures)

Jerry Lee Lewis
Dan Peebles
(Retna Pictures)

Rick Nelson
Richard Young
(Rex Features)

Gene Vincent
David Magnus
(Gene Rex Features)

1957

Dr John
Heungman
(Retna Pictures)

Marvin Gaye
David Corio
(Retna Pictures)

The Isley Brothers
Gems
(Redferns)

1958

George Clinton
Chris Clunn
(Retna Pictures)

Albert Collins
Elisa Ramos
(Retna Pictures)

Dion and the Belmonts
SIPA
(Rex Features)

Duane Eddy
Dezo Hoffman
(Rex Features)

Buddy Guy
Baron Wolman
(Retna Pictures)

**Cliff Richard and
the Shadows**
Dezo Hoffman
(Rex Features)

Smokey Robinson
Baron Wolman
(Retna Pictures)

Phil Spector
Baron Wolman
(Retna Pictures)

Ritchie Valens
Photofest
(Retna Pictures)

Link Wray
G. De Roos/Sunshine
(Retna Pictures)

1959

Roy Buchanan
Michael Putland
(Retna Pictures)

**Johnny Kidd and the
Pirates**
Dezo Hoffman
(Rex Features)

Carole King
Michael Ochs Archives
(Redferns)

Otis Redding
Michael Ochs Archive
(Redferns)

Joan Baez
(Rex Features)

1960

Al Green
Alan Messer
(Rex Features)

Ike and Tina Turner
Baron Wolman
(Retna Pictures)

The Ventures
Michael Ochs Archives
(Redferns)

1961

The Beach Boys
King Collection
(Retna Pictures)

1962

The Beatles
Robert Freeman
(Apple Corps Ltd)

Booker T. and the MG's
Baron Wolman
(Retna Pictures)

Bob Dylan
Michael Ochs Archives
(Redferns)

Bob Marley
Adrian Boot
(Retna Pictures)

Stevie Wonder
Marjorie Lyons
(Rex Features)

1963

Bee Gees
Dezo Hoffman
(Rex Features)

Manfred Mann
Dezo Hoffman
(Rex Features)

Lee 'Scratch' Perry
Brian Rasic
(Rex Features)

The Rolling Stones
Gered Mankowitz

Dusty Springfield
Dezo Hoffman
(Rex Features)

 **The Animals**
Dezo Hoffman
(Rex Features)

 **David Bowie**
David Bebbington
(Retna Pictures)

 **Eric Clapton**
(Retna Pictures)

 **Joe Cocker**
Roy Arenella
(Rex Features)

 **The Spencer Davis Group**
King Collection
(Retna Pictures)

 **Marianne Faithfull**
David Mcenery
(Rex Features)

 **The Kinks**
Val Wilmer

  **John Mayall**
Stills
(Rex Features)

 **The Moody Blues**
Michael Putland
(Retna Pictures)

 **Van Morrison**
Michael Putland
(Retna Pictures)

 **Pretty Things**
Dezo Hoffman
(Rex Features)

 **Simon and Garfunkel**
Photographer Unknown

 Rod Stewart
John Welsby
(Retna Pictures)

 **The Yardbirds**
Dezo Hoffman
(Rex Features)

 The Zombies
King Collection
Retna Pictures

 **Jeff Beck**
Baron Wolman
(Retna Pictures)

 **Marc Bolan**
Bill Orchard
(Rex Features)

 The Byrds
Dezo Hoffman
(Rex Features)

 Donovan
David Magnus
(Rex Features)

  **Flamin' Groovies**
Fin Costello
(Redferns)

 The Fugs
Michael Ochs Archives
(Redferns)

  The Lovin' Spoonful
David Magnus
(Rex Features)

 The Mamas and the Papas
(Redferns)

 Nico
SIPA
(Rex Features)

 Boz Scaggs
Jay Blakesberg
(Retna Pictures)

 The Seeds
Michael Ochs Archives
(Redferns)

 **Small Faces**
David Magnus
(Rex Features)

 The Who
Ray Stevenson
(Retna Pictures)

 The Bonzo Dog Doo-Dah Band
Dezo Hoffman
(Rex Features)

 **Tim Buckley**
Michael Putland
(Retna Pictures)

 **Buffalo Springfield**
Glenn A Baker
(Redferns)

 Captain Beefheart
Michael Putland
(Retna Pictures)

 **Cream**
King Collection
(Retna Pictures)

 **The Creation**
John Lyons
(Rex Features)

 **Julie Driscoll**
Barry Peake
(Rex Features)

 **The Electric Prunes**
Michael Ochs Archives
(Redferns)

 Grateful Dead
Peter Brooker
(Rex Features)

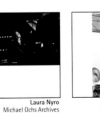 **Tim Hardin**
Michael Putland
(Retna Pictures)

Roy Harper
Adrian Boot
(Retna Pictures)

 **Jimi Hendrix**
Gered Mankowitz
(Retna Pictures)

 **The Incredible String Band**
Ray Stevenson
(Retna Pictures)

 Jefferson Airplane
Robert Altman
(Retna Pictures)

 **Love**
Michael Ochs Archives
(Redferns)

 **MC5**
Michael Ochs Archives
(Redferns)

 **Randy Newman**
Dezo Hoffman
(Rex Features)

Harry Nilsson
Michael Putland
(Retna Pictures)

Laura Nyro
Michael Ochs Archives
(Redferns)

Bob Seger
Pix International
Rex Features

Sly and the Family Stone
Neal Preston
(Retna Pictures)

Cat Stevens
Michael Clapton
(Rex Features)

The Troggs
R. Watson
(Rex Features)

Frank Zappa
Michael Putland
(Retna Pictures)

J.J. Cale
Michael Putland
(Retna Pictures)

Country Joe and the Fish
J. Bernard
(Rex Features)

 The Doors
Henry Diltz
(Retna Pictures)

 Fairport Convention
Photographer Unknown
(Courtesy Ashley Hutchings)

 Family
Michael Putland
(Retna Pictures)

Fleetwood Mac
Araldo Crollalanza
(Rex Features)

  **Janis Joplin**
Elliott Landy
(Redferns)

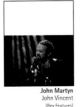 **John Martyn**
John Vincent
(Rex Features)

 **Moby Grape**
Michael Ochs Archives
(Redferns)

 **The Move**
King Collection
(Retna Pictures)

 **The Nice**
Graham Lowe
(Redferns)

Gram Parsons
Robert Altman
(Retna Pictures)

Pink Floyd
Jill Furmanovsky
rockarchive.com

Procol Harum
Baron Wolman
(Retna Pictures)

Soft Machine
Michael Putland
(Retna Pictures)

Steppenwolf
Dezo Hoffman
(Rex Features)

Ten Years After
Jim Selby
(Rex Features)

Traffic
G. Hanekroot/Sunshine
(Retna Pictures)

Vanilla Fudge
Michael Ochs Archives
(Redferns)

The Velvet Underground
Holland
(Retna Pictures)

Scott Walker
Michael Putland
(Retna Pictures)

1968

The Band
Elliott Landy
(Redferns)

Barclay James Harvest
John Madden
(Rex Features)

Blood, Sweat & Tears
Dezo Hoffman
Rex Features

Arthur Brown
Brian Moody
(Rex Features)

Can
Dean Belcher
(Retna Pictures)

Leonard Cohen
Marcel Hartmann
(Retna Pictures)

Creedence Clearwater Revival
Baron Wolman
(Retna Pictures)

Deep Purple
Fin Costello
(Redferns)

Free
Ray Stevenson
Retna Pictures

Rory Gallagher
Michael Putland
(Retna Pictures)

Genesis
(Rex Features)

Groundhogs
Michael Putland
Retna Pictures

Iron Butterfly
Globe Photos Inc
Rex Features

Jethro Tull
G. Hanekroot/Sunshine
(Retna Pictures)

Elton John
Terry O'Neill

Leo Kottke
Simon Ritter
(Redferns)

John Lennon
Peter King
(Hulton Getty)

Man
Fin Costello
(Redferns)

Steve Miller
Robert Altman
(Retna Pictures)

Joni Mitchell
T. Russell
(Redferns)

Mike Oldfield
Pictures Dmitriy Vlasenkov
(Retna)

Quicksilver Messenger Service
Herb Green
(Redferns)

Leon Russell
Peter Smith
(Retna Pictures)

Spirit
Pictures Paul Slattery
(Retna)

Status Quo
Chris Craske
Retna Pictures

Three Dog Night
Dezo Hoffman
Rex Features

Van Der Graaf Generator
G. Hanekroot/Sunshine
Retna Pictures

1969

The Allman Brothers Band
Michael Ochs Archives
(Redferns)

Amon Düül II
New Eyes/H. Schiffler
(Redferns)

Badfinger
Michael Putland
(Retna Pictures)

Syd Barrett
Gems
(Redferns)

Blind Faith
(Rex Features)

Blodwyn Pig
Dezo Hoffman
(Rex Features)

Chicago
David Thorpe
(Rex Features)

Alice Cooper
Rex Features

Nick Drake
Keith Morris
(Redferns)

Grand Funk Railroad
Michael Ochs Archives
(Redferns)

Humble Pie
Michael Putland
(Retna Pictures)

James Gang
Chansley Entertainment Archives

King Crimson
Michael Ochs Archives
(Redferns)

Led Zeppelin
Globe Photos Inc
(Rex Features)

Mott The Hoople
Robert Altman
(Retna Pictures)

Iggy Pop
Andy Chambers
(Retna Pictures)

Linda Ronstadt
Robert Altman
(Retna Pictures)

Santana
Baron Wolman
(Retna Pictures)

Slade
Dezo Hoffman
(Rex Features)

Yes
Studio G
(Rex Features)

Neil Young
David Peterson
(Retna Pictures)

Warren Zevon
Aaron Rapoport
(Retna Pictures)

1970

Black Sabbath
Gems
(Redferns)

Ry Cooder
Karen Miller
(Retna Pictures)

Crosby, Stills, Nash & Young
Ray Stevenson
(Retna Pictures)

Emerson Lake & Palmer
G. K. Hanekroot/Sunshine
(Retna Pictures)

Faces
Jill Furmanovsky
(Retna Pictures)

Fanny
Michael Putland
(Retna Pictures)

The J. Geils Band
Gems
(Redferns)

Gentle Giant
Gems
(Redferns)

Emmylou Harris
Michael Putland
(Retna Pictures)

Hawkwind
Michael Putland
Retna Pictures

Hot Tuna
Gems
(Redferns)

Little Feat
Michael Putland
(Retna Pictures)

Nils Lofgren
Patrick Ford
(Redferns)

 Magma
Michael Ochs Archives
(Redferns)

 Curtis Mayfield
Alice Arnold
(Retna Pictures)

 Paul McCartney
Richard Young
(Paul Rex Features)

 Mountain
Dezo Hoffman
(Rex Features)

 Todd Rundgren
Fotos International
(Rex Features)

Tangerine Dream
Michael Putland
(Retna Pictures)

 UFO
Bob Grant
Rex Features

 War
Yoram Kahana
Rex Features

Robert Wyatt
Jak Kilby
(Retna Pictures)

 ZZ Top
Jay Blakesberg
(Retna Pictures)

  1971
The Doobie Brothers
G. K. Hanekroot
/Sunshine
(Retna Pictures)

 Earth, Wind & Fire
Michael Putland
(Retna Pictures)

Focus
Yoram Kahana
(Rex Features)

 Gong
Gunn Press
(Rex Features)

Michael Jackson
Mark Anderson
(Retna Pictures)

 **Kraftwerk**
Tim Jarvis
(Retna Pictures)

 Lynyrd Skynyrd
Michael Putland
(Retna Pictures)

 Meat Loaf
Niels van Iperen
(Retna Pictures)

 Pink Fairies
Keith Morris
(Redferns)

 Bonnie Raitt
Michael Putland
(Retna Pictures)

Carly Simon
Richie Aaron
(Redferns)

 Thin Lizzy
Photographer Unknown
(Courtesy of Thin Lizzy Ltd.)

1972
ABBA
Nick Rogers
(Rex Features)

America
G. Hanekroot
(Retna Pictures)

 **Joan Armatrading**
G. Hanekroot
(Retna Pictures)

 Big Star
Dennis Kleiman
(Retna Pictures)

 **Blue Öyster Cult**
Matt Lis
(Rex Features)

 Jackson Browne
Gems
Redferns

Eagles
G. K. Hanekroot/Sunshine
(Retna Pictures)

Billy Joel
Drew Farrell
(Retna Pictures)

The Mahavishnu Orchestra
David Redfern
(Redferns)

Raspberries
Gems
(Redferns)

 **Lou Reed**
Niels van Iperen
(Retna Pictures)

The Residents
Nils Jorgenson
(Rex Features)

 Roxy Music
Michael Putland
(Retna Pictures)

Scorpions
Tony Mottram
(Retna Pictures)

 Gil Scott-Heron
Steve Callaghan
(Rex Features)

The Sensational Alex Harvey Band
Michael Putland
(Retna Pictures)

 Sparks
Phillipe Hamon
(Rex Features)

 Steely Dan
Neal Preston
(Retna Pictures)

 10cc
Harry Goodwin
(Rex Features)

Richard Thompson
Valerie Phillips
(Retna Pictures)

1973
Aerosmith
Lorne Resnick
(Retna Pictures)

Brian Eno
Martin Goodacre
(Retna Pictures)

New York Dolls
Ian Dickson
(Redferns)

 Suzi Quatro
Michael Putland
(Retna Pictures)

Queen
Michael Putland
(Retna Pictures)

 Rush
Fin Costello
(Redferns)

 Bruce Springsteen
Neal Preston
Retna Pictures

 Tom Waits
Bill Burt
(Rex Features)

 1974
AC/DC
Midori Tsukagoshi
(Retna Pictures)

John Hiatt
Youri Lenquette
(Retna Pictures)

 Judas Priest
Jay Blakesberg
(Retna Pictures)

 Kiss
Karen Fuchs
(Rex Features)

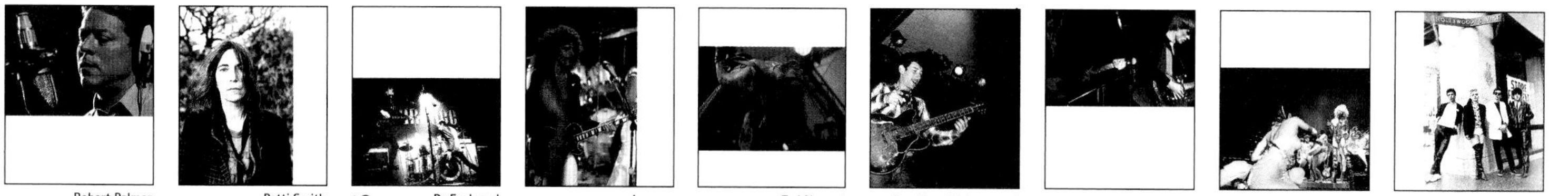

Robert Palmer
Adrian Green
(Retna Pictures)

Patti Smith
Youri Lenquette
(Retna Pictures)

1975

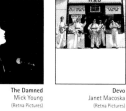

Dr Feelgood
Mick Gold
(Redferns)

Journey
Lynn McAfee
(Rex Features)

Ted Nugent
Pat Enyart
(Rex Features)

Jonathan Richman and the Modern Lovers
Pix International
(Rex Features)

Television
Michael Putland
(Retna Pictures)

The Tubes
Chris Capstick
(Rex Features)

1976

Blondie
Glenn A Baker
(Redferns)

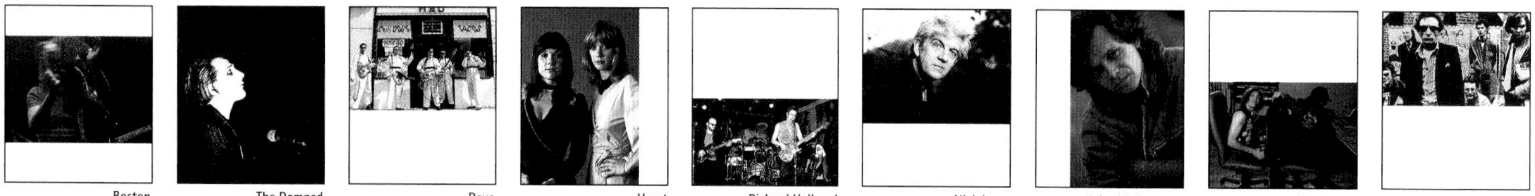

Boston
Michael Putland
(Retna Pictures)

The Damned
Mick Young
(Retna Pictures)

Devo
Janet Macoska
(Retna Pictures)

Heart
G. de Roos/Sunshine
(Retna Pictures)

Richard Hell and the Voidoids
Ebet Roberts
(Redferns)

Nick Lowe
Christopher Barker
(Retna Pictures)

John Mellencamp
Laura Levine
(Rex Features)

Motörhead
Tony Mottram
(Retna Pictures)

Graham Parker and the Rumour
Gems
(Redferns)

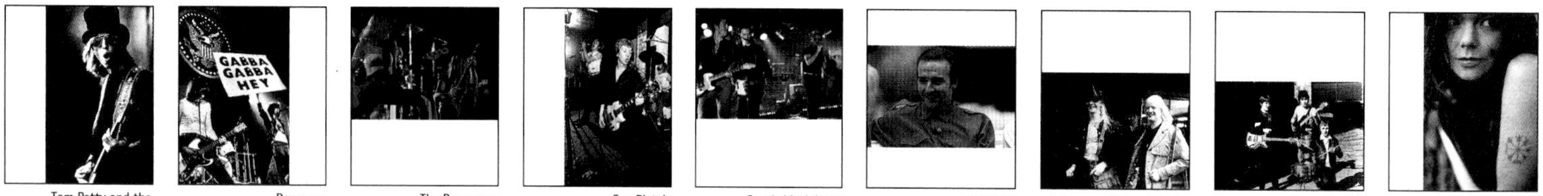

Tom Petty and the Heartbreakers
Adrian Boot
(Retna Pictures)

Ramones
Kees Tabak/Sunshsine
(Retna Pictures)

The Runaways
Cito Franco
(Rex Features)

Sex Pistols
Ray Stevenson
(Rex Features)

Southside Johnny and the Asbury Jukes
Larry Busacca
(Retna Pictures)

Ultravox
Mauro Carraro
(Rex Features)

Johnny and Edgar Winter
Michael Putland
(Retna Pictures)

1977

Alternative TV
Gems
(Redferns)

Björk
Austral International
Rex Features

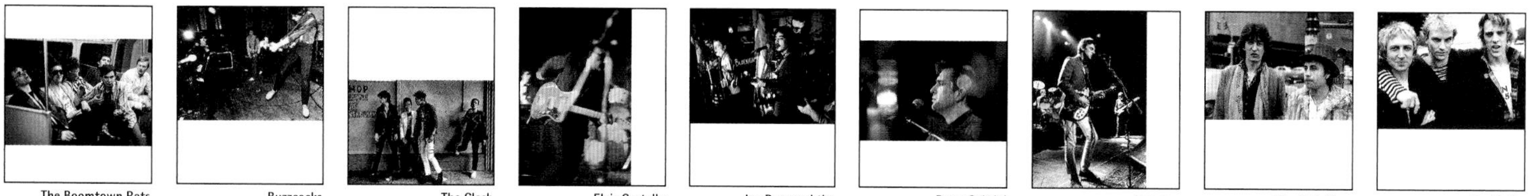

The Boomtown Rats
Adrian Boot
(Retna Pictures)

Buzzcocks
Ray Stevenson
(Retna Pictures)

The Clash
Adrian Boot
(Retna Pictures)

Elvis Costello
Paul Slattery
(Retna Pictures)

Ian Dury and the Blockheads
Adrian Boot
(Retna Pictures)

Peter Gabriel
Armando Gallo
Retna Pictures

The Jam
Jill Furmanovsky
(Retna Pictures)

The Only Ones
Michael Putland
(Retna Pictures)

The Police
Richard Young
(Rex Features)

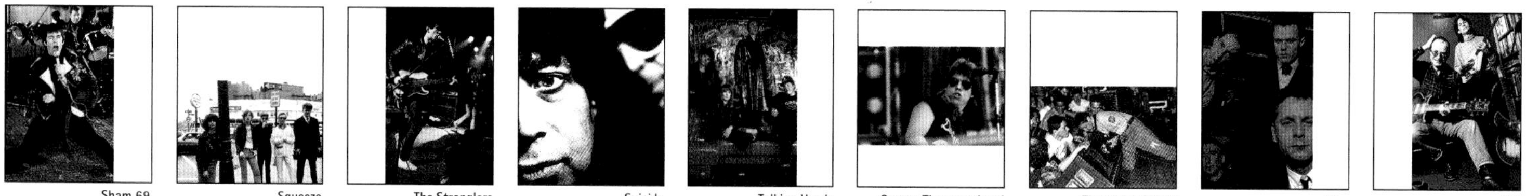

Sham 69
Sheila Rock
(Rex Features)

Squeeze
Adrian Boot
(Retna Pictures)

The Stranglers
Adrian Boot
(Retna Pictures)

Suicide
Gavin Evans
(Retna Pictures)

Talking Heads
Richard Corman
(Retna Pictures)

George Thorogood and the Destroyers
Adrian Boot
(Retna Pictures)

Throbbing Gristle
Michael Ochs Archives
(Redferns)

Wire
Bill Burt
(Rex Features)

XTC
Paul Rider
(Retna Pictures)

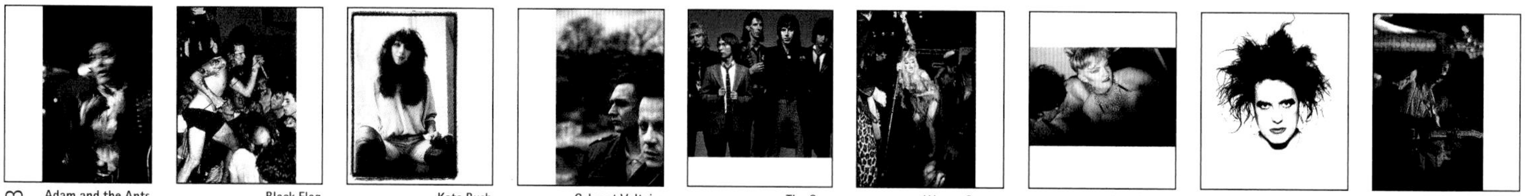

1978

Adam and the Ants
John Rogers
(Rex Features)

Black Flag
Ebet Roberts
(Redferns)

Kate Bush
Jill Furmanovsky
(Retna Pictures)

Cabaret Voltaire
A.J. Barrett
(Retna Pictures)

The Cars
G. De Roos
(Retna Pictures)

Wayne County
Ray Stevenson
(Rex Features)

The Cramps
Tony Mottram
(Retna Pictures)

The Cure
Steve Double
(Retna Pictures)

Dire Straits
Adrian Boot
(Retna Pictures)

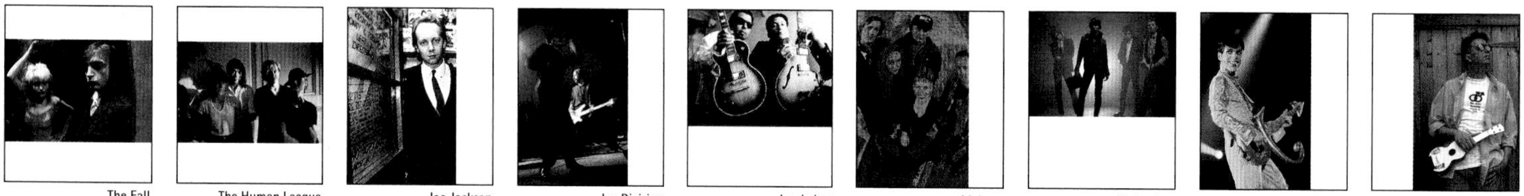

The Fall
Tim Bauer
(Retna Pictures)

The Human League
Fraser Gray
(Rex Features)

Joe Jackson
Ray Stevenson
(Rex Features)

Joy Division
Chris Mills
(Redferns)

Los Lobos
Cheryl Himmelstein
(Retna Pictures)

Mekons
Jay Blakesberg
(Retna Pictures)

Pretenders
Fin Costello
(Redferns)

Prince
Brian Rasic
(Rex Features)

Tom Robinson
Herbie Knott
(Rex Features)

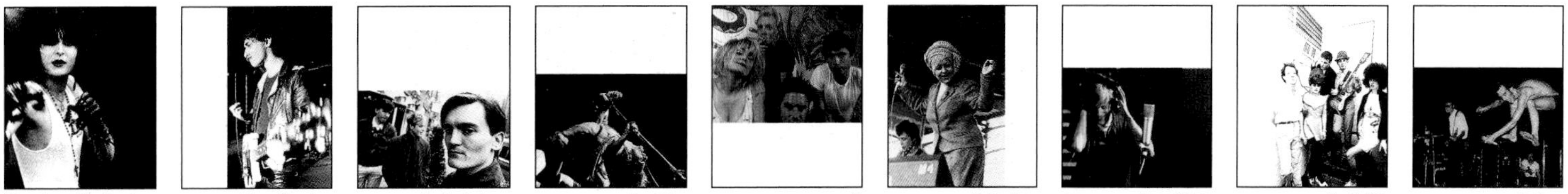

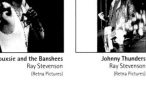

Siouxsie and the Banshees
Ray Stevenson
(Retna Pictures)

Johnny Thunders
Ray Stevenson
(Retna Pictures)

The Undertones
Tony Mottram
(Retna Pictures)

Van Halen
Ross Halfin
(Retna Pictures)

X
Ann Summa
(Rex Features)

X-Ray Spex
Mick Young
(Retna Pictures)

1979

Bryan Adams
Michael Putland
(Retna Pictures)

The B-52's
Adrian Boot
(Retna Pictures)

Bauhaus
Steve Rapport
(Retna Pictures)

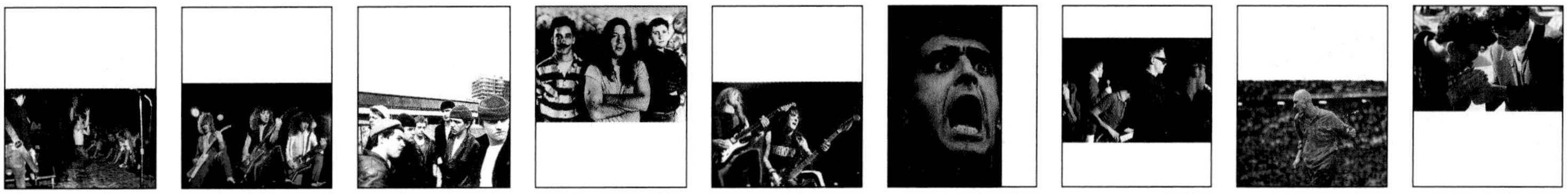

Dead Kennedys
Bob King
(Redferns)

Def Leppard
Sheila Rock
(Rex Features)

Dexys Midnight Runners
David Corio
(Retna Pictures)

Hüsker Dü
Glenn A Baker
(Redferns)

Iron Maiden
Tony Mottram
(Retna Pictures)

Killling Joke
Niels van Iperen
(Retna Pictures)

Madness
Ray Stevenson
(Retna Pictures)

Midnight Oil
Youri Lenquette
(Retna Pictures)

Orchestral Manoeuvres In The Dark
Youri Lenquette
(Rex Features)

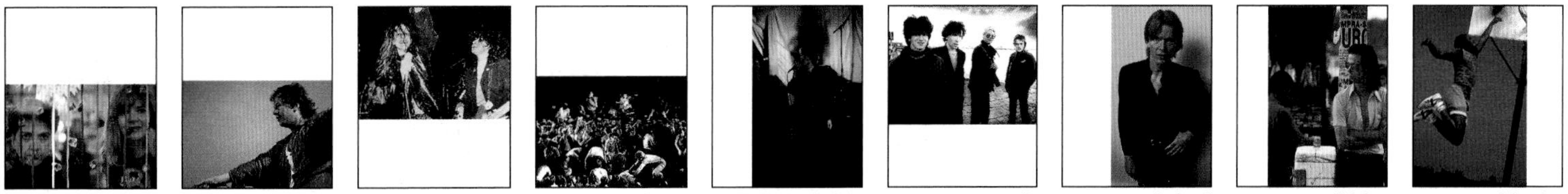

The Raincoats
Martyn Goodacre
(Retna Pictures)

Simple Minds
Brian Rasic
(Rex Features)

The Slits
Ray Stevenson
(Retna Pictures)

The Specials
Adrian Boot
(Retna Pictures)

The Teardrop Explodes
Steve Callaghan
(Rex Features)

U2
Paul Slattery
(Retna Pictures)

1980

Jim Carroll
Pix International
(Rex Features)

Nick Cave
Steve Double
(Retna Pictures)

Robert Cray
E. J. Camp
(Retna Pictures)

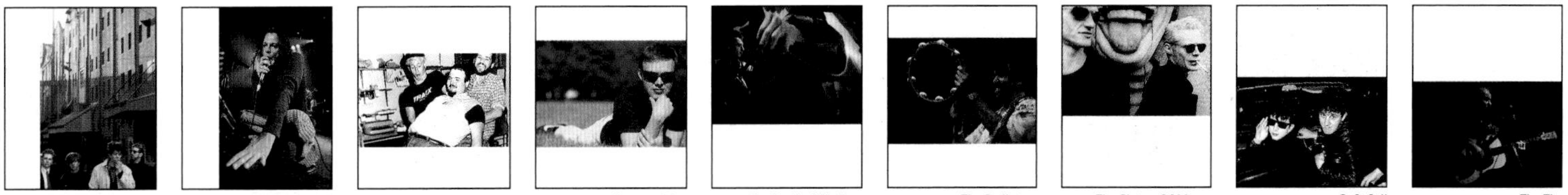

Echo and the Bunnymen
Joe Shutter
(Retna Pictures)

INXS
Brian Rasic
(Rex Features)

Minutemen
Photofest
(Retna Pictures)

Orange Juice
J Wohlfromm
(Rex Features)

The Psychedelic Furs
Henry Diltz
(Rex Features)

The Radiators
Leon Morris
Redferns

The Sisters Of Mercy
Martyn Goodacre
(Retna Pictures)

Soft Cell
Eugene Adebari
(Rex Features)

The The
Paul Slattery
(Retna Pictures)

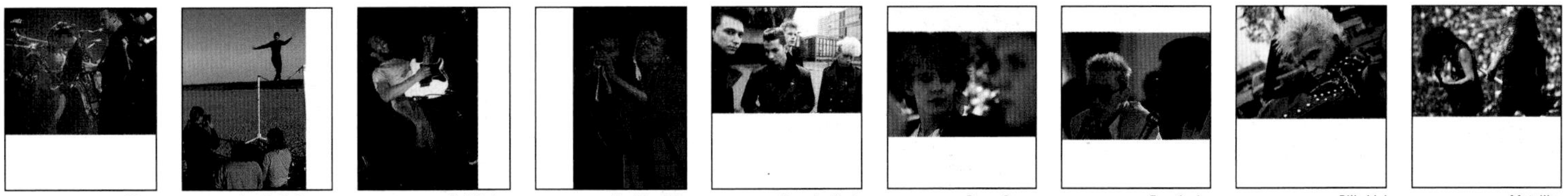

UB40
Ed Sirrs
(Retna Pictures)

1981

Laurie Anderson
Bill Davila
(Retna Pictures)

Bad Brains
Johnnie Miles
(Retna Pictures)

The Blue Nile
Peter Walsh
(Retna Pictures)

Depeche Mode
Pyke
(Retna Pictures)

Duran Duran
Michael Putland
(Retna Pictures)

Eurythmics
R. le Morvan
(Rex Features)

Billy Idol
Kevin Cummins
(Retna Pictures)

Metallica
Tony Mottram
(Retna Pictures)

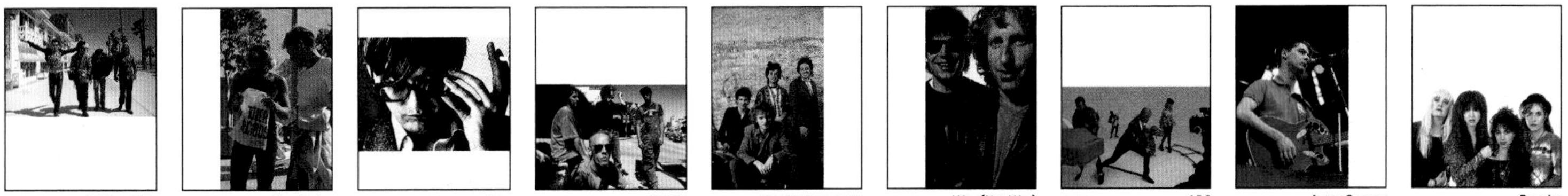

Mötley Crüe
Armando Gallo
(Retna Pictures)

New Order
Julian Barton
(Retna Pictures)

Pulp
Herbie Knott
(Rex Features)

R.E.M.
Andy Earl
(Retna Pictures)

The Replacements
Steve Marsel
(Retna Pictures)

Was (Not Was)
Steve Double
(Retna Pictures)

1982

ABC
Neil Matthews
(Retna Pictures)

Aztec Camera
Adrian Boot
(Retna Pictures)

Bangles
Howard Tyler
(Retna Pictures)

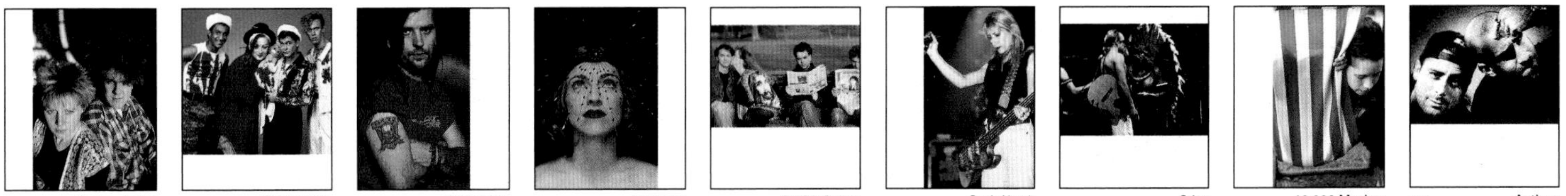

Cocteau Twins
Tony Mottram
(Retna Pictures)

Culture Club
G. de Roos/Sunshine
Retna Pictures

Steve Earle
Tony Mottram
(Retna Pictures)

Madonna
(Rex Features)

Prefab Sprout
Kevin Cummins
(Retna Picture)

Sonic Youth
Stephen Sweet
(Rex Features)

Sting
Neal Preston
(Retna Pictures)

10,000 Maniacs
Kevin Cummins
(Retna Pictures)

1983

Anthrax
Niels van Iperen
(Retna Pictures)

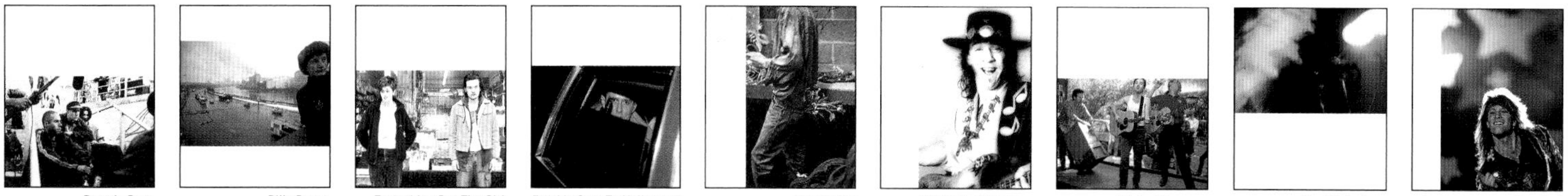

Beastie Boys
Scarlet Page
(Retna Pictures)

Billy Bragg
Adrian Boot
(Retna Pictures)

Everything But The Girl
Paul Rider
(Retna Pictures)

Frankie Goes To Hollywood
Walter McBride
(Retna Pictures)

The Smiths
Paul Slattery
(Retna Pictures)

Stevie Ray Vaughan
Robert Matthews
(Retna Pictures)

Violent Femmes
Fotex/Doormann
(Rex Features)

The Waterboys
Chris Clunn
(Retna Pictures)

1984

Bon Jovi
Le Segretain
(Rex Features)

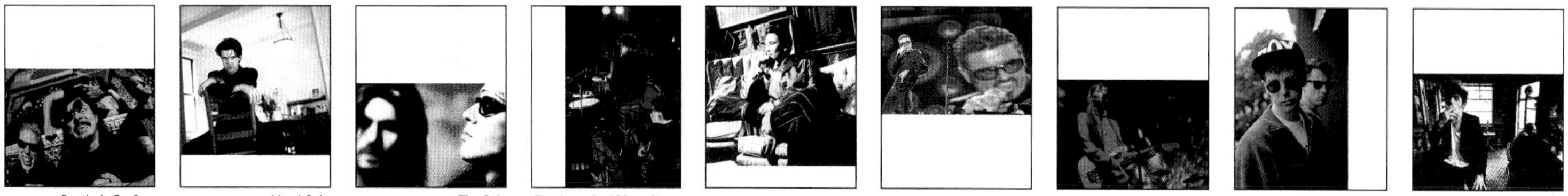

Butthole Surfers
Brad Miller
(Retna Pictures)

Lloyd Cole
Jeffrey Kane
(Retna Pictures)

The Cult
Niels van Iperen
(Retna Pictures)

The Jesus And Mary Chain
Michael Putland
(Retna Pictures)

k.d. lang
Greg Allen
(Retna Pictures)

George Michael
Brian Rasic
(Rex Features)

My Bloody Valentine
Paul Slattery
(Retna Pictures)

Pet Shop Boys
Paul Rider
(Retna Pictures)

The Pogues
Paul Spencer
(Retna Pictures)

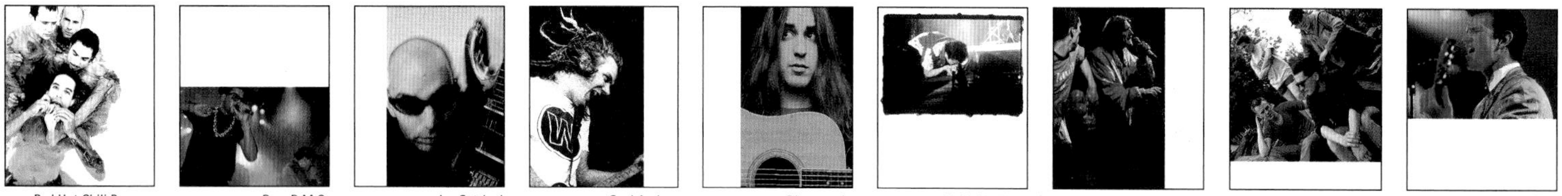

Red Hot Chili Peppers
Niels van Iperen
(Retna Pictures)

Run-D.M.C.
Normski
(Retna Pictures)

Joe Satriani
Niels van Iperen
(Retna Pictures)

Soul Asylum
Niels van Iperen
(Retna Pictures)

1985

Dinosaur Jr.
Matt Anker
(Retna Pictures)

Faith No More
Niels van Iperen
(Retna Pictures)

Happy Mondays
Kevin Cummins
(Retna Pictures)

The Housemartins
Tim Bauer
(Retna Pictures)

Chris Isaak
Camacho
(Rex Features)

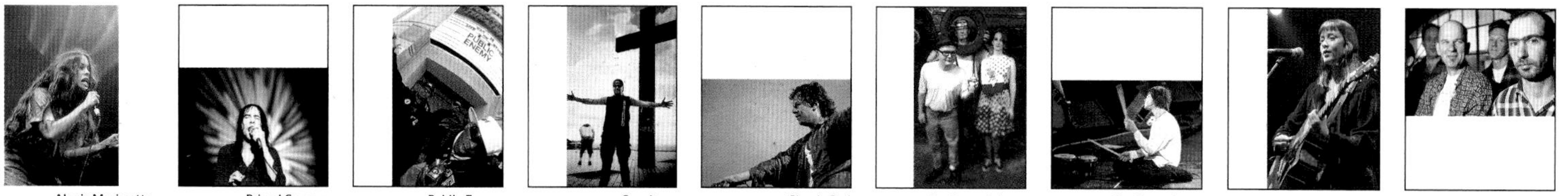

Alanis Morissette
George Chin
(Redferns)

Primal Scream
Drew Farrell
(Retna Pictures)

Public Enemy
Normski
(Retna Pictures)

Sepultura
Niels van Iperen
(Retna Pictures)

Simply Red
Chris Taylor
(Retna Pictures)

Southern Culture On The Skids
(Michael Benson)

The Stone Roses
Kevin Cummins
(Retna Pictures)

Suzanne Vega
Brian Rasic
(Rex Features)

1986

American Music Club
Erik Averbach
(Retna Pictures)

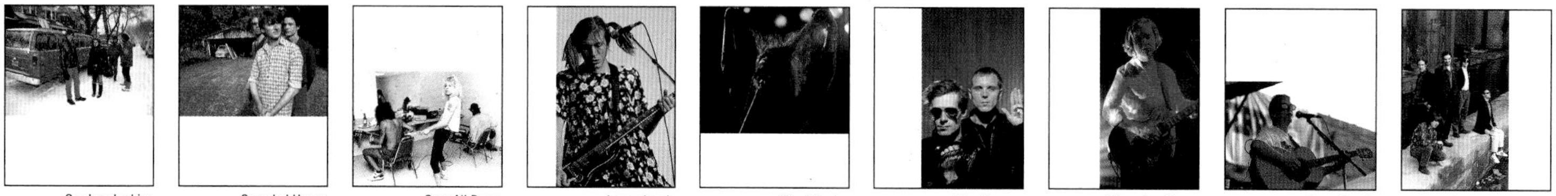

Cowboy Junkies
Chris Taylor
(Retna Pictures)

Crowded House
Andy Earl
(Retna Pictures)

Guns N' Roses
Ian Tilton
(Retna Pictures)

Lemonheads
RIP
(Retna Pictures)

The Mission
Paul Slattery
(Retna Pictures)

The Shamen
Steve Double
(Retna Pictures)

Throwing Muses
Karl Grabowski
(Rex Features)

1987

Mary Chapin Carpenter
Charles Steiner
(Retna Pictures)

Hothouse Flowers
Sheila Rock
(Rex Features)

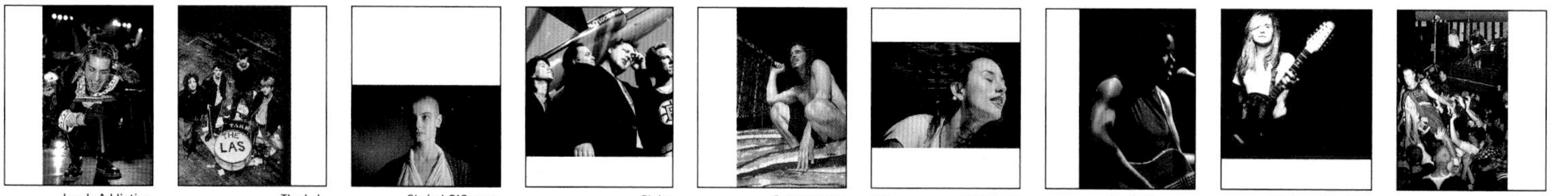

Jane's Addiction
Steve Jennings
(Retna Pictures)

The La's
Ronnie Randall
(Retna Pictures)

Sinéad O'Connor
J. Y. Legras
(Rex Features)

Pixies
Youri Lenquette
(Retna Pictures)

Soundgarden
Jay Blakesberg
(Retna Pictures)

1988

Tori Amos
Niels van Iperen
(Retna Pictures)

Tracy Chapman
Peter Brooker
(Rex Features)

Melissa Etheridge
Joseph Pluchino
(Retna Pictures)

Fugazi
Steve Eichner
(Retna Pictures)

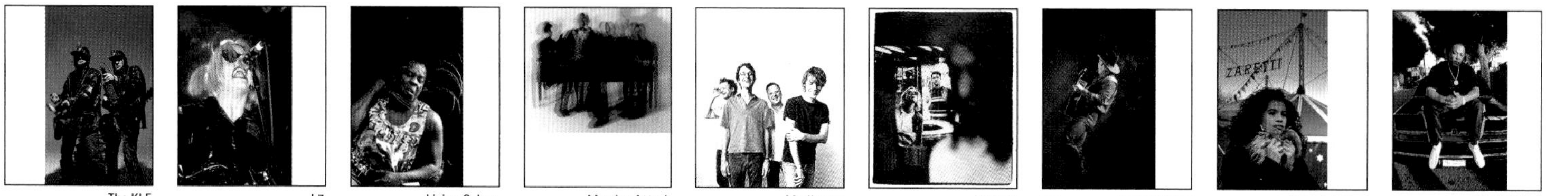

The KLF
Steve Double
(Retna Pictures)

L7
John Stephen
(Rex Features)

Living Colour
Ed Sirrs
(Retna Pictures)

Massive Attack
Karl Grant
(Retna Pictures)

Mudhoney
Anthony Saint James
(Retna Pictures)

Nirvana
Stephen Sweet
(Rex Features)

1989

Garth Brooks
Dave Hogan
(Rex Features)

Neneh Cherry
A.J. Barratt
(Retna Pictures)

Dr Dre
Jay Blakesberg
(Retna Pictures)

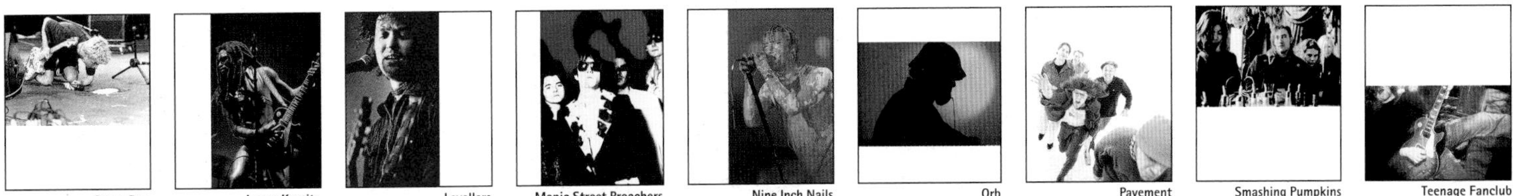

Green Day Jay Blakesberg (Retna Pictures)
Lenny Kravitz Scott Weiner (Retna Pictures)
Levellers Niels van Iperen (Retna Pictures)
Manic Street Preachers Colin Bell (Retna Pictures)
Nine Inch Nails Brian Rasic (Rex Features)
Orb Ian Tilton (Retna Pictures)
Pavement Guy Aroch (Retna Pictures)
Smashing Pumpkins David Tonge (Retna Pictures)
Teenage Fanclub RIP (Retna Pictures)

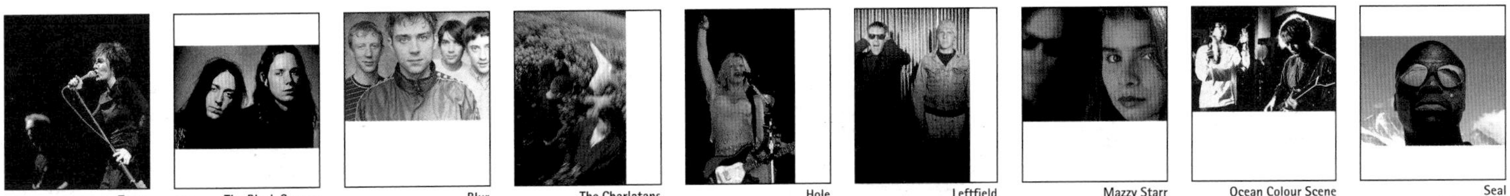

Texas Jon Super (Redferns)
1990
The Black Crowes Niels van Iperen (Retna Pictures)
Blur Midori Tsukagoshi (Retna Pictures)
The Charlatans Steve Double (Retna Pictures)
Hole Brian Rasic (Rex Features)
Leftfield Steve Double (Retna Pictures)
Mazzy Starr Steve Rapport (Retna Pictures)
Ocean Colour Scene Valerie Phillips (Retna Pictures)
Seal Adrian Myers (Retna Pictures)

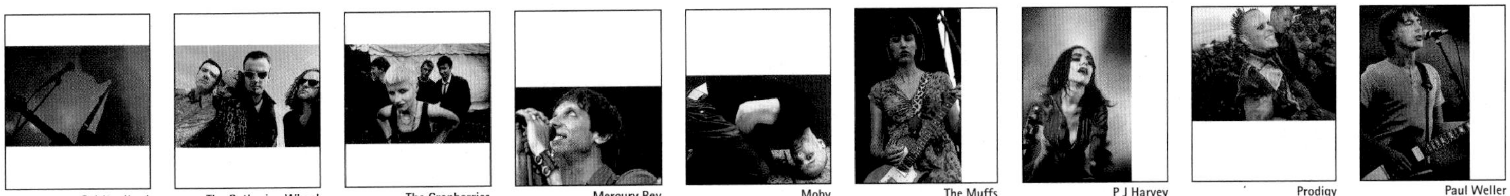

Spiritualized Steve Parker (Retna Pictures)
1991
The Catherine Wheel Greg Allen (Retna Pictures)
The Cranberries Niels van Iperen (Retna Pictures)
Mercury Rev Tung (Retna Pictures)
Moby Sonja Pacho (Retna Pictures)
The Muffs Tara Canova (Retna Pictures)
P J Harvey David Corio (Retna Pictures)
Prodigy Sutton Hibbert (Rex Features)
Paul Weller Niels van Iperen (Retna Pictures)

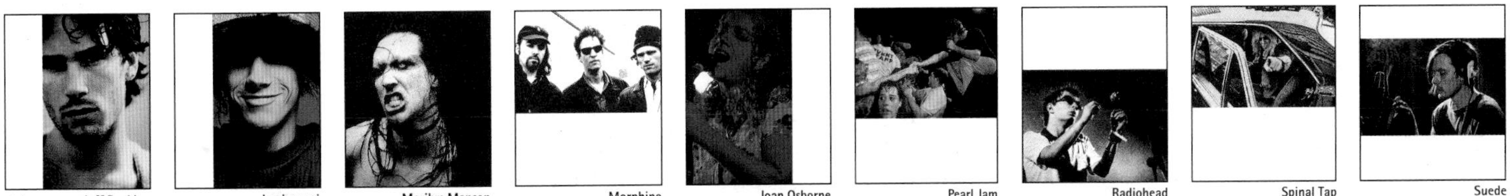

1992
Jeff Buckley Niels van Iperen (Retna Pictures)
Jamiroquai Ray Burmiston (Retna Pictures)
Marilyn Manson Niels van Iperen (Retna Pictures)
Morphine Niels van Iperen (Retna Pictures)
Joan Osborne Bernhard Kuhmstedt (Retna Pictures)
Pearl Jam Lance Mercer (Retna Pictures)
Radiohead Niels van Iperen (Retna Pictures)
Spinal Tap Martyn Goodacre (Retna Pictures)
Suede Herbie Knott (Rex Features)

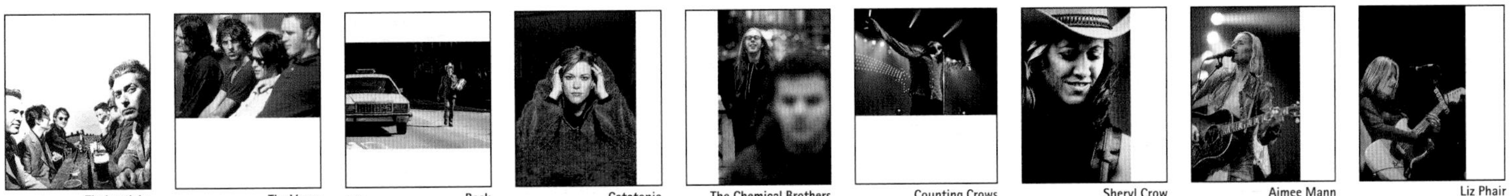

Tindersticks Franck Courtes (Retna Pictures)
The Verve Steve Rapport (Retna Pictures)
1993
Beck Bill Davila (Retna Pictures)
Catatonia Steve Double (Retna Pictures)
The Chemical Brothers Steve Double (Retna Pictures)
Counting Crows Tim Auger (Retna Pictures)
Sheryl Crow Niels van Iperen (Retna Pictures)
Aimee Mann Brian Rasic (Rex Features)
Liz Phair Ann Stern (Redferns)

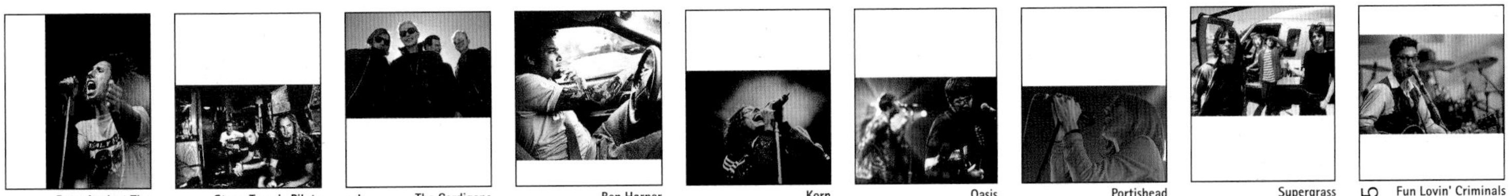

Rage Against The Machine Niels van Iperen (Retna Pictures)
Stone Temple Pilots Niels van Iperen (Retna Pictures)
1994
The Cardigans Martyn Goodacre (Retna Pictures)
Ben Harper Franck Courtes (Retna Pictures)
Korn Niels van Iperen (Retna Pictures)
Oasis Jill Furmanovsky (Retna Pictures)
Portishead J. Sutton Hibbert (Rex Features)
Supergrass Steve Double (Retna Pictures)
1995
Fun Lovin' Criminals Richard Young (Rex Features)

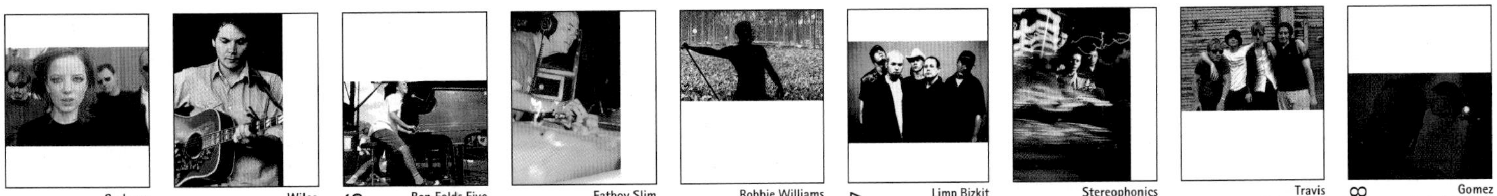

Garbage Steve Double (Retna Pictures)
Wilco Daniel Coston (Retna Pictures)
1996
Ben Folds Five Dennis Kleiman (Retna Pictures)
Fatboy Slim Antonio Pagano (Retna Pictures)
Robbie Williams Lee Carter (Retna Pictures)
1997
Limp Bizkit Kevin Estrada (Retna Pictures)
Stereophonics Corlouer (Rex Features)
Travis Spiros Politis (Retna Pictures)
1998
Gomez Antonio Pagano (Retna Pictures)

Philip Dodd would like to thank everyone who, wittingly or otherwise, helped shape this book: Sean Bodie and the Helter Skelter staff, Graham Brough, Chris Dennis, Paul Du Noyer, Dan and Jan Einzig, BP Fallon, Mark Gibbon, John Kent, Paul Krykant, Margot Lester, Greg Macdonald, Neil Ortenberg and Thunder's Mouth Press, Keith Richmond, Michelle Roques-O'Neil, Colin Rudderham, Boyd Stimson, Dave Suckling, Mark Taylor and Mick Watson. *The Book of Rock* is not intended to be a reference work; to learn more about any of the musicians in detail, consult the following highly recommended books: the original and still brilliant *Illustrated New Musical Express Encyclopedia of Rock* edited by Nick Logan and Bob Woffinden, Colin Larkin's vast *Encyclopedia Of Popular Music* (so vast it includes David Costa and Trees), Dafydd Rees and Luke Crampton's *Rock Stars Encyclopedia*, the *New Rolling Stone Encyclopedia of Rock & Roll*, Mark Prendergast's *The Ambient Century*, M.C. Strong's range of *Rock Discographies*, and the *Rough Guide To Rock* – even if, or especially as, they don't always agree with each other. *The Book of Rock* would not exist without the energy and vision of Colin Webb, founder of Pavilion Books, who oversaw the evolution of his original idea to this final printed version. In this he was supported by his colleagues Vivien James, Ben Donald, Tim Clarke, Terry Shaughnessy and Kate Oldfield, who gallantly completed the previous work of David Williams and Maxine McCaghy. At Wherefore Art?, David Costa was as inspirational as ever, ably supported by Rachel Godfrey, Sian Rance and the rest of the studio. Picture researcher Emily Hedges provided invaluable input, as did the eminently quotable Michael Heatley. Special thanks to Frédérique Bavouzet, now Alvarez, for playing me *Dark Side Of The Moon* at Pierrefiche one hot summer's day in 1973. And an extra special dedication to my wife Wan for her unwavering support and tolerance beyond the call of duty for a project that invaded many a high day and holy day.

Philip Dodd is a writer and publisher specialising in music and popular culture. As a publisher with Octopus Illustrated and Virgin Publishing, he was at the forefront of bringing rock'n'roll books into mainstream illustrated publishing, including titles like *The NME Rock'n'Roll Years*, *The Hendrix Experience* by Mitch Mitchell and John Platt, *The Electric Guitar* by Paul Trynka and BP Fallon's *U2: Faraway So Close*. He was the co-author of *Musical Instruments* and *The Encyclopedia Of Singles*, and with Dora Loewenstein created and compiled *The Rolling Stones: A Life On The Road*.

For all their help with the picture research for this book, Emily Hedges would like to thank: Glen Marks and Kathryn Jones at Rex; Andy Seal, Malcolm Collins and Richard Skidmore at Retna; and Dede Millar, Jon Wilton and Julian Ridgeway at Redferns.

David Costa would like to thank most of the entries in the book - not all - for their rich contribution to his life, probably none more than Buffalo Springfield for showing me the way, Trees for giving me the merest hint of a taste of the real thing, and The Beatles for enriching his current career. Thanks to Colin Webb and everyone at Pavilion, to a very special Sian Rance and team at Wherefore Art? ably assisted by Cachao, to Gered Mankowitz, image maker, contributor and friend, and of course to the matchless Philip Dodd - flattered by his use of the word 'inspirational' he returns the compliment and continues to envy Phil's wit, his writing, his limericks and his seemingly infinite frame of reference. He made the long haul effortless and pleasurable.

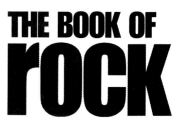

THE BOOK OF
rock

Spinal Tap The Fugs Squeeze Björk Jimi
Was (Not Was)
Travis Def Leppard ABC New Order Throbbing Gristle
Eddie Cochran The Jesus And Mary Chain
Cowboy Junkies Patti Smith George Thorogood and the Destroyer
Yes Marianne Faithfu
B.B. King Garbage J.J. Cale Pavement
Tracy Chapman Neil Young Status Quo Neneh Cherr
Rumour Frankie Goes To Hollywood
Tom Petty and the Heartbreakers
Ada
Aretha Franklin Joan Baez Al Green
Link Wray Bo Diddley The Creation Robert Cra
The Incredible String Band Cocteau Twins Devo
Lloyd Coles Ike and Tina Turner Vanill
Supergrass Hothouse Flowers Portishead Prefab Sprout
Dexys Midnight Runners
Ultravox Korn Marvin Gaye John Lennon
Elvis Costello Pretenders
The Beatles Pixies Steve Earle Bon Jov
X-Ray Spex
Talking Heads Moby Syd Barrett John Marty
ron Maiden The Cranberrie
XTC Joni Mitchell Billy Joel Wit
Dinosaur Jr. Tom Waits Dire Straits Cat Stevens Dr John Ech
Buddy Guy Linda Ronstadt U
Sham 69 Peter Gabriel Bob Seger Roxy Music
The Mamas and the Papas
Ocean Colour Scene Santana Fun Lovin
The Who Iggy Pop Massive Attack Ric
10,000 Maniacs Smokey Robinson
Lonnie Donegan Aztec Camera Grateful Dead
Prodigy Ten Years After Hot Tuna
The Psychedelic Furs Smashing Pumpkins The Fal
Rage Against The Machine
Earth, Wind & Fire Green Day Joh
Lynyrd Skynyrd Siouxsie and the Banshees Groundhog
Robert Wyatt Paul Weller
Pearl Jam Eagles Jonathan Richman and the Modern Lovers
Beck Guns N' Rose
Gene Vincent
Public Enemy Nick Lowe Fairport Convention